T0334003

Theorizing Cohesive Development

This volume proposes an alternative development paradigm to the existing capitalist extant one, and studies how it is distinctly different from the older system. Rooted in the principles of solidarity between humans, as well as between humans and nature, this alternative paradigm replaces the methodological individualism of capitalism by 'reciprocal altruism', a new logic of capital, to give pace and direction to the development process.

The essays in this volume highlight instances of various forms of solidarity that have emerged in the contemporary world – such as resistance movements of informal workers, the formation of an autonomous cooperative of self-employed waste pickers in India, called SWaCH, and Brazil and Cuba's experiments with social and solidarity economy (SSE) – to achieve long-sustaining cohesive development. They also provide recommendations as to how the state can mold its development process to the benefits of the marginalized communities especially in India and Bangladesh.

Featuring insights from leading experts in the field, *Theorizing Cohesive Development* will be an indispensable read for students and researchers of development studies, economics, political economy, political science and sociology, minority studies and Asian studies.

Sunil Ray is Professor of Economics. He was previously Director of A. N. Sinha Institute of Social Studies, Patna, India and Dean of School of Social Sciences and Head of the Centre for Economic Studies and Policy at the Central University of Bihar, India. He has been a visiting fellow at the Institute of Development Studies, Sussex, UK, and the Institute of Oriental Studies, Moscow, Russia. His papers have appeared in various national and international journals such as *Economic and Political Weekly*, *International Journal of Ecological Economics*, *Asian Survey*, *Saving & Development*, and *Capitalism Nature and Socialism*. He has authored several books, including *Protection and Industrial Growth in India* (1998), *Natural Resources Organization and Technology Linkages* (1997) and *Management of Natural Resources – Institutions for Sustainable Livelihood* (2008).

Neetu Choudhary is Adjunct Faculty with the School of Human Evolution and Social Change, Arizona State University (ASU), USA. She was also Fulbright Fellow, 2018–19, at ASU. Prior to that, she was Assistant Professor of Economics with the A. N. Sinha Institute of Social Studies, Patna, India. She has worked and published considerably on issues of nutrition, gender and informal workers' organizing.

Rajeev K. Kumar is Assistant Professor of Sociology and Social Anthropology at the A. N. Sinha Institute of Social Studies (ANSISS), Patna, India. His research focuses on tribal development and public health issues. Prior to joining ANSISS, he was Assistant Professor at the International Institute of Health Management Research, Jaipur, India, where he worked on numerous projects on public health and was also Assistant Editor of the *Journal of Health Management*. He is the author of one book and several research papers and articles.

Theorizing Cohesive Development

An Alternative Paradigm

Edited by Sunil Ray, Neetu Choudhary
and Rajeev K. Kumar

Routledge
Taylor & Francis Group

LONDON AND NEW YORK

First published 2020
by Routledge
2 Park Square, Milton Park, Abingdon, Oxon OX14 4RN

and by Routledge
52 Vanderbilt Avenue, New York, NY 10017

Routledge is an imprint of the Taylor & Francis Group, an informa business

British Library Cataloguing-in-Publication Data
A catalogue record for this book is available from the British Library

Library of Congress Cataloging-in-Publication Data
A catalog record for this book has been requested

ISBN: 978-1-138-58063-3 (hbk)
ISBN: 978-0-367-50129-7 (pbk)
ISBN: 978-1-003-04832-9 (ebk)

Typeset in Sabon
by Apex CoVantage, LLC

Contents

vi *Contents*

Contributors

Amiya Kumar Bagchi is Emeritus Professor, Institute of Development Studies, Kolkata, India, and Adjunct Professor, Monash University, Australia. His publications include *Private Investment in India 1900–1939* (1972), *The Political Economy of Underdevelopment* (1982), *Public Intervention and Industrial Restructuring in China, India and the Republic of Korea* (1987), *Capital and Labour Redefined: India and the Third World* (2002), *Perilous Passage: Mankind and the Global Ascendancy of Capital* (2005), and *Colonialism and Indian Economy* (2010).

Meghadeepa Chakraborty is Assistant Professor, Banasthali Vidyapith, Rajasthan, India. She has previously worked in the development sector. Her research interests include community development, rural and urban livelihood, and household livelihood strategies.

Lalatendu Keshari Das is Postdoctoral Fellow at the Indian Institute of Technology, Bombay, India. He has published in journals such as *Economic and Political Weekly* and *Sociological Bulletin*. His research focuses on the Marxist debate on capitalist development, political subjectivity, and the informal sector. Through this, he tries to understand issues ranging from social movements, agrarian change, and fisheries to ecotourism.

Abhijit Ghosh is Assistant Professor of Economics, A. N. Sinha Institute of Social Studies, Patna, India. His research interests include human development and related issues (education, health and food security), regional economics, local government and panchayati raj institutions, and applied econometrics. He has published extensively in reputed international and national journals, as well as in edited volumes.

Barbara Harriss-White is Emeritus Professor and Fellow of Wolfson College, Oxford, UK, and Visiting Professor at JNU, India. Her work focuses on field economics research on rural markets and development, and policies affecting Indian agriculture, commodity markets, informal economy and small towns. She also studies the various aspects of deprivation and their relationship to markets. She has published various books and papers.

Parvaz Azharul Huq is Professor and Former Chairman, Department of Public Administration, University of Rajshahi, Bangladesh. He is also Director of the Centre for Governance and Development Studies (CGDS), University of Rajshahi, Bangladesh. His research focuses on governance and development. He has published various articles in refereed journals and chapters in peer-reviewed books.

Antje Linkenbach is a long-term fellow at the Max Weber Centre for Advanced Cultural and Social Studies, University of Erfurt, Germany, and at the M.S. Merian – R. Tagore International Centre of Advanced Studies in the Humanities and Social Sciences 'Metamorphoses of the Political', Delhi, India. She has held teaching and research positions in Germany, Switzerland and New Zealand. Her expertise includes anthropological and sociological theory, anthropology of development and environment, social movements, justice and inequality, human rights, and indigenous rights.

Leandro Morais is an economist. He is Professor and Researcher at UNESP, Araraquara, Brazil; Coordinator of the Extension and Research Nucleus in Solidarity Economy, Creativity and Citizenship (NEPESC); Full Member of the International Scientific Committee of CIRIEC International and Member of the Task Force on SSE at the United Nations. He is also an international consultant and lecturer in the field of SSE, cooperativism, SDG, ecosystems, and international cooperation.

M. V. Nadkarni is Honorary Visiting Professor at Institute for Social and Economic Change (ISEC), Bengaluru, India. He was previously ICSSR National Fellow, Vice Chancellor of Gulbarga University, Karnataka, India, Chairman of the Editorial Board of the *Indian Journal of Agricultural Economics*, and Professor of Economics at ISEC.

Gail Omvedt is a sociologist and human rights activist. She has published numerous books on the anti-caste movement, Dalit politics, and women's struggles in India. She has been involved in Dalit and anti-caste movements and environmental, farmers' and women's movements, especially with rural women. She has also served as Dr Ambedkar Chair Professor at National Institute of Social Work and Social Sciences in Orissa, India; Professor of Sociology at the University of Pune, India; and Guest Professor at the Nordic Institute of Asian Studies, Copenhagen, Denmark. She was Senior Fellow at the Nehru Memorial Museum and Library, India, and former Chair Professor for the Dr B.R. Ambedkar Chair of Social Change and Development at IGNOU, India. She currently holds an ICSSR National Fellowship on the bhakti movement.

Bharat Patankar is a leading activist of the left-wing Shramik Mukti Dal and of the peasant movement in Maharashtra. He is one of the architects of equitable water distribution movement in Maharashtra, India. He has published extensively, including 20 English-language articles and books such as *Characteristics of Contemporary Caste System and Its Annihilation*, *Maharashtrache Shilpakar Nana Patil* (2002), and *Mudda Ahe Jag Badalnyaca* (1989).

M. Gopinath Reddy is Professor of Political Science and Public Policy at the Centre for Economic and Social Studies (CESS), Hyderabad, India. He is Principal Coordinator for the Division for Sustainable Development Studies (DSDS) at CESS. He has published extensively on decentralised governance, forest governance and livelihoods, and natural resources in the journals of *Development and Change*, *The Small Scale Forestry Journal*, and *Economic and Political Weekly* (*EPW*).

Rohini Sahni is former Professor and Head, Department of Economics, Savitribai Phule Pune University, India. She co-edited the volume *Prostitution and Beyond: An Analysis of Sex Work in India* (2008). She was also the Principal Co-Investigator of the First Pan India Survey of Sex Workers (2009–2013).

V. Kalyan Shankar is Assistant Professor at Symbiosis School of Economics, Symbiosis International (Deemed University), India. He was formerly a Fulbright-Nehru scholar at the India China Institute, The New School, USA, and ICSSR Postdoctoral Fellow at JNU, Delhi, India. He is also the recipient of the EXIM Bank IERA Award for the best doctoral thesis in international trade by an Indian national (2014). His research has been published in journals such as *Economic and Political Weekly*, *Higher Education*, *IIC Quarterly* and *WSQ*.

Joseph Tharamangalam is Emeritus Professor of Sociology, Mount Saint Vincent University, Canada, and Adjunct Professor of International Development Studies, St. Mary's University, Canada. His research interests include agrarian relations and peasant movements in India, religious pluralism and secularism, and more recently comparative studies of human development across Indian states and different countries. His academic papers have appeared in reputed journals such as *Critical Asian Studies*, *Journal of Peasant Studies*, and *Economic and Political Weekly*.

Preface

The most intractable challenge that human civilization confronts today is how to reverse the contemporary development narratives that reverberate a "catastrophe-like-situation". The mainstream development paradigm is the architect of the contemporary development narratives rooted in methodological individualism. The latter gives pace and direction to the former. However, the paradigm is inherently constrained to provide any opportunity to avert the impending civilization crisis growing out of deep inequality, poverty and ecological disaster. The principles of mutuality, cooperation and compassion and, above all, a culture of sharing find no place in this paradigm. While the rise in the misery of both humans and nature constantly demeans it, the paradigm appears to have been caught up into its own contradictions. Consequently, not only does it breed inequality and injustice, it has failed even to address the crisis that it has repeatedly produced, shaking its own foundation. These contradictions are inexorable. No technocratic approach accompanied by enormous scientific and technological breakthrough seems to be of any help to resolve them. The human race, as a consequence, is increasingly becoming polarized between the gainers, the powerful, the minority on the one hand and the losers, the powerless, the large majority on the other. The polarization has deepened over time, has grown sharper and is at its worst now. The material conditions of the majority that are needed to survive, sustain and grow on the planet earth are now more critical than ever. Furthermore, irreversible environmental changes due to crossing planetary boundaries has led to the destabilization of the earth system and threatening of life.

These crises have been motivating for us to explore an alternative development paradigm. We call it "cohesive development" and believe it is achievable based on the principles of solidarity between humans and between humans and nature. Cohesive development refuses to accept methodological individualism, replacing it with "reciprocal altruism" to give pace and direction to the development process. While one has to recognize that providing safe ecological space for humanity can never be decoupled from addressing human deprivation, which is accumulating at a planetary scale, we have no choice but to weave co-evolution of economy, society and nature into an alternative paradigm. It pronounces a new way of living that involves a renewed sense of shared prosperity and commitment to justice in a world which is finite.

This book is an outcome of the international seminar "Cohesive Development: An Alternative Paradigm?" organized by the A. N. Sinha Institute of Social Studies, Patna, during February 24–25, 2017. The intellectual motivation underlying this seminar stemmed from the paper authored by Sunil Ray, "Economics of Solidarity: Economics of the 21st Century", that appeared in the *Economic and Political Weekly* in 2012. The overwhelming response received from the scholars from different parts of the world is a testimony to their eagerness to seek an alternative development paradigm, such as the one the seminar had addressed with its own framework. Eminent academicians and scholars from Germany, the United Kingdom, Brazil, Canada, Bangladesh, and the Netherlands and, of course, India enthusiastically participated in the discussion and contributed to the proceedings of the seminar. We express our deep sense of gratitude to them.

We are grateful to Jan Breman for delivering the keynote address. Apart from delivering the inaugural address, Amiya Bagchi was immensely helpful at the initial stage while organizing this event. We are indebted to him for his unstinted support and cooperation. In addition to six technical sessions, a panel discussion and two special lectures were also organized, which were delivered by Barbara Harriss-White and Vandana Shiva. We express our gratitude to them. We take this opportunity to thank all the paper writers and presenters who join us in our endeavour to articulate an alternative development paradigm.

The help and cooperation extended by the faculty and staff of the A. N. Sinha Institute of Social Studies was immense. We would like to place on record their selfless cooperation for making the seminar a success. The doctoral students of the Institute played very important role in managing the programme. We profusely thank them for their contribution. Dr Ashok Choudhary, the then Chairman of the Board of Control of the Institute and Minister of Education, Government of Bihar, was a great source of inspiration for us to organize the seminar. We express our heartfelt thanks to him. We are grateful to the Government of Bihar, Department of Education and the Indian Council of Social Science Research (ICSSR), New Delhi, for providing us financial assistance to organize the programme. We express our deep sense of gratitude to Routledge Publications for having accepted to publish the seminar volume in its present form.

Sunil Ray
Neetu Choudhary
Rajeev K. Kumar

1 Introduction

Cohesive development as an alternative development paradigm

Sunil Ray

Never before has an historical moment been witnessed like that of current worldwide resistance movements, which are challenging the epistemological base of the mainstream development paradigm rooted in the capital system (capitalism). The capital system that designs the extant development paradigm has lost its appeal because of its devastating acts against humanity and nature. These acts have occurred to such an extent that it is inconceivable that the system could ever escape from its inevitable collapse due to its sharp internal contradictions. Its pathological symptoms are indicative of an entropic disorderly stalemated post-capitalist interregnum society (Streeck, 2017; Ghosh, 2017). Almost a century ago, Gramsci warned about interregnum and wrote little before the emergence of the saviour of capitalism that was threatened by its inevitable collapse under the burden of the Great Depression (Gramsci, 1971). It is Keynesianism, the saviour armoured with state welfarism, which has now taken the capital system to a level where it is left with crisis which is now endemic, cumulative, chronic and permanent – a depressed continuum indicating structural crisis (Antunes, 2010a, p16). But now no saviour, no escape route is in sight as a successor to save the same capital system that has ravaged civilizational principles of mutuality, cooperation and compassion. The common humanity is forgotten in the depth of inequality and injustice (Jahanbegloo, 2017a, p. xxx). The crisis is more civilizational than structural, in that the environmental crisis, the immediate fall-out of the capital system, is exacerbating the former. No entry of the destruction of production conditions consequent to the environmental crisis is given as an analytical component to the development paradigm which is based on the capital system.

Any attempt to refurbish the capital system based on the lessons drawn from the Keynesian intervention for its recovery from the Great Depression does not appear to be as useful as one hopes, even in the wake of 'Great Recession'. The worst of it is that it has been subverting the dialectics of human progress which is, historically speaking, determined by the co-evolution of nature and human society. Without valuing the importance of co-evolution, the capital system goes on reproducing itself even under the shadow of welfarism and has pushed the large majority, the deprived ones, to interregnum as mentioned earlier.

However, one has reasons to believe that such a state of hopelessness may cease to exist since the resistance movements (anti-systemic movements) the world over are clamouring for reversal of the mainstream development paradigm. The clamour for its replacement by the alternative development paradigm has been growing strong and becoming more palpable, especially during the neoliberal regime. What is epochal about it, as one learns from the resistance movements, is that 'mutual altruism' (reciprocal altruism), as against the self-interest of egoistic individualism of the extant (mainstream) development paradigm, has transcended as the founding principle of the alternative (new) development paradigm.[1] These movements have created space for building a collective understanding about the development objective for collective emancipation. As the space grows larger, the same collective understanding underscores the emergence of the alternative development paradigm as a natural choice that can change the world. It is an alternative development epistemology of the deprived, the powerless and the ones who are at the margins at all levels, including local, national and global (Ray, 2012). The mutual altruism as the founding principle of this new paradigm brings integration between humans on the one hand and humans and nature on the other based on the principle of solidarity while recognising the importance of the co-evolution of humans and nature. This is what I call 'cohesive development'. Before elucidating its conceptual framework, I discuss briefly why the extant development paradigm has failed and why attempting to resuscitate the same will also fail.

Failed paradigm?

Let us begin by saying that the mainstream development paradigm of almost all nation states of the globe is essentially rooted in the logic of capital that seeks to expand the capital circuit. Even if seen in the context of a welfare state, the instrumental role of 'welfarism' undeniably creates a passage for expansion of the latter. The truth is that surplus generation is the logic of capital under a capital system and the soul of the development paradigm. While the scope for obfuscating the development narratives, especially of the third world countries, under surplus value generation is more, the logic of capital under capital system controls, shapes and direct their development process. The quest for generating unlimited surplus value has reached its outer limits. Its fall-out is disastrous even for the capital system, which is facing a systemic crisis and encountering systemic disorder that has halted its further expansion (Cangiani, 2017). The accumulation of human misery, as a consequence, ridicules the development paradigm, which has lost its relevance to humanity, especially the deprived ones and nature. By not recognising the principles of co-evolution of human and nature, it has become less resilient.

The steep rise in the concentration of wealth on the one hand and wage stagnation and growing unemployment to a frightening scale on the other are exacerbating the crisis of the capital system. The perpetual shrinkage of the real economy (Antunes, 2010b, p. 19) has given rise to inner contradiction in the capital system at another level. And, if Piketty is found to be correct in his forecast of a still higher level of inequality, the capital system will further aggravate dichotomy in the economy for its survival. It may not matter if it is incompatible with the objective of the capital circuit to expand in the short run. The capital system has no other choice but to create more dichotomies at all levels of economic activity under global capitalism. In the process, it creates an 'underdevelopment trap' in which all regressive forces reinforce each other, leading to further peripheralisation of the deprived. The welfarist approach, especially of the third world countries, fails to counter the cumulative effect of their suffering and bring them out of the trap.

Joseph Stiglitz calls the capital system 'ersatz capitalism' in that, although it is at an advanced stage with entropic drift, it has failed to show the workings of a normal market economy (Zizek, 2017a, p. 29). The market economy can never avoid such an obvious outcome, leaving no reason to doubt the false epistemological construction of the development paradigm. It yields only contradictions that are of course inner but mature enough to weaken the capital system and endanger capital for being less valorised. The only route available for valorising capital is to subordinate use value to exchange value, such that the capital system fails to develop without a declining rate of the utilization of use value (Antunes, 2010a, p. 16). The uncontrollable expansion of capital oriented towards exchange value to the detriment of use value indicates ecological incompatibility with capital's mode of social metabolic reproduction (Mészáros, 2017).

Commodification, social metabolic order and divisibility

While competitive accumulation of capital determines the order of social metabolism and its reproduction, the current market society propelled by the forces of globalization has turned human behaviour into a commodity. Once this has been achieved, capital can penetrate everywhere to guide every human action and reduce everything to exchange relations by subjugating the non-commodified relations to commodification. It means that everything has an exchange value, a market value that invades every sphere of life, personal relations, families, community ties, health, education, civic life, law, politics etc. (Sandel, 2014). While exchange values of commodity feed the capital circuit, it subsumes humans and nature. The commodification of nature or subsumption of it to capital directs the emergence of the social metabolic order. Even the subsistence economy, which ensures its survival by basing its system of production on self-consumption, has shifted its production for sale and fostered privatisation of land resources (Nathan and Kelkar, 2012). The system has now witnessed the emergence of a new social arrangement and economic behaviour with growing social divisibility between the gainers and losers in monetised transactions that entail exchange value (Datta, 2009, pp. 64–66).

The loss of use value in exchange owing to the commodification of nature (or exchange of more ecological use value for less) is the fall-out of the logic of capital, which is one of the most significant capitalist distortions. Widening the space for the creation of more exchange value to the detriment of the loss of ecological use value for accumulation of wealth is increasingly threatening the survival conditions of all humans, let alone the poor and the disadvantaged. It has deepened the planetary ecological crisis and driven the earth system towards more hostile states from which it is difficult to return. It may lead to the disappearance of a safe operating space for humanity (Angus, 2015). The interest of humankind may cease to be indivisible.

The social metabolic order under the capital system encourages expropriation of nature, which is nothing but the appropriation of nature without exchange. In other words, it is appropriation minus equality in all exchange relationships (Foster and Clark, 2018). Appropriation without reciprocity, in which conditions of reproduction are not maintained, causes what is known as 'metabolic rift', a rift in the metabolic relation between humans and nature (Foster and Clark, 2018).[2] The cure can hardly be traced in von Liebig's (2018) 'law of replenishment' as elemental natural processes are ruptured. The rift grows larger and becomes a source that breeds inequality and debases nature. As nature (that provides production conditions) undergoes more transformation for creating more wealth by the logic of capital, the rift grows further. Two inescapable truths facing developing countries in particular are due to (1) the concentration of wealth in a few hands, and therefore, growing inequality and (2) the incessant degradation of natural resources (Ray, 2012).

The environmental inequality under global capitalism in addition to income inequality which is already in existence seems to have worsened the development scenario of the peripheral countries who are exporters of primary goods. It is arguably much worse than unfavourable terms of trade (in terms of relative prices) with the core countries. For example, a large comparative study implemented over many years clearly shows how Ecuador (a peripheral country because it exports primary goods) meets the demand of global capitalism at the expense of local environmental degradation. It further shows how the commodification of nature is associated with the increased social metabolism of the latest phase of global capitalism and how it has triggered socio-environmental movement in the country (Latorre et al, 2015).

This case exemplifies unequal ecological exchange, in that the energy exchange ratio or the value of the embodied energy is heavily biased against the periphery (Foster and Holleman, 2014).[3] While the argument of core–periphery relations in the international context of environmental degradation parallels the rural–urban context within a nation, core (urban) may be seen as growing at the expense of the periphery (rural). The growth of core-periphery relations is a natural corollary of the capital system in which capital has its own logic of expansion. Wallerstein argues why and how it goes on reproducing such relations for incorporating every economic transaction into the capital circuit even within a country (Wallerstein, 2004). It is the same social metabolic order that creates exchange value by means of unleashing forces of commodification in the periphery by transferring surplus to the core. Implicit in this development paradigm is unaccounted social cost that deepens the misery of both humans and nature.

Social cost

In the absence of any mechanism to absorb the cost incurred, the capital system externalises cost to society for its survival and growth. I have argued elsewhere that the socialisation of private cost forms an inherent but unstated logic of growth of private enterprise system under capitalism (Ray, 2010). One never knows how society pays for it owing to, for example, the metabolic rift that such a practice creates between humans and nature. Human misery, which surfaces in the form of inequality, deprivation, loss of employment and income, loss of ownership and control over assets and resources and more importantly loss of social cohesion, and nature's misery manifested in the form of its degradation entails cost to the society. Society may tolerate the social cost up to a limit, but once it exceeds the limit, the system fluctuates wildly and erratically and becomes chaotic. It may move far away from equilibrium (Wallerstein, 2004). When social cost is distributed it is always the poor and disadvantaged who bear the brunt of it (Swaney and Martin, 1989).

Even if the capital system succeeds in reorganising its production conditions, it can hardly internalise the cost. It has to continue to externalise its cost for its uninterrupted growth (Foster, 2002). It can do so until the social cost reaches the level of least tolerance. The destruction of production conditions by the capital system owing to the commodification of nature, described by O'Connor as the 'second contradiction of capitalism', entails cost to the economy and society (O'Connor, 1991).

Under the burden of the accumulated cost of the growing marginalisation of millions of people, who are outstripped from their possible economic gain that ensures sustainable livelihood, and nature, the question is, can the logic of capital ever rectify capitalist market distortions? This is a tautology, in that the capital system is expected to dispose of its own laws of survival and growth. However, such a tautology creates a 'democratic illusion', fostering false hope in the minds of the deprived. It masks the reality of domination, exploitation and brutal struggles and prevents the radical transformation of the society (Zizek, 2017b, p. 28). While examining how the substantive economy is under continuous and vicious attack of the formal economy under neoliberal globalisation, Federici observes,

> The recent phase of the neo-liberal globalization has produced a historic leap in the size of the world proletariat, through a global process

of enclosures that has separated millions from their lands, their jobs, their customary rights – by destroying subsistence economies and by separating producers from the means of subsistence by making millions dependent on monetary income.

(as quoted in O'Hearn and Grubacic, 2016)

The situation is catastrophic in that substantive freedom, as defined by Sen (Cangiani, 2017), of the great majority of humanity is lost. Global capital under the forces of globalisation divides humans, setting the people of countries against each other to see who can produce more cheaply by driving wages, working conditions and environmental standards to the lowest in order to survive in the war of all against all (Lebowitz, 2006). Much more dangerous is that it is splitting the social cohesiveness of the deprived, especially those of third world countries, creating a state of hopelessness. The epochal transcendence of Polanyi's double movement that created the social history in the 19th century is felt in the 21st century, when society has started protecting itself through resistance movements, as mentioned earlier, against the perils inherent in a self-regulated market system (Polanyi, 1944). The resistance movement has now found its expression in combatting not only economic deprivation, but also environmental degradation and all types of social discrimination, including gender, race and caste. In other words, divisiveness of any kind in any form which has been widening as a sequel to the onset of neoliberalism is now challenged world over (Ray, 2012). The development epistemology must now rest on, as one learns from the movements, different development coordinates.

Paradigm shift?

This suggests that the coordinates of transformation must change from the parts to the whole. In the old paradigm the dynamics of the whole in a complex system is understood from properties of the parts (Capra, 1996). The paradigm shift of development seeks reversal of the relationships between the parts on the one hand and between the parts and the whole on the other.[4] It suggests a radically different social metabolic order that corresponds to the reproductive order of a society which is sustainable and based on the principle of substantive equality and freedom (Mészáros, 2017). The process of substantive freedom finds its real expression only when the development paradigm rests on cooperation and solidarity between humans and humans and nature (Honneth, 2015; Ray, 2012).[5] The coordinates of transformation must arise from cooperation, not competition. The dialectics of the progress of human society is then governed by the law of reciprocal altruism, not methodological individualism. The logic of empathy will then find its meaningful articulation in the 'phenomenology of spirit' that recognises intersubjective plurality based on mutual and reciprocal sense of recognising each other's rights and duties (Jahanbegloo, 2017b, p. 74).

Cohesive development arises as an alternative development paradigm based on these new coordinates of transformation.

Cohesive development

The foundational norms of transformation based on cohesive development are located precisely at four levels. These include (1) reciprocal altruism at the individual level, as constituent of rationality of individual behaviour, (2) interdependence as a relational totality and structural relational totality, (3) no singularity of development to gravitate towards, and (4) the economics of solidarity (Ray, 2012). The alternative development paradigm that grows based on these norms must replace the logic of capital that has been working in the capital system with a new one that never controls labour. The production relations are then determined by the forces of cohesiveness. Capital will be structurally reoriented to serve the needs of social reproduction and happiness through decommodification of labour and nature (Gills, 2010). The new logic of capital in practice calls for new politics that empower the poor and deprived but *not* without disempowering the rich. The new politics to create new institutions must begin to defy the power structure on the one hand and institutionalise laws of cohesive development on the other.

The primary condition for cohesive development is social cohesion among individuals with a sense of community and commitment to the common objective based on collective understanding despite the differences that might exist between them. It is this common objective that binds individuals together. However, this can happen only if the common objective never falls in line with the existing power structure, which is undemocratic and exploitative, yielding powerlessness and deprivation of the majority. In other words, no social cohesion can ensure cohesive development as an alternative development paradigm if it fails to recognise the debilitating impact of the existing power structure on it. The irony, however, is that the power structure is never given an entry to the discourse on social cohesion and development as an analytical component by multilateral organisations such as the World Bank, the Organisation for Economic Co-operation and Development (OECD), the Club of Rome etc. (Colletta et al, 1999; OECD, 2012). Then how does one expect social cohesion to bring about cohesive development without changing the existing power structure that breeds inequality, disintegration and impoverishment? Jan Jensen may be right when he argues that this notion is primarily used by multilateral organisations to mask social inequality (Jane, 1998).

Hence, cohesive development, in the present context, is conceived as an alternative development paradigm that replaces the logic of capital as it works in the capital system with a new one that seeks to establish a radically different social metabolic order based on the principle of solidarity between humans on the one hand and between humans and nature on the other. Here reciprocal altruism, contrary to the methodological individualism of the mainstream development paradigm, shapes the development paradigm. While holding the people, the deprived, together, mutual (reciprocal) altruism affirms the achievement of common objectives based on collective understanding, with the key to substantive freedom or actual freedom residing in the 'apolitical' network of social relations, from market to family (Zizek, 2017b, p. 29). This holds well equally at all levels, including local, national and international. It also seeks to defy the existing power structure which acts as a deterrent to cohesive development. Reciprocal altruism also institutionalises the fulfilment of all the necessities of life, while equal space is created for all to harness their full potential and live with dignity. A new development paradigm is thus conceived which suggests deep structural change from the grassroots to bring about equity and justice while maintaining relational totality. Moreover, it never allows natural resources, the very base of the productive forces of the economy, to be exhausted beyond the limit where co-evolution of both human and nature stops. It is only within this framework that one may have reasons to argue that sustainable development is realisable.

The new logic of capital will never valorise capital, but recognise the 'self-valorisation' of workers. One can then see, as Negri argues, the theoretical possibility of proletarian independence within capital (Negri, 1984). Self-valorisation subordinates the power of capital of the capital system to give precedence to use value over the creation of exchange value. It defies capitalist mechanisms of accumulation and development (Negri, 2005).

Mutual cooperation and solidarity

The expansion of the domain of use value of the products and their transactions over exchange value creation implies expansion of the commons in this alternative development framework. As the commons expand, social products will provide more use value for the common satisfaction of needs (Lebowitz, 2016). While one has to examine, however, how the commons can expand to produce more use values, Rifkin's concept of 'collaborative commons' (Refkin, 2014) may not be as useful as it appears to be for the present task. It is true that this approach is opposite to two other forms of social organisation, including egoistic competition and the search for profit and centralised planning. However, overemphasis on the access of goods and services and excessive reliance on market relations and their forces determining the size of the commons to be shared by all participating individuals may infuse another dose of inequality to the already unequal society. When inequality rises between those who have access to the commons in the sphere of exchange and those who do not, collaborative commons may tend to collapse. One must not see expansion of the commons from the lens of the erstwhile Soviet system of socialism that failed to recognise individual initiative for change and development.

Equality may occur in the form of co-operatives of individuals or associated producers in any form guided by the values of mutual cooperation and solidarity and who create their own organisations within the framework of 'comprehensive co-operation' (Yang and Wen, 2011). The deprived ones may organise themselves into large subjects and negotiate and transact with the state and market, enabling them to respond to market forces. One may argue that this is an effective integration of both market and non-market forces. If the market economy based on competitive laws fails to repair the system, power-based political 'voice' is useful (Hirschman, 1970). This voice may force some institutions or organisations to exit. The non-market forces are then assigned the responsibility of combatting the logic of capital to purify the market of its capitalist distortions without taking an anti-market stance.

The recent experiences in Cuba and Argentina in developing workers' co-operatives provide insightful lessons in this regard.[6] The conversion of state-run institutions in Cuba into independent social enterprises (self-managed co-operatives) (Lebowitz, 2016; Marszalek, 2017) is an historic transition from a bureaucratic top-down approach to democratic governance while redefining commons for the benefit of all. It is important to note that gradually several activities, including the management of forests, fields, waterways, education, health, production etc. became part of this process. The institutions were socialised in that democratic governance of the community was infused and wealth is now made available to all (Durand, 2017).

The experience of Emilia Romagna, a region of four million people in northern central Italy, is equally rewarding. A network of consumers, farmers and worker-driven co-operatives has been in existence for the last 150 years based on 'reciprocity' (Lappi, 2006). This is another form of economic solidarity that shows how mutual insurance can transform the economic structure to create decent employment without assigning the responsibility for change to capital. In India, examples abound in the field of natural resource management. Here people in arid conditions brought back ecological resilience, recovering forest and grassland through their own efforts. They revived their rural economy, leaving no scope for capital to determine their success (Ray, 2012).

The process of emergence of self-organisation based on mutual cooperation and solidarity by means of maintaining mutually consistent relationships within the network gives rise to a 'niche economic structure'.[7] The construction of a niche economic structure brings about structural transformation without being led by the logic of capital of the capital system. It redefines the same being led by the forces of cohesive development based on solidarity and mutual insurance. The formation of a niche structure, which is a result of the process of emergence of self-organisation, indicates a shift from the old paradigm. In the old paradigm there exists a fundamental structure that gives rise to process. However, here each structure is seen as the manifestation of an underlying process (Capra, 1996). When the process emerges and networking multiplies based on development coordinates of cohesive development, nothing can stop the co-evolution of humans and nature. Civilisational growth may then be discernible, putting an end to the misery of both human and nature.

While the perspective of cohesive development as an alternative development paradigm as explained is embryonic, its footprint is traced in this chapter. Its irrefutable emergence based on solidarity between humans on the one hand and humans and nature on the other as a product of inexorable forces of history may have distinct impact on the evolutionary growth of human society and economy in the 21st century.

Overview of the contributions

Authors in this volume have systematically reasoned out why there can be no other alternative paradigm than cohesive development to free humans and nature from misery. While cohesive development is conceived in different ways by the authors, they convincingly argue that the dialectics of social change are going to take human society away from where it is now. Cohesive development as the present discourse explores needs to be acknowledged as an emerging development paradigm. It is this more than any other approach than can extricate human civilisation from its decay.

Gail Omvedt, in her chapter titled "Cohesive Development: Forging Theoretical Space for Alternative Developmental Paradigm", not only shows the contradiction between the laws of motion of capitalist development and cohesive development of humans and nature but also discusses repressive social structure and oppressed social groups. Both are antagonistic to the emergence of the alternative development paradigm. In relation to the existing development paradigm in the era of imperialist globalisation, she asserts, cohesive development would have to mean a complementary development of healthy human relations and productive forces on the one hand, and healthy prosperity of the rest of nature with which humans do their development activities on the other. According to her, the perspectives of Karl Marx and Jotiba Phule may be combined to achieve cohesive development. The main thread of Phule's perspective, which is the unbound relation of liberated humanity with nature, and Marx's understanding of metabolic rift that shows how disturbance in the circulation of matter between humans and soil in capitalist agriculture violates the condition necessary to lasting fertility of the soil, help her to conceive cohesive development. According to her, cohesive development is non-oppressive and non-extractive development between humans and humans and humans and nature. It is a process which is fundamentally based on renewable, environmentally enriching and decentralised production. Moreover, she suggests that the majority who are affected adversely by the existing system could rally around the general long-term interests of a cohesive, ecologically balanced, prosperous and healthy society. They must find a way to bring about cohesiveness among themselves, without which they cannot come up with alternative development paradigm of their kind. To forge a theoretical space for an alternative development paradigm, she proposes a unified theory that combines the history of people's contributions with the grassroots-level natural science experiments at both national and international levels.

Amiya Kumar Bagchi's chapter, "Enemies of Cohesive Development", which was his inaugural address at the "Cohesive Development: An Alternative Paradigm?" seminar, begins by defining what cohesive development means. According to him, it means the ability of human beings to develop their full potential. This attainment, while tracing back the history, has been central to the objectives of the founders of great religions such as Buddhism and Christianity and the thinking of all great men from Socrates to Karl Marx, Frederick Engels and Rabindranath Tagore. But from the outset of what is called civilisation, there have been individuals who have denied that the interests of any other human beings than themselves matter in the pursuit in their well-being. This appetitive pursuit of self-interest has become embedded in the concept of unregulated capitalism. With the unbridled pursuit of profit by the capitalist class, there have always been tendencies to concentrate and centralise capital, increasing the power of big capital. Consciously using media of mass communication and education, such individuals could exercise control over the thinking of ordinary people and persuade them to accept the highly unequal capitalist order. The author goes on to explain how the drive for what has been called bandwagon, snob and Veblen effects in consumption are added to the manipulative devices mentioned. The capitalist order, according to Bagchi, is in crisis. The currently ongoing Great Recession, fascist tendencies and the denial of the fundamental postulate of civil liberty of individuals have exposed the basic contradiction of the order. However, the author pins his hope on the protest movement that people around the world have been waging against the capitalist order. This may create conditions for cohesive development to emerge as an alternative development paradigm.

Antje Linkenbach, in her chapter "The Power of Audibility: Contestation and Communication as a Route to Cohesive Development", argues that cohesive development can be considered as an alternative to the existing concepts of development only when it is the result of respectful communication and debate based on the social recognition and parity of participation of all members of the larger society or nation, but also within particular groups. Under such circumstances, she maintains, cohesiveness will be characterised by diversity, multiperspectivity and multivocality. Then development will be redefined in multiple ways and probably stripped of the dominance of one of its core elements, namely economic growth. However, for such a debate to take place, social conditions have to be challenged to the effect that they allow identifying, criticising and overcoming existing intersecting social inequalities and injustices. They must provide space for productive confrontation, communication and negotiation at all levels of the society. For achieving cohesive development, apart from changing the socio-legal and political order, a basic condition is that the mind-set of the dominant sections of the people must undergo a change as well. The audibility of the marginalised is needed.

The author focusses on visions of a good life and a preferred future 'from below' as encountered in India based on three brief cases that include an indigenous group (the Adivasis), Himalayan hill dwellers and Dalit. Based on these studies, she illustrates how these marginalised groups have critically addressed issues like economic rationality and economic humans, alternative forms of economic activity, their relations to nature, gender relations, political participation and the local knowledge system. While their perceptions greatly differ from the mainstream, lack of audibility, she argues, shows deficit of democracy. Drawing inspiration from the Zapatista movement in the region of Chiapas in Southern Mexico, she suggests that democracy needs to be broadened by means of promoting a culture of listening. While mutual respect and solidarity between all sections of society guarantees audibility, according to her, cohesive development will be possible only if the "victims of underdevelopment" are transformed into subjects and into "conscious and active shapers of their history".

M. V. Nadkarni, in his chapter "A Genuine Social Democracy: The Only Way!", argues that cohesive development, which he defines as democratic, egalitarian and sustainable, can be realised only under social democracy. According to him, social democracy avoids the evils of both capitalism and socialism but incorporates the merits of both. Going further to draw merits from both ideological strands to see their compatibility with cohesive development, the author argues that capitalism breeds inequality to an unacceptable extent and has failed to ensure sustainable development. Hence, it is inherently impossible for capitalism to offer cohesive development. Equally problematic is communism, which is not democratic and lacks the inertia for economic growth and sustainable development. However, social democracy as a political philosophy provides scope for private capital to grow and contribute to economic growth. However, it has to function under the control of a democratic state. In capitalism, on the other hand, democracy functions under the control of capital. While drawing lessons from India, which, according to the author, functions under social democracy, the country has failed to meet the basic needs of the people, let alone democratic values. However, it hardly means India can never meet these objectives as constitutional obligations.

Joseph Tharamangalam's chapter, "Reimagining Socialism for the 21st century: Cuba's Experiments with Cooperativism and Solidarity Economies", shows a unique way of bringing about cohesive development based on field experiences in Cuba. He perceives cohesive development based on the principles of solidarity, which manifests in the form of cooperativisation and defies the myth called "There Is No Alternative" created by neoliberal capitalism. There is an alternative, and the author argues that the emerging forms of cooperatives offer the best alternative to a disastrous embrace of capitalism offered by the US and other 'friends' as the only route to prosperity. Tharamangalam envisages a 'cooperative road' to reforms as a model of 21st-century socialism. According to him, in their quest for a more sustainable model of development Cubans are exploring ways to 'rectify the errors' in their current model by formulating and implementing the needed economic and political reforms. In this struggle, the central questions, the author observes, are how to free the economy from such state control, implement greater decentralisation and democratisation of the system and provide greater freedom and incentives to its people to draw on the high levels of social and intellectual capital and traditions of solidarity. These are non-state forms of property and reimagination of the very idea of 'social property'. This is also a transition to forms of property and economic enterprises outside the state sector. They are self-employment and small business ventures – a model of solidarity economy organised as new forms of self-governing and self-managing cooperatives. The expanding space for the self-managed and democratically controlled solidarity economy independent of state control illustrates how cohesive development can be brought about.

Leandro Morais, based on Brazil's recent development experience, reposes his conviction in promoting the social and solidarity economy (SSE), which is instrumental for achieving cohesive development that sustains. It is a development model, which the author claims, is alternative to capitalism. In his chapter "Territorial Development and Social and Solidarity Economy in Brazil: Some Contributions to Cohesive Development", Morais explains how the viability of economic activity is rooted in the territorial dynamics under the influence of the socio-cultural values that differ from other territories. Once the notion of territoriality emerging from the interdependence of the economic sphere is accepted as a strategy to promote SSE, the author maintains that the endogenous process of development accelerates while it fosters consolidation of social capital within the territory concerned. The solidarity economy enterprises, run by the solidarity groups based on the principles of self-management and cooperation, have proved to be an innovative alternative for employment and income generation, especially for those who are socially and economically excluded. The author notes, in the context of Brazil, that not only the mode of engagement of these enterprises with production and processing, but also their proven accomplishments, activities in the field of services, finance, trade and exchanges have witnessed steady expansion over the years under the self-management of solidarity groups.

The significant aspect of the growth of SSE in Brazil is the creation of SENAES, a formal institutional organ that has gained entry into the federal government's pluriannual plans through its "Social and Solidarity Economy Program in Development". Actually, it marked the beginning of the process of institutionalisation of the public policy related to the promotion of the solidarity economy in the country. Although the SENAES could achieve considerable success in framing public policy in favor of SSE, resource crunch in addition to other problems are not yet removed from the trading channels and appear to have been posing formidable challenges for them to grow. However, according to the author, building networks based on the principles of solidarity as well as greater integration of economic transformation with the social, cultural and political changes will thwart these aberrations.

The chapter titled "Tracing Cohesive Development from Practice to Theory: Experience in Maharashtra" authored by Bharat Patankar argues how some recent experiments conducted by the people themselves in the state of Maharashtra have initiated the emergence of cohesive development. While the moorings of the society's evolution at the early stage was cohesive development of free human beings and unbound nature, the author argues that modern industrial society under capitalism has destroyed it and halted the process of change in that direction. This is glaringly so, especially when one recounts how agricultural practices have created an agro-ecological rift that has destabilised the living conditions of the farming community to an unbearable extent. Drawing lessons from the experiment that the people in some parts of Maharashtra conducted for drought eradication which, according to author, is a result of a particular kind of planning and practices of the ruling classes and castes, the author concludes that no lasting solution is discernible without cohesive development.

While the people live in an oppressive framework of caste, class, race and gender with a great deal of segmentation, their movement brought all of them together to eradicate the conditions that make the area prone to drought. Their novel experiment of creating fusion between traditional knowledge and modern science yielded an alternative development paradigm, in that solidarity between all stakeholders is established on the one hand, and between farmers and nature (land and water use) on the other. An alternative land–water relationship in terms of determining the exact requirement of water for agriculture could establish the relationship of equity that has a profound impact on sustainability. The emergence of such an alternative development paradigm in agriculture in different regions of Maharashtra, even by way of introducing renewable processes, epitomises the process that could sustain development based on the principles of cohesive development.

In his chapter titled "Towards Developing the Theoretical Perspective of Cohesive Development", Abhijit Ghosh seeks greater cohesion among those who are the victims of the economic order that exists today and the solidarity network of different resistance movements taking place around the world against the same order. Based on the insightful lessons he has drawn, especially from the conservation of common property resources, he argues how the powerless can sustain their livelihood by way of defying the regressive forces of change within the framework of consequentialism.

What matters most is to develop a solidarity network among the powerless to share developmental gains equally and improve their living conditions together.

Several other studies have also inspired Ghosh to develop the conceptual framework of cohesive development. He earmarked four strands to conceptualise them: (a) positional objectivity, (b) humanism, (c) institution, and (d) problematic. While each one is potentially rich enough to influence the course of cohesive development, the framework might lose its essence if complementarity between them is downplayed. The deeper understanding of concrete historical conditions of the current situation bears great significance in this regard. But no recognition is accorded to it in the mainstream development paradigm. Similarly, the author asserts, no development can take place if opportunities are created only for a few. This goes against humanism, the absence of which is antithetical to development. What is required, therefore, is to develop and make instrumental institutions that are appropriate for bringing about development without sacrificing human values.

Barbara Harriss-White, in her chapter titled "Formal, Informal, Social and Unsocial Economy: Waste and the Work and Politics of Women", critiques the concept of solidary economy and assesses the potential growth of social solidary organisations in India as an alternative model of development to capitalism. She takes the informal economy and the politics of subaltern women to examine it. For the second part, she uses ethnographic evidence from women's work in the waste economy of a South Indian town. She observes that the distinctive form of empowerment of women has failed to challenge both the logic and mode of expansion of capitalism, nor can it move against Polanyi's destructive market society.

The informal economy and collectivities such as tribal or caste association, which are SSE, are in tension with an insufficiently effective and ambivalent state. They operate through kin and work groups, debt bondage and authority over territory of small-scale capital invested in recycling, but they never challenge the logic of expansion of capitalism.

The informal waste economy develops as part of the local capitalist economy. Self-employment/petty production and trade in this field expands by multiplication rather than accumulation, as it does elsewhere. As elsewhere, waste is collectively regulated in a multiplicity of ways, in which social objectives operate under capitalism rather than in opposition or resistance to it. While Polanyi's three modes of exchange are not mutually exclusive, other social objectives (self-respect, better contracts) are more important than opposition to capitalism. The collective, self-managed activity of women in the 'everyday praxis' of caste and ethnicity seeks empowerment but in general social terms rather than in the immediate needs of waste work. Objectives such as respect and autonomy, or environmental responsibility, might form a platform for oppositional alternatives to capitalism in the future; but of this, in this town, she asserts, there is currently no sign. Rather they are antithetical to the growth of a solidary economy.

Contrary to what is observed by Barbara Harriss in her field-based study on the waste economy, Kalyan Shankar and Rohini Sahni's study on the same shows positive signs of solidarism and cohesive development. In their chapter titled "Integrating the Informal with the Formal: A Case of Cohesive Development in Urban Waste Chain", they show how the waste pickers can ally with other labour forms in the informal sector or workers in the formal sector and create a common work consciousness as the key to rallying all stakeholders. The process through which a functional prototype of formal–informal integration for waste collection has emerged in the city of Pune is insightful from the point of view of growth of a solidary economy. First, the waste pickers were collectivised to form a trade union of their own. Second, through the union, the waste pickers could reach out to other stakeholders of waste, the urban local body in particular, for safeguarding their economic and social interests.

An alternative model of governance emerged from this engagement and carved out a space for the informal waste pickers in the formal/municipal waste chains. The union was instrumental in enhancing internal cohesion between different stakeholders and paved the way for reforming the organisational and functional aspects of waste collection in the city. Besides curbing the presence of child labour in this trade, exploitative financial transaction with scrap dealers is eliminated due to the formation of an alternative credit channel by the union. The municipality endorsed the initiative of issuing identity cards to the waste pickers, which exemplifies solidarity. The entire process finally culminated into the formation of SWaCH, India's first wholly owned cooperative of self-employed waste pickers and other urban poor. It entered into a memorandum of understanding (MoU) in 2008. SWaCH illustrates how the journey of waste pickers is a model of cohesive development that upholds the interests of the state, citizens, waste pickers and the city at large. The authors argue that one must count its transformative potential that adds to the processes of inclusion and sustainability.

Neetu Choudhary, in her chapter "Organising among Informal Workers: Can Pragmatism Invoke Cohesive Development?", traces the emergence of solidarity in the contemporary world in various forms of informality. Its phenomenal rise, especially in the wake of the implementation of ruthless neoliberal policies, is the result of a drastic shift in labour relation associated with the changing production structure. Choudhary's paper is a qualitative reflection based on a survey of existing literature along with the author's individual interactions with the representatives from civil society organisations and trade unions from several countries. What is emerging, she observes, is a new form of organising which is not necessarily within the framework of class struggle and which is defined for long as trade union movement across the world. However, the informal workers' organising and their solidarity may be explained, she argues, in terms of 'pragmatism'. While it displays discontent against the onslaught of neoliberal capitalism through resistance and cooperation, it attempts to carve out space for it. However, it never challenges the hegemony of capital.

She argues that the trend of such a resistance movement of informal workers shows remarkable transformation in organising strategy of the workers in that they collude with the stakeholders who are perceived to be on the other side. It reflects a growing emergence of common interest that deepens by altering the ways workers' voices are expressed and negotiated. This process that seeks justice and space for everyone in the world under pragmatism has the potential to offer an alternative development paradigm by way of invoking cohesiveness among them.

Parvaz Azharul Huq, in his chapter "Does Community-Driven Development Empower the Powerless: The Case of Urban Bangladesh", emphasises power relations as an issue that needs to be addressed within the realm of cohesive development as an alternative development paradigm. While examining the participatory development process initiated through the community-driven development approach in Bangladesh, he observes how existing power relations determine what is possible to do. CDD is conceived within the confines of the three parameters of decentralisation, democratisation and collective action. These are all uncompromisingly basic requirements for cohesive development to come about. What is missing, however, is an explicit recognition of the unequal economic, social and political power relations that never allow the powerless to share development gains. The author explains it as "elite capture" that distorts the outcomes of the participatory processes to their benefit.

Huq has looked closely into the community-led participatory development process while investigating the functioning of the Urban Partnerships for Poverty Reduction (UPPR) project in Bangladesh, one of the largest in the world for urban poverty reduction. He shows how the logic of clientelistic and patronage politics has influenced the local governance process through shaping local government institutions. In other words, the author observes, the aim of such an intervention is actually to consolidate the local political power base instead of sharing power down to local levels following democratic decentralisation. This is, however, not true of all programme interventions. For example, group savings and credit programmes, community group activities for infrastructural development, could succeed to a significant extent in some areas. In any case, the author argues that unless the practice of co-opting the traditional power structure is stopped, cohesive development will be far off. No transformation as intended would be possible.

Lalatendu Keshari Das argues in his chapter, "Neo-community Formation, Contestation and Policy Making in India: Narratives from Chilika", how increasing fragmentation of the marginalised subaltern group helps capital to consolidate itself more and exercise more control over them. The redressal of sustainable livelihood of the marginalised subaltern group, as a result, remains far off. Hence, the choice left to them is to shift their approach towards cohesive development. This is what he has observed in his study on aquaculture activities in Odisha's Chilika Lake.

The lake was a traditional source of livelihood for a large number of subaltern groups belonging to several caste and sub-castes living around the lake. However, with the introduction of shrimp cultivation by the state government in collaboration with the corporate houses, efforts made earlier by the same government on behalf of the poor fishers were wasted. Worse, the state government changed the access to Chilika so that the majority of the culture source was allotted to the non-fishing caste. Along with it, shrimp cultivation was intensified. As a result, the traditional source of livelihood of all of the fishing community was hit hard. It gave rise to their resistance movement with the support of several civil society organisations. Meanwhile, judicial pronouncement clearly went against environmental degeneration owing to intensive shrimp cultivation.

However, despite the judicial pronouncement, shrimp cultivation continued. At the same time, movement that was organised some time ago gradually lost its steam. According to the author, this was mostly the result of fragmentation based on caste affiliation and the collaboration of some subcaste fisher groups with upper caste shrimp cultivators and local corporate houses. The divergent fishers' community could have maintained their cohesion, which would have protected them against the vagaries of capital. According to the author, it failed to do so and the anti-dispossession movement fell apart. Taking a cue from this case, the author asserts that the cohesiveness of capital cannot take over the fragmentation of the community and demolish their cooperative societies in Chilika for their sustainable livelihood. The fishing community may be left with no choice but to follow a cohesive development approach, as the present case study shows. It may mould state and direct capital for their interest.

Improving community networking is instrumental to bringing about cohesive development, Meghadeepa Chakraborty argues in her chapter titled "Community Network for Cohesive Development in Rural India: An Exploratory Study". In an attempt to examine if a cohesive development approach can offer an alternative development paradigm to capitalism, she extensively surveyed literature. She also undertook a field survey in four villages in four states in India. According to the author, no community can ever evolve without mutual respect for each other, trust, shared vision, negotiating with diversity etc. This is contrary to methodological individualism, which is the foundation of the growth of capitalism. The culture of social insurance, which insures that people in a community will lead a dignified life, is alien to it. However, caring for each other, an offshoot of a moral economy, does exist in the community notwithstanding the onslaught of the market economy. This is what Chakraborty found in her study conducted in the villages of (1) Anandwari (Rajasthan), (2) Bhoominagar (Gujarat), (3) Chetanagar (South Assam) and (4) Dhurlabwadi (North Tripura).

For instance, in Bhoomonagar village much diversity exists in the community in terms of caste and religion. Despite such differences, the author notes that people care for each other to the extent that they are proud of the fact, and their village has always maintained communal harmony and was never infected by divisiveness of any kind. The occupational interdependence and mobility within the village instantaneously bind them together. It has intensified social capital that helps the community endure any crisis they encounter. This provides collective efficiency, in that villagers seek redressal of their problem, for instance, indebtedness or scarcity of money, in the event of organising any social ceremony at the household level. However, sometimes the lack of trust and the domination of powerful people do not allow collective action to take root. Nevertheless, the author feels that if the poor are appropriately incentivised through state intervention by way of designing pro-poor policies, emergence of the process of cohesive development can never be challenged.

Gopinath Reddy, in his chapter "Implementation of the Forest Rights Act 2006 and Its Implications for Cohesive Development: The Case of Telangana and Andhra Pradesh", closely examined the Forest Rights Act of 2006 and found it had serious limitations in creating provision for the tribals to live in harmony with the forest. The author underscores that in practice the act has failed to undo the 'historical injustice' meted out to the tribal dwelling in the forest. They are yet again considered as 'encroachers' by the state in the post-liberalisation era. One of the noticeable flaws, as pointed out by the author, was that overemphasis on individual land rights over community rights adversely affected social cohesion that binds the tribals together and reinforces their well-being. Even access of the tribals to common land was denied by the state of Andhra Pradesh legally through a range of policies. While there were JFM/CFM (joint forest management/community forest management) committees to allow non-timber forest produce collection, the tribals hardly have legal rights to access to it.

The author has shown how provisions in the act are weak in practice to address their problems. Worse is the acquisition of land by the government in the name of development projects. This posed a serious obstacle to the tribals to assert their right to land. Another important clause in the act is that forest land titles assured under the act are inalienable and as such titles granted to the claimants have no absolute and alienable right over the property. The large-scale rejection of individual claims for the right to lands is another matter of serious concern and, hence, needs to be addressed in a systematic manner. As the author observes, several civil society organisations and political parties are mobilising the tribals to exercise their rights to land where they have been living for generations. However, much still needs to be improved in this area. At the same time, the state must design its development intervention to enhance the tribals' well-being without disturbing the harmony that exists between the tribals and the forest. The Forest Rights Act and its provisions must bring about cohesive development between the tribals and between the tribals and the forest. However, this is missing in the act.

Concluding remarks

Critiquing the extant development paradigm and its disastrous consequences lead one to explore its alternative. However, if the seed of development of the alternative is that of the old, the old is reproduced. True, the form of development may be different in such a situation, but it may not be desirable. Development aberrations could then worsen the misery of both humans and nature and deepen, in turn, civilisational crisis. The only way out is to seek for an alternative development paradigm, the new development seed, that could reverse the degenerative process. It is this that the present volume attempts to explore and to demonstrate how cohesive development could be the alternative development paradigm. It is indeed our hope that the unique engagement of this book will pave the way to open up fresh debate on development.

Notes

1 Several social movements took place in the recent past both at the national and the international level. While most of them were directed against globalization, environmental degeneration and racial and gender discrimination etc., they were all against the existing exploitative system (for a detailed discussion on these movements, see my paper titled "Economics of Solidarity: Economics of the 21st Century" [Ray, 2012]). The new social movements that are manifestations of the new social conflicts over autonomy, quality of life, human rights, political participation, environmental degeneration etc. are, needless to mention, finally shaped by the global capital system (Ci'sar', 2015). The Zapatista movement in Mexico and Buen vivir in Ecuador can be cited as some such historically significant social movements. These are not only resistance movements against globalization and the exploitative systemic order, but also have different cosmic vision that provides alternative development epistemology (Gudyuas, 2011; Burbach, Fox and Fuentes, 2013). The global justice movement is another such movement that counterposes an alternative conception of welfare and development to the ones advanced by the International Monetary Fund (IMF), World Trade Organization (WTO) etc. (Barker and Lavalette, 2015). The massive resistance movements organised by the peasants and Adivasis (tribals) in India in the recent past gives testimony to how solidarity between people from varying social, religious and economic backgrounds can develop collective understanding to achieve common objectives (Dhawale, 2018).
2 Marx referred to the 'spoliation', 'squandering' and 'robbing' of the earth in his theory of metabolic rift – according to which the extraction of soil nutrients from the land in capitalist agriculture and their shipment to the new urban industrial centres in the form of food and fibre, preventing their recirculation to the field, results in the rupture of elemental natural processes (Foster and Clark, 2018).
3 Actually, Odum has extensively dealt with it in the context of natural resources and agricultural produces being sold to the urban consumers. He argues that the value of these resources rural areas receive is much lower for value of the embodied energy and never incorporated into the monetary calculations of the value being received. (Odum, 1996).

4 In line with the conceptual revolution of quantum physics in 1930, the properties of the parts can be understood only from the dynamics of the whole (Capra, 1996).

5 While outlining three basic weaknesses of the classical model of socialism, Axel Honneth explains the process of expanding freedom in terms of (1) the freedom of individual in the public sphere, (2) the freedom which renders possible the democratic foundation of the collective will, and (3) the freedom from oppression in the intimate sphere (Honneth, 2015).

6 Cuba's success is partly derived from the kind of incentives provided elsewhere. In Argentina, factories abandoned during the financial crisis during late 1990s became sites of solidarity between workers and their local communities. (Marszalek, 2017).

7 The idea of construction of niche structure is developed based on the niche-constructing theory (NCT) that has originated as a branch of evolutionary biology. It emphasises the capacity of organisms to modify their environment and thereby influence their own and other species' evolution (Kendal et al, 2011) It differs from standard evolutionary theory (SET), according to which natural selection changes the environment for the species to change. However, according to NCT, species can change the environment through constructing niche structure (Kendal et al, 2011; Ray, 2016).

References

Angus, Ian (2015), "When did the Anthropocene begin . . . and why does it matter?" *Analytical Monthly Review*, Vol. 13, No. 5, September, p10.

Antunes, Richard (2010a), "The substance of the crisis: Introduction", in *Structural crisis of capital (Istvan Meszoras)*, Cornerstone Publications, Kharagpur, India, with the permission from Monthly Review Press, New York, p16.

Antunes Richard (2010b), op. cit., p19.

Barker, Colin and Michael Lavalette (2015), "Welfare changes and social movements", in *The Oxford handbook of social movements* (eds) Donatella Della Porta and Mario Diani, Oxford University Press, Oxford, pp711–728.

Burbach, Roger, Michael Fox and Federico Fuentes (2013), *Zed Book*, Zed Books Ltd, London, pp13–24 and 158.

Cangiani, Michale (2017), "Social freedom in the 21st century: Reading Polanyi", *Journal of Economic Issues*, Vol. LI, No. 4, December, p916.

Capra, Fritjof (1996), "System theory and the new Paradigm", in *Key concepts in critical theory ecology* (ed) Merchant Carolyn, Rawat Publications, Jaipur and New Delhi, pp334–341.

Ci'sar', Ond'rej (2015), "Social movements in political science", in *The Oxford handbook of social movements* (eds) Donatella Della Porta and Mario Diani, Oxford University Press, Great Clarendon Street, Oxford, UK, pp50–67.

Colletta, Nat J, Ghee Lim Teck and K Vitanen Anita (1999), *Social cohesion and conflict prevention in Asia-managing diversity through development*, The World Bank, Washington, DC, June, p2.

Datta, Amlan (2009), *Transitional puzzles*, Sage Publications, New Delhi, p64.

Dhawale, Ashok (2018), "Remarkable farmers' struggles in India: Some notes from Maharashtra and Rajasthan", *Agrarian South: Journal of Political Economy*, Vol. 7, No. 2, August, pp257–274.

Durand, Cliff (2017), "Cuba's new cooperatives", *Analytical Monthly Review*, Vol. 15, No. 8, p48.

Foster, Bellamy (2002), "Capitalism and ecology: The nature of contradiction", *Monthly Review*, September, pp6–16.

Foster, Bellamy and Brett Clark (2018), "The expropriation of nature", *Analytical Monthly Review*, Vol. 13, No. 12, March, p4.

Foster, Bellamy and Hannah Holleman (2014), "The theory of unequal ecological exchange A Marx-Odum dialectic", *The Journal of Peasant Studies*, Vol. 41, No. 2, March, pp199–233.

Ghosh, D N (2017), " 'The future of capitalism' Book Review 'How will capitalism end? Essays on a falling system' ", *Economic and Political Weekly*, Vol. L11, No. 48, December 2, P47.

Gills, Barry (2010), "Going south: Capitalist crisis, systemic crisis, civilizational crisis", *Third World Quarterly*, Vol. 31, No. 2, pp169–184.

Gramsci, Antonio (1971), *Selections from the prison notebooks* (eds and trans) Quintin Hoare and Geoffrey Nowell-Smith, London, Lawrence and Wishart, p276.

Gudyuas, Eduardo (2011), "Buen Vivir: Today's Tomorrow", *Development*, Vol. 54, No. 4, pp441–447.

Hirschman, Albert (1970), *Exit, voice and loyalty, responses to decline in firm, organization and state*, Harvard University Press, Cambridge, MA, London and England.

Honneth Axel (2015), *Die Idee sozialismus*, Suhrkamp, Frankfurt.

Jahanbegloo, Ramin (2017a), *The decline of civilization*, Aleph Book Company, New Delhi, pxxx.

Jahanbegloo, Ramin (2017b), op. cit., pp49–50.

Jahanbegloo, Ramin (2017c), op. cit., p74.

Jane, Jenson (1998), " 'Mapping social cohesion: The state of Canadian research', Ottawa, Canadian Policy Research Networks (from 'social cohesion: A dialectical critique of a quasi-concept' by Bernard, Paul, Department of Sociology, Université de Montréal)", www.omiss.ca/english/reference/PDF/pbernard.PDF (Accessed September 2018).

Kendal, Jeremy, Jamshid Tehrani and John Odling-Smee (2011), "Human niche construction in interdisciplinary focus", *Philosophical Transactions of the Royal Society*, Vol. 366B, pp785–792, http://rstb.royalsocietypublishing.org

Lappi, F M (2006), "A market without capitalists", *Alternet*, June, www.alternet.org/story/37920/a (Accessed September 2018) Market Without Capitalists.

Latorre, S, K Farrell and M J Alier (2015), "The commodification of nature and socio-environmental resistance in Ecuador: An inventory of accumulation by dispassion cases, 1980–2013", *Ecological Economics*, Vol. 116, August, pp58–68.

Lebowitz, Michael (2006), *Build it now: Socialism for the 21st century*, Monthly Review Press, Danish Book, New Delhi, p50.

Lebowitz, Michael (2016), "What is socialism for the 21st century?" *Analytical Monthly Review*, Vol. 14, No. 6, September, p84.

Marszalek, B (2017), "Stronger together", *Analytical Monthly Review*, October, p53.

Mészáros, Istvan (2017), "Capital's historic circle is closing – The challenge for secure exit", *Analytical Monthly Review*, Vol. 15, No. 9, p8.

Nathan, Dev and Kelkar Govind (2012), "Civilizational change, markets and privatization among indigenous peoples", in *Adivasi question, issues of land, forest and livelihood* (ed) Indra Munshi, Orient Black Swan, New Delhi, pp340–347.

Negri, A (1984), *Marx beyond Marx: Lessons on the Grundrisse*, Bergen and Gravy, New York.

Negri, A (2005), "Domination and sabotage: On the Marxist method of social transformation", in *Books for burning: Between civil war and democracy in 1970's Italy* (ed) A Negr, Verso, London.

O'Connor, J (1991), "Symposium on the second contradiction: Initial note and on contradiction of capitalism", *Capitalism, Nature and Socialism*, Vol. 3, No. 2 and 7, October.

Odum, H T (1996), "Environmental accounting: Energy and environmental decision – Making, New York: John Willey and Sons (From Foster, J. M and Holleman, H (2014); 'The Theory of Unequal ecological exchange: A Marx-Odum dialectic", *The Journal of Peasant Studies*, Vol. 41, November 1–2, and March, pp199–233.

OECD (2012), "Perspective son global development 2012: Social cohesion in a shifting world, (Summary in English)", www.oecd.org/site/devpgd2012/49067954pdf (Accessed September 2018).

O'Hearn, Denis and Andrej Grubacic (2016), "Capitalism, mutual aid, and material life understanding exilic spaces", *Capital and Class*, Vol. 40, No. 1, pp147–165.

Piketty, Thomas (2015), *The economics of inequality*, Harvard University Press, Cambridge, MA, London, England, Chapter Three, pp66–99.

Polanyi, Karl (1944), *The great transformation, the political and economic origins of our time*, Bacon Press, Boston, p76.

Ray, Sunil (2010), "Economic growth and social cost: Need for institutional reforms", *Economic and Political Weekly*, Vol. xlv, No. 14, April 3, pp17–20.

Ray, Sunil (2012), "Economics of solidarity, economics of the 21st century", *Economic and Political Weekly*, Vol. LVII, No. 24, June 16, pp39–48.

Ray, Sunil (2016), "Construction of niche structure for employment creation: Debating structural transformation", ANSISS Working Paper 01, A. N. Sinha Institute of Social Studies, Patna (Bihar), April.

Refkin, J (2014), *The zero marginal cost society: The internet of things the collaborative commons and the eclipse of capitalism*, Palgrave Macmillan, New York, pp18–19, (from Zizek, Slavoj, op. cit.)

Sandel, Michael (2014), "The marketization of life will be a challenge for India", *Interview, Times of India*, January 26.

Streeck, Wolfgang (2017), *How will capitalism end?* Juggernaut Books, New Delhi, p35.

Swaney, A James and A Martin (1989), "The social cost concepts of William Kapp and Karl Polanyi", *Journal of Economic Issues*, Vol. 111, No. 1, March.

von Liebig, J. (2018), "1862 preface to the Agricultural chemistry", *Monthly Review*, Vol. 70, No 3, July–August, pp145–150 and letters on modern agriculture, London, Walton and Maberly, 1859 (From Foster, J. B. and Clark, B. (2018); "The robbery of nature, capitalism and the metabolic rift" Vol. 16, No. 4 and 5, July–August, p18.

Wallerstein, Immanuel (2004), "After developmentalism and globalization what? Keynote address delivered at the conference on development challenges for the 21st Century", Cornell University, October 1.

Yang, S and T Wen (2011), "Nongmin Zuzhihua de kunjing yu pojie (The predicament of and solution to farmers' organisation) Renmin Huntan (peoples' Forum)

29, 44=5 (from Yan Hairong and Chen Yiyuan (2013): Debating the rural co-operative movement in China, the past and the present", *The Journal of Peasant Studies*, Vol. 40, No. 6, pp955–981.

Zizek, Slavoj (2017a), *The courage of hopelessness*, Penguin Random House, Great Britain, UK, p28.

Zizek, Slavoj (2017b), op. cit., p32.

2 Cohesive development
Forging theoretical space for alternative developmental paradigm

Gail Omvedt

In relation to existing developmental paradigms in the era of imperialist globalization, cohesive development would have to mean a complementary development of healthy human relations and productive forces as well as the healthy prosperity of the rest of nature with which humans do their developmental activities. Two perspectives that could aid understanding for achieving this cohesive development and that are presented in the earliest period of the history of capitalism are those of Karl Marx and Jotiba Phule.

Although Marx and Phule were contemporaries in different parts of the world – Marx was in Europe during the period of emerging capitalism and Phule was in feudal India, there are important similarities between the two. India, a colony of the most powerful capitalist, imperialist country at that time, had already been undergoing industrial development under the domination of British imperialist capital. Its working class in cities like Mumbai and Kolkata had started a working-class movement, shaped under the leadership of Narayan Meghaji Lokhande, who was leading activist of the Satyashodhak movement led by Phule. Lokhande was a founder of the trade union movement in India. India had already become the part of the world capitalist market in terms of export of commodities in the form of raw materials and goods produced by industry and agriculture, and import of finance and industrial capital as well as goods produced by industry, mainly from Britain, but also from other imperialist countries. Phule has vividly described the adverse effects of this capitalist exploitation on the village artisan-produced goods in the caste-based hierarchy of all Indian villages in his *Whip of the Farmer*. He also wrote about how the investments of the British banks in building big dams in India was for extracting a large amount of profits for these banks and not for the betterment of the Indian farmers.

Marx dealt with these same processes as part of the world capitalist system but also included the development of capitalism in the pre-capitalist colonial countries. This was the common thread between Marx and Phule. They both had analyzed the caste system in India and had talked about the effects of the development of capitalism in colonial India on the caste system. In his books *Slavery* and *Whip of the Farmer*, Phule deals with his understanding of the materialist concept of the history. One of his resources was Darwin's book. His analysis of Indian history brings forward his different concept of materialism, in which knowledge becomes a material force when it functions as an instrument of domination. His understanding goes nearer to Marx's point in the "Theses on Feuerbach," where he points out that consciousness also becomes an objective force. In short, they were in different locations and milieus but dealing broadly with common problematics from the standpoint of moving towards liberated humanity.

In *Capital* Vol. I Marx says,

> Capitalist production, by collecting the population in great centers and causing an ever-increasing preponderance of town population, on the one hand concentrates the historical motive power of society; on the other hand, it disturbs the circulation of matter between man and the soil, i.e., prevents the return to the soil of its elements consumed by man in the form of food and clothing; it therefore violates the conditions necessary to lasting fertility of the soil. By this action, it destroys, at the same time, the health of the town laborer and the intellectual life of the rural laborer. By while upsetting the naturally grown conditions for the maintenance of that circulation of matter, it imperiously calls for its restoration as a system, as a regulating law of social production and under a form appropriate to the full development of the human race.

He concludes by saying, "Capitalist production, therefore, develops technology, and the combining together of various processes into a social whole, only by sapping the original sources of all wealth, the soil and the laborer."[1]

Here, Marx is talking about the exchange of matter between humans and nature along with the basic point about healthy ecology and ecological balance. Today his propositions are more than proved in terms of the importance of generalizing organic farming and renewable-based decentralized industrialization. Jotiba Phule, in his *Whip of the Farmer*, talks about the importance of the exchange of matter between forests and agriculture in terms of maintaining the primary productivity of the land, and exchange of matter between humans and various natural resources like water, forests etc. He criticizes the capitalist ways of industrial intervention in agriculture, forests, water, and other natural resources.

Marx's concept of alternative society was not very clear, and he envisaged converting private ownership of capitalist productive forces into social ownership, obviously implying no change in the relation between humans and nature, as he himself discusses in the earlier quoted extract.[2] Yet, the contradictions in his theory definitely help us in developing a theory for an alternative developmental paradigm based on healthy and interdependent relations of free humanity and nature.

Jotiba Phule, on the contrary, looks towards nature and human relationships in a more holistic manner. He includes the abolition of caste and gender exploitation along with economic exploitation into his concept of cohesive development. He also deals with various components of nature like forest, water, agriculture, etc. as renewable resources on the basis of which cohesive development could take place in a decentralized manner. Phule is ahead of his time when talking about gender liberation and liberation from the caste system while bringing forward the ideology of taking pride in doing menial manual work for the creation of new humane productive forces. His concepts about the land–water relationship concern using water in a volumetric way that depends upon the needs of various crops and basing development on renewable-based products. The combination of moving towards liberated humanity and an unbound relation with nature is the main thread in Phule's perspective.[3]

There are many inventions which have taken place all over the world and many experiments conducted by farmers, technologists, and scientists, and their combined efforts could prove the truth of the theory for bringing about cohesive development in reality.

Problematic posed by contradictions in existing society and forging a theoretical space

Existing society has contradictions that pose a problematic for the emergence of theory. These include:

- The contradiction between the laws of motion of the capitalist mode of production and the cohesive development of humans and nature.
- The contradiction between the caste system, racial oppression, or oppression of particular communities and the creation of ecologically balanced cohesive society.
- The contradiction between patriarchy and women's creative participation.
- The contradiction between the model of development of the established society and the emergence of the new model of an alternative developmental paradigm.

In order to theorize development, these contradictions must themselves be theorized as fundamental and perhaps irreconcilable. If we do not center these contradictions, we cannot develop a cohesive theory of cohesive development – because there is no cohesion in the social system created by humans which could otherwise have come up with a unanimous developmental model. If every section of society comes up with a different model of development based on the particular interests of that section, then this unanimity becomes impossible. On this background there could be only one alternative, that the majority of the society could rally around the general long-term interests of a cohesive ecologically balanced prosperous and healthy society. In this case, those who don't agree with this based on their short-term interests will definitely oppose it and will try to foil efforts of this majority. This could be done by only one section of society which is at the helm of the social-economic system which prevails today and which only cares for its own immediate interest of benefiting from the existing structure by remaining at the helm.

If this is the only possible alternative, then it becomes very clear that we can have a model of cohesive development but cannot have cohesion in the existing society for bringing it into reality. This cohesion can come in only one way, by converting a section of society at the helm of the existing socio-economic structure to agree with the long-term interests of human society as a whole, including themselves. This appears to be an impossible task.

So, on this background we can define cohesive development in a way which takes note of these realities. It could be defined in the following ways:

- Cohesive development is development which has a program for bringing about a healthy coexistence between humans and nature.
- It is a development of a relation of a non-oppressive, non-extractive, non-exploitative kind between humans and humans, and humans and nature. It allows every individual to have freedom for one's unlimited development, which is a precondition for the development of all.
- It is a process which not only brings about a qualitative change in relations between humans and humans, and humans and nature, but also makes human society and nature prosperous in a healthy manner.
- It is a process which is fundamentally based on renewable-based non-polluting, environmentally enriching and decentralized production processes under the decision-making of people operating them directly and these decentralized production groups of people. This point takes cognizance of the contradiction between state and people, between political society and civil society, in which state/political society dominates people divided by class, caste, gender, religion, race, community etc.
- This process could only walk on two legs – one is a process of abolishing exploitative, domineering, divisive relations between people and bringing about cohesiveness among them, and the other abolishes the contradictions between ecology and production, between health and production, between agriculture and industry, and between production and nature as a whole.

All this envisages the deeper and precise understanding of the content of contradictions among people, understanding of contradictions between humans and nature, and understanding nature in such a way that enables humans to have healthy relations with nature by basing their production processes and mode of production on that understanding.

Process of research and development for cohesive development

If we properly understand Phule, then it becomes obvious that he is talking about mutually enriching natural processes between forest, rainfall, and water; between land and water; between naturally created biomass and fertile land, etc. If one proceeds based on this mutually enriching process and theorizes this process, coupling it with mutually enriching processes between humans and nature, then it gives us a qualitatively different direction for developing a theory for cohesive development.

One can take an ironic example in the transformation in the methods of cultivating agriculture in India. Up to the late 1960s, cultivation of agriculture undertaken by the farmer was basically what one today defines as "organic agriculture." This organic agriculture was a process developed through the practice and thinking coupled with that for ages. It did not require any investment, which becomes necessary today for converting a soil which has lost primary productivity into organically developed fertile soil. With the so-called green revolution starting, adopted by the state in India, this method of cultivating agriculture was destroyed, and along with that, all the previous existing components required for that kind of cultivation were also destroyed. Today, the state has gone a full circle, and it is advised now that farming methods should shift towards organic farming! But, in the existing situation, all those components which were easily available for organic farming are nonexistent. That is why it becomes a costly and Herculean task to create those components again for the purpose of generalizing organic farming. Individual examples of organic farming today could be brought in practice only with heavy investment in the beginning of the transformation process from chemical farming to organic farming.

The same is true for the relationship between land and water. This relation in the past was based on a kind of volumetric water use and on the process of increasing productivity of both land and water. A theory was implicit in this process but was never developed, and the state wants to go from totally non-productive and destructive process of land–water relations to volumetric water supply and increasing the productivity of water and land. This is happening on the background that there is no integrated theory based on old practices and wisdom coupled with modern scientific methods. So, the experiments and bureaucratic efforts for cohesive development of the land–water relationship become an impossibility.

If we delve into the history of making implements, building houses, bridges, roads, and dams, producing colors, making medicines etc. we find the process of transformation from naturally available renewable and healthy material to nonrenewable, fossil, and harmful chemical materials that comes with these processes. Even energy production has traveled a similar route. Therefore, not one single serious research project has been invested in by the state or any other institute into developing renewable processes by applying the developments in basic scientific inventions. So if somebody now says that for building long-lasting roads, instead of using steel grid, a grid made out of woven material from natural fibers can be sewn together in a honey-combed structure, people would not believe it or mock it. People *are* doing experiments in various fields but without any social, state, or institutional support. No establishment wants rigorous research in this field. We can take another example of frame structures (RCC) made out of 3-inch diameter timber instead of steel and concrete, which also would not be believed or would be mocked by people and the establishment. Although people are successfully experimenting in this field, thorough and full-fledged research will take place only if the majority of society or the state and institutes support the research proposal.[4]

We can go on giving examples like this, but the main point is to change the policy and support it wholeheartedly on behalf of society. Therefore, it becomes a policy question. Mere experiments undertaken with the help of meager resources are not going to change the scenario. Only if various social initiatives are supported by the majority of society will there be policy changes in the research and development field. What is involved in such policy changes is opposition based on the immediate interests of the established controllers of the mode of production and production processes. They are going to be at loggerheads with the new policy. Again, one has to state here that non-cohesiveness in society becomes instrumental for maintaining non-cohesiveness in the field of human–nature relationships and ecology.

Today's development and cohesive development

Since the advent of capitalism based on modern industry, the process of exchange of matter between nature and humans has gotten disturbed in such a way that much more matter is taken from nature for processing into the goods used by humans than is returned to nature. Not only that, whatever is returned is poisonous to humans as well as to nature. This has created massive deforestation, resulting in a sharp increase in barren and drought-prone land, creating vast tracts of landmass heading towards desertification. This process has emitted into the atmosphere poisonous substances which has created a process of global warming, which in turn has an effect resulting in rising of the sea level. All the rivers and streams have become the reservoirs of poison-containing water flows. The creation of capitalism has entered into the field of destruction of the conditions of production, the raw materials and natural resources functioning as the stock of the raw material. In short, capitalism has dug its own grave not only in terms of creating a dispossessed proletariat and other working masses who would abolish capitalism, but also in terms of its own existence as a mode of production by making production itself impossible. This has given rise by the controllers of capital to the trend called "green capitalism." Any production is based on transforming or processing resources which are available in the earth or in the biosphere, both renewable and non-renewable. If capitalist production relies upon non-renewable fuels whose resources are pollutive and finite, than the current capitalist condition of production is going towards irreparable damage and depletion, which will make capitalist production itself impossible.

Green capitalism is concerned about global warming, deforestation, pollution, the poisoning of the land, water, and sea, but also about shifting towards renewable-based production. Whatever is coming forward today in the form of wind energy, solar energy, sea wave energy, biofuels, etc. is a creation of this concern. But here too there is a big problem. It is in terms of using matter coming from fossil fuels for erecting the structures to produce energy or other things. This matter is again coming from fossil fuels! It is because of this that capitalism is getting entangled into the same process of adverse exchange of matter between nature and humans. It also cannot resolve the contradiction within its ranks, that of a major section of the controllers of capital, that because of their immediate interest they do not want to shift from fossil to renewable fuels because their monopoly is based on natural gas, coal mines, metal mines, and metal and plastic industries. Given this situation, it is clear that the capitalist mode of production itself cannot solve the contradiction of adverse exchange of matter between humans and nature, poisoning nature on the one hand and developing productive forces on the other.[5]

One more thing which makes existing development based on capitalist interests difficult is the use of caste exploitation, race exploitation and gender exploitation etc. for reducing the value of labor power. Division of laborers based on these exploitations is usurped by capitalism for pushing this division to the extremes. It uses racially exploited and caste-exploited populations for low-paid "dirty" and unprotected jobs and creates a mass of men and women who can only stay alive with the help of the remuneration they are getting in very bad conditions. On the other hand, it creates a section of the working class and middle class who receive better life security, better working conditions, and better living standards. Because of this division of laborers and the insecurity of maintaining the jobs which one has, people's struggles against pollution, the poisoning of water, and the destruction of nature cannot become strong or move in a determined direction. Almost all the energy of the working masses is spent on maintaining the status quo of life security.

Another side of this process is the increasing hierarchy, divisions, and consolidation of social groups which prevent cohesiveness from being achieved by the majority affected by the existing system. So unless and until they find a way to bring about this cohesiveness, they cannot come up with the alternative of cohesive development of their own, which could be called as alternative developmental paradigm. Without cohesiveness, each section of the working masses based on class, caste, gender, race etc. continues thinking and asking for change based on their sectional interests, because as a group they cannot go beyond the sectional interest and think about a cohesive development of society in which they would have a prosperous space and non-exploitative life. We observe this process today both in advanced capitalist countries and in developing or underdeveloped countries.

To overcome this lack of cohesiveness, a theory is needed to discover the basic reasons for the division of laborers as well as provide a practical program for cohesive development. This program would not only include the satisfaction of the short-term interests of each section but would also include the long-term interests of all the groups. This is not an easy task to complete. It requires multidisciplinary efforts that bring together understandings based on social sciences, natural sciences, etc. However, there is no other way than to address this task and come up with a practical program for alternative developmental paradigm. This paradigm could become the basis for transforming the state, the social formation, and the mode of production operating today.

Forging theoretical space

For forging theoretical space for an alternative developmental paradigm, the task can only be accomplished by combining a multidisciplinary and a multi-linear theoretical approach. This approach entails transforming the experiential knowledge of people into a theory and the theoretical approach for transforming abstract theoretical understanding into a practical program for bringing an alternative developmental paradigm in reality. This would require a historical review of the people's contribution, which could become the basis for gaining intuition for creating a new theory of this kind. It also would require the study of various experiments in the field of natural sciences undertaken by grassroots groups, institutions, people's science networks, and scientists. At the same time, one has to process all this into a unified theory which would enable guidance in practice. This cannot be accomplished without the collective efforts not only at the national level but also at the international level. In fact, the concept itself encompasses global and local together in a live relationship. Though numerous contributions can provide many intuitions of theoretical development, they are either piecemeal or they deal with only one of the aspects of the alternative developmental paradigm in a disjointed manner.

Practically speaking, one has to realize that we have not dealt with the beginnings of the task for forging a theoretical space for an alternative developmental paradigm. We have to start from scratch, and it requires the brainstorming of the various concerned scientists, technicians, and people doing social practice in relation to this task.

Notes

1 Karl Marx, *Capital*, Vol. I, International Publishers, New York, fourth printing, 1972, 505–507.
2 Ibid., p. 763.
3 Jotirao Phule, *Collected Works*, Maharashtra Rajya Sanskruti Mandal, Bombay, 1959.
4 Suhas Paranjpe and K.J. Joy, *Sustainable Technology: Making the Sardar Sarovar Project Viable*, Centre for Environment Education, Ahmedabad, 1995.
5 Deshka Paryavaran, Paryavaran Kaksh Gandhi Shanti Pratisthand, June 1982.

3 Enemies of cohesive development

Amiya Kumar Bagchi

Cohesive development defined

Let us try first to roughly understand what cohesive development might mean. We can be helped by the root word 'cohesive'. It is something that coheres. Coheres with what? Development of what? Development of human beings. Thanks to the work of United Nations Development Programme (UNDP) and scholars such as Amartya Sen and Martha Nussbaum, even economists recognize that development does not only mean a rise in income, although that is important when a person is earning much below what would be necessary for her to obtain nutrition, education and health care to be able to lead a decent life. So development will mean that all these necessities should cohere with each other. But we are concerned with more than that. This kind of development must apply to everybody. That means that the requirements of all beings must cohere with one another. But we cannot stop there. The development must also be sustainable. We are all painfully aware of the ravages caused to Spaceship Earth by the unlimited greed of human beings, which has led them to mine non-renewable resources at such an accelerating speed as to lead to global warming and climate change.

Dreams of cohesive development

Almost from the very beginning of what is called civilization, that is, the invention of agriculture, domestication of animals and handicrafts, society has become hierarchical, and resistance to that hierarchy has also arisen. Among the great religions, Buddhism and Christianity were partly the result of resistance to the inequality of man and man. In our country, waves of the Bhakti and Sufi movements were evidence of such resistance. In Europe the Lollards, that is, the followers of John Wycliffe, the rebellious priest of fourteenth-century England, and the peasant rebels of Germany in the sixteenth century led by Thomas Münzer were voicing and fighting for a more egalitarian society. Almost at the same time, Thomas More was writing his *Utopia*, portraying a non-existent but possible egalitarian society. In the next century, the English Civil War witnessed an explosion of egalitarian demands by the Diggers and Levellers.

People continued to dream of a better, a more egalitarian society as capitalism dug its talons into human solidarity.

Ernst Bloch in his *The Principle of Hope, vol. 2* (p. 471) quoted John Ball, a prominent Lollard: 'The earth belongs to nobody, its fruits belong to all'.
Karl Marx and Frederick Engels wrote in *The Communist Manifesto*:
'In place of the old bourgeois society with its classes and class differences there arises an association in which the free development of every individual is the condition for the free development of all' (Marx and Engels 1969[1848], p.127).

Nearer our own time, Rabindranath Tagore formulated a dream for India (and all other countries) in two poems, one of which is called 'Prayer', in which he wanted every person to hold his/her head high and dare to express his/her thought freely (Chaudhuri 2004).

Self-centred objectives of enemies of cohesive development

All these dreams are being continually shattered in a class-divided society, and the shattering of those dreams has assumed horrific dimensions in the current world, in which semi-fascist rulers have come up in the United States, Britain and several other countries including India. A truly cohesive society was fractured, of course, as soon as a labouring class and private property were invented. Along with that a species of human beings came up who regarded their own greed as the only compass for their behaviour. Perhaps the earliest expression of that was given by Callicles in his debates with Socrates in Plato's *Gorgias* (Plato 1937).

'Socrates [to Callicles] Once more, then, tell me what you and Pindar mean by natural justice. Do you not mean that the superior should take the property of the inferior by force; that the better should take the worse, the noble have more than the mean? . . .

'Callicles. Yes; that is what I was saying, and I still aver' (ibid, pp. 547–8).

'Callicles. I plainly assert, that he who would truly live ought to allow his desires to wax to the uttermost, and not to chastise them; but when they have grown to their greatest he should have courage and intelligence to minister to them and to satisfy all his longings. And this I affirm to be natural justice and nobility' (ibid, p. 551). Examples that readily occur to us are Rupert Murdoch, who married four times, almost always women much younger than he – the last time in 2016 at the age of 86; Donald Trump who has married three times, again often women much younger than he, and is known for his outrageous views on women; and Vijay Mallia, who lived it up as chairman of United Breweries and Kingfisher Airlines and likes to be surrounded by glamorous women.

Before the advent of capitalism, all social systems put some restraint on greed or the desire for profit so that in Karl Polanyi's words the economy was embedded in society. As Polanyi (1944, p. 46) put it:

> The outstanding discovery of recent historical and anthropological research is that man's economy, as a rule, is submerged in his social relationships.

The first, controlled phase of capitalism

Even under capitalism the unbridled drive of the profit motive was curbed in the nineteenth century by what Polanyi called a double movement, because the drive met social resistance and the ill-health of the workers was counter-productive even from the capitalists' point of view (see also Atiyah 1979). Marxists would put it differently: apart from the capitalists' own interest, workers' movement in the core metropolitan countries and the rise in wages caused by the joint effect of 40 million Europeans (the largest mass migration in history) overseas, the resulting tightness of the labour market and the fear of the growth of socialism caused new measures of social insurance to be put in (Bagchi 2005a, chapters 7 and 16). The upward movement of wages and standards of living of workers in the metropolitan lands was resumed, after the disasters of the interwar period, in the era of the so-called golden age of capitalism (between 1945 and 1971).

The beginning of neoliberal capitalism

But the sustained rise in wages and continuance of near-full employment led to a decline in profits, and the capitalists began their counterattack. Trade unions were demonized and wherever possible broken up. The fear of the spread of communism, which had partly restrained the capitalist powers of North America and Europe, was removed with the terminal decline of the economic and political prowess of the USSR. The advent of Ronald Reagan and Margret Thatcher completed the victory of the neoliberal regime in the core countries. Meanwhile Third World countries, especially of Latin America and Sub-Saharan Africa, were struck by the debt crisis resulting in their subjugation to the dictates of the IMF and World Bank. The usurers' structural adjustment policies set the per capita incomes back to where they were in 1960 or even earlier.

Just like all earlier class-divided regimes, the neoliberal regime also tried to exert its *ideological hegemony* through education, nurture, propaganda and consumption habits. In the area of education, the period saw the resurgence of a Eurocentric view typified by the work of North and Thomas (1973) and Jones (1981) (for a critique, see Bagchi 2005a, chapter 1). In the area of economics the period saw the virtual obliteration of Keynesian macroeconomics, replaced first by neoclassical economics, with its methodological individualism, and then by so-called rational expectations implying perfect foresight. In the general equilibrium framework of neoclassical economics, as typified by, for example, Debreu (1959), every economic agent is an island, maximizing his own utility for all conceivable future, with no link with any other economic agent. All participants in the game of capitalist imperialism is brainwashed to make him/her believe in this absurd proposition.

Neoliberal capitalism has made particular targets of children, stimulating their greed and often also rousing their violent instincts (Schor 2005). Children covet toys and goods that their peers and often the better-off children buy, putting pressure on the budgets of their parents. We also read in the papers some child shooting his/her playmates or classmates because he/she is annoyed with them or their parents because they refuse to listen to their demands. The easy availability of guns not only in the USA but also in most other countries has smoothed the path of this kind of violence. Of course, thanks to the proliferation of electronic media portraying all kinds of sexual behaviour including child abuse, large numbers of children, especially in poor countries like India, are trafficked to satisfy the unnatural appetites of the customers. That kind of trafficking, along with the trafficking of women, has become a multi-billion dollar industry.

Of course, propaganda is mainly directed towards the adult population. This propaganda can often take the form of feeding false information to the public and suppressing the correct information. The propaganda war by the US-led coalition of western powers reached new heights during the Thatcher–Reagan era of neoliberalism (Herman and Chomsky 2002).

The basic characteristics of their 'propaganda model' as set out by Herman and Chomsky (2002, p. 2), as one in which the inequality of wealth and power plays the crucial part, can be understood by combining three of the basic ideas adumbrated by Marx, the Marxists and other radical writers (including, of course, Chomsky and Herman in their other writings). The first idea is that under capitalism two laws operate, unless they are countered by resistance of the workers or liberal defenders of free competition as against oligopolies. These two laws are those of concentration and centralization of economic power. In most areas of commodity production, economies of scale in production, finance, marketing and advertising will enable a large firm to cut the cost of production, raise finance on more favourable terms and reach the buyers on a wider front than a small firm can. Economies of scale in production are best exemplified by the three-fifths law in process (ore refining and chemical industries), namely, that as the volume of a vessel doubles the surface area increases only by approximately three-fifths, thus conferring a cost advantage to the owner of the larger container. This plus the advantage in raising finance that a larger firm generally enjoys will allow it to take over smaller firms and thus economic power will be centralized in fewer hands. The process of centralization was accelerated as a market for firms developed in the 1960s (Manne 1965; Shleifer 2000). The second proposition is that the dominating ideas in a society are the ideas of the ruling class. The third strand of the argument is that despite advances made by some ex-colonial countries in economic and human development, the world is dominated by the imperial countries led by the United States. The fourth, relatively recent strand of the argument is that the ideas of neoliberal liberalization have gripped the ruling classes of the subordinate countries, and the latter have done their best to inculcate them among the labouring population. Herman and Chomsky applied their propaganda model to the US ruling class, but it can be applied to the relation between media, corporate power and the state in every market economy. Moreover, the suppression or exclusion of relevant information, the deliberate channelling of disinformation and the concentration of media and corporate power have been taken much farther in the twenty-first century.

There is a reciprocal relationship between the media and the government. In Britain, successive prime ministers from Tony Blair to David Cameron, and leaders of opposition (would-be prime ministers) have taken care to cultivate Rupert Murdoch, chairman of News Corporation, and arguably the most powerful media magnate in the world (Wheatcroft 1996). That kind of deception and false propaganda was the basis on which Ronald Reagan and George H. W. Bush conducted wars in Nicaragua, a proxy war in Iran and the first war against Iraq, which reached its apogee in the second Gulf War against Iraq in 2003.

The case of the rise of Tony Blair illustrates the power of news management by the rulers of neoliberal capitalism. In 1996, Blair's press secretary Alistair Campbell badgered the news media to give priority to Blair's speech (he was still only the opposition leader) at the Labour Party Conference. As Wheatcroft put it, 'This went beyond spin-doctoring. It was news management worthy of a none-too-democratic Balkan state, or of some Third World country rejoicing in the "new information order.'

In India, most of the media have been controlled by big business houses for a long time. For instance, *The Hindustan Times* has been controlled by the S.K. Birla Group. The control of media by big business houses reached a new height when Mukesh Ambani, the richest man in India, acquired Network 18, a huge conglomerate of electronic and print media. On 29 May 2014, Reliance Industries Ltd (RIL) announced it would be acquiring control in Network 18 Media & Investments Ltd, including its subsidiary TV18 Broadcast Ltd. The board of RIL approved funding of up to Rs. 4,000 crore to Independent Media Trust (IMT), of which RIL is the sole beneficiary, for acquisition of control in Network 18 and its subsidiaries (Bamzai 2014).

Even without direct control by a particular business group, newspapers in India have published news which was planted by a business house or politician in lieu of a fee. This 'paid news' has been published in English-language as well as vernacular newspapers (Guha Thakurta 2011). Newspapers have lied on behalf of corporations. For example, when farmers were committing suicide in their thousands because they could not recover the cost of cultivating Bt cotton, *The Times of India* wrote an editorial praising Bt cotton and denying that any deaths had taken place because of the cultivation of the genetically modified seed marketed by Monsanto (Sainath 2012).

As the degree of control of media by business houses has increased, so has the vulnerability of journalists employed by them. For instance, In June 2013, it was reported that the *Forbes India* editor Indrajit Gupta was fired after he refused to accept a severance package without consulting his lawyers. After the initial firing, the managing editor was forced to quit, and the following day, two other staff were also forced to quit due to severance issues. The Press Club, Mumbai, condemned the incident. The CEO of Network18 Group said that the problems were due to the restructuring of the Network18 Group with the merger of FirstPost.com and *Forbes India* (www.thehindu.com/news/national/forbes-india-editors-sacked-for-demanding-stock-ownership/article4795699.ece accessed 17/12/19). More recently, *The Hindustan Times* 'shelved' its editions and bureaus, from 9 January 2017, in Kolkata, Bhopal, Indore, Ranchi, Allahabad, Varanasi and Kanpur without offering any explanation. As a result, all the journalists associated with those editions lost their jobs (Samrat 2017).

People caught in the neoliberal order are always compelled to consume, often beyond their real needs and paying capacity, because of social pressures. These social pressures have been captured as snob, bandwagon and Veblen effects. Although the snob and Veblen effects are characteristic of the rich, the poor are also caught up in its snare. The consumerist behaviour of the Indian rich, as the behaviour of the rich elsewhere, can be explained by combining bandwagon, snob and Veblen effects (Veblen 2005[1899]; Leibenstein 1950; Bagwell and Bernheim 1996; Bagchi 2005b). Let us first see how Leibenstein (1950, p. 109) distinguishes between these effects:

> By non-functional effect is meant that portion of the demand for a consumers' good which is due to factors other than the qualities in the commodity. Probably the most important kind of nonfunctional demand is due to external effects on utility. That is, the utility derived from the commodity is enhanced or decreased owing to the fact that the commodity bears a higher rather than a lower price tag. We differentiate this type of demand into what I shall call the 'bandwagon effect,' the 'snob effect' and the 'Veblen effect'. By the bandwagon effect, we refer to the extent to which the demand for a commodity is *increased* due to the fact that that others are also consuming the same commodity. It represents the desire of people to get into the 'swim of things' . . . By the snob effect we refer to the extent to which the demand for a consumers' good is *decreased* owing to the fact that that others are also consuming the same commodity (or others are increasing the consumption of the same commodity). This represents the desire of the people to be exclusive; to be different; to dissociate themselves from the 'common herd'. By the Veblen effect we refer to the phenomenon of conspicuous consumption; to the extent to which the demand for a consumers' good is increased

because it bears a higher than a lower price. We shall perhaps emphasise the distinction between the snob and the Veblen effect – the former is a function of the consumption of others the latter is a function of price.

The bandwagon effect is not a characteristic of the rich. It primarily characterises the behaviour of those who are trying to keep up with the Joneses. They are the kind of people who would flaunt a Gucci bag knowing it was a fake. Here we are concerned with the rich who want to signal their superior status through conspicuous consumption.

Anecdotal evidence suggests that Veblen effects may be significant for luxury goods. According to one marketing manager, 'Our customers do not want to pay less. If we halved the price of all our products, we would double our sales for six months and then we would sell nothing. Indeed *The Economist* (1993) emphasises that 'retailers can damage a glamorous good's image by selling it too cheaply'. A recent article in the *Wall Street Journal* noted that 'a BMW in every driveway may thrill investors in the short run but ultimately could dissipate the prestige that lures buyers to these luxury cars'.

(Bagwell and Bernheim, p. 349)

This status-seeking behaviour of the rich also has policy implications. When the US government imposed a tax on luxury goods, 'Rolls Royce, Jaguar, and BMW [each ran] promotional campaigns in which they offered to reimburse customers for the full amount of the luxury tax' (ibid, p. 352).

Of course, the major exploitation of workers takes place in the production process. As Marx and Engels (1976[1845–46], p. 83) wrote:

Competition separates the individuals from one another, not only the bourgeois but still more the workers before individuals can unite.

This competition is constrained by worker solidarity and other bonds of social cohesion. The relentless attack on workers under neoliberalism and mounting unemployment, however, have shattered most of those bonds and left them prey to new modes of exploitation, such as flexiwork, rationing of employment and home-based work.

Apart from Veblen effects and the inter-working class conflicts, there is the seductive power of a hierarchical society in which a mere Wally Simpson, an ordinary American woman, can marry the king of England. So why should another ordinary woman who imbibes the values of that society and behaves according to values of that society not aspire to own a decent house and other good things of life, such as a rich husband, a decent house, a television set and a car, even though she belongs to the working class? Carolyn Steedman's mother originated from Lancashire labour aristocracy, namely weavers, migrated to London after the textile industry fell into bad times during the 1930s and ended up as a manicurist for rich ladies. She was a 'good mother' although her children were illegitimate, with a rather irresponsible husband. She voted Conservative, saved ferociously for a house which she never bought and left £40,000 in 1967, a tidy sum for a university professor at that time (Steedman 1986). One can understand how Margaret Thatcher could find solid support in the British working class from this story of Steedman's mother.

The final weapon in the hands of the capitalists, of course, remains the state. The fact that capitalism is facing a renewed crisis, especially since the eruption of the financial recession triggered by the subprime crisis in the United States, is exemplified by the emergence of semi-fascist rulers in the United States, Britain, Israel, Turkey, India and the Philippines.

Georgi Dimitrov, addressing the Seventh World Congress of the Communist International, described the class character of fascism 'as the open terrorist dictatorship of the most reactionary, most chauvinistic and most imperialist elements of finance capital'.

Capitalism and fascism

Capitalism bares its fascist fangs when it suffers a major crisis such as a steep rise in unemployment or a severe decline in real earnings of ordinary people, as it did during the Great Depression, when Nazism, starting in Germany, overwhelmed most of Continental Europe west of Soviet Russia. Again with continuing high levels of unemployment and job insecurity during the recent Great Recession, it threw up leaders like Theresa May and Donald Trump, who himself as a multi-billionaire is part of the problem. Trump became president of the United States riding on the discontent of the white working class and the racism latent in the mind-sets of a substantial section of the whites (Hossein-Zadeh 2017). The fascist intentions of Trump became clear early in his presidency. He banned the entry of Muslims from seven countries – Iraq, Iran, Syria, Libya, Somalia and Sudan. On 28 January he exploded during a friendly call from the Australian prime minister, Malcolm Turnbull, asking him to accept 1250 refugees, calling it a dumb deal (Thrush and Innis 2017). As judge after judge refused to let Trump implement his refugee ban, he vowed to have his way at last (Shear, Kulish and Feuer 2017). On 29 January he fired Acting Attorney General Sally D. Yates for defying his order (Shear, Landler and Apuzzo, 2017). Trump nominated the conservative Federal Appeals Court Judge Neil Gorsuch to the Supreme Court (Williams 2017), but Gorsuch refused the appointment because of Trump's derogatory remarks about judges.

While openly fascist and racist parties have come to power in Ukraine, Hungary and Poland, and while British Prime Minister Theresa May has professed openly racist views (Seymour 2016), people have been protesting against these fall-outs of neoliberalism from movements like Occupy Wall Street to daily protests against the incredible Donald Trump all over the

United States and in major European capitals. The only hope is that ultimately such protesters will prevail, because many of the perpetrators are out to destroy what is left of human civilisation.

Bibliography

Atiyah, Patrick. 1979. *The Rise and Fall of Freedom of Contract*, London: Oxford University Press.

Bagchi, Kumar. 2005a. *Perilous Passage: Mankind and the Global Transformation of Capital*, Lanham, MD: Rowman & Littlefield.

Bagchi, Kumar. 2005b. Foreword, in Thorstein Veblen 2005[1899], ed. *The Theory of the Leisure Class*, New Delhi: Aakar Books.

Bagchi, Kumar. 2016. Neo-liberalism and imperialism, pp. 1099–1120 in Immanuel Ness and Zak Cope, eds. *The Palgrave Macmillan Encyclopedia of Imperialism and Anti-Imperialism*, New York: Palgrave Macmillan.

Bagwell, Laurie Simon and B. Douglas Bernheim. 1996. Veblen effects in a theory of consumption, *American Economic Review*, 86(3): 349–373.

Bamzai, Sandeep. 2014. RIL deal-Network18: Is Mukesh Ambani the new media mogul? *India Today*, 14 January.

Bloch, Ernst. 1986. *The Principle of Hope*, Vol. 1, translated from the German by Neville Plaice, Stephen Plaice and Paul Knight, Cambridge, MA: MIT Press.

Chaudhuri, Sukanta. 2004. *Selected Poems of Rabindranath Tagore*, New Delhi: Oxford University Press.

Debreu, Gerard. 1959. *Theory of Value: An Axiomatic Analysis of Economic Equilibrium*, New Haven, CT: Yale University Press.

The Economist. 1993. The luxury goods trade, *The Economist*, 8 June, pp. 90–98.

Guha Thakurta, Paranjoy. 2011. "Paid news" and the transformation of the media, pp. 24–28 in Buroshiva Dasgupta, ed. *Market, Media and Democracy*, Kolkata: Institute of Development Studies Kolkata and Progressive Publishers.

Herman, Edward and Noam Chomsky. 2002. *Manufacturing Consent*, New York: Pantheon Books.

Hossein-Zadeh, Ismael. 2017. The class dynamics in the rise of Donald Trump, *Counterpunch*, 3 October 2016 (URL:www.counterpunch.org/2016/10/03/the-class-dynamics-in-the-rise-of-donald-trump/, accessed on 19.1.2017)

Jones, Eric. 1981. *The European Miracle: Environments, Economies, and Geopolitics in the History of Europe and Asia*, Cambridge: Cambridge University Press.

Leibenstein, H. 1950. Bandwagon, snob and Veblen effects in the theory of consumers' demand, *Quarterly Journal of Economics*, 64(2): 183–207.

Marx, Karl and Frederick Engels. 1969[1848]. Manifesto of the communist party, p. 137 in Karl Marx and Frederick Engels, eds. *Selected Works*, Moscow: Progress Publishers.

Manne, Henry G. 1965. Mergers and the market for corporate control, *The Journal of Political Economy*, 73(2): 110–120.

Marx, Karl and Frederick Engels. 1976[1845–46]. *The German Ideology*, Moscow: Progress Publishers.

More, Thomas. 1516. *Utopia*, Planet PDF edition.

North, Douglas and R. P. Thomas. 1973. *The Rise of the Western World: A New Economic History*, Cambridge: Cambridge University Press.

Ollmann, Bertell. 1971. *Alienation: Marx's Conception of Man in Capitalist Society*, Cambridge: Cambridge University Press.

Plato. 1937. Gorgias, pp. 505–587 in B. Jowett, trans. *The Dialogues of Plato*, Vol. 1, Introduction by Raphael Demos, New York: Random House.

Polanyi, Karl. 1944. *The Great Transformation*, Boston, MA: Beacon Press.

Sainath, P. 2012. Reaping gold through cotton, and newsprint, *The Hindu*, 10 May.

Samrat. 2017. 'Malicious and unjust': Powerful business houses and journalists, *Economic and Political Weekly*, LII(4): 13–19.

Schor, Juliet. 2005. *Born to Buy: The Commercialized Child and the Consumer Culture*, New York: Scribner.

Seymour, Richard. 2016. Theresa May's Le Pen moment, *Jacobin*, October 2016 (URL: www.jacobinmag.com/2016/10/theresa-may-ukip-conservative-speech/, accessed on 21.2.2017).

Shear, Michael D., Nicholas Kulish and Alan Feuer. 2017. Judge blocks Trump order on refugees amid chaos and outcry worldwide, *New York Times*, 28 January.

Shear, Michael D., Mark Landler, Matt Apuzzo and Eric Lichtblau. 2017. Trump fires acting attorney general who defied him, *New York Times*, 30 January.

Shleifer, Andrei. 2000. *Inefficient Markets: An Introduction to Behavioral Finance*, New York: Oxford University Press,

Steedman, Carolyn. 1986. *Landscape for a Good Woman: A Story of Two Lives*, London: The Virago Press.

Thrush, Glenn and Michelle Innis. 2017. U.S.-Australia rift is possible after Trump ends call with Prime Minister, *New York Times*, 2 February.

Veblen, Thorstein. 2005[1899]. *The Theory of the Leisure Class: An Economic Study of Institutions*, reprinted, with an introduction by Amiya Kumar Bagchi, New Delhi: Aakar Books.

Wheatcroft, Geoffrey. 1996. The paradoxical case of Tony Blair, *The Atlantic Monthly*, 277(6): 22–40.

Williams, Pete. 2017. Trump nominates Federal Appeals Court Judge Neil Gorsuch to Supreme Court, *NBC News*, 1 February.

4 The power of audibility

Contestation and communication as a route to cohesive development

Antje Linkenbach

1. Cohesive development – implications and promises

Imagining 'cohesive development' as a new paradigm means turning away from a focus on economic growth and giving priority to an integrative, social perspective on development. Such a perspective invites one to look at the social composition of society and explore the conditions under which a form of development can be achieved, one that takes the diverse and heterogeneous nature of voices and aspirations existing in society into account.

This contribution, therefore, focuses on three concepts – *cohesion, difference* and *development*. In the first part the chapter explores how these concepts are being defined and interpreted within the disciplines of sociology and anthropology, what the relevant debates evolving around these concepts are and how these debates merge in the paradigm of cohesive development. In the second part the article will draw attention to regionally and socially marginalized groups in India and their 'capacity to aspire'.[1] This section will reveal the plurality and heterogeneity of visions for a 'good life' and the ways to shape the future. The chapter concludes with reflections on the social and political conditions for audibility and parity of participation within the wider project of cohesive development.

1.1 Cohesion – an ambivalent concept

The various ways 'cohesion' is defined and interpreted in the social sciences has recently been revisited by scholars on request of international organizations like OECD and World Bank (Norton and de Haan 2013; Larsen 2014; Mold et al. 2016). These institutions have started to promote social cohesion as a normative idea and essential condition for the functioning of society based on equity and justice. The scholars observe that in the relevant literature social cohesion is first and foremost linked with ideas of group, community and belonging: It is a measure of 'the extent of community that exists in a society';[2] it relates to 'the total field of forces which act on members to remain in the group';[3] and it refers to a 'set of social processes that help instil in individuals the sense of belonging to the same community and the feeling that they are recognized as members of the community'.[4]

But what characterizes a group or a community, what is needed for individuals to feel they belong? For an answer to this question it is worth recalling the work of French sociologist Emile Durkheim. For Durkheim social cohesion is a key concept, even though in his own research he laid the main focus on processes of *erosion* of social cohesion, on social anomie, observable in the context of the socio-economic transformations towards modern capitalist societies.[5] While in primitive societies 'mechanic solidarity', based on similarity in lifestyle, (religious) worldview and normative and value orientations (*conscience collective*), provides the glue which holds the individuals together, in complex societies difference supersedes similarity. In societies characterized by division of labour, it is economic interdependence and thus 'organic solidarity' that functions as precondition for social cohesion. However, because of the significant economic and social differences between the individual members in complex societies, conflicts seem to be inevitable and social cohesion comes under threat; thus Durkheim's main question is how to restore it. Contemporary debates still move within the Durkheimian framework: On the one side we encounter conflict – or class-oriented approaches (related to the critical Marxian tradition), in which social cohesion is seen as a transformative socio-economic and political project, where normative ideas and conceptions of social order are subject to constant negotiation, debate and even struggle. On the other side are bourgeois-conservative approaches focussing on cohesion through acceptance of and submission to given economic and social conditions, as well as through compliance with moral standards defined by conventions and authorities, thus advocating a certain form of collective consciousness.

Given this background, participants in a debate on 'cohesive development' as a new paradigm have to take a stance. While social cohesion inevitably refers to a minimum of shared values, norms, and ideas, the question of how to reach such a consensus in modern globalized societies is a valid and an urgent one. Should a consensus be reached by re-inventing homogeneity? Should we demand an authoritative state to push conservative or even racial ideologies to promote and preserve conformity? Do we want social cohesion at the risk of exclusion and xenophobia? History provides us with many examples of how social cohesion was attempted through exclusionary practices, violence and even ethnic cleansing, and contemporary political systems are not immune against violent forms of homogenization. In light of this fact and to counter inhuman policies, social cohesion has to be grounded differently. Norton and de Haan argue that for the concept of social cohesion 'to be useful as a policy tool to support progressive developmental change, it needs to avoid a bias to the established social and political order and a bias to cultural and social homogeneity' (2013:4). This leads us back to the first approach, and departing from this, cohesive development must be understood as an *inclusive* socio-economic and political transformative project.

First, it is imperative to realize and acknowledge the existence of multiple and intersecting forms of *difference* in a society – differences on the economic, social, political and cultural levels (class, wealth, ethnicity, caste, language, race, gender), which may lead to deep social divisions and cleavages, hampering mutual recognition, respect and people's sense of community. The second task is to find ways to adequately deal with such differences and to establish conditions and create spaces in which different groups of people can come together in an attempt to develop a consensus regarding normative and practical commonalities. The definition of social cohesion given by the OECD reflects awareness of this problem:

> A cohesive society works towards the well-being of all its members, fights exclusion and marginalization, creates a sense of belonging, promotes trust, and offers its members the opportunity of upward mobility.
> (OECD, Perspectives on Global Development
> 2012, 2011: front page)

Democratic states raise the claim to strive for social cohesion and to create an environment which makes people feel they belong and want to participate. However, in most cases the main political procedures follow a *top-down* approach. Definitions, policies and strategies are the subject of debate and contestation between ruling parties, interest groups and all those exerting power in society. Civil society organizations (as particular interest groups) may be part of the debate, but whether their demands are taken seriously depends on the strength of these organizations within the sociopolitical arena. In contrast, the weaker sections, the minorities, the marginalized and excluded, those without a significant lobby within a certain society, are hardly audible. For the most part their voices are seldom raised, not unless these groups join in protest movements and challenge the established structures with non-parliamentary means. Nevertheless, more often than not these protests and other forms of expression are ignored, or suppressed and silenced by police, security organs of the state, even the military.

Therefore, social cohesion – and thus cohesive development – as a democratic project can only succeed if – in a first step – the particular conditions in a society provide opportunities for members from the various socioeconomic and cultural backgrounds to communicate their perspectives, aspirations and demands in a *bottom-up* process of *symmetric participation* in negotiations about the future of society, respectively their own future within the society. What is required is the experience of all social groups not only to have a voice but also to be widely heard and get resonance.

1.2 Difference – a challenge to hegemony

Contemporary societies are nation states within a globalized world. On the one hand, as nation states they are part of larger international economic, financial and political networks, treaties and legal frameworks, thus having to sacrifice some of their national autonomy to external supra-national institutions.[6] On the other hand, nation states – often already marked by cultural diversity – experience 'global cultural flows' of people, goods, capital and images,[7] with the effect that internal homogeneity is weakened. Both movements make the nation states particularly 'vulnerable' to both external influences and internal contestations and conflicts. In the present context it seems appropriate to have a closer look at the dynamics and possible conflicts emerging out of internal differences.

Individuals (and groups) differ because of their *social positioning*, a sociological term that points to apparently pre-given forms of belonging like race, ethnos, gender, but also class (Anthias 2002; Yuval-Davis 2006). However, categories of affiliation are not simply objective factors but also socially constructed. They gain their evocative power only via identification or disassociation in the process of self-perception or perception through one's Others. Social positionings acquire their significance through their embeddedness in structures of power or powerlessness given in a society. These structures are providing the scope in which a person can or cannot seize opportunities (e.g. regarding education, participation), whether s/he has access to influential offices or not. Thus they are co-constitutive of practices and feelings of inclusion or exclusion, of being in the centre or at the margins of society. Furthermore, individuals are not characterized by only one status-position in society; they belong to different and overlapping categories at the same time. Therefore it is important to take into consideration the *intersectionality* of status-positions, which often strengthens inclusion or exclusion and is decisive for the sense of belonging of individuals or groups, their agency and degree of participation in social negotiations and decision-making.

When talking about difference, special attention has to be given to *cultural dimensions* as one particular form of belonging. This is especially important in the context of a debate on development. Very often cultural factors are made responsible for a country's (a people's) low economic performance and are seen as blockage on the road to progress. Amartya Sen warns about believing 'that the fates of countries are effectively *sealed* by the nature of their respective cultures', because this 'would be not only a heroic oversimplification, but it would also entail some assignment of hopelessness to countries that are seen as having the "wrong" kind of culture' (Sen 2004:38). Contemporary anthropologists have deconstructed an essentialist and constraining conception of culture, which dates back to the American anthropology of the late 19th and the early 20th century.[8] While early anthropologists understood culture as homogenous, a-historical and bounded totality, pre-determining the way human beings can act and perform in society, contemporary scholars underline the openness, historicity, fluidity and heterogeneity of culture.[9] These heterogeneous, dynamic and interrelated ways of symbolically relating to and acting in the world represent meaningful and transformative forms of social praxis, merging creativity and constraint.

Against this background of intersecting social positionings and cultural particularities of individuals and groups within a given society it seems plausible that various social actors articulate different, competing, some-times conflicting ideas and dispositions. While certain cultural forms and expressions claim and hold hegemonial status, alternative perspectives, imaginations and practices do exist – even though often only at the margins. Difference means necessarily plurality, heterogeneity and multivocality.

1.3 Development – a powerful discourse and praxis

Social positioning of individuals and groups and the degree of cultural diversity of a society or a nation state play a significant role when it comes to ideas/ideals and strategies of development. The answer to the question of what counts as development, what are the means and end of development varies widely and is often the subject of contestation and conflict. In this context a related question arises: How far are the visions and aspirations of the diverse groups within a society represented in national and global development planning and decision-making? How far are social, legal and political structures in place, which can contribute to the implementation of alternative visions? The answer to this query requires a closer look into the discourses and practices of development.

During the period of decolonization after World War II development started to become a powerful and compelling discourse and praxis, first among the countries of the West; later it was also adopted and advanced by nations from the global South. Critics diagnosed development as 'religion of modernity' (Rist 1997:21), as a 'salvific process' with redemption as its ultimate goal (Pieterse 2001:25); others saw it as a concrete utopia, a dream of the 'kingdom of abundance' (Escobar 1995:4), inciting 'collective hope' (Rist 1997:19).[10] Although it was possible to follow different approaches to development and to debate its forms, development as such was never called into question.

The history – or as Wolfgang Sachs calls it, the 'archaeology' – of the development discourse and its associated practices is well documented from a critical perspective, and there is no need to re-narrate it.[11] However, I would like to emphasize a particular aspect that I consider important for the debate on cohesive development, namely the emergence of discourses about alternative development, or alternatives to development, and their relation to the so-called mainstream approach. Mainstream development was based on the conviction that so far 'underdeveloped' societies or nation states have to follow a uni-linear route towards economic growth, industrialization, technological efficiency and institutional modernization, considered beneficial for all sections of society. The failure of national development strategies and their promise of poverty reduction and socio-economic improvement for all, as well as the experience of the finiteness of nature, initiated a process of critique and protest in the countries of the Third World and among particular groups in the West.[12] Fuelled by postcolonial and anthropological debates on culture and agency (see earlier), these critical voices recognized cultures as valuable assets and no longer as obstacles in the process of development;

they also acknowledged individuals and groups as capable social actors and participants in the development process and no longer as subservient, passive recipients of development aid. Out of these critiques visions of 'alternative development' evolved, demanding peoples' participation in defining goals and strategies of development, a focus on sustainable and respectful use of nature, fulfilment of basic needs, self-reliance and social and gender equality.

However, alternative development, as a primarily *reactive* endeavour, never turned into a clearly designed theoretical and practical programme. It was the mainstream discourse turning self-critical, which started to successively absorb the alternatives, that way revising and modifying its own approach.[13] While retaining economic growth as a necessary condition for development, the final goal of development became defined as *well-being of all*, as capacity of human beings to lead long, creative and fulfilling lives – thus integrating a normative-ethical perspective emphasizing human development and capabilities (see for example Millennium Development Goals, United Nations 2000). Mainstream development agencies started to directly interact with the 'subjects' of development and even acknowledged more direct democratic procedures as favourable for the new participatory approach. 'Sustainable development' as a new key phrase claimed that care for nature was to become an integral part and core concern of development (see Report of the WCED Our Common Future, 1987; see also the 2030 Agenda for Sustainable Development).

To allow for (some) critical perspectives and to acknowledge insights and demands of those who are considered the target groups of development and incorporate these into development planning proved a fruitful enterprise of institutions operating in the field of mainstream development. An evaluation of the World Bank's Indigenous Knowledge for Development Program, for example, praised that the Bank had recognized the intrinsic value and significance of local knowledge in the development process 'not only because it offers some obvious solutions to local problems but also because it is an important component of the identity and spirit of a people' (Davis and Ebbe 1993:8). Seen in the light of such previous efforts it seems that the recent debate on *social cohesion* launched by the OECD and the World Bank is an ingenious and foresighted attempt of development agencies to get to grips not only with the diversity of societies and nations, but first and foremost with the growing *awareness of difference* among those who are the subjects of development and with their will to self-determination.

However, a crucial question remains: To what extent do the self-critical and constantly evolving mainstream debates and practices of development truly embrace, incorporate and implement alternative visions or how far are they just empty rhetoric? Do mainstream approaches really try to do justice to alternative ideas or do they rather accept the limitations set by the existing, hegemonic economic and political ideologies and the neoliberal capitalist framework? The answer is not surprising. A closer look reveals that despite its alternative rhetoric, mainstream development approaches move within established ideological and practical parameters and do not opt for basic structural transformations: Firstly, mainstream development is still development from above. The final goal of development and the decisions about strategies, programmes and projects regarding how to reach that goal are taken by so-called experts in the headquarters of global development institutions or by national governments; participation of the people concerned is often limited to information, consultation and involvement in implementing projects decided upon by outsiders.[14] Secondly, although economic growth is no longer propagated as the paramount goal of development, it is now seen as its major *means*. Development is considered not to be possible without economic growth, which is perceived as the sine qua non for poverty reduction and for human development. Thirdly, democracy in its existing representative form does not easily allow for the political involvement of citizens, especially in marginal (rural) areas. Although in many countries law prescribes decentralization and devolution of power, in practice it still remains a largely unrealized potential, as for example in the case of India. Fourthly, the international political, economic and financial order and the global power structures and dependencies remain unquestioned. Governments of developing countries have to follow international policy agendas like the Washington Consensus to get support for their development projects, which themselves follow the logic of economic growth, are largely oriented towards what is claimed to be the national interest or 'greater good' and often ignore the vital needs of marginal groups. This leads to the fifth and last point, which concerns sustainable development as a unique way of 'both violating and healing the environment' (1992b:29). Development is now being legitimized by splitting nature into two: a resource to be commercially used and exploited and a vulnerable, endangered environment that needs to be protected. In both scenarios the preferences and aspirations of the people living in close interrelationship with the natural resources are disregarded.

The critical examination of the concepts of cohesion, difference and development allows for the following conclusion: To promote cohesive development as a new paradigm and hence advance a social and integrative approach to development requires taking into account 'deep diversity', multi-perspectivity and multi-vocality in a society and giving the various social agents the opportunity to communicate and negotiate their perspectives, aspirations and demands in a bottom-up process of symmetric participation. However, the current structure of the international order is not favourable either for weak nation states or for the weaker and marginalized sections within a nation state to be recognized as equal partners in processes of defining and planning development. Especially the marginalized groups – in the Indian context: Dalits, Adivasis, the urban poor and others, as for example people in remote regions – are not sufficiently included. While these groups often have elaborate visions of how they want to live as individuals and/or groups and speak up via civil society organizations, political society activities[15] and non-violent protests, their voices are largely ignored. In India the '*conditions* of listening' are in principle in place;[16] however, for the creation of cohesive development, considerable changes in the socio-legal and political order as well as in the mind-set of the dominant social sections are basic preconditions. The willingness of those in power to *actually* listen to the perceptions of the suppressed, to accept their voice as a 'voice of authority' (Burghart) and to engage in a symmetric dialogue about defining and pursuing development has to be enforced. What is needed is the *audibility of the marginalized*.

2. The 'good life': aspirations, 'preferred futures' and the question of audibility of India's marginalized sections of society[17]

Within the critical development discourse scholars of *development ethics*, in particular, criticize the *top-down* way in which mainstream development is defined and implemented, and the perceptions and the agendas of the people concerned are ignored. These scholars request a genuine *bottom-up* approach, and – by sidestepping the biased notion of development – encourage particular culture- or group-specific definitions of 'good life' as well as the creation of social spaces to implement the alternative visions. One of the pioneers of development ethics, the American philosopher and political theorist Denis Goulet, proposed to ask: 'What exactly is the good life and the just society and the proper stance towards nature?' and he is convinced that 'very different answers will be given by people with different belief systems, or philosophies of life, or cultural explanations of the meaning of life and death' (Goulet 1990). In a similar way, Amartya Sen and Martha Nussbaum argue that development is neither a value as such, nor value-neutral; it is 'value-relative': 'without some idea of ends that are themselves external to the development process . . . we cannot begin to say what changes are to count as development' (Nussbaum and Sen 1987:1; see also Sen 1984, 2000). Ends and values that are meant to guide the development process are not separate from particular ideas of 'good life' and therefore are only to be defined through the experiences of the people concerned.[18]

In the following I will briefly present three case studies from India and illustrate the particular visions of indigenous groups (Adivasis), Himalayan hill dwellers and Dalits for a good life and a preferred future, which goes along with the desire of being acknowledged as citizens and full members of society in all their particularity and difference. However, I want to add a word of caution. To argue for self-defined ideas and strategies of 'good life' and for equal participation of hitherto marginal groups in debates on cohesive development does not mean falling into the trap of overlooking group-internal conflicting views due to status and gender inequalities, as well as possible processes of essentialization of culture in the service of identity politics. Especially indigenous groups have been largely romanticized. The focus these groups put on their own indigeneity and the way they communicate their cultural particularities (e.g. their quasi-communicative relation to nature) is probably a necessary, conscious political move. It functions as some sort of 'strategic essentialism' (Spivak 1990) in the struggle for indigenous rights and the right to be heard.

2.1 Adivasis

Indian Adivasis are concentrated in particular regions of India and have different colonial and post-colonial histories, religious allegiances and traditional ways of life. Their current socio-economic and political situation within the Indian nation state has to be understood in this wider context. Adivasis traditionally lived in close relationship to the natural environment and are therefore immediately affected by so-called national development projects like construction of hydroelectric dams, extraction of minerals and large-scale industrialization, but also by projects aimed at the conservation of nature. Many of these projects force Adivasis to sacrifice their land, forests and water for the 'greater good', and with that their well-being and often even their cultural integrity. As a result Adivasis have to face displacement and forced resettlement and are insufficiently rehabilitated and often impoverished. In the following part on indigenous visions I refer primarily to the experiences of Adivasis in Chota Nagpur (Central India), one of the most mineral-rich and industrialized areas of the country.

In spring 2015 Adivasis from Andra Pradesh, Chattisgarh, Jharkhand and Odisha and members of Adivasi solidarity groups from Germany joined in a 'Dialogue on Adivasi Experience and Perspectives for Development' in Kalunga (Odisha).[19] The dialogue attempted to reach out to the Adivasi world of experience and tried to learn about indigenous visions through experience-near language. The dialogue succeeded in bringing up concepts and ideas that emerged directly from local contexts. These were expressed in the vernaculars, and the language was often idiomatic. The imaginations and aspirations voiced by the Adivasi participants are interrelated with their actual life-worlds and living conditions in such a way that specific experiences apparently create specific visions and ideals.

- The experience of *marginalization, deprivation, suffering* and *humiliation* leads to aspirations for a *fulfilled life*. Adivasi keywords (here and in the following translated from local idioms): happiness – fullness – fulfilment – dignity – peace – creativity.
- The experience of *exploitation, destruction* and *disrespect of nature* creates the demand for ownership and (re-)gaining *control of the local environment*, considered as the basis of Adivasi life. Adivasi keywords: full possession of/full rights to/control over forest, water, land – fullness of life for the whole environment – a dignified life in harmony with the cosmos.

- Experience of *social and political neglect* results in *gender awareness* and the demand for *parity in participation*. Adivasi keywords: equality and respect for all – participation of all – equal participation of women.
- Experience of *devaluation* of the Adivasi way of life encourages the *recollection of Adivasi social values* and leads to *awareness of Adivasi cultural belonging*. Adivasi keywords: sharing – cooperation – solidarity – unity – security – protection of culture – wisdom – (local) knowledge – practices – language.
- Experience of *power structures and heteronomy* triggers the demand for *self-determination* as precondition for socio-political autonomy and the chance to live a life without interference (from others). Adivasi keywords: independence – self-rule – self-reliance – self-sufficiency.
- Awareness of *legal discourses* and experience of *legal possibilities* result in the conviction that Adivasis have the *right* to demand and fight for a self-determined life in dignity. Adivasi keywords: rights – fundamental rights – constitutional rights – special provisions – knowing about acts.
- Adivasis have learned that in order to *succeed* they must always be *alert and prepared* and able to develop their capabilities: Adivasi keywords: awaken – vigilant – education – elementary education – all kinds of knowledge.

The 'Dialogue' has illustrated that Adivasis want to pursue their particular way of life as recognized and respected subjects and citizens within the socio-political framework of the Indian nation state. They want their ways of life – considered as 'good life' – to be acknowledged as an equal option of human existence and they themselves to be treated as equals. The dialogue also gave evidence that Adivasis are fully aware of their *rights* to intervene as equal partners in all democratic processes. In its modern articulation as human rights or constitutional rights, the concept of rights derives from non-indigenous contexts but has meanwhile become a genuine part of local Adivasi discourses; it thus functions as a 'bridging concept'. The concept of rights, however, is an ambivalent tool. It can be used as an instrument for getting justice and obtaining parity in participation, while at the same time it can function as a barrier to equality. Right as legal system comes with its own language, procedures and representatives, and is thus not easily accessible for marginalized people with fewer economic resources and less formal education. For Adivasis to make use of legal possibilities (cultural) *translation* processes are needed as well as constant training and support from the side of civil society/solidarity organizations.

2.2 *Himalayan hill dwellers*

The following case study refers to the Uttarakhand movement for state autonomy that emerged in 1994/95 in the Central Himalayan regions of Garhwal and Kumaon – then part of the North Indian state of Uttar Pradesh.

Unfortunately, this movement did not succeed in the way participants had hoped for, even though the new state of Uttaranchal (later renamed in Utta-rakhand) was established in 2000. One reason for the failure was a lack of coherence in the political strategies and actions of those involved.[20] How-ever, Himalayan hill dwellers developed a unique socio-political imaginary and translated perceptions of and demands for what they considered a 'good life' into a pioneering message of political participation, social justice and self-determination.

Hill farmers complained that for too long political decisions had been taken in Lucknow, the distant capital of Uttar Pradesh, by those not famil-iar with the special geographical and social conditions in the Himalayan hills and not interested in its development. Even in the regional government services and administrative bodies the majority of employees in higher- and medium-rank positions were said to be unconcerned 'outsiders'. Emerging out of the critique of the political and administrative structures three core notions were showing up in the projections of a proposed Uttarakhand: *self-determination, proximity* and *transparency.*

The natural environment has always been a key concern of the hill popu-lation, as their economic security is largely dependent on an agro-sylvo-pastoral way of life. Yet, since the late 19th century the regional political and environmental history has been characterized by state control over vital resources like forest and water. One of the main claims of hill dwellers was therefore to regain control and management of the natural resources. That included stopping the flow of resources and profits into the plains and mak-ing use of them by establishing processing industries in the region itself, implementing small hydro-electric projects and promoting tourism at cer-tain places. But all this, so said the demand, should be done on a *small scale* and in a sustainable way, without being destructive to human beings and the environment. As another pillar of economic advancement hill farmers envisioned the increase of productivity through moderately introducing new technologies, (cash) crops and new animal breeds, and the establishment of proper marketing facilities. They hoped that these efforts would bring employment, financial and social security and infrastructural development to all districts of the region – this way creatively *modifying, but not totally transforming* the Pahari agro-pastoral way of life characterized by a close interconnection of humans and nature.[21]

While self-determination and proximity were the keywords for restruc-turing the economic space, they were also seen as valid for reorganizing the political and social spaces. In an autonomous state the capital with the main administrative bodies and the jurisdiction should be near and within the reach for the citizens. Educational institutions like primary and secondary schools were to be located within the vicinity of even remote villages, safely approachable by roads and paths during the whole year for children of all status groups. The same holds for hospitals and health centres where proper treatment should be given to males and females from all social strata.

Having experienced corruption and neglect from the side of politicians, administrators and those working in educational and welfare institutions, people from Garhwal and Kumaon further saw the need to create modes of direct control and intervention. Proximity facilitates transparency. With proximity of institutions and services, the decision makers and those who own certain responsibilities would have to step out of their anonymity and could be addressed and criticized by the citizens in face-to-face communication and interaction. A *personalized* way of negotiation and policy making was seen as a safeguard against corruption and the breaking of promises. Proximity and comprehensibility were considered foundational for what Anthony Giddens calls 'dialogic democracy', 'a form of politics 'which does not focus on the state, but helps to create and to strengthen a close relationship between autonomy and solidarity' (Giddens 1994).

Apart from the economic and political aspects of autonomy quite a few people – especially younger ones – reflected on the question of regional particularity and identity. With the equality of life chances, with education and social advancement, so their argument, Uttarakhandis could hope not only to achieve social recognition from others but also to develop a positive self-image and self-esteem, based on a distinct socio-cultural sense of belonging. Being recognized as an equal part of the pan-Indian society, cultural traits may serve as markers of difference – not to promote ethnic seclusion, but to emphasize the feeling of distinctness and particularity and to stabilize the conviction to add positively to the cultural plurality of India.

Himalayan hill people have convincingly illustrated that they neither see development equated with unconditional progress and economic growth nor reject modern achievements in favour of tradition. They themselves wanted to define what counts as development or as a good life and how to achieve it. They opted for a self-determined and distinct form of modernity, in which people carefully re-structure socio-economic life, while paying respect to nature and the particular sociality prevalent in the hills (see also Linkenbach 2000).

At this point I want to evoke again Denis Goulet, the pioneer of development ethics. He makes a plea for what he calls 'development from tradition'; however, he cautions for misinterpreting the term. He argues that people following this paradigm do not automatically reject aspects of the mainstream development goals but

> view modern technology or modern rationality systems or the primacy given to improving consumption or physical comfort in a radically different way from those who assume that these things are unconditionally good in themselves and not subject to the scrutiny of another set of values.
> (Goulet 1990, online interview)

According to Goulet, opting for an alternative to mainstream development does not mean to be anti-modern, but to be selective in what one considers appropriate and worthwhile of being integrated into one's own existing set of preferences. To put such aspiration into praxis, a certain degree of audibility, bargaining power, but also consistency in political action is required.

2.3 Dalits

The term Dalit is widely used as self- as well as external designation for historically disadvantaged (stigmatized) groups in India, which are officially categorized as Scheduled Castes (SC). The general term encompasses a heterogeneous section of the Indian population, which differ with respect to occupation, social and economic status, religious affiliation and local tradition; these differences have increased (ironically) because of antidiscrimination policies, new opportunities in urban contexts and processes of self-assertion and struggle. The positive developments for some should not obscure the existing conditions of exclusion and physical and mental humiliation many Dalits still have to endure, especially those who live in rural areas and/or have to follow polluting occupations and are economically weak.

In two workshops conducted in 2014, which focused on marginalization, humiliation and 'negative sociality' in India, the participating Dalit scholars and activists emphasized that Dalits regularly experience the ambivalence of anti-discrimination policies.[22] They argued that these policies are, on the one hand, absolutely beneficial for the hitherto excluded section of society, but that, on the other hand, improvements result in new forms of marginalization. The education system was often mentioned as a prime example as it brings new orders of ranking and segregation into social relations.[23] Stigmatization continues for example through welfare schemes in schools (free food, free learning material for Dalit), disrespectful treatment by teachers and professors and degrading housing (hostel) conditions. With regard to rural areas Dalit scholars point to the ineffectiveness of land reforms. Despite being a generally positive intervention, land distribution to Dalit does not always help to improve their economic condition. The distributed land often proves to be insufficient, of bad quality, and sooner or later farmers are again driven into the debt trap and end up as (semi-)bonded labourers.

Many Dalits are very proud of their long history of struggle (*sangarsh*)[24] and they are very much aware of their constitutional and human rights and the possibilities to obtain justice through law. However, similar to Adivasis, they recognize the ambivalence of law, as it needs knowledge, self-reliance and financial resources to make proper use of it. In addition, anti-discrimination laws are constantly under attack, as the very recent ruling by the Indian Supreme Court intended to weaken the Scheduled Castes/Scheduled Tribes Prevention of Atrocities Act shows (see Fuchs 2018). Despite drawbacks Dalits make sure that the struggle to get justice through law will go on. The song of Ganesh Ravi, a Dalit activist from Palamau (Jharkhand), demonstrated this impressively during the aforementioned workshop. The song urges a boatman to row and row into the distance, envisioning a better future, unmindful of the past.

Dalit imaginaries of a 'good life' are less specific; they are also varying and follow different lines of discursive justifications. For Martin Fuchs (2009) the major differences are between a hegemonic, particularistic (casteist) position and a subaltern perspective with a universalistic grounding. In the words of Gail Omvedt (1994): The difference lies between integration into the Hinduist system on the one hand, and autonomy on the other. Dalit visions for the future are based, in the first case, on improvement of one's own status within the hierarchical Hindu social order. This may include economic and social advancement, abandonment of polluting activities (occupation, food-habits) and adoption of practices and rituals related to high caste Hindus (e.g. marriage practices). However, status improvement of one group often goes along with new forms of exclusion oriented towards those who are now considered of lower rank. The second, subaltern and autonomous way comes with a critique of the Brahmanical worldview and often is further enhanced by attempts at religious liberation and conversion and by universalist-ethical ideas of human dignity and equality. This path, nevertheless, leads again into different directions. Some Dalits have opted for anti-hierarchical forms of Hinduism like *bhakti*; others joined universalistic religious denominations like Christianity or Ambedkarite Buddhism. In both cases confirmation of one's humanity and worth is grounded in transcendental relationships; either they confirm equality of human beings before god, or equality is seen as universally inscribed into human social nature.

In the different forms of perception of a 'good life' one aspect is expressed very clearly and drives all forms of self-assertion of Dalits as core motive: It is the search for recognition as fellow human beings, seen as a precondition for self-esteem and self-respect. Dalits strive towards the abolishment of stigmatization and of all discriminations connected with this; these include physical and mental violence, sexual harassment, forced labour, landlessness and exclusion from public and religious spaces and functions and from prestigious occupations.

2.4 The 'good life' – dimensions and preconditions

Grassroots visions for a 'fulfilled life' recall (with varying focus) the importance of a perspective that re-locates human beings into nature, emphasizes social relationality, dignity and (self-)respect, but also conveys awareness of the essential preconditions for the realization of local aspirations, particularly a certain degree of self-determination, capabilities, rights and entitlements. The crucial importance of relating ethical (normative) claims to political demands for capabilities (education, health) and entitlements (right over land, control over natural resources) has been highlighted by Amartya

Sen. A person's entitlements 'are the totality of things he can have by virtue of his rights', and a person's capabilities therefore consist of the sets of 'functionings' s/he can achieve, according to the personal, material and social resources available to her or him (Sen 1984, 2000; see also Vizard 2001).

In order to enable individuals and groups to function in a way that has been envisioned in local imaginaries, radical structural changes in the social, political and economic arenas are needed. The currently most visible form of self-assertion worldwide is that of indigenous peoples, and many countries encounter intense fights for indigenous self-determination based on self-defined projects of a 'good life'. It seems worthwhile to mention, at least briefly, that such fights have already yielded some success. In Bolivia and Paraguay, for example, indigenous conceptions of the 'good life' became part of the political discourse under the Spanish slogan *Buen vivir*.[25] Both countries have adopted the concept, which is said to represent the indigenous 'cosmovision', as state and government objectives in their constitutions. Raul Prada Alcoreza, former minister and professor of political science, Bolivia, explains:

> The concept does not split mankind from nature and has an inseparable interconnection between the material life of reproduction and the production of social and spiritual life. Men and women, together with nature, are part of the Mother Earth and there is a communion and dialogue between them mediated by rituals in which Nature is understood as a sacred being.
>
> (Prada [Alcoreza] 2013:145)

Discontent with the mainstream way of conceptualizing and implementing development equally shows in the term 'life projects', which stems from indigenous groups in Paraguay. They claim the right of indigenous individuals and groups to pursue a life 'according to their own preferences and aspirations', and they argue that their visions of the world and the future are '[p]remised on densely and uniquely woven "threads" of landscapes, memories, expectations and desires' (Blaser 2004:26).

In Bolivia and Paraguay the constitutional recognition of indigenous rights, the move from anthropocentric to cosmocentric visions of preferred futures and the acknowledgement of plurality and multi-vocality goes along with a transformative political programme targeting existing structures in many areas of life. Raul Prada Alcoreza from Bolivia indicates that besides changes towards a 'plural economy', a major transformative endeavour is geared towards political and administrative restructuring: decentralizing administration, forming institutions from the bottom up, responding to territorial demands of the various regions in the country. In short, the system of government is meant to be 'participatory democracy, with social participation and control, including the exercise of direct democracy, delegated democracy and community democracy' (Prada [Alcoreza] 2013:150, 153).[26]

3. Concluding remarks: audibility and radical democracy

Evoking the 'power of audibility' has two different aims: firstly, to indicate that marginalized individuals and groups require the capabilities as well as the opportunities to speak up and to communicate their aspirations for a good life and social advancement – not only with the help of mediators (like advocacy organizations), but also on their own. Secondly, marginalized individuals and groups must experience that their visions and demands are heard, understood and considered legitimate by the wider society and so can trigger societal debates and, by using legal and political avenues, can ultimately lead to transformative practices. However, the ideological and structural conditions in a country like India are anything but favourable for creating spaces for debates and strategies of cohesive development.

Apparently, the most basic obstacle in India is long-established mindsets. Human social interactions are navigated by underlying assumptions about the *conditio humana*, and each society is characterized by particular, deeply ingrained structures and beliefs regarding the status of human beings and the way relationships in society should work. These beliefs can be thoroughly complex and ambivalent, in accordance with the different (hegemonic, alternative) perspectives existing in a social formation. In India this ambivalence shows in the tensions between positions that emphasize human equality and general human dignity and those that rigidly deny these qualities to members of certain sections of society. Discriminatory ideas justify exclusionary and humiliating attitudes and practices, especially against Dalits and Adivasis. Dalits – seen from the still dominant brahmanocentric perspective – are considered outside the *varna* system, stigmatized as polluting and therefore not allowed to equally participate in many aspects of public and private life. Dalits target such a mind-set with their struggle for recognition and by increasingly making use of the judicial system. The history of Dalit movements and the constitutional recognition Dalits receive today give evidence of the possibility of normative social transformation and practical change through constant protest and struggle.

In contrast and despite constitutional provisions, Adivasis do not feel recognized at all. Unlike Dalits, who were linked to the mainstream society through negative forms of sociality (inclusion by exclusion), Adivasis had not been part of the wider society, and in former times most of them did not even aspire to be. Only since the colonial period did the remote tribal areas become increasingly accessible by way of infrastructure building, commerce and forest policies. Penetration into the tribal space accelerated on the part of the British colonizers but also Hindu merchants and non-tribal agriculturists in search for land. Adivasis became integrated into the modern economy as labour force and bonded labour, and the women through prostitution. In independent India tribals are largely seen as obstacles of development. Their way of life, their outlook, their distinct humanity is devalued and not considered suitable for the modern world. For many, Adivasis represent a

primitive past, and although Adivasis have learned to articulate their interests and viewpoints and engage in protest campaigns, the mainstream society often refuses communication and does not take their claims seriously.

Making use of the law and engaging in civil (political) society activities
are legitimate attempts to alter other peoples' outlook and to initiate normative and social change. However, it seems worthwhile to ask how far democratic structures can be used (or modified) to provide opportunities to make
marginal voices audible and to include so far excluded sections in debates
on cohesive development and in decision-making processes. We probably
have to seriously consider democracy 'from below' as an avenue to audibility and participation. Bolivia and Paraguay have chosen this path and D.S.
Sheth proposed this route for India already 30 years ago.

> For the politics of alternative development to emerge, the corresponding
> theory should be primarily rooted in the *problematique of democrati-*
> *zation*. More specifically, the idea of alternative development must be
> explicitly integrated with the idea of democracy and such integration
> must allow the criteria emerging from the ground to shape the very
> conception of alternative development.
>
> (Sheth 1989:69)

In the last two decades scholars and activists in India engaged in a vigor-
ous debate on the deficits of Indian democracy, encouraging a rethinking of
democratic institutions and practices. At the heart of an agenda for political reform are demands for de-centring politics through the devolution of
power to panchayati raj institutions on the village and district level and
about reducing unequal access to political and financial resources and information. Although decentralization and self-governance has been ensured in
the 73th/74th Constitutional Amendment of 1992 or Panchayati Raj Act
and in the Provisions of the Panchayats (Extension to Scheduled Areas)
Act, 1996 (PESA), it has not created the desired effects in political practices. Democracy 'from the ground' seems still only an aspiration, as it also
became obvious in the example of the Uttarakhand movement.

The most radical ideas regarding a process of 'democratization of democracy' developed out of the Zapatista movement in the region of Chiapas in
Southern Mexico. The movement appeared on the scene of global activism
in 1996 by organizing the First Intercontinental Encounter for Humanity
and against Neo-Liberalism. Following Thomas Olesen the Zapatista idea
of radical democracy includes three dimensions: broadening, delegation and
deepening of democracy (Olesen 2006). *Broadening of democracy* refers to
the extension of democracy beyond the political arena; Zapatistas aim for
democratic control in politics, economics, cultural systems and civil society.
Delegation of democracy circumscribes the creation of autonomous spaces
to govern independently from the state – in the case of Chiapas it means
securing a certain degree of autonomy for indigenous peoples and granting

them the possibility to rule according to tradition (continuous consultation, aiming at consensus). The concept of *deepening of democracy* presupposes civil society not as a terrain but as a target of political action. Thus it aims for politicization of civil society, for an empowerment of civil society through social action, activism and movements.

In the context of broadening democracy, Zapatistas explicitly demand a *culture of listening*. In a communiqué issued in the year 2000 they formulate: 'We want to find a politics that goes from the bottom to the top, one in which "to rule by obeying" is more than a slogan' (quoted in Olesen 2006:138). With *rule by obeying* Zapatistas refer to the relation between government and citizens. It implies, on the one hand, governing through listening, obeying the ideas of the citizens; on the other hand it involves that citizens are empowered to permanently evaluate government work, to criticize and even reverse political decisions if they are not in accordance with the mandates given by the electorate.[27]

Taking into consideration India's marginalized groups, the idea of radical democracy or democracy from below seems to resonate with their visions and hopes. Linking radical democracy with the question of cohesive development, three aspects have to be highlighted:

1   Democracy from below must be based on mutual respect and solidarity with regard to all sections of society. Only then will it be possible to include people with different positionalities in a *symmetric poly-vocal dialogue* on goals and means of development, and guarantee them audibility.
2   Democracy from below must aim for political structures, which allow collaborative decision-making, transparency, permanent evaluation and control of the governing agencies by the citizens ('rule by obeying' the electorate).
3   Radical democracy always builds on (gets input from) *protest and struggle in its local and trans-local forms*. Many local movements are also part of transnational movements and networks and give each other mutual support in their demands and practices of protest.[28]
4   Creating and establishing a symmetric dialogue on the basis of cultural and social diversity within a society is a major challenge. Scholars have pointed towards the communicative potential of 'translation'.[29] Translation here is not meant in its linguistic but in its cultural dimension. It is the mutual attempt of social actors to make their own specific problems, discourses and practices comprehensible to other persons and groups. Such an endeavour is possible because nobody lives in an isolated and closed space; social and cultural groups are open, porous and fluid, they provide contact areas, which allow the discovery of commonalities in outlook and practice. In the words of Boaventura Santos: 'Through translation work, diversity is celebrated, not as a factor of fragmentation and isolationism but rather as a condition of sharing and solidarity' (2006:133).

I will conclude by modifying a statement voiced by Denis Goulet with reference to Paolo Freire: Cohesive development will only be possible if the 'victims of underdevelopment' will transform into subjects, and into 'conscious and active shapers of their history' (Goulet 2006:63).

Notes

1 This expression has been coined by Arjun Appadurai (2004).
2 Boehnke, Klaus, et al., quoted in Social Cohesion in Eastern Africa, 2016:2.
3 Festinger, quoted in Norton and de Haan 2013:11.
4 French Commissariat General du Plan, quoted in Norton and de Haan 2013:11.
5 See Durkheim's studies *Suicide* 2006 (French orig. 1897) and *The Division of Labour in Society* 2013 (French orig. 1893).
6 For a definition of the nation state see Giddens 1993:311–312. For the role of states in the international world order, respectively the cosmopolitan nation state see e.g. Held 1995; Archibugi and Held 1995; Archibugi, Held and Kohler 1996. For nation states and the international legal frameworks see e.g. Hayden 2005.
7 See Appadurai's framework of global cultural flows, termed 'scapes' because of their fluidity: ethnoscapes, mediascapes, technoscapes, finanscapes, ideoscapes (Appadurai 1990).
8 Most famous is the definition of Edward B. Taylor who sees culture as a 'complex whole which includes knowledge, belief, art, morals, law, custom, and any other capabilities and habits acquired by man as a member of society' (1920:1).
9 For critique of the traditional concept of culture see e.g. Wicker 1997; Fuchs 2000.
10 For a discussion on development and environmentalism as utopian beliefs see Linkenbach 2009.
11 See the aforementioned works of Rist, Escobar, Nederveen Pieterse; see also Sachs 1992a.
12 In India scholars working at the Centre for the Study of the Developing Societies (CSDS), Delhi (such as D. S. Sheth, Rajni Kothari, Vijay Pratap), engaged in the alternative discourse. Sheth was founding editor of the journal *Alternatives: Global, Local, Political*. Kothari founded *Lokayan* (dialogue with the people), a forum and a movement for alternatives in politics and development, in 1980. The ecological perspective was brought in by the work of Anil Agarwal and others from the Center for Science and Environment, Delhi. They initiated the 'Citizens' Reports' on the state of the Indian environment; the first report was published in 1982 (see Agarwal, Anil, Chopra, Ravi and Kalpana Sharma 1982), others followed. Critique from an eco-feminist perspective was first voiced by Vandana Shiva (1988).
13 An example for such an apparently progressive approach to development is the report Making Democracy Work for Pro-Poor Development 2003. One of the authors of this report is Manmohan Singh, economist and former finance minister (1991–1996) and prime minister of India (2004–2014); see Singh (2003).
14 Rodgers, Hartley and Bashir (2003:330) have listed different possible levels of participation regarding use of local resources: *Passive* – receive information; all decisions made by outsiders. *Information* – communities feed information to external decision makers. *Consultation* – communities discuss issues with outsiders, who take local views into account. *Functional* – communities, all members or certain groups, undertake activities driven by outsiders. *Interactive* – communities participate in planning activities and become full stakeholders. *Total* – ownership of the resource by local communities, full rights of decision-making and implementation.

15 The term political society was coined by Partha Chatterjee (2001) to conceptualize the political engagement and movements of those who are not part of 'civil society' (understood as institutions of associational life that are Western in origin), of those who are marginalized and often claim their rights out of illegal spaces.

16 In an essay on teachers' protest in Nepal during the Panchayat era Richard Burghart argues that in a hierarchical social structure with no civil society, the 'conditions of listening' have to be created by first generating 'the moral space in which subjects can publicly criticise' (2008:317).

17 The notion 'preferred futures' was coined by Javeed Alam (1999).

18 Martha Nussbaum, in particular, is known for her neo-Aristotelian perspective on a theory of the 'good'. She criticises John Rawls who considers some primary goods ('basic essentials') as prerequisites to carry out one's place in life; these goods are liberty and opportunity, wealth and income. Instead she argues with Aristotle that wealth and income do not have any independent significance; they are only useful for something. Together with Amartya Sen she therefore warns that we cannot properly estimate the worth of distributable goods until we have an account of the functioning towards which these goods are useful (Nussbaum 1987). Nussbaum develops an 'outline sketch' of the good life, an 'account of what it is to be a human being', which she grounds in basic anthropological assumptions (Nussbaum 1990:225). While the list has been criticized as being patronizing and 'imposed' onto others, Nussbaum rejects the critique and argues that her list is open to amendments and additions, includes perspectives from non-Western cultural contexts (e.g. of Indian women) and allows for many concrete specifications.

19 See the report of the workshop *Adhikaar* – 'Rights', *khushaalii* – 'happiness', *sampuurn jiivan* – 'fullness of life' 2015.

20 The movement was a well-organized, decentralized struggle without formal leadership; mobilization work was basically carried out by government employees, journalists, social activists and, importantly, by women of all ages and from all status groups. In 1998/99 I talked with social activists, intellectuals and village men and women in Garhwal and Kumaon and learned that – in a more or less elaborated way – they had developed ideas and hopes regarding how to form of the new state and how to improve their life within the new state. For an account of the vision of an imagined Uttarakhand in the context of the autonomy movement and for course and result of the movement see Linkenbach 2002; for the history and politics of the movement see also Kumar 2000.

21 For a description of the interconnection of humans and nature in the Central Himalayas see Linkenbach 2007.

22 I refer to the findings of two workshops conducted in Ranchi (Jharkhand) and Delhi in September 2014 on the topic of on "Marginality, Humiliation and Social Recognition among Dalits, Muslims and Adivasis (Tribes) in India". The workshops were organized by Valerian Rodriguez, University of Mangalore, India, and Martin Fuchs, Max-Weber-Kolleg, University of Erfurt, Germany. Invited speakers were, among others, scholars and activists from the communities concerned. The contributions of Adivasi members support the arguments I presented before in part 2.1.

23 Relevant arguments were made by P. Ramajayam (Tiruchirapalli), N. Sukumar (Delhi), Shankar Das (Jharkhand).

24 For Dalit struggles see for example Omvedt 1994, 1995; Fuchs und Linkenbach 2003; Fuchs 1999.

25 See Gudynas 2011. The vernacular versions for 'good life' are, for example: '*sumak kawsay*' (Quetchua), '*nandereco*' (Guarani), '*suma qamana*' (Aymara). *Buen vivir* is seen as an umbrella term, and what exactly is included in this expression depends on particular regional and cultural conditions. So has Ecuador laid

the focus on rights, while Bolivia emphasizes ethic principle and cultural diversity. *Buen vivir* is the subject of constant debate; it is not considered a static concept but is meant to indicate a process.

26 Here is not the place to explore and evaluate success or failure of political restructuring in Bolivia or Paraguay.

27 For more information on the Zapatista movement see e.g. Ramirez 2008; Mignolo 2011, chapter 6.

28 For the internationalization of movements and movement networks see Kurasawa 2004.

29 For the concept of cultural translation see Bachmann-Medick 2006; Fuchs 2009.

References

(2015), *Adhikaar* – 'Rights', *khushaalii* – 'happiness', *sampuurn jiivan* – 'Fullness of life': Report and Thematic Resumé of the 'Dialogue on Adivasi Experience and Perspectives for Development', Saturday, 28 February and Sunday, 1 March 2015 at Nava Jagriti Centre, Kalunga, Odisha, India. Organised jointly by ASHRA, Rourkela, and Adivasi Koordination, Germany. *sarini* Occasional Papers 11.

Agarwal, Anil, Chopra, Ravi and Kalpana Sharma, eds. (1982), *The State of India's Environment: The First Citizens' Report*, New Delhi: Centre for Science and Environment.

Alam, Javeed (1999), *India: Living with Modernity*, New Delhi: Oxford University Press.

Anthias, Floya (2002), 'Where do I belong? Narrating collective identity and translocational positionality', *Ethnicities* 2(4), 491–514.

Appadurai, Arjun (1990), 'Disjuncture and difference in the global cultural economy', *Public Culture* 2(2), 1–23.

—— (2004), 'The capacity to aspire: Culture and the terms of recognition', in: Vijayendra Rao and Michael Walton (eds.), *Culture and Public Action*, Stanford, CA: Stanford University Press, 59–84.

Archibugi, Daniele and Held, David (1995), *Cosmopolitan Democracy: An Agenda for a New World Order*, Cambridge: Polity.

Archibugi, Daniele, Held, David and Kohler, Martin, eds. (1996), *Re-imagining Political Community: Studies in Cosmopolitan Democracy*, Cambridge: Polity Press.

Bachmann-Medick, Doris (2006), *Cultural turns: Neuorientierungen in den Kulturwissenschaften*, Reinbek bei Hamburg: Rowohlt.

Blaser, Mario (2004), 'Life projects: Indigenous peoples' agency and development', in: Mario Blaser, Harvey A. Feit and Glenn McRae (eds.), *In the Way of Development: Indigenous Peoples, Life Projects and Globalization*, London: Zed Books; Ottawa: International Development Research Centre, 26–44.

Burghart, Richard (2008), 'The conditions of listening: The everyday experience of politics in Nepal', in: C.J. Fuller and Jonathan Spencer (eds.), *The Conditions of Listening: Essays on Religion, History and Politics in South Asia*, New Delhi: Oxford University Press, 300–318.

Chatterjee, Partha (2001a), 'On civil and political society in post-colonial democracies', in: Sudipta Kaviraj and Sunil Khilnani (eds.), *Civil Society: History and Possibilities*, Cambridge, England: Cambridge University Press, 165–178.

Durkheim, Émile (2006), *On Suicide, translated by Robin Buss* with an introduction by Richard Sennett and notes by Alexander Riley, London, England: Penguin Books.

———, (2013), *The Division of Labour in Society*. 2nd ed. (ed. by Steven Lukes), Oxford: Macmillan Education – Palgrave.

Escobar, Arturo (1995), *Encountering Development: The Making and Unmaking of the Third World*, Princeton, NJ: Princeton University Press.

Fuchs, Martin (1999), *Kampf um Differenz: Repräsentation, Subjektivität und soziale Bewegungen. Das Beispiel Indien*, Frankfurt am Main: Suhrkamp.

——— (2000), 'Universality of culture: Reflection, interaction and the logic of identity', *Thesis Eleven* 60, 11–22.

——— (2009), 'Reaching out; or, nobody exists in one context only – society as translation', *Translation Studies* 2(1), 21–40.

Fuchs, Martin and Linkenbach, Antje (2003), 'Social movements', in: V. Das (ed.), *Oxford India Companion to Sociology and Social Anthropology* (2 Vols.), New Delhi: Oxford University Press, 1524–1563.

Fuchs, Sandhya (2018), 'Indian Supreme Court curbs one of the world's most powerful anti-discrimination laws'. www.opendemocracy.net/en/openindia/indian-supreme-court-curbs-one-of-world-s-most-powerful-anti-discrimination-/; last accessed 15–12–2019.

Giddens, Anthony (1993), *Sociology* (2nd ed. Fully rev. and updated), Cambridge: Polity Press.

——— (1994), *Beyond Left and Right: The Future of Radical Politics*, Cambridge: Polity Press.

Goulet, Denis (1990), *New Ethics of Development*. Interview by Mike Gismondi. Aurora online with Denis Goulet. http://aurora.icaap.org/index.php/aurora/article/view/51/64; last accessed 15–12–2019.

——— (2006), *Development Ethics at Work: Explorations 1960–2002*, London and New York: Routledge.

Gudynas, Eduardo (2011), 'Buen Vivir: Today's tomorrow', *Development* 54(4), 441–447.

Hayden, Patrick (2005), *Cosmopolitan Global Politics*, Aldershot: Palgrave.

Held, David (1995), *Democracy and the Global Order. From the Modern State to Cosmopolitan Governance*, Cambridge: Polity Press.

Kumar, Pradeep (2000), *The Uttarakhand Movement: Construction of a Regional Identity*, New Delhi: Kanishka Publishers.

Kurasawa, Fuyuki (2004), 'A cosmopolitanism from below: Alternative globalization and the creation of a solidarity without bounds', *European Journal of Sociology/Archives européennes de sociologie* 45(2), 233–255.

Larsen, Christian Albrekt (2014), *Social Cohesion: Definition, Measurement and Developments*, Institut for Statskundskab, Aalborg Universitet, Aalborg. CCWS working paper no. 2014–85. http://vbn.aau.dk/files/207548602/85_2014_CAL.pdf; last accessed 10–04–2018.

Linkenbach, Antje (2000), 'Anthropology of modernity: Projects and contexts', *Thesis Eleven* 61, 41–63.

——— (2002), 'Shaking the state by making a (new) state: Social movements and the quest for autonomy', *Sociologus* 52(1), 77–106.

——— (2007), *Forest Futures: Global Representations and Ground Realities in the Himalayas*, Ranikhet: Permanent Black.

——— (2009), 'Doom or salvation? Utopian beliefs in contemporary discourses on development and ecology', *SITES. A Journal of Social Anthropology and Cultural Studies* 6(1), 24–47.

Mignolo, Walter (2011), *The Darker Side of Western Modernity: Global Futures, Decolonial Options*, Durham and London: Duke University Press.

Mold, Andrew et al. (2016), 'Social Cohesion in Eastern Africa, United Nations Economic Commission for Africa, Subregional Office for Eastern Africa'. www. uneca.org/sites/default/files/PublicationFiles/social_cohesion_in_easterndragolov DraDraDragolov_africa_fin_eng.pdf; last accessed 10–04–2018.

Norton, Andrew and de Haan, Arjan (2013), *Social Cohesion: Theoretical Debates and Practical Applications with Respect to Jobs*, Background Paper for the World Development Report 2013. http://siteresources.worldbank.org/EXTNWDR2013/ Resources/8258024-1320950747192/8260293-1320956712276/8261091-13486 83883703/WDR2013_bp_Social_Cohesion_Norton.pdf; last accessed 10–04–2018.

Nussbaum, Martha C. (1987), *Nature, Function, and Capability: Aristotle on Political Distribution*, World Institute for Development Economics Research of the United Nations University; WIDER working papers; 31. www.wider.unu.edu/ sites/default/files/WP31.pdf; last accessed 15–12–2019.

――― (1990), 'Aristotelian social democracy', in: R. Bruce Douglass, Gerald M. Mara and Henry S. Richardson (eds.), *Liberalism and the Good*, New York and London: Routledge, 203–252.

Nussbaum, Martha C. and Sen, Amartya (1987), *Internal Criticism and Indian Nationalist Traditions*, World Institute for Development Economics Research of the United Nations University; WIDER working papers; 30. www.wider.unu.edu/ sites/default/files/WP30.pdf; last accessed 15–12–2019.

OECD (2011), *Perspectives on Global Development 2012: Social Cohesion in a Shifting World*, OECD Publishing, Paris, (Summary in English). https://doi.org/ 10.1787/persp_glob_dev-2012-en; last accessed 03–04–2018.

Olesen, Thomas (2006), 'Global democratic protest: The Chiapas connection', in: Ingo K. Richter, Sabine Berking and Ralf Mueller-Schmid (eds.), *Building a Transnational Civil Society: Global Issues and Global Actors*, Houndmills, Basingstoke: Palgrave Macmillan, 135–155.

Omvedt, Gail (1994), *Dalits and the Democratic Revolution: Dr. Ambedkar and the Dalit Movement in Colonial India*, New Delhi: Sage.

――― (1995), *Dalit Visions: The Anti-Caste Movement and the Construction of an Indian Identity*, New Delhi: Orient Longman.

Pieterse, Jan Nederveen (2001), *Development Theory: Deconstructions/ Reconstructions*, London et al.: Sage Publications.

Prada, Raul (2013), 'Buen Vivir as a model for state and economy', in: M. Lang and D. Mokrani (eds.), *Beyond Development: Alternative Visions from Latin America. Permanent Working Group on Alternatives to Development, Quito*, Ecuador: Fundacion Rosa Luxemburg; Amsterdam, NL: Transnational Institute.

Ramirez, Gloria Munoz (2008), *The Fire and the Word: A History of the Zapatista Movement*, Translated by Laura Carlsen with Alejandro Reyes Arias, San Francisco: City Lights Books.

Rist, Gilbert (1997), *The History of Development: From Western Origins to Global Faith*, London and New York: Zed Books.

Rodgers, William, Hartley, Dawn and Bashir, Sultana (2003), 'Community approaches to conservation: Some comparisons from Africa and India', in: Vasant K. Saberwal and Mahesh Rangarajan (eds.), *Battles over Nature: Science and the Politics of Conservation*, New Delhi: Permanent Black, 324–382.

Sachs, Wolfgang (1992a), *Zur Archäologie der Entwicklungsidee*, Frankfurt/Main: IKO-Verlag.

——— (1992b), 'Environment', in: Wolfgang Sachs (ed.), *The Development Dictionary: A Guide to Knowledge as Power*, London: Zed Books, 26–37.

Santos, Boaventura de Sousa (2006), *The Rise of the Global Left: The World Social Forum and Beyond*, London and New York: Zed Books.

Sen, Amartya (1984), *Resources, Values and Development*, Cambridge, MA and London: Harvard University Press.

——— (2000), 'Capability and well-being', in: Stuart Corbridge (ed.), *Development. Critical Concepts in the Social Sciences*, London and New York: Routledge.

——— (2004), 'How does culture matter?' in: Vijayendra Rao and Michael Walton (eds.), *Culture and Public Action*, Stanford, CA: Stanford University Press, 37–58.

Shelton, H. Davis and Ebbe, Katrina, eds. (1995), *Traditional Knowledge and Sustainable Development: Proceedings of a Conference sponsored by the World Bank Environment Department and the World Bank Task Force on the International Year of the World's Indigenous People, held at The World Bank, Washington, DC, September 27–28, 1993*, Washington, DC: The International Bank for Reconstruction and Development/The World Bank. http://documents.worldbank.org/curated/en/517861468766175944/pdf/multi-page.pdf; last accessed 15–12–2019.

Sheth, D.L. (1989), 'Catalyzing alternative development: Values, the knowledge system, power', in: Poona Wignaraja and Akmal Hussain (eds.), *The Challenge in South Asia: Development, Democracy and Regional Cooperation*, Tokyo: The United Nations University; New Delhi: Sage, 61–74.

Shiva, Vandana (1988), *Staying Alive: Women, Ecology and Survival in India*, New Delhi: Kali for Women.

Singh, Manmohan et al. (2003), *Making Democracy Work for Pro-Poor Development: Report of the Commonwealth Expert Group on Development and Democracy*, London: The Commonwealth Secretariat. https://sas-space.sas.ac.uk/5847/143/2003_Making_Democracy_Work_For_Pro-Poor_Development.pdf; last accessed 15–12–2019.

Spivak, Gayatri C. (1990), *The Post-colonial Critic*. ed. by Sarah Harasym, New York: Routledge.

Taylor, Edward (1920 [1871]), *Primitive Culture* (Vol. 1), New York: J. P. Putnam's Sons.

United Nations General Assembly (2000), Resolution adopted by the General Assembly 55/2. United Nations Millenium Declaration. https://www.un.org/en/development/desa/population/migration/generalassembly/docs/globalcompact/A_RES_55_2.pdf; last accessed 17-03-2020.

Vizard, Polly (2001), *Economic Theory, Freedom and Human Rights: The Work of Amartya Sen*, London: Overseas Development Institute (OD); Briefing paper. www.odi.org/sites/odi.org.uk/files/odi-assets/publications-opinion-files/2321.pdf; last accessed 20–12–2019.

Wicker, Hans Rudolf (1997), 'From complex culture to cultural complexity', in: P. Werbner and T. Modood (eds.), *Debating Cultural Hybridity. Multi-Cultural Identities and the Politics of Anti-Racism*, London: Zed Books, 29–45.

Yuval-Davis, Nira (2006), 'Belonging and the politics of belonging', *Patterns of Prejudice* 40(3), 197–214.

5 A genuine social democracy
The only way!

M. V. Nadkarni

Introduction

Cohesive development, as the concept note on the seminar has pointed out, is one that aims at achieving solidarity or harmony between nature, people (labour), and capital. One may add that as far as people are concerned, there has to be solidarity between different sections (be they economic classes or ethnic/cultural groups) of people and between people of the present generation and people of future generations. Solidarity with nature, both on the part of people and capital, means sustainable or environment-friendly development. The ideal of cohesive development is expressed in the ancient Indian prayer in Sanskrit – *Sarve bhadraani pashyantu, maa kashchit dukkhamaapnuyaat,* which means: 'May all be secure, may not any one suffer.' If any people, even if only a few, become worse off as a result of a development project that benefits many or a few, then such people who are worse off should be adequately compensated and rehabilitated. Every individual counts; none should suffer. That is the ideal to be attained. Even where deprivation is only relative and not absolute, the disparity should be minimised and not reach unacceptable levels. Cohesive development cannot be only in economic terms, and cannot be attained at the cost of human freedom and democratic rights.

Why only a social democracy can deliver cohesive development

The question is, what system is most likely to deliver such development? Cohesive development, defined as development which is democratic, egalitarian, and sustainable, can be realised only under a social democracy. Capitalism cannot achieve it as it creates an unacceptable amount of inequalities. Both liberty and equality are equally important basic conditions for a democracy. Capitalism also cannot ensure sustainable development, since its unbridled motive of profit maximisation prevents it. In addition, communism cannot ensure cohesive development, because it is not democratic. It is no less obsessed with economic growth and accumulation than capitalism is, and as such cannot promote sustainable development. Social democracy on the other hand avoids the limitations of both capitalism and communism. It is democratic and ensures both liberty and equality. It gives scope to private capital and for incentives to grow, but subjects it to democratic norms to ensure an egalitarian and sustainable development. In a social democracy, capital has to function under the control of a democratic state; with capitalism, democracy functions under the control of capital.

Though private enterprise is needed for growth, unbridled capitalism cannot be the answer as it unleashes serious and unacceptable levels of disparity and deprivation, and through its tendency for reckless depredation of natural resources, including the pollution of air and water, it endangers the wellbeing not only of the future but also of present generations. A strong state is needed to control these tendencies. But communism cannot be the alternative, because even if it may have succeeded in meeting basic needs, it deprives people of their basic democratic rights and freedoms. A human being's aspirations go much beyond meeting the bare needs of food and shelter, which communism has failed to understand.

Social democracy is the golden mean between capitalism and communism. It achieves a reconciliation between liberty, which is the basic principle of a capitalist democracy, and equality, which is the basic principle of communism. It is not just a compromise between capitalism and communism, but it avoids the weaknesses of both and tries to have the positive points of both. It allows scope for private capital and market forces, but they have to operate under the control and supervision of a democratic state. The state has, of course, a prominent role under social democracy, but it cannot be suffocating as under communism, since it has to be a democratic state. Accepting the principle of liberty or freedom is vital to a democracy, but it does not mean that the state has no right to intervene in the interest of promoting equality. Absolute liberty is not possible in any society with multiple individuals, groups and interests, not even under a capitalist democracy.

A social democracy also accepts the ideals of socialism, along with democracy of course, particularly the commitment to reduce extreme inequalities in income and wealth to what is morally acceptable. In other words, it strives to ensure democracy and meaningful freedom for all. When private enterprise is given scope, it is not possible to wipe out all inequality in income and wealth due to the need to give incentives both for work and accumulation or investment. A social democracy has, therefore, to at least ensure that *all* people have access to basic minimum needs in respect of food, clothing, shelter, health security, and free and universal access to primary and secondary education, which is uniformly of good quality for all children. A social democracy should necessarily be a welfare state. It has a commitment also to provide jobs for all who seek them and avoids unemployment. Cohesive development has no meaning without full employment.

A social democracy, therefore, requires resorting to progressive taxation of income and wealth of the rich on the one hand, and social expenditure to meet the basic needs of the poor on the other. It is practical enough to realise that redistribution of income has to take place along with economic growth, by enlarging the size of the cake and not just by redistributing the given cake. The compulsion of economic growth arises, especially in developing countries, because it is easier to meet basic needs and provide social security for *all* under conditions of growth than under stagnation. The less well-off should at least enjoy additions to their income and welfare in absolute terms in the course of growth, and eventually even in relative terms. An important condition for this is that additions made to national income are not all appropriated by those few who already have the lion's share of it.

Advocates of capitalism or neo-liberalism argue that the increase in inequality that takes place under economic growth is necessary to provide incentives for growth and should not matter so long as absolute gains accrue to the poor and help them to move into the middle class. Under capitalism, it is argued, even a manual labourers' son can become a millionaire, provided that equal and fair opportunities to rise are given to all and they are not obstructed by feudal forces. It is the business of a social democratic polity to ensure such opportunities to all without discrimination. That is why social democracy, even while permitting a fair scope for capital to function freely, at the same time tries to see that such freedom is used in a responsible way which promotes the welfare of all and does not curb the freedom of and opportunities for the weak.

Arguments for unqualified incentives for capital need to be critically assessed. This is because, in this scenario the rich tend to walk away with most of the increase in GNP, and inequality persists and keeps growing. We may not be able to draw a precise line or *Lakshman Rekha* of what inequality is permissible, but it is clear, as John Rawls (2001: 42–43) has pointed out, that the extent of inequality permitted should be justifiable in the sense of being helpful to the least advantaged, indirectly at least. Today, a mere eight top billionaires of the world have more wealth than the bottom 50 per cent of the world population, and the bottom 50 per cent of the world population has just 0.2 per cent of the world's wealth, according to the Oxfam report. The "CEO of India's top information firm" is reported to earn "416 times the salary of a typical employee in his company".[1] Is such an extreme disparity necessary to provide incentives for initiative and enterprise?

What is equally worrying is that quite a few enthusiasts of freedom of enterprise and 'ease of doing business' look upon environmental regulations as obstructions. They persuade the government to relax them and give quick clearances to development projects and investment proposals in the interest of economic growth, without a thorough social and environmental impact assessment. For them the care of the environment is secondary to development.[2]

Flaws in neo-liberalism and Gandhi's solution

There are major flaws in the defence of neo-liberalism. It is not that capital alone requires incentives. Production of wealth is a collective enterprise in which labour, state and society at large contribute significantly. They too need incentives to give their best. Moreover, all the accumulated wealth of a person is not earned as a result of his or her enterprise. Much of it may be inherited. Inherited wealth contributes significantly to inequality, as Thomas Piketty (2014) has shown. He calls the system which has generated it as 'patrimonial capitalism'.

Mahatma Gandhi was keenly conscious of the reality of capitalism generating great inequalities in income and wealth. He advocated the principle of trusteeship for the owners of wealth, which is to be used for the benefit of the society, particularly of the deprived. Gandhi was wary of a dominating state, as it could lead to oppression, and preferred private philanthropy and non-governmental organisations (NGOs) to provide free education and health care for all. But he was also aware that not many rich would follow his principle of trusteeship. For such people, he did not mind taxing their excess wealth not used for philanthropy and using the tax proceeds for the welfare of the poor. However, the welfare state of his conception was not a centralised dominating state, but a decentralised democratic state meeting the needs of people in a responsive way.[3] It allowed private enterprise but not inequality. He would not allow disparity based even on merit, since he said that the remuneration of a lawyer should not be much above that of a manual labourer. A social democracy committed to reducing inequality significantly through taxing the rich (with possible exemption for genuine philanthropy) and meeting the basic needs of the people would thus be very consistent with Gandhian principles. Gandhi did not see socialism as merely a system of state ownership of the means of production. For him, such a system was an excuse for totalitarianism. Democracy was important to him for preventing the state from becoming too dominant, and that is why he did not like any system of centralised democracy distanced from easy accessibility to people. He wanted a decentralised democracy which is accessible and responsive to people.

Social democracy has to be a welfare state

Social democracy and welfare state are two expressions of the same system. Democracy guarantees rights to freedom, security and property for all, safeguarding negative civil rights. On the other hand, welfare state 'enables actual involvement and participation', making democracy a matter of actual realisation for all, and 'safeguards positive civil rights and liberties', guaranteeing rights to food, shelter, health, education and work. Social democracy gives equal priority or value to negative rights (like rights to life, freedom and property), and positive rights (like rights to food, education and health). In a social democracy, the state has the right to intervene in the distribution of income, wealth and welfare, making it more equal (Petring et al. 2012: 13–14).

An interesting issue under social democracy is to demarcate the respective spheres of private and public sectors. Since even the private sector is under the supervision and control of the democratic state under social democracy, the question of demarcation between the two spheres is *not* of crucial significance. However, a useful criterion could be whether profit maximisation is suitable for certain spheres and instead the goal of social service is more important. Health and education should clearly come under the public sector; even if the private sector is allowed here, it should be subject to the norms and discipline imposed by the state. It is not beyond the ingenuity of countries like India to give enough scope to the private sector and yet make it contribute to cohesive development. A system of allowing only a marginal scope for the private sector, such as for tea-stalls, will not contribute to development of any kind.

Social democracy essential for India

Since social democracy originated in the highly developed Nordic countries, which offered a classic example of its operation, a doubt may arise if it is suitable for developing countries like India. Even in Europe, welfare states have come under tremendous pressure from neo-liberalism and have tended to cut back on the expenditures on health and education. Since the need to ensure cohesive development is all the more urgent in the developing countries, however, social democracy is more suitable for them than capitalism or communism. One could also add that social democracy is more relevant and urgent here than even in the developed countries. Yes, poverty and inequalities are high in such countries, but that is precisely why social democracy is needed more there. In fact, in principle at least, many of these countries, including particularly India, have already accepted social democracy as the ideal political framework. If India can make a success of it, other countries will also follow. One may even say that developed countries could politically afford to go back from social democracy to neo-liberal regimes as they have already (almost) wiped out mass poverty and deprivation, but this cannot be the case for countries like India. India has no political option to give up the social goals of reducing inequality and meeting basic needs of all, including health and education, and take up neo-liberalism as its ideological foundation. Any government which gives up these goals will be thrown out in the elections. Indian democracy has that robustness.

The ideals and values of social democracy are built into the very Constitution of India. The very first paragraph of the Constitution, the Preamble, "resolves to secure for all its citizens:

Justice (social, economic and political),
Liberty of thought, expression, belief, faith and worship,
Equality of status and opportunity,
and to promote Fraternity assuring the dignity of the individual
and the Unity and integrity of the Nation."

What is more, it announces itself as a "Sovereign, Socialist, Secular and Democratic Republic". In other words, it is a clear commitment to be a social democracy. The task is to fully and sincerely implement this spirit of the Constitution.

However, there have been many a slip between the cup and the lip, from the beginning. Even before independence, nationalist leaders like Gopal Krishna Gokhale had asked the government to implement a policy of free, compulsory and universal education for boys and girls in the age-group of 6–14. This was not agreed to by the then British government. But what is ironic is that even after nearly seven decades after independence, universal and free primary and secondary education of good quality still remain a dream to be realised, though agreed to in principle. Jawaharlal Nehru, the first prime minister of India, was both an ardent democrat and a socialist. He had the full power and capability to launch India on a firm path of social democracy. But even he could not do justice to it. Nehru identified socialism with state ownership of means of production. He wanted to build up the foundation of a modern industrial economic power by launching modern iron and steel mills and major irrigation projects so that India could catch up with the West in economic development before long. He admired the Soviet model of socialism and its success in becoming a modern nation and economic power through state enterprise. But the real foundation of a strong social democratic nation consists of the level of education and health of all citizens, which needed state enterprise much more than iron and steel mills, which could well have been handed over to the private sector. However, a huge network of government schools and private aided schools had developed during Nehru's regime which provided practically free education of a fairly good quality. But the goal of compulsory and universal education for both boys and girls even at the primary level could not be achieved. Indira Gandhi also could not achieve it, but she took a major step in the direction of social democracy by nationalising major banks, which made bank credit accessible to the small business owners including farmers. She contributed to the democratisation of the economy thereby, which also enabled her to launch the Green Revolution in agriculture. In turn it created self-reliance in food and laid the foundation for food security for the poor without having to import food grains.

The economic reforms since 1991 and the wave of neo-liberalism they created are what truly reversed whatever trend existed towards social democracy in the country. They affected the education and health sectors quickly, in both of which the private enterprise for profit started increasing significantly. Data from the India Education Surveys show that the enrolment of students in the private unaided schools, which was only 5.1 per cent of all the students at the primary level in 1986, increased to 8.5 per cent in 1993 and further to 15.0 per cent in 2002. In the middle schools, the increase was higher still, from 8.4 per cent in 1986 to 11.2 per cent in 1993 and to 18.4 per cent in 2002. The increase was highest in the case of secondary schools: from 6.0 per cent in 1986, to 9.2 per cent in 1993, to 20.1 per cent in 2002.[4] The share of private unaided schools has further accelerated after 2002. This is worrisome because while the fees are restricted and low in government and private aided schools, there is rampant profiteering in private unaided schools in the name of higher quality of education provided by them. On the other hand, the government schools, subject of course to exceptions, are not attractive because of indifference to quality. In the health sector also, private nursing homes and hospitals have proliferated including chains of corporate hospitals, turning health care into a business for maximising profit. Even where natural delivery is possible and safe, caesarean section is alleged to be prescribed in private maternity hospitals. Even if no such mischief takes place, health care is denied to those who cannot afford to pay hefty fees.

The main objective of the 1991 economic reforms was to step up the rate of growth, beyond the earlier so-called Hindu rate of growth. However, it is not enough for the state to just leave economic growth to private enterprise and forget about it. The state has to influence the nature of economic growth, too, and not concentrate only on stimulating a higher rate of growth. The issue of the rate of growth is secondary compared with the capacity of growth to promote employment, remove poverty and improve the welfare, especially of the hitherto disadvantaged. The growth has to be egalitarian, and the first requirement to make growth egalitarian is to generate more jobs. Mahatma Gandhi had suggested an alternative development paradigm years ago, which included a way of growth based on small-scale and labour-intensive production, with a decentralised village-oriented economy, which was also environment-friendly and sustainable (Nadkarni 2015). It still has some relevance even if not taken up for wholesale implementation. There is room for labour-intensive employment-creating enterprises even in a system which allows larger capitalist enterprises. In this matter, however, recent experience has been very disappointing. Between 1991 and 2011, the growth rate of GNP is reported to have been 7.7 per cent per annum, but the growth of jobs was a mere 0.3 per cent per annum (Joshi 2016: 60). This jobless character of growth was bound to aggravate inequality as never before. According to the *Global Wealth Report 2016* compiled by the Credit Suisse Research Institute, after Russia, India is the second most unequal country now in the world, with the top 1 per cent of the population owning nearly 60 per cent of the total wealth. This is clearly an unacceptable level of inequality for any democracy.

We had noted earlier that inequality in income and wealth can be dealt with by progressive taxation of the rich on the one hand and a high level of social expenditure to improve the welfare of the poor on the other. India has one of the lowest tax to GDP ratios in the world. There was some increase in this ratio in India from 8 per cent in 1970 to 9.8 in 1990, but the trend was reversed for a while thereafter, with the ratio declining to 8.7 per cent in 2000. Fortunately it picked up later, having increased to 11 per cent in 2014. The ratio was as high as 39.1 per cent in Cuba and 26.3 per cent in Sweden in 2014 (see Table 5.1).

If the tax effort is low, social expenditure cannot be high either. Public expenditure on education in India as a proportion of GDP was a mere 1.9 per cent in 1970 but increased to 3.8 per cent in 1990 and has remained the same in 2014. In contrast, Cuba's public expenditure on education was 10.8 per cent of GDP in 2014, and it was 7.7 per cent in Sweden. Public expenditure on health as a proportion of its GDP has increased in India slightly, from 4 per cent in 1990 to 4.7 per cent in 2014, but it remains low in comparison with other countries (see Table 5.1).

There is thus a case in India for stepping up both tax effort and social expenditure. Marginal rate of income tax on the highest slab of income in India was only 30 per cent until recently, and now a surcharge of 10 per cent

Table 5.1 Major Fiscal Indicators of Social Commitment

Sln	Country	1970	1980	1990	2000	2010	2014
I. Tax revenue (% of GDP)							
1.	China $	–	12.6	15.0	12.6	17.9	18.7
2.	Cuba #	–	–	–	–	37.9	39.1
3.	France	18.6	19.2	18.6	23.2	21.9	23.2
4.	United Kingdom	23.0	23.9	24.2	26.1	25.4	25.0
5.	India	8.0	8.9	9.8	8.7	10.5	11.0
6.	Sweden	19.3	16.5	21.9	30.0	27.1	26.3
7.	United States	11.8	12.1	10.4	12.9	8.6	11.0
II. Public expenditure on education (% of GDP)							
1.	China	1.4	1.9	1.7	1.9	–	–
2.	Cuba	–	8.4	7.1	7.7	12.8	10.8
3.	France	3.2	4.3	4.5	5.5	5.7	5.5
4.	United Kingdom	5.0	5.1	4.1	4.3	5.9	5.7
5.	India*	1.9	3.0	3.8	4.3	3.3	3.8
6.	Sweden	–	6.6	5.3	6.8	6.6	7.7
7.	United States	–		4.8	5.5	5.4	5.2
III. Health expenditure, total (% of GDP)							
1.	China	–	–	3.5	4.6	4.9	5.5
2.	Cuba	–	–	5.2	6.1	10.2	11.1
3.	France	–	–	10.1	9.8	11.2	11.5
4.	United Kingdom	–	–	6.7	6.9	9.5	9.1
5.	India	–	–	4.0	4.3	4.3	4.7
6.	Sweden	–	–	8.0	8.2	9.5	11.9
7.	United States	–	–	13.1	13.1	17.0	17.1

Sources:

$ China Statistical Yearbook 2016, Government of China: National Bureau of Statistics China;
* Budgeted Expenditure on Education, Department of Higher Education, Ministry of Human Resource Development, Government of India;
# www.ascecuba.org/recent-developments-in-cuban-public-finance/ accessed 12/12/19; World Development Indicators 2016, World Bank data website.

of the income tax was imposed in the 2017–18 budget for incomes of 50 lakh to 1 crore rupees and of 15 per cent of income tax for incomes above 1 crore. In the 2018–19 budget, the standard deduction was restored, but a health-education cess of 4 per cent has been imposed, almost offsetting each other. Except for this, direct tax rates on income were kept unchanged. The marginal rates of income tax on high slabs have been higher in other countries than in India (see Table 5.2).

In India there has been no serious effort at taxing wealth and reducing inequalities in wealth, though this inequality has been increasing significantly (Anand and Thampi 2016). It is not that a progressive income tax precludes a wealth tax. Both can be levied in a balanced way. There is a

Table 5.2 Personal Income Tax Rates (allowances not included)

Country	Tax Rate	Individual Income Tax Slabs (local currency)
India	0%	<250,000
	5%	250,000–500,000
	20%	500,000–1,000,000
	30%	1,000,000 and above
		+ Surcharge of 10% of IT for incomes of 50 lakh to 1 crore and of 15% of IT for incomes of 1 crore and above*
China	3%	<1500
	10%	1500 to 4500
	20%	4500 to 9000
	25%	9000 to 35,000
	30%	35,000 to 55,000
	35%	55,000 to 80,000
	45%	80,000 & above
France	0%	<9700
	14%	9700 to 26,791
	30%	26,791 to 71,826
	41%	71,826 to 152,108
	45%	152,108 & above
UK	20%	<31,785
	40%	31,786 to 150,000
	45%	150,000 & above
Sweden	30%	<420,800
	50%	420,800 to 602,600
	55%	602,600 & above
US	10%	<9225
	15%	9226 to 37,450
	25%	37,451 to 90,750
	28%	90,751 to 189,300
	33%	189,301 to 411,500
	35%	411,501 to 413,200
	39.60%	413,201 and above

Sources: online government websites

* As proposed in the Government of India Budget for 2017–18 presented on February 1, 2017.

strong case at least for taxing wealth held in the form of precious metals and jewellery, though the risk of evasion is high. India had levied an estate duty or inheritance tax in the past, but this was given up since the rate was very low and the effort involved in tax collection was not considered worthwhile. Since inherited wealth is the major way of perpetuating inequality, it should not escape taxation. It need not be very high, however, since it should not act as a deterrent to accumulation. But subject to a suitable exemption, a marginal tax rate some 20 per cent on inherited wealth in the highest slab, including on gold and jewellery, should be adequate.

If taxing the rich is one side of social democracy, ensuring the basic needs of people is its other side. Both the union (central) and state governments have a plethora of social welfare schemes administered by over a dozen 'line' departments. In my state of Karnataka, about 50 such schemes are said to be in operation. Some of these, like the Public Distribution Scheme (PDS) for providing food grains at subsidised price and the Mahatma Gandhi National Rural Employment Guarantee Scheme (MGNREGS), are well known and widespread. There are also other schemes like health insurance and health assistance, old age pensions, special assistance for targeted groups, and scholarships for Scheduled Caste and Scheduled Tribe students. A study in Karnataka by Rajasekher et al. (2016) of 29 selected schemes (excluding PDS and MGNREGS) made some interesting observations. They are:

1   Social security policies are not consistent and coherent.
2   The quantum of social security provided is not sufficient.
3   A large number of schemes are in existence introduced at different times for different purposes; they are not universal and are implemented by too many departments to enable co-ordination. The beneficiaries have often to undergo too many hassles to be eligible for benefits. There are delays and missed targets. Beneficiaries sometimes do not know the schemes – what benefits they offer and whom to approach.

Exasperated by the complexity of such schemes and the administrative costs involved, the Government of India has proposed for public discussion a universal basic income (UBI) in the *Economic Survey 2016–17*. A full chapter (9) is devoted to explaining its justification. The proposal is to do away with most of the welfare or social security schemes, and in their place make an unconditional transfer of a basic minimum income to all households to their bank accounts, at least to those below the poverty line if not all. This will, it is hoped, remove poverty at one stroke at much less cost and plug the leakages involved in administering the variety of schemes.

Even if the UBI were to be adjusted for rise in the cost of living index every year, the proposal hardly meets the requirements of a social democracy. In the absence of a universal and free primary and secondary education and of a universal health insurance, such a basic income may meet food needs but not the needs of education and health for all. The goal of social democracy goes much beyond meeting minimum calorie requirements of all. Moreover, the cash income may not all be spent on basic needs. In a patriarchal society like India's, the man of the house may spend some of it for daily booze. The poor are often indebted in the face of emergencies, and the first charge on cash income received may be to repay the loans taken with hefty interest. The basic income may not often be enough even for the poor, in which case the employment guarantee will be a great help, but if that is stopped, the poor will be quite helpless. So if a UBI is launched it should not be in replacement of existing welfare schemes, though admittedly there is a need for some simplification or rationalisation of the plethora of schemes.

If India has to become a genuine social democracy as per the Constitution, it is not enough just to provide basic food security and guarantee of unskilled employment for the poor, though that is the minimum necessary expected of any country. There is an urgent need to drastically reduce costs and improve the quality of education and health care. In both, there is a great chasm between the services provided under the public sector, which are availed of by the general public or the poor, and what is provided at high cost by the private sector to the rich. A universal good-quality free education for all means an equal start in life and equal opportunities for all. It is a great leveller. A poor-quality education for the poor disadvantages them from the beginning. According to *Annual Status of Education Report (Rural) – 2014*, brought out by Pratham Education Foundation, only 48 per cent of the children in Standard IV could read a vernacular text prescribed for Standard II, and the proportion was even lower at 24 per cent for texts in English. The proportion was calculated by taking the weighted average of the figures for both government and private schools. The performance in government schools was still worse. The same story is repeated when performance in basic arithmetic was taken. The proportion of Standard IV children who could divide a three-digit number by a one-digit number with carryover was as low as 26 per cent. An important step was taken by the Government of India by passing the Right to Education Act 2010, under which a child has a right to be admitted to a neighbourhood school, even if under private management, free of charge if his or her family is below the poverty line. The fees of the child would be paid by the government. There has been some resistance to this act from private management, but the governments – both central and state, have stood their ground. Recently, guidelines under the act have been issued to all the schools by the central government, making it mandatory for them to achieve minimum learning outcomes by the end of the academic year for each class. The minimum outcome indicators have been laid down by the National Council for Education Research & Training (*Deccan Herald*, Bengaluru, March 6, 2017, p. 7). This step should make the schools more serious in improving education standards.

The access to health care is also quite poor in India, as seen from the comparative statistics provided by the World Development Indicators. Maternal mortality ratio (per hundred thousand live births) in India was as high as 181 in 2014, compared to China's 28. Births attended by skilled medical staff was only 52 per cent in 2008, compared with China's 100 per cent in the same year. Access to improved sanitation was only 40 per cent in India in 2014; even in Bangladesh it was higher at 60 per cent, let alone China with 75 per cent. Health care costs are exorbitantly high in India, particularly in private clinics and hospitals. The reputation of health care under the government is not very good even among the poor, and they don't mind raising loans from relatives or private money lenders to have reliable health care from private sector. This makes the poor very vulnerable to medical emergencies. Nothing short of placing the health service under the public sector as in UK, Canada and Cuba is required to meet India's health care needs. A poor state of education and health is not consistent with an India committed to being a social democracy as per its constitution.[5]

There is a large measure of political acceptance of both democracy and socialism in India. Socialism does not mean communism or state ownership of the means of production. Nor does socialism mean populism and freebies at the time of elections. Socialism is ending poverty and extreme inequality and providing equal opportunities for all. It requires free and universal good-quality education, particularly at the primary and secondary levels. Even in the US, education at this level is uniform, free and universal. We don't have it in spite of all our socialist sloganeering. We do not need a bloody revolution to make India a genuine social democracy. We only need to implement our constitution sincerely.

Notes

1 These figures have been as quoted by the editorial 'Monstrous Inequality' in *Economic & Political Weekly* (*EPW*), Vol. LII (3), January 21, 2017, p. 7.
2 Ramaswamy R. Iyer warned against this approach: 'The holders of "primacy of development" argument would say "yes, the protection of the environment is important, but not at the cost of development". Let us reverse that proposition: Can we really have development at the cost of environment?' Iyer (2014: 20).
3 A decentralised democratic state in Gandhi's vision was not vertically or hierarchically structured, but consisted of all villages as centres horizontally connected in widening circles both with other villages and co-ordinating nodal points. For a full discussion, see Nadkarni et al. (2018).
4 These figures are as quoted in Vaidyanathan (2007: 28).
5 The 2018–19 Budget of Government of India (GOI) has proposed a National Health Protection Scheme, committing the government to provide coverage of Rs. 5 lakh per family per year for secondary and tertiary hospitalisation for 10 crore poor families (about 50 crore people). The budget allocation for this is not commensurate with this commitment. There are health care schemes in several states also providing some insurance for hospitalisation expenditure. The National Health Policy 2017 of the GOI recognised that a catastrophic level of medical expenditure would push down an entire household below the poverty line. Hence the emphasis has been on financial assistance by way of insurance. There is, however, a crying need also to improve the quality of service and infrastructure

under government health care provision, particularly under primary health centres (PHCs). There is a significant shortfall in the availability of medical officers and nursing staff at these PHCs in almost all states, particularly in states such as West Bengal, Chattisgarh, Jharkhand and Bihar (Srinivasan 2018). If the quality of health and education under the government sector is improved, it will significantly improve the lives of the poor because they would not have to depend on the unreasonably expensive private sector.

References

Anand, Ishan and Anjana Thampi (2016). 'Recent Trends in Wealth Inequality in India', *Economic and Political Weekly*, LI (50), December 10, pp. 59–67.

Iyer, Ramaswamy R (2014). 'Environment and Development: Some Thoughts for the New Government', *Economic and Political Weekly*, XLIX (25), June 21, pp. 19–21.

Joshi, Vijay (2016). *India's Long Road: The Search for Prosperity*. Gurgaon: Allen Lane (Penguin).

Nadkarni, M V (2015). 'Gandhi's Civilizational Alternative and Dealing with Climate Change', *Journal of Social & Economic Development*, 17 (1) (Springer), January–June, pp. 90–103.

Nadkarni, M V, N Sivanna and Lavanya Suresh (2018). *Decentralised Democracy in India: Gandhi's Vision and Reality*. Routledge.

Petring, Alexander et al. (2012). *Social Democracy Reader 3: Welfare State and Social Democracy*. Berlin (English edition): Friedrich-Ebert Stiftung.

Piketty, Thomas (2014). *Capital in the Twenty-first Century*. Cambridge, MA: Harvard University Press.

Rajasekher, D; K S Manjunath; R Manjula (2016). *Improving the Delivery of Social Security Benefits in Karnataka: A Review of Application and Submission Procedures of Government Social Security Schemes*. Social and Economic Change Monographs 47. Bengaluru: Institute for Social & Economic Change.

Rawls, John (2001). *Justice as Fairness: A Restatement*. Edited by Erin Kelly. Cambridge, MA and London: Belknap Press of Harvard University Press.

Srinivasan, R (2018). 'Medicare Is Not Healthcare', *The Hindu*, February 11, p. 13.

Vaidyanathan, A (2007). *Private Sector in Education* (Dr C D Deshmukh Memorial Lecture). Hyderabad: Council for Social Development.

6 Reimagining socialism for the 21st century

Cuba's experiments with cooperativism and solidarity economies

Joseph Tharamangalam

I. Introduction

The international seminar recently organized by the A. N. Sinha Institute of Social Studies (ANSISS) in Patna critically examining an alternative paradigm of "cohesive economy" could not have come at a more critical historical juncture. Historically such a search began during the rise of capitalism, the "great transformation" that changed all previously known paradigms about how societies organize their economies. Since the time of Marx the dominant alternative paradigm has been "socialism", its actual *avatar* in several countries in the 20th century offering considerable hope to people across the world. But such hopes could not be sustained in the aftermath of the precipitous implosion of the system almost everywhere even before the end of the century. There followed a reassertion of an even more aggressive neoliberal capitalism with the arrogant *mantra* of "There Is No Alternative" (TINA). This system has held sway across the world over quarter of a century. The disastrous and inhuman consequences of neoliberal capitalism have been increasingly felt across the world, also well researched and documented. These include rising inequality and an extreme concentration of wealth unseen since the 1930s within and across countries, environmental destruction reaching unsustainable levels, and the scandal of a billion people living in poverty and hunger in the midst of unprecedented opulence, and this despite the World Bank's "war on poverty" over a decade.[1] The vibrant social protest movements that arose across the world in response to this situation – from the *Arab Spring* to the *Occupy Wall Street Movement* – are now more muted, but more middle-level movements (scattered as these may be) have persisted, and even increased, across the world, searching for and experimenting with an alternative paradigm, conceived in somewhat different ways and called by names such as "cohesive development", "solidarity economy", or more generally "social and solidarity economy".[2]

  This chapter focuses on Cuba, arguably the only country still sustaining its socialism (and successfully so in terms of achieving the basic goals and values of the revolution) but that is now at a turning point. While global commentators show a sudden surge of interest in the aftermath of the passing away of the *Maximum Leader* Fidel Castro (*El Commandante*), within Cuba the debate has been going on at least since the sudden crisis it faced in the early 1990s following the collapse of the Soviet bloc socialist countries, Cuba's only patrons and trading partners. The precipitous collapse of what has since been called "20th-century socialism" almost everywhere forcefully brought home major deficits in that model. For Cuba, now facing near collapse and even mass starvation, the need to rethink and reform its socialist system was not just a theoretical or ideological issue but one of its very survival. Cubans were forced to seriously address the issue of how to reform its system in order to put it on a more efficient and sustainable basis. The country quickly launched various reforms, especially during the "Special Period" in the early 1990s, mostly aimed at economic survival,[3] and with such success that the immediate crisis was largely overcome in just a few years. But the end of the Special Period saw not a weakening but an intensification of the debate, as the need for more far-reaching changes to the Cuban model became widely accepted in the country. At the same time, Cuba's leaders, policy makers, and intellectuals (as well as the majority of its people, from all the evidence I have been able to find) are desperately and boldly struggling to sustain the core values of the Cuban revolution – social justice, human dignity for all its citizens, and freedom from hunger – and to resist the forces that are at work to turn Cuba into a marginal partner in the global neoliberal capitalist system. In this task they feel emboldened by the growing disillusionment with the neoliberal system (nowhere more so than among its own neighbors and friends in Latin America) and its disastrous effects across the world, mentioned earlier.

The chapter is organized as follows. This introduction is followed by Part II that briefly discusses the theoretical assumptions and issues underlying the "solidarity paradigm" being debated (and put into practice) in many parts of the world. Part III focuses on Cuban socialism, its successes, and its deficits. Part IV reviews Cuba's reforms and the continuing debates about its transition to "21st-century socialism" with a special focus on the expanded and relatively independent space being made available for cooperatives (*co-ops*) as the preferred instruments for the Cuban transition. Part V concludes the chapter by raising some final questions about the prospects of the changes. I argue that Cuba has a fair chance of success with its reforms, especially the forms of solidarity economies, but that the project of "downsizing the state" has its limits in that the state's role will continue to be critical in providing the legal and institutional framework as well as oversight for the new co-ops and other new institutions. Finally, it will be argued that the model of 21st-century socialism envisioned by Cuba will not necessarily lead to any significant decentralization and democratization of state power or diminution of the special role played by the powerful Communist Party.

II. Theoretical assumptions and debates

The search for a new paradigm assumes the rejection of both the capitalist and the 20th-century socialist paradigms. To begin, it rejects the very assumption about human nature that is supposed to provide the philosophical basis for a capitalist, market economy – a self-seeking, utility-maximizing, amoral, and instrumentally rational *homo economicus* (by definition a sociopath) who is disembedded from society. In contrast to this, the new paradigm reaffirms the idea that the true human is a *homo socialis (socius)* and *moralis*, living within society and its normative and moral structures, cooperating, mutually dependent, and supportive – as shown by evolutionary biology, anthropology, sociology, and history.[4]

Second, it seeks to address "the social question", the rupture of society and its economy that followed the rise of capitalism, "the great transformation" (Polanyi, 2001). It wants to bring back societal control over the economy and over the provision and protection of the common good, instead of leaving these vital societal tasks to a mythical self-adjusting market, an "invisible hand".

Third, there is a rethinking of the relationship between state and society with particular reference to the role of "civil society". Despite the myth about the self-regulating market, it has been clear that capitalism and the capitalist market do not exist apart from and independently of the (capitalist) state. Similarly, socialism has been backed by a "socialist state", its 20th-century incarnation generally taking the form of an all-encompassing ("totalitarian" according to critics) state. A reformed 21st-century socialism seeks to downsize the state (though not in the neoliberal sense) by reducing state control over both the economy and society as a whole. As will be discussed later, Cuba is now focusing considerable attention on the first, its agenda on the second dimension remaining more ambiguous.

The attempt to free the economy from state control brings into focus the question of what constitutes "social property". Marx saw the first task in constructing socialism as that of socializing the means of production. But he seems to have paid little attention to what institutional form "socializing the means of production" was to take except to suggest a short period of the dictatorship of the proletariat that would shape the future "socialist man" and his institutions until the state would finally wither away. Ever since the Bolshevik revolution, socialist property has, in fact, taken the form of ownership and control of all property by a centralized, all-encompassing, and controlling state. As is now recognized by all, including Cuban reformers, this has been one of the major flaws of 20th-century socialism. It is widely recognized that such control of the economy by the state has suppressed the autonomy, creativity, innovation, and enterprise of individuals and communities.[5] Whether workers in such a system are also controlled and alienated in a manner similar to those in capitalism is an issue generally not addressed or debated by left scholars, but the general discontent among workers in the socialist countries, from Poland to Cuba, points to the need to examine this issue afresh. In any case, the current Cuban debate does address the issue; Cuba has started to open space for "social property" outside the direct control of the state.

Finally, and related to the earlier discussion, there is a new critique of the "mistake" made in conflating "market" with "capitalist market". That markets can exist outside capitalism is being acknowledged; even as Cuba has been opening limited but increasing space for such markets, the final forms and extent of free markets within a socialist system are still being debated.

III. Cuban socialism: achievements, deficits, and current debates

Cuba's achievements

Cuba's remarkable achievements in human development (HD) have been the focus of my research in the last ten years (e.g., Tharamangalam, 2010). Here I draw on my work to highlight a few of these. I have followed the HD approach and the measures used by the *United Nations Development Program* (UNDP) to gauge achievements in social security, general well-being, and human quality of life.[6]

First, Cuba is a rare example of a country in the Global South that has practically eliminated "hunger", as defined and measured by the *International Food Policy Research Institute* (IFPRI) that produces the annual *Global Hunger Index* (GHI). The following quote from a group of US researchers will, I hope, provide an appropriate prelude to looking at the GHI scores.

> With all the authority of hindsight, it is important to analyze and criticize the methods Cuba has chosen to eradicate hunger . . . But we should never lose sight of the fact that the Cuban revolution declared, from the outset, that no one should go malnourished. No disappointment in food production, no failed economic take-off, no shock wave from world economic crisis has deterred Cuba from freeing itself from the suffering and shame of a single wasted child or an elderly person ignominiously subsisting on pet food. No other country in this hemisphere, including the United States, can make this claim.
>
> (Benjamin, Collins, and Scott 1984, 180)

Cuba does not figure in the GHI; its score in the GHI is less than 5, the threshold below which the level of hunger in a country is deemed to be too low for inclusion in the index (*International Food Policy Research Institute* or IFPRI, 2016). The GHI uses a composite index of four parameters: malnutrition, childhood wasting (the proportion of children under age five with low weight for their age), stunting (the proportion of children under five with low height for their age), and under-five child mortality rates, problems that have long been eliminated in Cuba. Note that this is not to deny severe shortages of many consumer goods in Cuba or the very low purchasing power of Cuba's people. This, in fact, is what is unique about the Cuban "model", its ability to guarantee basic security and services with little wealth and low per capita income.[7]

To be noted also is the fact that many Cubans (including some university professors I know) went hungry during the Special Period when Cuba's GDP and especially food availability saw a steep decline. People ate whatever they could find; birds and animals disappeared even from the Havana's zoo, and Cuba's cattle population saw such a steep decline that Cuba still suffers from severe shortages of milk and especially beef. The shortage of milk was so severe during the Special Period that the meagre supply available, supplemented by imported milk powder from China, was reserved exclusively for children through the country's well-functioning ration shops. It is remarkable that there was no famine, no serious malnutrition, and practically no slow-down in its path of HD. Indeed, Cuba's success in overcoming the catastrophic crisis (often compared to the 1929 crisis in the US) is not only one of the most remarkable achievements for a state and society in recent times, but also a testimony to the value of social solidarity, cooperation, and mutual help, buttressed by a robust institutional framework. The key to its success seems to have been its ability to mobilize a well-organized and educated population to undertake various innovative and creative measures, including those aimed at attaining self-sufficiency in sustainable forms of food production. There is yet another irony (an unforeseen yet benevolent one) about the effect of the food and fuel shortages – an even healthier population that is caused by lower food consumption and greater physical activity (in addition to the high-quality medical care) in the absence of cars, buses, tractors, chemical fertilizers, and other oil-drinking instruments. Scientists who have studied this phenomenon have reported that the period of the shortages saw a significant decline (as much as a third or more) in deaths attributed to diabetes, coronary heart disease, stroke, and all causes.[8]

Second, Cuba is known for its exceptional achievements in education and health. It would not be an exaggeration to say that Cuba has perhaps the most educated and healthiest people of any country in the world (Gasperini, 2000); for example, the highest number of doctors and even of PhDs (in all disciplines including the hard sciences) per unit population. Indeed, in some critical measures of HD such as infant mortality rates, life expectancy, access to food security, and access to basic health care, Cuba outperforms the US (with per capita GDP that is about seven times higher). Cuba's health care system ensures that every child at birth is weighed, measured, and assigned to a neighborhood pediatrician for continuous monitoring and care. Special hospitals provide care for women with difficult pregnancies. My research team visited one in Havana more than once. Needless to say, we were impressed.[9]

During the past 25 years Cuba has been showcased several times for its exceptional achievement in health or education by international agencies such as UNDP, the *United Nations Children's Fund* (UNICEF), and the *Food and Agricultural Organization* (FAO), even by the World Bank, though unbeknownst to Cuba's critics abroad, especially in the US. To give one example I have noted elsewhere (Tharamangalam, 2008), in 2006 the *World Wildlife Fund's* (WWF) Living Planet Report explained that Cuba had achieved high HD (greater than 0.8) with a sustainable ecological footprint of less than 1.8 hectares, the only country to have done so. The latest example I have seen comes from the World Health Organization (WHO), which named Cuba the first country to have eliminated mother-child transmission of the HIV virus.[10]

Summing up this section, I argue that Cuba's achievements are of immense human and world-historical significance in two respects. First, Cuba has shown that the terrible suffering of one-fifth of the world's people, the acute hunger of 200 million children under five (United Nations Children's Fund or UICEF, 2007), many dying untimely and painful deaths, is needless and can be eliminated without turning the poor countries of the Global South into Western-type industrialized high-consumption societies. Second, Cuba has shown a path of ecologically sustainable development that is of great relevance for every country in the planet, as it will forcefully confront (sooner rather than later) the reality of the unsustainable nature of the conventional development path premised on continuous GDP growth and increasing consumption (unless they begin to colonize other planets, as suggested by Stephen Hawking).

The deficits and debates

We have already seen that the rude shock inflicted by the crisis of the Special Period triggered a process of rethinking Cuba's own model of socialism and an attempt to identify its deficits. Extensive and nation-wide debates and discussions followed, especially in conjunction with two recent Congresses of the Communist Party (PCC) in 2011 and 2016. What, then, are the issues/deficits that Cuban analysts have identified?

First and foremost, large sections of Cuba's people are tired of the endless shortage of consumer goods, the meager and declining ration entitlements (though still producing among the best health outcomes anywhere), and their low purchasing power and standard of living. Young Cubans in particular (especially those with relatives in Miami, mostly White Cubans), bombarded with visions of the lifestyles of the American middle class, aspire to see higher economic growth and prosperity, greater economic opportunities for themselves and their children, and greater opening and participation of Cuba in the global economy, including more trade. They also aspire to greater social and political freedoms, unrestricted freedom and ability to travel abroad (some restrictions already lifted), more democratic freedoms to participate in the political system, and greater decentralization of power. The focus of the debate is to interrogate and identify the systemic factors that hinder the achievement of these goals.

The over-centralized and tightly controlled state

As noted earlier, the state, as constructed in 20th-century socialism, produced mixed results; on the positive side, provision of social welfare and social safety nets for all, but on the negative side suppression of individual and community initiatives and rights, the worst of which were seen under Stalin, Mao, and other similar leaders who seized power in the century's great "peasant wars" and revolutions. Cuba followed the Soviet model, though a more benign version in many respects, and was not free from some of the now well- recognized deficits of that model.[11] But first, it is important to acknowledge the fact that in Cuba a strong and proactive state has played a critical role in sustaining national security and stability as well as in the provisioning of basic public goods and the promotion of science and technology. Yet today the deficits and failures of this model are being intensely debated and identified. These include (1) a bloated bureaucracy and its reach over the entire economic, social, and political system and the attendant problems of inefficiency, corruption, and black market, in tandem with a diminution of personal, local, and group initiatives, incentives, enterprise, and innovation. One negative consequence of this is the slow progress with the project of greater decentralization and local development, caused especially by the severe scarcity of financial and other resources at the local level and the low capacity of local democratic organizations to address daily problems and needs;[12] (2) technocratic styles of command and control and relative lack of debate, democratic control, and checks and balances. A Cuban commentator noted that bureaucrats exercise more power than elected representatives do. He then remarked (tongue-in-cheek), "they are very clever at finding a problem wherever there is a solution"; (3) an excess of non-productive employment in the state sector (up to 1.5 million may be redundant), now seen as unsustainable; (4) suppression of the market, even at the local level, and of people's ability to barter, exchange, and trade, an issue that has already been partially addressed; (5) unsustainable levels of free goods and services offered by a patronizing state regardless of and independent of specific citizen contributions, with a negative influence on motivation to work and on productivity and economic development. Many of these must be familiar, as neoliberals have never stopped condemning these practices as hampering economic freedoms and free markets.

A democratic deficit?

Is there also a democratic deficit in Cuba? If so, is it serious, as claimed by several US administrations that have used the claim to justify their illegal blockade? A short answer to this complex question needs to make two points. First, there are different models of democracy; the US model is by no means the ideal or the standard. Cuba's "People's Democracy" is a more effective, participatory, and vibrant form of democracy if democracy is to be understood as a system designed (and backed by appropriate institutional mechanisms and procedures) to represent the interests of the majority of the voting population.[13] By contrast, the US system of "democracy" can be seen as one in which state policy is blatantly tilted in favor of a small *corporate* elite, "the one percent", as claimed by the "Occupy Wall Street" movement, a claim backed by considerable empirical data (Burd-Sharps et al., 2008, CBO, 2011; Tharamangalam, 2011; Picketty, 2014). Furthermore, the Cuban system guarantees to all citizens such basic human rights as the right to food, employment, education, and basic health care – again in sharp contrast to that of the US. Once this basic point has been made, we are in a better position to deal with the deficits in Cuba's system, which basically is built on the same Soviet model despite some differences and its more benign features. Not only does the Cuban state control the means and instruments of production of both the material goods and the ideological and intellectual goods, but state power is also concentrated in a small elite at the top who also controls the powerful armed forces and the Communist Party (PCC). Freedom of the press, as well as of writers and artists, is highly restricted. The few national and regional newspapers are controlled by the PCC and/ or its affiliates such as the "Young Communist League". According to some reports, the new spate of artistic creativity unleashed by the excitement of the revolution made Fidel Castro nervous. In response he issued his famous injunction to the artists and the intellectual class: "Within the Revolution, everything; outside the Revolution, nothing",[14] a restriction that finds its place in Article 39 of the 1976 Constitution. Article 53 further stipulates, "all organs of the mass media are state or social property". There are also other important questions including the dominant role of the PCC and the pervasive "mass organizations" under its umbrella such as the "Committee to Defend the Revolution (CDR)", which keep watch on all social activities, severely restricting independent civil society activism. It is noteworthy that Arnold August (2013), an expert on Cuban democracy and generally an admirer of Cuba's participatory democracy, has pointed to a possible imbalance between two founding principles in the constitution. While Article 3 stipulates, "sovereignty lies in the people from whom originates *all the power of the state* (emphasis added), Article 5 states that the Communist Party of Cuba is "the highest leading force of society *and of the state* (emphasis added). If the PCC functions apart from the state and cannot interfere in matters of the state and its administration as Cuba's leaders and theoreticians claim, how can it be also "the highest leading force of the state"? August (pp. 189–90) admits, "this is not an easy balance to maintain", but he also implies that maintaining such a balance has been the Cuban tradition, something that makes the Cuban system different from the Soviet one.

It is interesting to note that in the workshops and conferences dealing with the reforms we generally find our Cuban colleagues and commentators very vocal in critiquing the economic deficits of the model but much more muted and indirect in addressing the political, democratic deficits. They tend to blame the corrupt bureaucracy for many of the problems, sidestepping the fact that the bureaucracy has been an integral part of the Cuban state system. Nevertheless, there is recognition of the need for greater decentralization, freedoms, and rights for individuals and communities and greater democratic control of the state and participation in policy making. "People's participation", always an ideal and a slogan, is once again an issue of policy debate, deepening it by strengthening the institutional framework as a new priority.

IV. Reform and transition: the central role of cooperatives[15]

The reforms that began in the 1990s towards a transition to forms of property and economic enterprises outside the state sector have recently been accelerated. The focus of attention has now moved to a model of solidarity economy organized through new forms of self-governing and self-managing cooperatives, free from state control. These "principal instruments of the Cuban transition" are favored by not only the old generation of revolutionaries and socialists, left intellectuals, and the governing elite, but have been studied and found to be quite promising by independent observers and researchers from Cuba and from across the world. For the first time, these have also moved into the manufacturing and service sectors. Yet, despite the prolonged debates and consultations conducted during the two important Congresses of the PCC (far more widespread, free, and open during the sixth Congress in 2011 than during the seventh Congress in 2016),[16] and despite the formulations of basic guidelines, already approved by these Congresses, the Cuban state is slow and cautious; it has yet to finalize an overall legal and institutional framework and has been very slow in approving new cooperatives. While some observers, especially from outside Cuba, are critical of the 'slow pace of reform' there is a strong argument in favor of some caution to avoid the pitfalls of many former socialist countries in the Soviet bloc (see later) which implemented similar reforms without first creating an appropriate legal and institutional framework.

Principles and guidelines[17]

The set of basic principles and guidelines, as approved by the two recent Party Congresses, include the following: (a) transfer as many economic activities as possible to the non-state sector; (b) but do this in the most "socialized" way possible in order to sustain the country's socialist achievements and to preserve the core values of the socialist revolution; (c) with these aims the state is still mandated to control and concentrate on core economic activities, the "commanding heights" of the economy, and to continue the public provisioning of education, health, and other basic services as well as guarantee social protection for vulnerable groups who may be negatively affected by the new reforms.

Even as the concept of social property is being redefined, some reforms have already been implemented. Small privately owned businesses have been functioning since the 1990s; foreign investments in some sectors like tourism now form part of the Cuban economy though within government-approved rules and partnership arrangements. Even the hiring of wage labor, still controversial, is now allowed to a limited extent. Nevertheless, the preferred choice for the future are cooperatives, more compatible with "socialist property".

Cooperatives in Cuba: history and current status

Cooperatives in Cuba are at least as old as its socialist system and the early land reforms, but these have been exclusively in the agricultural sector until recently. But even these have had an uneven trajectory, depending on changing state policies. As the government made an early move to adopt a Soviet model of state-owned, large-scale, and high-input farms with the aim of increasing sugar production for export, some of the early ones merged into the state farms. However, the cooperative movement persisted, experiencing a spurt of growth when a well-organized and active movement of small farmers, *Associacion Nationale de Agricultores Pequenos* or ANAP (which was to become one of the most influential and independent civil society organizations in Cuba and active to this day) took the initiative to organize relatively more independent co-ops from below with voluntary membership of small farmers. The early *Credit and Services Cooperatives* (CCS) were aimed at facilitating the acquisition of machinery, credit, and other inputs while retaining individual ownership of the land and working the land individually. In 1976 some of the CCS made a move to a higher stage of cooperativism by pooling their lands together to produce collectively with the aim of maximizing efficiency and productivity. The members of these *Agricultural Production Cooperatives* (CPAs) are collective owners of the land and equipment. A new period of cooperativism began during the Special Period. Beginning in 1993 the Soviet model of state-controlled farms and agri-businesses were dismantled and transferred to the workers, formed into cooperatives called *Basic Units of Cooperative Production* (UBPCs). These lands are held as "usufruct", the state still retaining ownership while these are farmed and managed by the co-ops collectively and democratically. I have visited a few, most of them successful and generating incomes for their members about three to four times higher than what they earned as state employees, in fact, much higher than those earned by state-employed professionals such as doctors and academics. One of these, in Alamar in the outskirts of Havana (Organopónic Vivero Alamar), has now become well known across the world as a model of organic urban agriculture). Its members were very proud to keep saying: "one day we went to bed as workers, but woke up next morning as owners and managers of our farm". It produces its own organic fertilizers (including earthworms) from locally available material.

By 2007 the cooperative sector managed about 45% of the total land and 64% of all agriculture, 37% of these by the UBPCs (Diaz, 2016). The non-state sector, dominated by cooperatives, now produced most of Cuba's staples for internal consumption – 86% of rice, 97% beans, and 85% milk. Notably, they also provide a variety of social benefits for members and their families: over a million people. I was at the Alamar co-op on a day when the neighborhood medical team was making its scheduled visit to the co-op community center, where it stayed all afternoon attending to the health needs of the workers and their families, their clients.

The new co-ops

Finally, Cuba has now embarked on its experiment with newer forms of cooperatives in the urban/industrial sector, self-managed and independent of state control but within the framework of the new guidelines. These began with the transfer of some state-owned enterprises to workers who were organized into cooperatives, basically holding the enterprise and its equipment as usufruct on favorable terms – rent-free and with state subsidies and tax concessions. A second type of voluntary co-ops from below is also encouraged, but is still at an initial stage in its development.

During my most recent visit to Cuba in June 2016 I participated in a week-long seminar-cum-field visits with an international team of specialists in co-ops. We visited seven of the new types of urban co-ops, two in manufacturing and the rest in services ranging from restaurants and taxi services. We also held an extensive presentation and discussion session with a group of young men, all friends from the same neighborhood community, and "drop outs" from school, now preparing a plan to launch their own co-op. These men told us that they were determined to stay in their community and to not look for employment elsewhere. They were planning to open a bakery, which will also arrange to make home deliveries of their products to households in the community.

It was striking to hear that the members of practically all of these new co-ops were now making incomes that were four to five times higher than when they were employees of the state in the same factories. Evidently, they were happy and enthusiastic about this. However, despite some discussion in answer to our questions, it remained unclear what the source of this increase was. We were left to guess that though there may have been some increase in labor productivity, most of the increase must be attributed to a smaller portion of the produce being siphoned off by the state. The co-ops are democratically controlled, their managers elected by the members. They also benefit from government subsidies and concessions. They do not pay rent for the building and equipment though they must pay for electricity and other utilities. Interestingly, they set aside a portion of the income for social protection of their members – for pension plans, paid vacations, and so on, a fact that points to the possibility of decentralizing the provision of public goods, even education and healthcare. One co-op that produces bamboo products offers social services in return for the free rent and other concessions they receive. They offer free training, apprenticeship, and employment opportunities for young people who have left school.

All these co-ops and their members are eagerly waiting for the laws and constitutional provisions that will assure them security and long-term stability.

V. Conclusion: from de-stating to "bringing the state back in"?

Cuba is at a critical juncture in its long journey towards socialism. Having withstood numerous problems and existential threats, it must now address its latest threat arising from the long-term effects of the weaknesses of its own model of 20th-century socialism. As mentioned earlier, several positive factors – the country's exceptional resilience, levels of solidarity, and the massive and collective effort to overcome the crisis – have helped to sustain its remarkable achievements in education, health, and social and food security. Nevertheless, the crisis did trigger a rude awakening leading to the still continuing process of reimagining and rethinking its own socialist system. The reforms launched during and after the crisis have opened up sections of its economy, accommodating forms of property outside the state-owned sector. But the pressure to move to a system that promises higher economic growth and greater prosperity for its citizens has only intensified.

Even as Cuba is moving to implement more reforms, its policy makers are eager to tread this path without abandoning the core values of the country's socialist system and sustaining its achievements. To this end, an attempt is being made to give a central role to cooperatives; the principles and guidelines for these have now been worked out and approved by recent Congresses of the Cuban Communist Party, the *de facto* decisive policy-making body in the Cuban system. The new co-ops, seen as the most "socialist" form of property outside state ownership, are to be given preferential treatment by the state. Nevertheless, the long-promised legal and institutional framework has not yet been finalized. There is considerable speculation and suspicion about this delay, fed also by the fact that in contrast to the widespread popular participation that was encouraged by the authorities during the sixth Party Congress in 2011, the seventh Congress in 2017 was more controlled and secretive. The explanation from above seems to have been that all the inputs from the popular bodies had already been received, the top policy makers now studying these extensively and moving forward cautiously.

It appears that even as the state is being downsized in some respects (e.g. transferring state property to co-ops), the state will be "brought back in" in other respects. According to some observers, there are some good reasons why the state must continue to matter (Bateman, 2016). First, there is ample empirical evidence that (a) systems have collapsed when states became weak, and (b) high levels of social well-being have generally been associated with well-governed (and democratic) states. The experience of the former socialist countries in the Soviet Union and Eastern Europe offer some salient lessons here. In the absence of a robust legal framework and state oversight, public property, transferred to varieties of "pseudo-cooperatives" quickly came into private, and even criminal, hands. Determined to preempt such errors, Cuba's policy makers want to ensure that the state will continue to provide the needed legal and institutional framework. Indeed, this is true of capitalism too, as was shown earlier – despite the myth of neoclassical economics that the entrepreneur is apart from and independent of the state, the capitalist state provides the legal and institutional framework for capitalism, buttressed by state power. In the Cuban case, this has involved a certain paradox: a reform process that begins with downsizing the state ends with the imperative to bringing a robust state back in.

In conclusion, our analysis leads us to believe that Cuba's path to a more viable form of 21st-century socialism has a reasonable chance of success. It has considerable strengths it can draw on: valuable experience with varieties of cooperatives (including understanding of their weaknesses), traditions of social support and solidarity, continuing state support, and finally high levels of accumulated social, human, and intellectual capital. How democratic and decentralized the transformed Cuban state will be remains an open question, however. The concentration of political power in the hands of a small group at the top is a long-established tradition over half a century. Add to this the critical role of the Cuban Communist Party whose moral and legal authority is enshrined in the Cuban constitution. While the PCC is not an electoral party, not only does it control the numerous mass organizations in the country, but the fact has always been that the top power holders in Cuba since the revolution have always occupied top positions in the Party, the president himself being general secretary of the Party. However, the renewal process in general, and the expanding space for the self-managed and democratically controlled *solidarity economies* that are independent of state control, point to the possibility of a reformed and renewed form of "21st-century socialism".

Notes

1 These facts are well documented by reputed scholars such as Thomas Picketty, as well as by major international organizations such as the UNDP (see its annual Human Development Reports published since 1990), the Oxford Poverty and Human Development Initiative (OPHI) which publishes its *Multi-dimensional Poverty Index* (MPI), also used by the HDRs, and the International Food Policy Research Institute (IFPRI) which produces the *Global Hunger Index* (GHI). For an introduction to "The Poverty and Development Problematic" see Tharamangalam (2017).

2 There is a worldwide network of organizations engaged with such economies, receiving support from international organizations such as the International Labour Organization (ILO). For an overview of the work of these solidarity organizations see Fonteneau et al. 2011.

3 The "Special Period in Time of Peace" was a period of emergency and austerity measures declared by Fidel Castro in response to the crisis which saw a sudden and steep fall in the country's GDP, import capacity, food availability, and calorie intake. See among others Uriarte (2002, 2004). The immediate measures included the legalizing of the US dollar (leading to a dual currency system, still in existence), opening of the country to tourism and to some limited foreign investments, dismantling of the Soviet model agricultural system, and launching of a campaign for organic farming and urban agriculture.

4 Even today large parts of people's economies in the informal sector – family economies including unpaid child and elderly care, the substantial remittances being sent by migrant workers to their families and relatives (*manna* from heaven in the words of a recent [2015] *Economist* article) – can be seen as functioning within the sphere of such solidarity economies, something to which economists pay little attention. The *Economist* article says that India alone received over $70 billion; in the small state of Kerala remittances amounted to about 36% of its GDP. These huge amounts are sent from the hard-earned incomes of migrant workers whose motivations could not have been anything but supporting their families, i.e. compassion, and solidarity with their families.

5 It is well known how such a centralized state, combined with the role played by a "vanguard" communist party, led to some of the worst forms of totalitarian and oppressive dictatorships under such dictators as Stalin and Mao.

6 On the human development approach, see the many works of its pioneers such as Amartya Sen and Mahboob Ul Haq. Sen's widely read book *Development as Freedom* (Sen, 1999) provides an easily readable overview of this approach. Since 1990 the UNDP has brought out its annual *Human Development Reports* (*HDRs*) which provide detailed measures of HD indicators such as life expectancy, literacy, infant mortality rates, etc. that cover most of the countries of the world. The UNDP also has other related publications.

7 It is noteworthy that one of the important points to emerge from the *HDRs* and the other measures referred to earlier is the absence of any close relationship between economic growth, on the one hand, and HD, poverty alleviation, and elimination of hunger on the other. India offers a good case study in this respect as high economic growth (EG) has been exceptionally slow in translating into HD and reduction of hunger. India figures very poorly in most of these measures and consequently in the GHI in general, its record even worse than that of Bangladesh, Nepal, and Sri Lanka. India is home to a quarter of the world's hungry, the single largest pool of hungry people in any country in the world. Examining the structural roots of this, the historically entrenched structures of inequality and exclusion (e.g. caste) is critical for assessing India's political economy, its development path, and its model of democracy. See the many writings on this by scholars such as Amartya Sen, especially Dreze and Sen. I have made a modest attempt to deal with some of these in my comparison of HD in Kerala and Cuba (2010) and in India and China (2014). In sharp contrast to the Indian path, both Cuba and China took early and radical steps to dismantle such structures, thus creating the pre-conditions for more inclusive HD. Kerala took some modest steps, more radical and decisive than India in general, and with very good outcomes in terms of its HD achievements.

8 See, for example, Shiffman, 2013.

9 For more details on these see my earlier paper (Tharamangalam, 2010). A recent study on food insecurity by the US Department of Agriculture reported that 50.2 million Americans (15% of the population), including 17.2 million children

(one in four), were food insecure in 2009 (Nord et al., 2010). Another study (NCBR, 2010, 2) stated that the number of people seeking emergency food assistance each year through food banks has increased 46% since 2006, from 25 million to 37 million, the highest numbers seen in the organization's 26-year history. For my take on the US situation see Tharamangalam, 2011.

10 IFPRI, 2016, GHI, 2016 http://uncova.com/who-declares-cuba-first-country-to-eliminate-mother-to-child-hiv-transmission. accessed December 2019

11 Two factors may help to explain why Cuba did not become the kind of brutal dictatorships of the Soviet or Chinese types. First is the leadership of Fidel Castro, an extraordinary and charismatic person and an idealist, committed to what he saw as the humanist goals of the revolution, and second a more effective form of socialist democracy in which a variety of peoples' organizations helped to provide a degree of checks and balances (Tharamangalam, 2010, August, 2003, Roman, 2003).

12 This issue was highlighted and discussed in detail at a three-day seminar in 2007, organized by my research team in the provincial town of *Sancti Spiritu* with the participation of representatives and staff of the local government. The local government had considerable autonomy to pursue local development policies but was severely constrained by lack of funds.

13 Several researchers from outside Cuba have done extensive fieldwork on the Cuban model of democracy (and its effectiveness in this respect). See especially August (2013), Roman (2003), and Saney (2002). See also my discussion of human development in Cuba (Tharamangalam, 2010)

14 This observation is based on a meeting with Cuban writers in Havana during my field trip to Cuba in 2005.

15 For this section I draw on my earlier fieldwork in Cuba, but especially on two workshops on Cuba's cooperatives I attended in 2016 in Halifax, Canada, and in Havana, Cuba. The paper presenters in both were scholars and researchers on Cuban cooperatives, many of them from Cuba. See especially Pineiro (2016a), Diaz (2016), and Durand (2016).

16 Based on information provided by the Party Congress, the draft guidelines for the Congress were discussed by people at all levels, from the grassroots to the Parliament (*The National Assembly of People's Power*); from December 1, 2010, to February 28, 2011, there were 163,079 meetings with 8,913,838 participants who contributed 3,019,471 separate inputs. This resulted in the modification of 68% of the original guidelines and the addition of 36 new guidelines and a final total of 311 (August, 2013).

17 For this section I draw especially on two workshops on Cuba's cooperatives I attended in 2016 in Halifax, Canada, and in Havana. Several of the papers presented in both were by Cuban as well as non-Cuban international scholars who have been researching cooperatives in Cuba. The second workshop also included visits to some new cooperatives in Havana, where we also held conversations and interviews with members and managers of these co-ops.

References cited

August, Arnold. 2013. *Cuba and its Neighbours: Democracy in Motion.* Black Point, NS, Canada: Fernwood Publishers.

Bateman, Milfred et al. 2016. "The importance of local institutional support for cooperative development in Cuba: Policies", paper presented at workshop on "Cooperatives in Cuba", St. Mary's University, Halifax, Canada, April 2016.

Benjamin, Medea, Joseph Collins, and Michael Scott. 1984. *No free lunch: Food and revolution in Cuba today.* San Francisco: Food First Books, Institute for Food and Development Policy.

Burd-Sharps, Sarah, Kristen Lewis, and Eduardo Borges Martins, eds. 2008. *The measure of America: American human development report 2008–2009*. New York: Columbia University Press.

Congress of the United States: Congressional Budget Office (CBO). 2011. *Trends in the distribution of household income between 1979 and 2007.*

Diaz, Beatriz. 2016. "Cooperatives in Cuba's economic model". Center for Global Justice. Available at www.globaljusticecenter.org/papers/cooperatives-within-cubas-current-economic-model, accessed December 2019.

Durand, Cliff (edit). 2016. *Moving beyond capitalism*. London: Routledge.

The Economist. 2015, September 3. *Remittances: Like manna from heaven.* Available at http://cdn.static-economist.com/sites/default/files/imagecache/1872-width/images/2015/09/articles/main/20150905_fnp503.jpg, accessed 19 December 2019.

Fonteneau, Benedicte et al. 2011. *The reader 2011: Social and solidarity economy: Our common road towards Decent Work* (2nd ed.). Turin, Italy: International Training Centre of the ILO.

Gasperini, Lavinia. 2000. "The Cuban education system: Lessons and dilemmas". *Country Studies: Education and Management Publication Series* 1.5. Available at siteresources.worldbank.org/Education/Resources/278200-1099079877269/547664-1099080026826/T, accessed December 2019.

Harnecker, Camila Pineiro. 2016a. "Visions of socialism guiding the current changes in Cuba". In Durand (edit).

———. 2016b. "Cooperatives in CUBA' new socio-economic model: What has been done and what can be done", paper presented at workshop on "Cooperatives in Cuba", St. Mary's University, Halifax, April 28–29.

International Food Policy Research Institute (IFPRI). 2016. *Global Food Policy Report 2016*. Washington, D.C. "http://dx.doi.org/10.2499/9780896295827%20accessed%20on%20November%2015"http://dx.doi.org/10.2499/9780896295827 accessed on November 15, 2017.

Northern Colorado Business Report [NCBR]. (2010). "USDA reports hunger reaching record high". Viewed on 21 November 2010 (http://www.ncbr.com/article.asp?id=54681).

Nord, Mark, Alisha Coleman-Jensen, Margaret Andrews and Steven Carlson. (2010). "Measuring food security in the United States: Household food security in the United States", USDA, Economic Research Service.

Polanyi, Karl. 2001. *The great transformation: The political and economic origins of our time*. Boston: Beacon.

Roman, Peter. 2003. *People's Power: Cuba's Experience with Representative Government*. New York: Rowan and Littlrfield Publishers.

Saney, Isaac. 2002. *Cuba: A Revolution in Motion*. Halifax: Fernwood, and London: Zed books.

Sen, Amartya. 1999. *Development as freedom*. New York: Anchor Books.

Shiffman, Richard. 2013. "How Cubans' health improved when their economy collapsed". *The Atlantic*, April 18. Available at www.theatlantic.com/health/archive/2013/04/how-cubans-health-improved-when-their-economy-collapsed/275080/, accessed December 2019.

Tharamangalam, Joseph. (edit). 2006. *Kerala: The paradoxes of public action and development*. New Delhi: Orient Longman.

———. 2008. "Can Cuba offer an alternative to corporate control over the world's food system?" Paper presented at the "20th Conference of North American and Cuban Philosophers and Social Scientists," Havana, 26 June. Available at the

Center for Global Justice: www.globaljusticecenter.org/es/papers/can-cuba-offer-alternative-corporate-control-over-world%E2%80%99s-food-system-0, accessed December 2019.

———. 2010. "Human development as transformative practice: Lessons from Kerala and Cuba". *Critical Asian Studies* 42.3: 363–402.

———. 2011. "Occupy Wall Street: Poverty and rising social inequality interrogating democracy in America". Global Research, December 13.

———. 2015. "Amartya Sen in Beijing: Comparing Human Development in India and China", in Roy, Ash Narain, and George Mathew (edit.) *Development, Decentralization, and Democracy (festscift for MA Oommen)*. Delhi: *Orient Blackswan*.

———. 2017. "The poverty and development problematic". In Henry Veltmeyer and Paul Bowls (edit) The Essential Guide to Critical Development Studies. Routledge. Available at www.routledge.com/The-Essential-Guide-to-Critical-Development-Studies/Veltmeyer-Bowles/p/book/9781138049970, accessed December 2019.

Thomas Piketty (2014), *Capital in the Twenty-First Century*. Translated by Arthur Goldhammer. Cambridge, Massachusetts: Belknap Press of Harvard University Press.

United Nations Children's Fund (UNICEF) 2007. The state of the world's children 2008. New York: UN Publications.

Uriarte, Miren. 2004. "Social policy responses to Cuba's economic crisis of the 1990s". *Cuba Studies* 34: 105–136.

———. 2002. *Cuba: Social policy at the crossroads*. Boston: Oxfam America.

World Health Organization. 2015. "WHO declares Cuba first country to eliminate mother-to-child HIV transmission". Washington, DE/Dublin/Bonn. Available at http://uncova.com/who-declares-cuba-first-country-to-eliminate-mother-to-child-hiv-transmission, accessed December 2019.

7 Territorial development and social and solidarity economy in Brazil

Some contributions to cohesive development

Leandro Morais

Introduction

The local generation of jobs and income from the social and solidarity economy (SSE) constitutes one of the elements that can contribute to territorial development since it revitalizes the economy, especially in more vulnerable areas with low economic dynamism and high poverty rates. It is therefore one of the pathways that contribute to *cohesive development*, as described in the concept note of the important cohesive development seminar in Patna, India.

In Latin America, there is a process of creating a plurality of forms of SSE, each based on their history and socioeconomic characteristics. Indeed, in this region, there is an increasing volume of literature addressing the existence and importance of the SSE and its various practical actions (Morais, 2013, 2015). More recently, some of it draws attention to the role of the SSE in matters of public policies, created as a mechanism to face unemployment, poverty, social exclusion, and inequality – structural characteristics of this territory.

In fact, the construction of new proposals for territorial and social development and productive and economic organizations is viable and could be fostered by public policies, with special attention to social entrepreneurs that strengthen regional ties. However, we cannot forget that they are actions created from the "bottom up", that is, from territorial experiences to adverse situations.

The success of these alternative experiences of production and community organization in the territories depends to a great extent on their ability to integrate processes of economic transformation and cultural, social and political changes, building networks of cooperation and mutual support, which presupposes a progressive participation in instances of formulation and implementation of public policies based on the idea of co-construction of these policies.

This chapter intends to show that territorial development can occur even from small actions, especially in socially and economically disadvantaged territories. In other words, it aims to develop a brief theoretical and conceptual discussion about territorial development and discuss the connections between SSE and the possibilities of territorial development, from the Brazilian experience.

1. Territorial development: some theoretical-conceptual considerations

The concept of "territory", which is becoming more useful and widely mentioned, has acquired a "polysemic" character (Ortega, 2008, p. 51). Cassiolato and Szapiro (2003) conceive territoriality from the idea of "specific interdependences of economic sphere", defined not only as location of economic activity. In the view of these authors, an activity is entirely territorial when its economic viability is rooted in "assets" which include social practices and relationships not available in other places and which cannot be instantly created or imitated in places that do not have them. This is the notion referred to as territorial development.

Therefore, it has to do with "endogenous" development of economies with territorial dynamics, based on cooperation, learning, tacit knowledge, specific technical knowledge and expertise, culture, and synergistic interrelationships. The idea of endogenous development is based on the view that productive systems consist of a set of material and non-material factors that allow for local and regional economies to adopt different paths for economic growth and social development. The routes to be followed by these economies depend so much on internal resources as their adjustment or exploitation depend on the stimuli of macro, regional, industrial, and other sectoral policies.

In this perspective, as mentioned by Putnan (2000), the fundamental explanation for endogenous development relies on the high degree of social capital found in the communities in which the actions are practiced. In other words, the organizational capacity of the society is fundamental in its process of development. By "social capital", the author means the "capital" that refers to the characteristics of social organization, such as trust, rules, and systems that contribute to increasing the efficiency of society, facilitating coordinated actions. In his view, more than identifying high social capital, the important thing is to know if the local-territorial-social organization leads to a strong capacity of cooperation around the collective project.

Rephrasing it, when referring to local and territorial development, we must consider the importance of the following dimensions: (a) economic: related to the creation, accumulation, and distribution of wealth; (b) social and cultural: implies quality of life, equity, and social integration; (c) environmental: refers to the natural resources and to the sustainability of medium- and long-range projects; and (d) political: refers to aspects related to territorial governance, as well as to the independent, sustainable collective project.

Navarro-Yañes (1998) conducted deep bibliographic research on the topic and, from this research, he pointed out three main lines of argument to show the importance of the local context in new opportunities for development: (a) connected to the recognition of the social basis for development and its knowledge about local capacities; (b) referring to the relevance of a local identity, fundamental to the consolidation of what Abramovay (1999) called a "guiding idea", around which a territorial pact of the community must occur, in search of its development, and (c) connected to the action of the state, in the sense of decentralizing public policies in the local context.

Within this context, the policies that are able to stimulate a route of development gain strength, while the public policies are the instruments of strengthening or even forming a proactive culture of development with a local basis. In these terms, the innovating focus of such public policies would be centered, on the one hand, on the idea that the development project must be built from below, and, on the other hand, that it must be based on a "territorial pact", mediated and articulated by the key actors (government, organizations of producers, unions, business associations, etc.).

After these initial considerations, we think it is possible to advance toward a systemic conception of territorial development or, as mentioned by Paula (2008), "Integrated and Sustainable Local Development" or "Desenvolvimento Local Integrado e Sustentável – DLIS".

In this perspective, we understand territorial development (sustainable and integrated), as based on a tripod: (a) "social capital", (b) economic development, and (c) conservation of natural resources. Such elements are understood as important for thinking about cohesive development in our analytic perspective.

2. Territorial development and social and solidarity economy: potentials and harmonious connections

SSE is a field of growing importance in many areas of discussion and practice, in the governmental context of public policies in their several manifestations, in multilateral organizations, as well as among researchers in the area, in Brazil and throughout the world. The International Labour Organization (ILO) considers SSE "a concept designating enterprises and organizations, in particular cooperatives, mutual benefit societies, associations, foundations and social enterprises, which have the specific feature of producing goods, services and knowledge while pursuing both economic and social aims and fostering solidarity" (ILO Regional Conference, Johannesburg, South Africa, 2009).

However, there is no consensus regarding the definition, measurement, and organizations that it includes.

In practice or in academy, there are at least three broad perspectives of understanding the SSE at the global level: (a) those who understand it as an another model of development (antagonistic to capitalism); (b) those who understand it as a form of precariousness of formal employment (standard employment, like "false cooperatives", called *coopergatos* in Brazil), and

(c) those who understand SSE as an instrument of socio-labor insertion, although immersed in the hegemonic capitalist system.

In this perspective, we adopt in this chapter the definition suggested by Morais (2013), by which solidarity economy refers to solidarity economy enterprises (SEE) and to the policies supporting the inclusion of social and labor groups that are typically excluded economically and socially. This is because in Brazil, solidarity economy has been, in recent years, an innovative alternative for generating work and income and also a method for promoting socio-occupational inclusion. It involves diverse economic and social practices, which include activities for the production of goods, providing services, solidarity finances, exchanges, fair trade, and solidarity consumption. Thus, although many of these experiences depict a "symbolic confrontation" with the capitalist hegemonic model, we understand that many of these practices occur within this system.

In this direction, according to Fraisse (2006), the emergence of territorial policies of SSE represent an interesting case of construction of a "new" area of local public action. In his view, the emergence of territorial policies of SSE offers a "historic opportunity" for consolidation and renewal that gives SSE its deserved place as a "legitimate component of a plural economy, entitled to have a considerable weight in the logic of local development" (p. 243).

In this sense, França Filho (2006), when listing public policies for territorial development and SSE, states that it concerns the construction of territorial strategies of development within the context of the promotion of new economic dynamics, based on the construction and strengthening of "socio-productive local circuits" integrated to the fabric of social, political, and cultural relations of a place.

We can see, therefore, that the policies of SSE represent specific operating actions for creating job opportunities and income, as they are based on a "strategic conception of territorial development". The strategic concept comes from the idea that territorial development is the result of collective, collaborative, and participatory actions for social and productive mobilization of the territory, with wider socioeconomic and political impacts that articulate themselves in a specific territory.

In Silva's view (2009), the enterprises of the solidarity economy are based on local action rooted in the community, understood as the sharing of the same territory and belonging to a net of common relationships, which favors a territorial development strategy through its strengthening. And it is precisely this rooting, shown as the local space in which they are inserted, that will promote direct relationship with the development of the local community, empowering the endogenous capacities and human and material resources.

However, it is important to emphasize that such an idea cannot neglect the importance of political economics adopted at the federal level. On the contrary, these must be thought out and implemented in such a way as to contribute to the successful achievement of territorial policies. After all, crucial matters such as interest rates, levels of investment, exchange rates, as well as the percentage of taxes paid to the municipalities and expenses with specific local policies, are decisions taken at the federal level and may either sponsor the actions, programs, and projects for territorial development or make them impossible to accomplish.

3. Brazilian experience: some contributions

The Brazilian labor market presents serious structural problems related to its historical background of slavery and to how the transition to wage employment occurred in Brazil. Informal work and high rates of unemployment, besides exclusion, are mentioned as the main problems, particularly of specific segments; the country's heterogeneity, income inequality, and so on are other relevant factors.

Within contexts of high unemployment rates, especially for more vulnerable groups that experience significant material deprivation of means of survival, some other sources of work and income can be found. One of these alternative ways is SSE.

According to Paul Singer, Former National Secretary of the Social and Solidarity Economy National Secretariat (SENAES), structural changes to the economic and social order that have occurred in the world in the last decades have undermined the traditional model of the capitalist relationship of work. The increase in informality and the process of loss of formal relations of work have been confirmed as a tendency in an environment of mass unemployment. On the other hand, the deepening of this crisis opened the way for the rise and advancement of other types of organization of work, which is a consequence, mostly, of the necessity of workers to find alternatives to generate income.

It is possible to observe some experiences that have been multiplying and spreading themselves in several territories, related to practices of territorial development through instruments of SSE. They express the attempts of society to find new ways of facing unemployment, absence of income, as well as lack of opportunities at the traditional economic spheres.

For Coraggio (2003), the "popular economy" already exists in the territories. Denied and excluded with adjectives such as "underground", "black", and "informal", it has always existed. However, it has gained greater strength in the present, in the face of the persistence and seriousness of the crisis. And it is oriented, progressively, by the need of survival of those who are excluded. In this context, the popular economy begins to register empirically learned strategies, disseminating models of action that allow us to respond to some of the elementary demands in their respective territories.

Cocco (2006) characterizes these experiences as a "productive multitude" and "radically democratic", within a "set of singularities that cooperate among themselves" and align themselves with the idea of productive mobilization of the territories, aiming at the social territorial development through the emergence of new political subjects and the constitution of common interests.

Such initiatives lead to knowledge, skills, notions, and principles that were acquired over time and that give sense and identity to a set of practices that generate economic, organizational, and articulation policies. These experiences emerged in different local contexts and are characterized by a rich repertoire of technical-productive practices and of economic and social organization.

In an international context, some countries allow the verification, in practice, of some experiences which contribute to territorial development, since the implementation of SSE. It is valid to say that the enormous variety of experiences in Latin America, including in highly heterogeneous regions, are well known.

3.1 SSE and the construction of the public policy in Brazil

In Brazil, the use of the term SSE is not consensual, although the organizations that act in the interface between the economy and society are an increasingly acknowledged social phenomenon. As for the sphere of *praxis*, we can see a wide spectrum of actors and legal arrangements that are set up in this field, although the cooperatives are easiest to find and the ones with the greatest tradition in the country.

The SSE has its own norms, rules, and codes and is made up of symbolic disputes and contradictions among individuals and member groups. In this sense, in order to start understanding the concepts and theories that underlie the bibliographic production that is presently disseminated in Brazil, it is necessary to understand, even if only in a synthetic way, the different studies that make up the country's scientific field. It is important to mention that, except for the studies in the sphere of cooperatives, the scientific discussion in the field of SSE is relatively recent, and although it uses different names (social economy, solidarity, third sector, NGOs, etc.), the number of studies that support initiatives from civil society that have socioeconomic characteristics has been constantly increasing. Hence, some of the trends have been classified as the following, as suggested by Serva and Andion (2006): (a) studies about "cooperativism", (b) the current trend of the "third sector", and (c) the current of solidarity economy.

In this article, we adopt the perspective of the solidarity economy, a constituent part of the SSE. For SENAES (2015),[1] the term "solidarity economy" is defined as a "set of economic activities organized and performed in mutual cooperation by male and female workers by means of self-management". Economic activities can be understood as the activities related to the production of goods, provision of services, solidary finances, fair trade, and solidary consumption. "Solidary organizations" refer to the cooperatives, associations, self-managed companies, solidary groups, exchange groups, etc., deriving from the idea of "solidary economic enterprises", which are simple or complex organizations, of collective character, in which workers from urban and rural environments exercise self-management of their enterprises and can or cannot have legal registration for the practice of their economic activities.

According to Leite (2011), when analyzing the characteristics of SSE in Brazil, several aspects deserve attention. Among them, first, the author mentions the number of enterprises; the organization of debate forums; the creation of entities within the movement (FBES, CONAES,[2] among others); the set of demands and proposals that have consolidated SSE as a project; the capacity to press the government for the creation of SENAES and the adoption of a public policy of SSE; the relationship with popular movements.

Second, the author stresses that SSE presents itself as a manifestation of extensive reach, either in territories – considering that "the movement spreads itself throughout the country, affecting several regions at the same time, just as the countryside and the city" – or in the different population groups that constitute them (men, women, young people, the elderly, retired). "[I]n social terms, [however,] it is restricted to groups that are in the margins of the work market" (p. 2), that is, the segments that are socially excluded or are factory workers, usually low-skilled, and those who are in more advanced age groups, who work for factories that went bankrupt.

Third, Leite (2011) states, "the capacity of organization that the movement has built is considerable" (p. 2), keeping in mind the creation of SENAES, of the technology incubator for popular cooperatives (ITCPs), and of forums, even though the author also indicates certain fragilities that are inherent to the solidarity economy movement in Brazil, as we shall see later.

According to Fraisse (2006), as already announced, the emergence of territorial policies of SSE represents an interesting case of construction of a "new" area of local public action. In his view, the emergence of territorial policies of SSE offers a "historic opportunity" for consolidation and renewal that gives SSE the place it deserves as a "legitimate component of a plural economy, entitled to have a considerable weight in the logics of local development" (p. 243).

Thus, an important question is the relationship between public policies of SSE and territorial development. In this perspective, França Filho (2006), when listing public policies for local development and SSE, states that it concerns the construction of territorial strategies of development within the context of the promotion of new economic dynamics, based on the construction and strengthening of "socio-productive local circuits" integrated to the fabric of social, political and cultural relations of a place.

We can see, therefore, that the policies of SSE represent specific operating actions for creating job opportunities and income, as they are based on a strategic conception of territorial development. The strategic concept comes from the idea that territorial development is the result of collective, collaborative, and participative actions for social and productive mobilization of the territory, with wider socioeconomic and political impacts that articulate themselves in a specific territory.

In Silva's view (2009), the enterprises of solidarity economics are based on local action rooted in the community, understood as the sharing of the same territory and belonging to a net of common relationships, which favors a local development strategy through its strengthening. And it is precisely this rooting, shown as the local space in which they are inserted, that will promote direct relationship to the development of the local community, empowering the endogenous capacities and human and material resources.

However, it is important to emphasize that such an idea cannot neglect the importance of political economics adopted at the federal level. On the contrary, these must be thought out and implemented in such a way as to contribute to the successful achievement of territorial policies. After all, crucial matters such as interest rates, levels of investment, exchange rates, as well as the percentage of taxes paid to the municipalities and expenses with specific local policies, are decisions taken at the federal level and which may sponsor or, on the contrary, turn the actions, programs, and projects for local development impossible to accomplish.

In *praxis*, this "new" principle of action towards development has as its basis the interrelationship of, mainly, three kinds of policies: (a) sectoral: aiming at permanent improvement in the efficiency and productivity of the productive sectors, through actions for training, education, and technological innovations, etc.; (b) territorial: ways of administering and managing the endogenous resources (labor, natural resources, and infrastructure), aiming at the formation of a favorable local surrounding environment; and (c) environment: through actions for the conservation of natural resources and through ecological concerns, considered of strategic value in issues of local development.

In this context policies that can stimulate a development path are emphasized, while public policies are the instruments for strengthening or even creating a proactive culture of development through local basis. In these terms, the innovative focus of such public policies should be centered, on the one side, on the idea that the development project can be built from "below", and on the other, that it must be based on a "territorial pact", mediated and moved by the articulation of key actors (government, organizations of producers, cooperatives, unions, business associations, etc.).

Another aspect that reinforces the connection between SSE and local development refers to its characteristic of transversality. According to Morais (2013), SSE does not refer only to the economic problem, as it may also involve other issues, such as sociability in the territories, citizens' political participation, the degree of associative organization, environmental preservation, and the reinforcement of cultural identities. This fact is pointed out by Souza (2012), who defends the "multidimensional" and "multi-territorial" character of the actions in the field of SSE.

In Brazil, SENAES, created in 2003, is the institutionalization of the public policy on SSE. Regarding the rise of SENAES, it is good to remember that although SSE began to constitute itself in a more representative way since the 1980s with the creation of several cooperatives, self-managed companies, and other similar enterprises, a space for discussion and national articulation started to be created during the activities of SSE in the First World Social Forum. Some national entities, along with the government of Rio Grande do Sul, decided to form a Brazilian Work Group on SSE in order to organize the activities of SSE at the World Social Forum II and III, gathering several initiatives of national entities and of organizations and international networks related to the topic. The Brazilian Work Group of SSE became a national and international reference for the activities related to the World Social Forum and even for other activities.[3]

As mentioned before, one of the structuring axes of the policies of SENAES is the idea of the connection of SSE with territorial development. Among the important projects developed were the "Solidary Economic Ethnodevelopment of the Quilombola Communities" and the "Project for Promotion of Local Development and Solidarity Economy", as well as the "Local Brazil Program", along with the *inter sectorial articulations* of SENAES in local and territorial development, the contributions of the Secretariat in the "National Program of Sustainable Development of Rural Territories – PRONAT", as well as the "Territories of Citizenship Program" and "Program of the Agenda 21 of the Environment Ministry". Other important advances were the creation of a National System of Information in Solidarity Economy – SIES; several courses and meetings for both training, social, and professional qualification and popular and solidarity education; a National Program of Technological Incubators of Popular Cooperatives – PRONINC; programs of social technologies and solidarity economy; and several projects and programs in solidarity finances (community banks, solidary funds etc.) and in solidary trade (fair and solidary trade, fairs, etc.).

Since the emergence of SENAES (2003), until the present, the Secretariat, through the Social and Solidarity Economy Program in Development, was gradually included in the federal government's pluriannual plans and constituted the beginning of the process of institutionalization of the public policies of a solidarity economy in the country, which is the legal framework of SSE in construction. There were also strategies for expansion of state and municipal public policies of a solidarity economy, as well as the emergence of the Public Centers of Solidarity Economy and the Parliamentary Front of Solidarity Economy. The emergence and strengthening of the National Conference of Solidarity Economy and the National Council of Solidarity Economy were also important.

We should mention the more recent "Programa de Desenvolvimento Regional, Territorial Sustentável e Economia Solidária" (Program of Regional, Sustainable Territorial Development and Social and Solidarity Economy) (2012–2015). This program intends to expand the strategy of regional/territorial action of the federal government, which has, in the last few years, gained strength and consistency for the widening of the options of generation of job and income.

In this perspective, since the creation of SENAES, several actions were taken to respond to the main demands of the SSE enterprises, the most important of which are access to financial services, infrastructure services, and knowledge and increased trade.

The Programa de Desenvolvimento Regional, Territorial Sustentável e Economia Solidária had several goals and initiatives planned for the period between 2012 and 2015. Its objectives are directed towards two areas: (a) fostering and strengthening SSE and (b) strengthening the institutionalization of the National Policy of SSE. Other objectives are the federative articulation and integration of the promotion policies of solidarity economy initiatives in the sustainable territorial processes of development based on solidarity.

To achieve these goals, SENAES will base its action upon the following initiatives: (a) development and dissemination of social technologies that are appropriate to SSE; (b) training of workers, agents, trainers, multipliers, and public managers of SSE; (c) implementation and consolidation of community banks of development, solidary rotational funds, and support to cooperativism of solidary credit; (d) incubators, sponsoring, technical assistance, and support to SSE and its networks and chains of production, trade, and consumption; (e) promotion of the adaptation of credit policies to the demands and characteristics of SSE; (f) promotion of access to governmental purchases of goods and services from SSE; and (g) promotion and strengthening of fairs, fixed locations, and facilities for trade of goods and services of SSE.

Additionally, among the public policies for SSE is the National System of Fair and Solidary Trade (SNCJS). The SNCJS is an important construction that permits the creation of a system of public recognition of the products and services of solidary economy, in such a way as to guide the market and the consumers in the selection of companies, technologies, and products with the attributes of social, economic, and ecological sustainability, in the valorization of more inclusive and socially fair market practices (Antunes & Conti, 2019).

The results and effectiveness of these policies are entirely unknown. This is in fact a topic that needs focus and attention. It is necessary to elaborate methodologies and monitoring processes to evaluate the impacts of the public policies of SSE.

More recently, the last national survey was completed and published in "A Economia Solidária no Brasil: umaanálise dos dados nacionais", coordinated by Gaiger (2014). Besides providing the characterization of the SSE in Brazil after 13 years of public policies undertaken by SENAES, this survey can serve as a starting point for the necessary creation of mechanisms for evaluating these policies.

Based on this survey, there are 19,708 SEE and 1,423,631 associate members. Of these, almost 55 percent are in the rural zone, while 34.8 percent are in the urban area and 10.4 percent of the SEE is simultaneously in rural and urban zones. By regions of Brazil, 41 percent of the SEE is in the northeast, 17 percent in the south, 16 percent are in the north and the same in the southeast, and 10 percent in the center west. As for the organization of the SEE, a wide predominance of associations can be observed, representing 60 percent of the SEE, 30.5 percent of the informal groups, 9 percent of the cooperatives, and less than 1 percent of the mercantile societies.

Other interesting data refers to the main collective economic activity of the SEE. Of the SEE, the main economic activity is production (56.2 percent), followed by consumption (20 percent), commercialization (13.3 percent), provision of services (6.6 percent) and, last, the exchange of goods and services (2.2 percent) and savings, credit, and solidarity finances (1.7 percent).

From the point of view of the importance of the income to the associate members, the survey shows that the SEE represent the main source of income for the associate members mainly when the economic activities are the providers of services or work for third parties, followed by trade and production.

Regarding the distribution of the SEE by sectors of economic activity:

a   30.6 percent are in manufacturing industries: manufacture of textile artifacts, manioc flour, and derivatives, production of cakes and sweets, production of honey products and manufacture of clothing;

b   27 percent in the primary sector: rice cultivation, horticulture, corn cultivation, bean cultivation, cattle raising for milk;

c   3 percent industrial services of public utility: collection and selection of recyclable materials, plastic recycling, collection, treatment and distribution of water;

d   1.6 percent in financial activities: rotation funds, rural credit cooperatives, solidary credit, community banks, and cooperatives of mutual credit.

Another relevant topic found in this survey has to do with the "Gordian knot" of the SEE, that is, the difficulties in distributing financial resources, which fosters inadequate conditions in society. From the total of SEE, 77 percent did not look for creditor financial aid during the 12 months prior to the collection of data for the survey. Of these, 42 percent did not look for it because they did not need it, while 35 percent of them did not contract them because they were afraid to go into debt. Still, from the total number, 12 percent looked for credit but were not able to get it (Gaiger, 2014; Morais, 2015a).

Besides this, it is important to register a serious problem found along the discussion of the issue of public policies of the solidarity economy in Brazil: the tight budget of SENAES. This fact is actually recognized by SENAES itself, in Documento Oficial de 2012[4] – the annual budgets are not sufficient to respond to the needs of the advancement of the solidarity economy in Brazil. According SENAES, budget expansion is a fundamental condition for the expansion and consolidation of public policies in the entire national territory. This situation also highlights the limits of the instruments of operationalization of the policy, as well as the technical and administrative limits and the insufficient physical facilities of the Secretariat.

Recently, Brazil's political, economic, and institutional crisis (2016) has led to a period of apprehension in the field of SSE in Brazil, taking into account the "fiscal tightening" and the reduction in public budgets, as well as the insertion of SENAES into the former Ministry of Work and Employment (actually Ministry of Labor and Social Security – www.mtps.gov.br) and the inherent political instability in these times of change of the government (from Dilma to Temer).

However, SENAES and the entire movement for SSE in the country still struggles and can, in fact, celebrate, not only the approval of Law no. 12690 of 2012,[5] which regulates the organization and functioning of work cooperatives and institutes the National Program of Promotion to the Cooperatives of Work – PRONACOOP, but also the recent unanimous approval of the Law Project of Solidarity Economy (PL 4685/2012), in August 26, 2015, in the Commission of Agriculture, Cattle Raising, Supply and Rural Development (CAPADR) by the House of Representatives. The law, which establishes definitions, principles, guidelines, objectives, and composition of the National Policy of Solidarity Economy, creates the National System of Solidarity Economy and qualifies the SEE as holders of rights. Through this victory, the PL 4685 moved and was approved on to the Commission of Constitution, Justice and Citizenship (CCJC) in November 2017.

4. Final considerations: some lessons learned

The debate concerning the SSE encompasses a large diversity of opinions and directions that go from simple practices of subsistence to those that see SSE as a new model of development in opposition to the hegemonic capitalist model. There are also critics who see it as another face of the increase in job insecurity in the labor market, such as some experiences of false cooperatives. In this article SSE refers to the possibilities of social and labor insertion of disadvantaged groups of the population from actions based on self-management, popular and community participation, solidarity finance, etc., elements that indicate a "symbolic confrontation" against the hegemonic capitalist system but which still do not allow it to become the "new" model of development, antagonistic to capitalism.

Despite this theoretical, conceptual, ideological, and practical dispute, the SSE is a phenomenon that has been gaining increasing economic, social, and political visibility. One of its novelties is the way it has been impacting public policy planning, since its subjects – organizations and entities – seek recognition, institutionalization, and support for projects and activities.

The public policies of SSE (or, in some cases, the supporting instruments, since not all of them are constituted as such),[6] when intending to generate work and income, therefore, to support certain *problem-groups*, do this by taking into account (a) potential impacts in the local place in which they act, since, when generating income, they also boost the economy in the territory; (b) the possibility of associating it to the social programs of reduction of poverty and misery, besides the programs that involve economic aspects (income generation), social aspects (improvement of the conditions of education, of sanitation, of housing etc.), technical aspects (qualification of labor), and environmental aspects (guaranteeing greater sustainability in the territories in which they act), which also includes a wider relationship – not observed yet – among the ministries (in the context of the federal policies) and secretariats (state and municipality policies); (c) connection or promotion of practices of a solidarity economy aiming at the generation of work by the public sector, in activities demanded by the state, such as the public purchase of products of cooperatives or associations from small producers, purchase of school uniforms from cooperatives, and so on.

However, public policies of support to the SSE do not advance by themselves. They must be articulated to the wider scope of functioning of the macroeconomic policies of their respective country, or in other words, they must be coherent with the more general goals of socioeconomic development in the country. In this sense, the credit conditions, the interest rates, the volume of resources destined to research, advising, development of technologies, and market guarantee (public budgets, for example) – measures, to a great extent, taken in the federal context – must satisfy the objective of supporting and protecting the SEE. To achieve this, they must be state policies, with an institutional and regulatory framework to guarantee them as such.

Another aspect refers to the absence of mechanisms and instruments to evaluate and monitor the policies. The view is that, to achieve greater efficiency and effectiveness in the programs, projects, and actions for a solidarity economy, it is necessary to step further, towards facing the challenge of evaluating and monitoring this set of public policies that contemplate the "sector", in such a way as to contribute to its better planning and subsequent advancements.

Also, from the microeconomic point of view, there are inherent problems in the functioning of the SEE (*modus operandi* of their activities), considering that their experiences are marked by intrinsic fragilities, as well as by the fragmentation of their actions. To understand this, let us consider a practical fact. In a recent survey done by SENAES between 2013 and 2014 and systematized by Rêgo (2014), the SSE presented the following difficulties: lack of working capital and difficulties in obtaining credit; insufficient trade structure; high cost of transportation and substandard conditions of roads for outflow of products; interference of middlemen and monopolies that pose obstacles to their insertion; difficulties in the maintenance of regularity of supply; difficulty in finding clients on a wide enough scale and dependency on public purchases; inadequate prices; and lack of registration for commercialization. However, the most curious aspect is the low number of SEE that trade among themselves, considering that only 17.7 percent of the SEE participate in the networks of commercialization, production, consumption, or credit; in other words, that keeps economic relationships with their fellows in the solidarity economy. This fact points to a contradiction in the solidarity economy that must be dealt with.

Another point is that SENAES constitutes an international example of success of public policy in favor of SSE, keeping in mind the scope of its programs, as well as the contribution to the achievement of legal advancements, such as the already mentioned approval of PL 4685. However, the low volume of resources destined for this governmental policy, on the one hand, makes it unfeasible to advance these policies and reiterate the intrinsic fragilities in this field of action and also suggests the reduction of its degree of autonomy to take certain decisions. On the other hand, they do not allow for advancements in following these policies and its effective results.

As observed by Boaventura de Sousa Santos (2002), the success of these alternative experiences of production and community organizations in the territories depends, to a large extent, on their capacity to integrate processes of economic transformation and cultural, social, and political changes, building networks of collaboration and mutual support, which presumes a progressive participation in the spheres of formulation and implementation of public policies, based on the idea of co-construction of these policies.

Notes

1 www.mte.gov.br/ecosolidaria, accessed 30/12/19.
2 FBES – Fórum Brasileiro de Economia Solidária; CONAES – Conferência Nacional de Economia Solidária.
3 During the organization of World Social Forum III activities, within an environment that pointed to the election of the candidate of the Partido dos Trabalhadores for the Presidency of the Republic, this Work Group planned to hold an expanded national meeting to discuss the role of SSE in the future government (Lula). This meeting was held in November 2002 and during it, the decision was taken that a letter to the elected president should be written, suggesting the creation of a National Secretary of Solidarity Economy. Also, in this meeting it was decided that the First National Plenary Session of Solidarity Economy would be held in December. The First Plenary, attended by over 200 people, endorsed the November 2002 letter and decided to hold the Second National Plenary during the Third World Social Forum to discuss the creation of a Brazilian Forum of Solidarity Economy – FBES. This plenary enabled the beginning of a debate and deepening of the political platform for the strengthening of a solidarity economy in Brazil. This platform is a set of priorities related to the solidary finances, the legal framework for the enterprises of SSE, the training, the education, the networks of production, trade and consumption, and the democratization of knowledge and technology and social organization of SSE. The Second National Plenary was held in January 2003 and could count on the participation of over 1,000 people, making possible the deepening of the political platform of SSE. This plenary decided to constitute the FBES in another National Plenary, while this should be preceded

by state meetings to prepare the national discussion and elect the delegates to it. FBES was created in June 2003, in the Third Plenary, at the same moment of creation of SENAES in the Ministry of Work and Employment. The Forum started to have the role of main speaker with SENAES, in the sense of presenting demands, suggesting policies, and following the implementation of public policies of SSE.

4 Available at: http://portal.mte.gov.br/data/files/8A7C812D3ADC4216013AFAF EB3962C74/BALAN%C3%87O%20A%C3%87%C3%95ES%20SENAES%20 2011%202012.pdf

5 www.planalto.gov.br/ccivil_03/_Ato2011-2014/2012/Lei/L12690.htm, accessed 30/12/19.

6 It is understood that there is no pattern/model of public policies for SSE; in fact, in some municipality-level experiences, we cannot speak of public policies but rather of instruments of support to certain activities.

Bibliographic references

Abramovay, R. Agricultura familiar e o desenvolvimento territorial. Revista da Associação Brasileira da Reforma Agrária. São Paulo, vol. 29, jan-agosto de 1999. Available at: https://wp.ufpel.edu.br/ppgdtsa/files/2014/10/Texto-Abramovay-R.-Agricultura-familiar-e-desenvolvimento-territorial.pdf

Antunes, D.; Conti, B. O comércio justo e solidário na política pública federal: histórico e perspectivas. In: Mercado de trabalho: conjuntura e análise. Brasília, IPEA, 2019. Available at: < https://www.ipea.gov.br/agencia/images/stories/PDFs/ mercadodetrabalho/190722_bmt_66_economia_solidaria_o_comercio_justo_e_ solidario.pdf>.

Cassiolato, J.E.; Szapiro, M. Uma caracterização dos arranjos produtivos locais de micro e pequenas empresas. In: Lastres, H.M.; Cassiolato, J.E.; Maciel, M (Orgs). *Pequena empresa*: cooperação e desenvolvimento local. Rio de Janeiro: RelumeDumará-IE-UFRJ, 2003.

Cocco, G. Mobilizar os territórios produtivos: para além do capital social, a constituição do comum. In: Cocco, G.; Silva, G. (Orgs). *Territórios produtivos*: oportunidades e desafios para o desenvolvimento local. Brasília. Sebrae, 2006.

Coraggio, J.L. *Sobrevivencia y otras estrategias en LAC*: La perspectiva desde lo local, 2003. Available at: www.coraggioeconomia.org/jlc/archivos%20para%20 descargar/sobrevivenciyotrasestrategias.pdf, accessed 19/12/19.

Fraisse, L. Os desafios de uma ação pública a favor da economia social e solidária. In: França Filho, G.; Laville, J.L.; Medeiros, A.; Magnen, J. (Orgs). *Ação Pública e Economia Solidária*: uma perspectiva internacional. Porto Alegre: Editora UFRGS, 2006, pp. 237–244.

França Filho, G. Economia popular e solidária no Brasil. In: França Filho, G.; Laville, J.L.; Medeiros, A.; Magnen, J. (Orgs). *Ação Pública e Economia Solidária*: uma perspectiva internacional. Porto Alegre: Editor UFRGS, 2006, pp. 57–72.

Gaiger, L. (Org). *A Economia Solidária no Brasil*: uma análise de dados nacionais. São Leopoldo – RS: Editor OIKOS, 2014.

ILO. Partnerships for Decent Work Newsletter, No. 30 (June), Geneva: PARDEV, ILO, 2012.

Leite, M.P. *Cooperativas e trabalho: um olhar sobre o setor de reciclagem e fábricas recuperadas em São Paulo*. Faculdade de Educação e Doutorado em Ciências Sociais/UNICAMP, Campinas/SP, 2011.

Morais, Leandro. *As políticas públicas de Economia Solidária (ESOL):* avanços e limites para a inserção sociolaboral dos *grupos-problema.* Campinas: IE-UNICAMP, 2013 (PhD. Thesis).

Morais, Leandro. *Social and Solidarity Economy and South-South and Triangular Cooperation in Latin America and the Caribbean:* Contributions to Inclusive Sustainable Development. Géneve: ILO, 2014. Available at: www.ilo.org/wcmsp5/groups/public/–ed_emp/–emp_ent/–coop/documents/publication/wcms_546401.pdf, accessed 19/12/19.

Morais, Leandro. *Por la necesidad de pensar políticas públicas integradas para el campo de la Economía Social y Solidaria:* la experiencia brasileña. Géneve: ILO, 2015a.

Morais, Leandro. *Social and Solidarity Economy (SSE), South–South and Triangular Cooperation and Social and Solidarity Finance (SSF):* harmonious and promising connections. UNRISD Workshop: Social and Solidarity Finance: Tensions, Opportunities and Transformative Potential, Geneva, 2015b. Available at: www.unrisd.org/ssfworkshop-morais, accessed 19/12/19.

Navarro-Yañes, C. *El nuevo localismo.* Município y democracia en la sociedad global. Córdoba, España: Diputación de Cordoba, 1998.

Ortega, A.C. *Territórios deprimidos:* desafios para as políticas de desenvolvimento rural. Campinas: Editor Alínea, 2008.

Paula, J. *Desenvolvimento Local Integrado e Sustentável.* São Paulo: SEBRAE, 2008.

Putnan, R. *Comunidade e democracia:* A experiência da Itália moderna. 2nd ed. Rio de Janeiro: FGV Editor, 2000.

Rêgo, D. *A natureza da comercialização naeconomia solidária:* a contribuição dos grupos de consumo responsável. Salvador: UFBA, 2014 (Dissertação de Mestrado).

Santos, Boaventura. Preface. In: Santos, B. (Org) *Produzir para viver:* os caminhos da produção não capitalista. Rio de Janeiro: Civilização Brasileira, 2002.

Serva, M., Andion, C. A economia social no Brasil: panorama de um campo em construção. In: Uralde, J.M. *La Economia Social em Iberoamérica:* um acercamiento a su realidad. Madrid: MTAS/FUNDIBES, 2006, pp. 39–86.

Silva, S. *Economia Solidária e políticas públicas de desenvolvimento local:* uma análise de dois programas de gestão pública no Brasil. In Revista Perspectivas em Políticas Pública.

Souza, A. Política pública de economia solidária e desenvolvimento territorial. In: *Boletim Mercado de Trabalho:* conjuntura e análise. Brasília: IPEA e MTE, no. 52, agosto de 2012, pp. 63–70.

8 Tracing cohesive development from practice to theory

Experience in Maharashtra

Bharat Patankar

Cohesive development could be defined as a positive, ecologically friendly development for free humanity, where nature remains unbound and unharmed. Such development could be traced right from the time when women in various parts of the world invented "agriculture." Like ghatasta-pana in Maharashtra, during what is called as Nav-ratra in dussera, women always related their own reproduction, their involvement in the repro-duction of human beings from their womb, and nurturing them with the regeneration in a natural regenerative process. Another kind of basis for this proposition comes from the studies of matrilineal Sanghagana societies during the times of early Vedas. Up to late 1960s, before the generalization of the modern capitalist method of agriculture, women in the toiling farmer family were performing the skilled function of choosing the ears of crops based on their knowledge of seeds and preserving for next sowing season using natural pest control methods. They were the experts in horticulture and in cultivation of the vegetables, too. This remains an area in which much more research work is needed. However, this ecologically friendly and humanity-centered cohesive development could be seen as the historical theme on which most of early human societies prospered. It could be traced right up to the emergence of male-dominated societies and the democra-cies like gana sanghas in India. It could be said that most of the history of human society largely shows a pattern of cohesive development as the basis of human practice and relations with nature.

Even after the emergence of the state-dominated societies in India and the caste system following that, Adivasi culture and social-economic practices related to development maintained a limited pattern of cohesive develop-ment. The caste mode of production is a unique exploitative system which, as Dr. Babasaheb Ambedkar said, is based on graded inequality creating division of laborers preventing them from coming together for the abolition of the caste system. Therefore, development after the emergence of caste system became bound up with the exploitation of caste-oppressed peo-ple along with gender exploitation. It is more difficult and complicated to organize a united struggle, as against sectional movements, to eradicate the caste mode of production. Nonetheless, the relationship between the methods of cultivation and small-scale artisan production with natural resources were eco-friendly. The use of forests, water, sea, and other resources was also based on the balance of healthy exchange of matter between humans and nature. Jotiba Phule, the first modern crusader against the caste system, dealt with this in detail in his *Whip of the Farmer*. Marx also stated that the exchange of matter between humans and nature started becoming unhealthy with the growth of capitalism. Every exploitative mode of production has these contradictory situations in its system. Analysis of these contradictions should help in the critique of which positive aspects to carry forward and which negatives practices to abolish.

The real blow to cohesive development was dealt by the emergence of modern industrial society in the form of capitalism. But even then, most of the agrarian societies in the world, including India, maintained the theme of cohesive development up to the late 1960s, when fertilizers, seeds, and implements, among other things, were taken away from the farming communities by capitalism. Farming communities maintained only partial glimpses of cohesive development within the oppressive framework of caste, class, race, and gender exploitation. If you look at the world scenario today, even these traces of development practice are absent in any social fabric.

At the same time, people's struggle for drought eradication, equitable water distribution, organic agriculture, and the use of wind and solar energy could be experienced in a different manner. Companies today can create an alternative developmental paradigm based on the experiences of their predecessors and of the various technologists, scientists, and agriculturists who brought forward various methods, which could be woven into the practices towards the unfolding of this alternative.

Experiments done by farmers and activists together for deciding the exact requirement of water for agricultural production could form the base of a minimum prosperous livelihood. This is one way that people can move from the themes of an alternative developmental paradigm towards a way of livelihood consistent with cohesive development. The struggle by the villagers of Raigad district in the Konkan region of Maharashtra who were encroached upon by coal-based power plants by Ambanis with the help of the government is one example. Raigad villagers had been practicing novel agricultural practices consistent with cohesive development. They proposed a full alternative plan of generating the same amount of energy with more employment based on renewable processes.[1] In this example, after six years of struggle, the people defeated the government and Ambanis, getting back their land which was transferred to Reliance Energy Limited (REL) the name of the company. And this happened before people of Singur in West Bengal, who had also waged a similar fight against land acquisition for the proposed Nano factory of Tata Motors, got back the land.

These examples of people's movements and people's experiments show that theory and practice go together impacting each other and through this inter-related process a more comprehensive theory as well as practice could be developed.

From solving the problematic posed by the concrete situation to the theoretical alternative

This story of going from practice to theory could be told based on the movement for eradicating drought in the eastern part of western Maharashtra. It is a story of tenacious struggle from 1983 to the present period. The struggle of people in a drought-prone area started as protection from extreme drought conditions, which required more than 99% of people in the area to go on living wages from employment guarantee scheme work, depend on tankers sent by the government for drinking water, and sell their cattle or obtain a takavi loan for fodder which the government would put on their land records. However, the struggle also started for complete eradication of drought and stopping the repeated dependence on government props. During this time, a team of young Marxist-Phuleite-Ambedkarites-feminist men and women of Shramik Mukti Dal and others came together to work with the people's movement. The movement talked with people about the history of drought and discussed what they think about its eradication. Based on these discussions and on people's experience and action, they understood that people themselves in their own way know about the reasons of increasing drought, and they have attempted to conserve water to eradicate drought. They also understood that people do not want to continue this life based on almost continual dependence on employment guarantee scheme, tanker water, and selling of draft animals. They want to change the situation so that they can achieve freedom from drought and move towards a self-reliant and prosperous livelihood. Based on this education and discussion, the movement contacted the peoples' science movement in Maharashtra,[2] who started exploring the problem with the whole drought-prone tehsil of Khanapur and its residents. They worked on discovering ways to regenerate degraded forest, to explore those places in the area where integrated watershed development could be done, and to investigate re-enlivening the rivers and aquifers from the effects of ruthless sand excavation.[3] They also explored ways to regenerate and update the methods of agriculture and land–water relationship that were already in place and to determine the minimum quantity of water and land required to support the minimum prosperous livelihood of the family.[4] Based on this study and the discussions with the constituents of the people's science movement, a primary basic alternative was formulated not only for eradicating drought but also for creating a self-reliant livelihood based on organic agriculture and renewable-based decentralized small industry. This was proposed as an alternative to fossil-based centralized big industry, replacing steel with wood, synthetic fibers with natural fibers, and fossil-based energy with renewable-based energy. The process continued to deepen and be experimented with widely in various fields.

Finding out the basis for alternative developmental paradigm

A conscious social practice of the people in the movement and activists coming together with technologists and people in scientific research work led to an alternative developmental paradigm along with its theoretical basis and practical program. They arrived at the following conclusion:

- The drought is not a natural calamity or inevitable natural phenomenon but a creation of the wrong practices of human beings involved in various planning and production processes. In today's society dominated world over by the capitalist mode of production, the main responsible institutions for creating the drought situation are the state and the government. There is a difference between low-rainfall areas and drought-prone areas. Low-rainfall areas are not necessarily always drought-prone areas. Investigating the history of today's drought-prone areas, one will discover that the mode of living practiced by people in low-rainfall areas was radically different from that of people in high-rainfall areas. In low-rainfall areas, people brought the land under cultivation only along the banks of streams, rivulets, and small rivers, where the soil layer is relatively deeper. They created a series of small dams on these flows and removed water by diverting it from these small dams to irrigate the land. Because they reserved a large area for forest cover and grass cover to herd sheep and cattle, rainwater harvesting was much better. In the valleys of these small streams, they dug wells for irrigating the lands at somewhat more distance from the banks. In years of higher rainfall, more than sufficient production in agriculture took place and the surplus was stored under houses or inside their thick walls. At the same time, fodder was also saved. Both of these were used during the lean years protect them from drought. This pattern was broken in the pre-British period because of either exorbitant taxes in-kind or looting by the fighting warlords. In the post-British modern period, because all produced goods were brought into a commodity market and taxes were to be paid in monetary terms, people in low-rainfall areas had to raise cash crops. The growth of population and spread of the cash crops made them change their mode of life from the one based on herding sheep and cattle and on prosperous agriculture based on organic farming, with captive water used for minimal necessary irrigation. The areas for herding and forest began to be used for agriculture, resulting in the diminishment of rainwater percolation and the depletion of underground water. This process led to the droughts of modern times, which continue to increase in frequency.

Based on this conclusion, a new theoretical understanding arose: a drought situation is created by a particular kind of planning and the practices of the ruling classes, castes, and the state. To change the situation, one has to study the new social-economic and ecological conditions and implement measures for eradicating drought. This can only be achieved with a holistic alternative developmental process that includes methods of agriculture, methods of changing the nature of the land–water relationship, and industrial development that affects the situation of water availability and land use.[5]

Out of the study of the modern situation, activists and people came to the understanding that there has to be a thorough and generalized program for local watershed development and water conservation. There should be a change in the methods of water use and finding out the water requirement. As a result, experimentation in the field of agricultural production was undertaken to decide the minimum amount of water sufficient for producing the required goods in agriculture, which would become the basis for minimum prosperous livelihood for a five-member family unit. It was discovered that 18 tons of dry biomass is required for the minimum prosperous livelihood of a five-person family, and it would require at least 5000 cubic meters of assured water for having a sufficient production equivalent to 18 tons of dry biomass. Part of this biomass would be for consumption of the family itself, in terms of vegetables of various kinds and food grains and fodder for the cattle, and part of it would be a cash crop for purchasing the basic needs in the market, such as seeds, fertilizers, nutrients, farm implements, clothes, medicines, education of a new generation, etc. If minimum water is to be used, one has to know how its quantity could be minimized. Experimentation proved that if the organic content of the soil meets the standard which maintains the primary fertility of the soil, then its water-retaining capacity increases, which would minimize the quantity of water required. It was also determined that in low rainfall areas, even for this minimum water requirement local rainfall water harvesting would never suffice. So, the water should be brought in from the heavy rainfall areas after considering the overall minimum water requirements of that area's minimum prosperous livelihood. This conclusion led the movement to propose a combination of organic farming, conjunctive use of exogenous and local water, and equitable water use rights for those families who are landless, marginal farmers, or small landholders. These sections should receive equitable water amounting to the requirement for the production for making minimum prosperous livelihood possible. That is the amount which comes up to the 5000 cubic meters based on experiments done by the movement itself.[6]

These findings became the basis for equitable water distribution to achieve eradication of drought for all the families living off agriculture. This proposal was put forward based on studies of the Krishna valley for replanning the water use and water distribution pattern. Giving them equitable water use rights brings crores of people out of drought. This means that landless, marginal farmers, small landowners, and large landholders will get the same amount of water required for producing the minimum amount of things necessary for creating a minimum prosperous livelihood for a five-person family.

It means there would be sharing of land and water by the landless and landholders, by marginal farmers and small holders and big landholders. This process lays the basis for land redistribution based on fulfilling a minimum prosperous livelihood and achieving equitable use of both land and water.

After tenacious struggles of more than 30 years, people in western Maharashtra became victorious by forcing the government to sanction the replanning of land and water use based on equitable water, which was a path-showing experiment sanctioned principally in 2005. After undergoing various debates and discussions in terms of scientific and economic soundness and the technical possibility of bringing this replanning into practice, the alternative model was finalized, giving the right to minimum prosperous livelihood to all families in two tehsils, Atpadi and Tasgaon, in western Maharashtra. Changing the unequal use pattern of water and the dumping of thousands of families into permanent drought by keeping them away from water rights was the biggest achievement of this alternative planning. This is the first experiment in India of its kind, which will be implemented with a closed-pipe delivery system, alternative water supply, and equitable water rights to all the families.[7]

The theoretical conclusion and the alternative for drought eradication are not limited to only drought-prone areas. Because of the study involved in finding this alternative, one has to think about organic methods of enriching the soil and maintaining its primary productivity, and at the same time increasing its water-retaining capacity. These findings are applicable in any area where we want to increase productivity of water and land both by maintaining the ecological balance and maintaining exchange of matter between humans and nature in a balanced and healthy way.

This process led the activists and the participating technologists and scientists to the problematic of the relation between agriculture and industry. If we are going to base our agriculture and land–water relationship on organically enriching the soil and keeping the water healthy, then it becomes obvious that this cannot happen without changing the nature of industry. To achieve healthy water and soil, polluting and fossil-based industry must be eliminated, substituted with an industry based on farm products and renewable natural resources. The search to discover inventions and technological alternatives was made possible by the movement.

1 Replacing steel with small diameter timber, which has been given a preservative treatment, for constructing buildings, small dams, bridges, etc.
2 Replacing synthetic fiber with treated natural fiber, thereby these fibers could be used for replacing steel grids with grids of natural fiber, replacing fossil-based insulating material with slabs of nonwoven fabric, and also replacing synthetic fiber ropes with treated natural fiber ropes.
3 Adopting a policy of investing more funds into developing small wind, solar energy, and electricity-producing units in a decentralized manner in all the villages and cities, in the same way finding out the way to use

small diameter timber and natural fiber material for making windmills and solar units.

4   Creating a chain of production of organic fertilizers and material which gives a boost to the crops for growing healthy, strong, and fast and at the same time starting the regeneration process of micronutrients, organisms, and things like earthworms in the soil.

5   Researching the more modern forms for producing biofuels like bio-diesel and the ways to produce these in small scale units so that people can come together to create such units in a decentralized manner.

   a   As an experiment, a building using small diameter timber for the frame structure of a big hall was erected. The hall, which has been standing for the last 25 years, measures 40 by 20 feet and is covered by a roof of thin sheets of a hybrid of natural fibers and synthetic material. The same process was used to build a two-story residential building with stable, which has also been safe and standing for the last 20 years. These structures could be replicated only if the policy in building construction changes by adopting the new policy. One can change from a combination of a hybrid of 90% material coming from natural and renewable resources and 10% from fossil material to 100% material from natural renewables.

   b   Production of natural renewable material and synthetics in the field of pipelines also was a successful experiment.

   c   Long-lasting flows with heavy traffic are built with concrete using a steel grid. Instead of this, an experiment used a grid of natural fiber material, which tested successfully.

All these experiments could come into general use, but this will only happen when the government is forced to take a policy of allocating a large amount of funds for research and development in this direction instead of for atomic research and fossil-based material used for development. The people's struggle along with the strong demand from technological and scientific community in support of this struggle can achieve this change in government and state policy. Until this happens, development based on the cohesiveness of people and the cohesiveness of nature and humans will be impossible.[8]

Remarkable successful struggle of people for cancellation of coal-based power projects of Ambanis by giving renewable-based alternative

In Alibag district on the west coast of Maharashtra, people had converted the salty land on the banks of the Arabian sea into non-salty land. They did this by inventing a method of desalinating it every year and by building structures for training the seawater in such a way that it doesn't spread onto this land. This is a very innovative method of doing highly productive agriculture on this kind of land. People take 25 quintals of rice per acre, which is very good productivity. At the same time they have inland ponds in the same area in which they do fish agriculture. The government sanctioned coal-based power projects of Ambanis and Tatas on this land, despite the fact that there was non-productive land available near the same location. Twenty-two villages and more than 3000 hectares of land were going to be affected, with people being displaced. There was a strong and tenacious struggle against the proposition of starting highly polluting industries, not only for the areas where they are situated but also for areas 30 or 40 kilometers away from the power plant.

Men and women together had indefinite sit-ins lasting for 30 days or sometimes more than two months in front of the collectorate, which had become a seat of officers of Tata and Ambani for getting hold of the required land. When the issue of the debate between government and the peoples' struggle had shifted to the state government, people had long marches on foot for 30 kilometers, 40 kilometers, and up to Mumbai for more than 100 kilometers, finally forcing the state government to examine the whole proposition of starting these industries. They were forced to consider an alternate site on unproductive land and alternative proposals for renewable-based production of electricity in the same area without this kind of land acquisition. People were finally successful in reverting the land acquisition process (in which land had already been handed over on record to the project of Ambanis and Tatas) by getting the ownership of the land back in the hands of farmers. This happened based on alternatives put forward by the movement called "for a beautiful and prosperous Konkan." Though this example is not widely publicized, it had taken place before the Supreme Court had reverted the process of land acquisition in Singur in West Bengal.[9]

Struggle for stopping the commercial sand excavation from the Yerala river bed and constructing a people's dam called "Bali Raja"

This is one more example of fighting against the process causing the depletion of ground water and escalating drought in a drought-prone area, proving the capability of the farming community to build a small dam and maintain it for drought protection.

Yerala river starts from a drought-prone area and meets Krishna river in an area with an average rainfall in the range of 350 mm per year. As far as the per capita water availability is concerned, from all sources in its sub-basin on the average is around 500 cubic meters. The minimum requirement per capita for not being forced to migrate is 1000 cubic meter per capita. This river has a thick sand layer which is usually chosen as high quality sand by builders and contractors. But at the same time, it functions as an aquifer to be used by people after the flow of the river stops after the winter season. It has been functioning as a source of water for irrigated agriculture because of this. Ruthless sand excavation started in this river, particularly after the frequency of drought increased and the pumping of the water from the river bed kept increasing as well. Because of the excavation up to the deep layer measuring even 20 feet, the quality of this sand as an aquifer was hampered markedly. This became additional reason for escalation of the drought situation because the quantity of water for drinking and minimum irrigation to sustain families on the bank was lost. People organized to stop this excavation in a very determined way and started to obstruct the contractors from taking away the sand. They started lying in front of the trucks and telling the drivers to go on their bodies if they wanted. This forced the collector to pay attention to the problem.

Meanwhile, farming communities along the bank, along with the activists, surveyed the riverbed throughout Khanapur tehsil and recorded the information from observations. Based on this, they came to the conclusion that the water in the riverbed was being depleted in direct proportion to the amount of sand excavation. They also recorded the amount of irrigated land and crops grown in that land along the banks of the river before this kind of sand excavation started. After the study, it was proposed to the collector that there should be a ban on auctions of this kind in the Yerala river and sand should be only used for building houses of local people within 8 kilometers of the river bank. Excavating sand only up to 3 feet could be allowed, and monetary income coming from the sand excavated like this on a permit system for local house building should be used for building a series of small dams, which could help with drought protection as well become a seal which prevents sand excavation.

The residents had a tenacious, long-drawn-out struggle supported by movements all over Maharashtra, scientists, technologists, and people experiencing the same situation along the banks of other rivers. Out of the income from the sand used for the first 3-foot layer, people themselves started building the dam. This was opposed by the government, who said, "who are the people who build the dam like this? Government is the only authority which could build the dam." There was a struggle to achieve freedom of people to eradicate drought if government is not doing its job, and the definition of democracy is people's freedom to achieve their cohesive development with nature. Finally, Bali Raja dam was sanctioned and built by the people, helped by students in colleges and high schools and progressive people. This example established the fact that if government and the state are not studying and finding a solution for drought eradication, people should study it and find the solutions and take planning and implementation in their own hands by achieving cohesive unity among themselves for cohesive development of nature and humans. Here, people's intuitions, experiences, and understanding of the history of the river was combined with technologists and scientists, which developed into a new alternative.[10]

Alternatives of small dams to large dams

The movement also became involved with the dam-affected problems of rehabilitation and resettlement. The water from large dams like Koyna, Urmodi, and Tarli in western Maharashtra was planned to be given to the drought-prone areas for drought eradication. While developing a struggle for equitable water distribution and conjunctive use of water, the people's movement started thinking about big dams as a cause of displacement of the farming communities in their submergence area. It was understood from a study of this situation that displacement of the dam evictees and drought eradication necessitating water from the higher rainfall areas are organically related to each other. The movement for dam evictees for developmental rehabilitation could be related to the movement for drought eradication and equitable water distribution. These two sections of society, which are usually pitched against each other though originating from the toiling farming community, came together. and developmental rehabilitation before the dam stores the water and drought eradication with equitable water distribution became a combined slogan of both sections. This is the rarest of examples of this kind of unity. A cohesion among the majority of the toiling people required for cohesive development could be achieved only in such a way.

Through the experience and the study of particular dams, the movement arrived at an alternative to the dams proposed by the government, which would submerge a much smaller cultivable area and residential area. Such an alternative was given for Uchangi dam in Kolhapur district of Maharashtra. Three smaller dams were proposed that would store the same amount of water as the larger dam, which would avoid 50% of the original proposed displacement.[11]

The same kind of study was carried out by technologists and experts along with activists as an alternative to the celebrated Sardar Sarovar dam, which would avoid 75% of the displacement. As well as freezing the dam height at 100 meters, it was proposed to move water through the canals to the northern Gujarat and Kutch, storing this water in reservoirs larger than required for storing local rainfall. The water would then be used throughout the year to irrigate the area to eradicate drought. A tour of meetings and dialogue with the people in the command area was planned, resulting in agreement of the local people to the alternative. However, the proposal could not be implemented because it was not accepted by the then representatives of the

Sardar Sarovar dam evictees' organization. You can see the result today. Not only is the 100 meters of dam height completed, but the dam height will be increased to the proposed level, submerging the area according to the original plan. This is a revealing example for understanding what should not be done and what should have been done.

Many examples of going from practice to theory could be given. But the point to be noted here is that the alternative paradigm for cohesive development could be achieved through the unity of people and a cohesive process of exchange of matter between nature and humans in a healthy way. Of course, there is no fully developed theoretical understanding of the new paradigm which would enable us to have a practical plan for bringing cohesive development into reality. It has to develop through the thinking and practice of the people in various areas of India and the world, because this process is not one that can be developed behind the closed doors of the intellectual world. It is instead necessary to bring together people's intuitions and experiences with the theorizing and planning ability of the intellectuals, technologists, and scientists. Neither side can go ahead without enriching each other. This is a very important and inevitable cohesion of the two worlds of the mode of living that has become necessary and inevitable.

Here what we can say is that we have developed the concept of Jotiba Phule of ecologically balanced development of natural resources and agricultural production in a healthy way and the concept of Karl Marx, who says,

> All the progress in capitalist agriculture is a progress in the art not only of robbing the laborer but of robbing the soil; all progress in increasing the fertility of the soil for a given time, is a progress towards ruining the lasting sources of that fertility. The more a country starts its development on the foundation of modern industry like the United States, for example, the more rapid is this process of destruction. Capitalist production, therefore, develops technology and the combining together of various processes into a social whole, only by sapping the original sources of all wealth – the soil and the laborer.

As a solution to this, he says,

> [capitalist production] destroys at the same time the health of the toiling laborer and the intellectual life of the rural laborer. But while upsetting the naturally grown condition for the maintenance of that circulation of matter it imperiously calls for its restoration as a system, as a regulating law of social production, and under a form appropriate to the full development of the human race.[12]

Yet in his best-known formulations, such as the "negation of negation" and "expropriators are expropriated" passage in *Capital* – he emphasizes the socialization of the existing capitalist mode of production without mentioning the need to transform that production process itself with respect to the exploitation of land and nature, as well as the human–ecological balance. "The knell of capitalist private property sounds. The expropriators are expropriated. The capitalist mode of appropriation, the result of the capitalist mode of production, produces capitalist private property. This is the first negation of individual private property, as founded on the labour of the proprietor. But capitalist production begets, with the inexorability of a law of Nature, its own negation. It is the negation of negation. This does not re-establish private property for the producer, but gives him individual property based on the acquisition of the capitalist era: i.e. on co-operation and the possession in common of the land and of the means of production produced by labour itself." In subsequent Marxist theory and practice, this neglect has often been replicated, despite Marx's own assertion otherwise, that "robbing the laborer" is always linked with "robbing the soil."

Because of the conclusion of analysis of *Capital*, Marx himself says elsewhere that revolution of changing the capitalist system is to convert privately owned means and sources of production to a socialized form of means of production. For him, it was the negation of the negation. But in the previous paragraph, he notes that unless and until the process of sapping the soil and the laborer is transcended, it will be impossible to establish a completely new social production. This new production can only be based on using renewable natural resources and renewable products from the soil with healthy ecological balance to establish the prosperity of soil and humans. This could be further developed based on a new orientation of analysis of imperialist globalization of today, a Herculean task which all of us should engage ourselves in. Let us hope that people become successful in bringing cohesion among themselves, barring the exploiters, and in combining the intelligence of people and intellectuals to generate a new theory.

Notes

1 Sharmik Mukti Dal Booklet (2007), "Towards a Prosperous and Beautiful Konkan: An Alternative Energy Plan to the Proposed Power Projects in the Konkan".
2 Joy, K.J. (1984), "Vignyan Yatra in Khanapur Taluka: Beginning of a New Search", unpublished document.
3 Joy, K.J. and Rao, N. (1988), "The Great Sand Robbery and Impending Ecological Disaster", *Economic and Political Weekly*, Volume 23, Issue 33, pages 1669–1671.
4 Phadke, Anant and Patankar, Bharat (2006), *Integrated Water Resource Management: Asserting the Right of Toiling Peasantry for Water Use*, New Delhi: Sage.
5 Omvedt, Gail and Patankar, Bharat (1991), "Movement for Water: Takari Peasants Struggle in Maharashtra", *Economic and Political Weekly*, Volume 26, Issue 15, pages 955–956.
6 Paranjpe, Suhas and Joy, K.J. (2000), *Panlot Kshetra Vikasacya Navya Disha; Sadhan Saksharta, Shasvat Vikas, Samanyayi Vatap*, Mumbai: Maharashtra Krishi Shikshan va Sanshodhan Parishad.

7 Minutes of the meeting with the principal secretary of irrigation, Maharashtra government, 22/6/2016 and 7/9/2016.

8 Paranjpe, Suhas and Joy, K.J. (1995), "Sustainable Technology: Making the Sardar Sarovar Project Viable, Part III: Energy Self-reliance and Sustainable Prosperity", Centre for Environment Education.

9 Patankar, Bharat (2008), "Struggle against Singur Pattern and SEZ: An Example and its Prospects", paper for National Conference on Special Economic Zones, Economic and Social Perspective, September 18–20, Indian Academy of Social Sciences, Allahabad, Indian Institute of Advanced Study, Shimla.

10 Marathi booklet published by the movement, Bharat Patankar, Uchangi dharanala paryay (Alternative to the Uchangi dam), published by Shramik Mukti Dal, Ajara, 1999.

11 Paranjpe, Suhas and Joy, K.J. (1995), "Sustainable Technology: Making the Sardar Sarovar Project Viable, A Comprehensive Proposal to Modify the Project for greater Equity and Ecological Sustainability", Centre for Environment Education.

12 Karl Marx, Capital, Vol. I, International Publishers, New York, fourth printing, 1972, 505–507.

Reference

Sharmik Mukti Dal Booklet (2007), "Towards a Prosperous and Beautiful Konkan: An Alternative Energy Plan to the Proposed Power Projects in the Konkan", Kasegaon: Shramik Mukti Dal.

9 Towards developing the theoretical perspective of cohesive development

Abhijit Ghosh

I. Introduction

> It was the best of times, it was the worst of times . . . it was the season of
> Light, it was the season of Darkness, it was the spring of hope, it was the
> winter of despair.
>
> (A Tale of Two Cities, Charles Dickens)

What the first few lines of *A Tale of Two Cities* illustrated about London
and Paris 200 years ago resonates today as world's present situation has
emerged. The recently published Oxfam's report[1] shows that the wealth of
eight men is equal to the wealth of 3.6 billion people! This 3.6 billion is not
merely a number. It comprises the poorest half of the world population, who
are compelled to live in sub-human conditions. The deprivation is so acute
that this section is virtually crippled without being able to function in their
daily lives.[2] The peasantry, particularly in the south, are the worst sufferers,
due to the increasing integration of the domestic economy with the global
economy (Amin 2012). More than three billion people, roughly half of the
world population, who are engaged in the primary sector, are constantly
facing threats to their existence due to the policy dictated by international
organizations. Neither can they continue with the same primary sector nor
can they be absorbed into other sectors. This has aggravated the unemploy-
ability condition of the economy, in particular of the developing countries.[3,4]
This has resulted in a growing inequality, more than has been seen in recent
history.

In such a situation, invoking 'cohesive development' may sound utopian,[5]
if one goes by its literal meaning. A definite question must be asked – cohesive development for whom and for what? The word 'development' is itself
an abstract conception if not properly defined. The human development
paradigm is advocated by economists and social scientists like Amartya
Sen, Mahbub-ul Haq, and Martha Nussbaum, who have pointed out that
improvement of human welfare does not merely depend on income. It also
depends on a set of non-income parameters that determine the quality of

life, such as the right to a healthy life, the right to education and gathering knowledge, and the right to acquire resources that are essential for a decent standard of living.[6] These rights are defined as *basic* and *minimum essential*. The denial of these basic rights falsifies the relevance of the existing development paradigm and gives reason to search for an alternative paradigm that ensures a dignified life for all.

The simmering discontent across the world with the onslaught of globalization has given rise to the resistance movement, may it centre on the degradation of natural resources, right to food, right to employment, right to dignified life, right to equality, or right to environmental protection (Ray 2012). The struggle waged by Latin American countries, including Cuba, and by movements all over the world show that people are seeking an alternative paradigm.[7] It echoes the significance of building solidarity among people to seek a comfortable space for living with dignity. This kind of resistance movement is visible not only on the global scale but also at national and local levels (Amin 2012). The local-level movements have gained momentum due to the ceaseless implementation of privatization and liberalization policy that have been grabbing and destroying common property resources (CPRs). CPRs are the most significant source for livelihood generation of the rural poor. Since the present economic system cannot ensure the basic needs of the poor, the shrinking CPRs makes the poor more vulnerable. However, the rural community is not the mute spectator of the aggression of neo-liberal economic order. Rather, they have built a strong resistance against this onslaught.

This chapter intends to take the CPRs as an area of contestation among various interest groups to meet their individual interest. The contestation is how the vulnerable section can resist the attack to break their private domain and destroy their livelihoods. The chapter reviews works on CPRs, describing how the *commodification* process, intensified by the forces of globalization, brings CPRs under its hold and how primitive capital accumulation in the classical sense is being perpetrated to all sections of marginalized people. On the other hand, the conservation of CPRs by people together at the local level creates positive externalities leading to dismantling existing power relations. This resistance emerges as social capital that can defy the regressive forces. Having gathered lessons from these studies, the chapter aspires to develop a conceptual framework of cohesive development which is, to the best of our knowledge, largely missing in the literature.

The rest of the chapter is organized as follows: the next section describes approaches to the commons as an alternative. It also presents a few studies which show the practices as a lesson for cohesive development. Based on the lessons of different studies, the third section of the chapter develops the conceptual framework of cohesive development. The fourth section concludes the study, identifying some barriers to cohesive development.

II. Commons as an alternative

Approaches to commons

In India, where around 60 to 70 per cent of the population lives in rural areas, common property resources, including forests, water bodies, coastal fisheries, rivers, and mangroves, have been a traditional source of livelihood (Dasgupta 2005). This list is not exhaustive. No individual has exclusive property rights over the CPRs, which are accessible to the whole community (Jodha 1986). Beck and Ghosh (2000) noted that despite vast regional variations in India, apart from being an important source of income generation for the rural poor, women and children are mainly engaged in the work of CPRs. Therefore, the preservation of the commons is very important for the rural community from the gender perspective as well. However, the implementation of liberalization and pro-market policy has been destroying their CPRs with the help of the state and thus systematically excluding poor people from the access to it.

Gordon (1954) first exposed the economic theory of open access. His interpretation was that open access resources are overused. Therefore, it is better to restrict its use given its finite size. Hardin (1968) later termed it as 'the tragedy of the commons'. However, it was debated that Hardin has made a grounds for private ownership of resources or at least 'centralized management system of the resources'. However, Harvey (2012: 68, cited in Öztürk et al. 2014), deals with this issue otherwise. He explains that individual utility-maximizing behaviour and private property rights create the tragedy of the commons. This fundamentally reflects on the failure to protect the common interest by allowing individual property rights. Therefore, the question is to find 'creative ways' to serve the community interest. This creative way, as Öztürk et al. (2014) argues, in the present situation is manifested through resistance – collective actions of people to the market forces.

Öztürk et al. (2014) also noted three important approaches to the commons: (i) the commons as social practice, (ii) the commons beyond the domain of private and public, and (iii) the commons as an emanatory notion. The first and third ideas are interconnected since they emphasize hard work, joint action, and cooperation. The kind of behaviour that emerges as social practice produces what Giddens (1984) refers to as the conditions in which agents are able to reproduce the resources. The privatization process grabs natural commons to make more profit without any control by the state. The curtailment of the commons takes place at the cost of the group or community to produce value or assets for a few through privatization (Öztürk et al. 2014). Ostrom (1990) proposes some principles for effective management of local CPRs. Institutional change is one of the main principles for the effective monitoring of CPRs. However, the power relation built into the institution has not been considered (Ray and Bijarnia 2007). The existing power relation bears important implications for the outcome of CPRs.

While capitalism tends to turn everything into a commodity,[8] CPRs are not left untouched by this. Neo-liberalism has intensified the process of commodification through globalization, resulting in CPRs, as a source of livelihood of the poor, being greatly curtailed. Commodification has become a natural phenomenon under the current neo-liberal economic order. This has threatened the existence of CPRs on which the dependency of poor rural people has been immense. Against commodification, the preservation of CPRs appears to be a strong alternative for the development of the poor. This development is essentially cohesive in nature since it promotes and nurtures the idea of cooperation. This advances a kind of kinship and caring mind-set for the community to which one belongs. This can ultimately fight against the onslaught of CPRs.

Numerous studies clearly establish this case. However, since it is not possible to evaluate all of this research, we instead have chosen a few studies which seem to best forward the case for cohesive development.

Why are the commons important?

Öztürk et al. (2014) show how smallholders' rural families of Turkey have built resistance to the ongoing commodification of agriculture being imposed in the Turkish economy. This commodification has been implemented by neo-liberal policy dictated by the World Bank by cutting input subsidies, putting in place a price control mechanism, and paving the way for the entry of international capital. The entry of capital, with the help of the state, into the rural area severely shrinks the natural commons and has a significant impact on the rural hinterland. Against this aggression of capital, the rural community has built resistance to save their livelihood and social relations. This resistance has two distinct characters. Firstly, peasant families managed to retain their autonomy by not selling their land to the capitalist and agri-business entrepreneurs. This has led to strengthening the kinship and other ties across socio-geographical space. Secondly, the families have developed a kind of social practice that directly defies the logic of capital by developing a non-commodity circuit. Thus, the example of Turkey presents a locus of resilience through developing 'solidarity networks' based on the social commons. This resistance exemplifies a third-order social arrangement which is quite distinct from the state intervention as well as the profit-making logic of private capital.

In a series of studies, Jodha (1985, 1986, 1990, 2000) shows how poor households rely on CPRs for their livelihood options in India. He also shows that the decline of CPRs creates danger for the very subsistence of these households by degradation of a community asset. This also leads to the erosion of environment-friendly survival options for the people.

Ray and Bijarnia (2007), examining village commons of two villages in Rajasthan, critically explored how the institutional structure could influence significantly the development achievement. The village, which could renovate existing institutions by altering the power relation, had achieved a higher institutional outcome in terms of equity. This renovation was possible due to the effective participation of the villagers. The alteration is important for the sustainability of the village commons given the wide socioeconomic heterogeneity. Any service provided externally that is authoritarian in nature can never eliminate the discriminate character of the institution; compare this to the outcome being achieved through the active participation of people. Mishra and Kumar (2007), while studying the pastureland of Rajasthan, also underscore the significance of institutionalization of CPR management. They show how the major benefits of CPRs go to the dominated groups' panchayati raj institution. Therefore, the need is to understand the underlying rural dynamics that prevent the proper management of CPRs.

Kurien and Vijayan (1995) examined how fishermen of Kerala expand their income base without choosing the technology of free market. The system is so developed that it creates a communitarian feeling and caring system that itself produces a kind of positive externality, even under the great strain of the market mechanism's fierce attack. Because of this connection, the authors put forward the case for institutionalizing such examples for their sustainability.

Beck and Ghosh (2000) studied seven villages of West Bengal across different agro-ecological zones. They found that 12 per cent of the income of poor households is contributed by CPRs. The authors insightfully commented that CPRs might be considered a backward source for an economy if new policy being designed for promoting the modernization and industrialization would absorb the poor people who depend solely on CPRs. Since the present economic order fails to do so, CPRs are to be conserved as an alternative source of livelihood generation. They also put forward the case for institutional mechanization to protect CPRs.

Iyengar (1989) studied 25 villages of Gujarat spread over different geophysical regions. The study reveals the significant depletion of CPR land, which has a strong implication for village life. He prescribed some policies that emanated from the study. Firstly, he suggested stopping privatization of land except for housing. Secondly, a regulatory mechanism should be in place. Village-level institutions like Village Panchayat may play a vital role in this context. He categorically mentioned that no external organization could do this work effectively. The requirement is to reorient the panchayati raj institutions so that they can promote and protect CPRs.

Bon (2000), examining the management of three types of common property resources – communal forests, grazing lands, and gravity flow irrigation systems – concludes that community management of CPRs by rural poor and state agencies may complement each other to build effective institutions. In this context, collective action may emerge as a powerful response to the dichotomy between private and state-owned resources.

We have cited a few studies on CPRs, just to promote an understanding of how different mechanisms of CPR management can uphold the spirit of cohesive development at the local level, defying the logic of capital advanced by international organizations such as the IMF and the World Bank. Some clear insights have emerged from the studies cited: (i) CPRs constitute a major part of income for the rural poor, (ii) there is a continuous decline and degradation of CPRs leading to depletion of the environment, (iii) the over-riding of CPRs needs to be controlled by devising regulatory mechanisms and strengthening local-level institutions such as panchayati raj institutions, (iv) power relations built into the institution should be broken, and (v) community develops a social practice beyond the logic of market and the intervention of state to sustain their basic livelihoods.

The main finding, however, of all the studies reflects upon the immense capacity of the local-level community to build a resistance against the onslaught of the existing economic order. Öztürk et al. (2014) distinguishes this resistance into two categories. First is direct resistance against commodification by nurturing and innovating traditional practices through developing a localized market relation and integrating the resource management. The second is indirect resistance. Strategic in nature, it emerges through income differentiation – being employed outside of the agricultural sector. This helps protect their land from being sold off.

This resistance generates the social capital which comes out from the society. Historical evidence shows how human resistance wins out over strong power like imperialist forces.[9] However, it is also important, as mentioned earlier, to interconnect these practices to the national- and international-level resistance movement. Otherwise, the sustainability of all of these practices may be questioned and compromised. This helps conceptualize the model of cohesive development.

III. Conceptual framework

Based on the understanding derived from the various studies, this section attempts to conceptualize the notion of cohesive development. Four ideas are proposed here that conceive cohesive development: (a) positional objectivity, (b) humanism, (c) institution, and (d) problematic.

a. Positional objectivity

Sen (1993), in a seminal contribution, put forward the idea of positional objectivity. Objectivity emphasizes the object without any reference to the context, what Nagel (1986) termed 'a view from nowhere'. However, as Sen argues, objectivity defined as position independent – not a view from nowhere – has a certain advantage, but in social science, positional objectivity is certainly important. Positional objectivity emphasizes objectivity as perceived from a definite position (Sen 1993). The sun is objectively much larger than the moon. But "the sun and the moon look similar in size" from the earth (Sen 1993, p. 128). Hence, we observe a solar eclipse. Sen explains this claim by saying that although the sun is much larger than the moon in size, which is scientifically proven, this fact cannot explain the occurrence of the total solar eclipse. How can the 'tiny' moon cover the 'huge' sun? The answer can be drawn from the following 'positional claim'. From the earth, the sun and moon look similar in size. The claim is based on a positional observation – the observation from the earth.

This idea has immense implications in social science. Sen (ibid) presents a comparative picture of the health status of Kerala and Bihar. Kerala, the most developed states of India, has achieved the highest level of life expectancy at birth, whereas Bihar lags far behind. But a field survey reports a very low level of morbidity with extremely high rate of mortality in Bihar. Sen, disentangling this scenario, indicates towards the self-perception – 'the point of view of the persons themselves'. In other words, in social science analysis, the contextualization turns out to be very significant. The model or method justified for Kerala might not be applicable to Bihar.

This implies that the examples illustrated in the previous section cannot be replicated in other cases. The adaptation of any methodology must depend upon the prevailing 'concrete' historical condition of the region concerned. The conceptualization of cohesive development must recognize the prevailing condition. Therefore, positional objectivity is an important dimension of cohesive development.

b. Humanism

The idea of humanism has attracted many philosophers over the centuries. Not only for philosophers and for the academic community, the popularity of humanism transcends across society. In the late eighteenth and nineteenth centuries, humanism gained popularity and turned out to be the most influential idea during the Enlightenment era. The Protestant movement against the orthodoxy of Christianism upholds the spirit of humanism. In India, the emergence of Buddhism in ancient India and Sufi and Bhakti movements in the fourteenth century reflects a kind of resistance against social oppression. This resistance also espouses the idea of humanism.

Jean-Jacques Rousseau wrote, 'Man is born free, and everywhere he is in chains' in his *Du Contrat Social* (Bagchi 2000). But who chains man? In the next sentence, Rousseau (1762, p.2) replied, 'Here's one who thinks he is the master of others, yet he is more enslaved than they are'. Human production is not only meant for self-consumption but for exchange as well. This particular characteristic of production distinguishes human species from the rest of the animals (Sayers 2017). This same capacity has brought immense segregation within human civilization through ownership of the means of production, which leads to the alienation of human beings.[10] This, as Marx said, isolates all basic aspects of a human being and prevents the fulfilment of potential. In other words, the labourer who produces goods does not possess or control the goods (Heinrich 2013). Thus under capitalism, a human being becomes an object. Polanyi (1957), in the same line of argument in his magnum opus *The Great Transformation*, depicted how the market-based economy was 'disembedded' from the society and cultural sphere. This leads to the subordination of social life into the mere economic realm in order to meet the requirement of capital (Clark and Longo 2017). Before the advent of capitalist society, economic systems were embedded within institutions and cultural practices. In other words, economic activity was a function of the social organization. The endless motive of capital accumulation transforms all human relations into 'money relation'. Therefore, the present economic order deepens the alienation (Clark and Longo 2017).

Luis Althusser criticizes the idea of humanism that Marx developed as the 'Theory of Alienation' and levelled it as not Marxist.[11] The basic idea of Althusser was that humanism emanates from the social relations prevailing in the society. Therefore, humanism dominates by the ideology of the ruling class.[12] He distinguishes two kinds of humanism: class humanism and socialist humanism. Socialist humanism, as Althusser termed, is an ideological concept, promoting personal humanism, while class humanism is scientific. On the other hand, two distinct groups of theorist adopt the approach of humanism. The first group mainly consists of psychoanalysis, which concentrates on the 'fractured self' of humans, ignoring the cohesive identity of humanism. The second group, influenced by Marxism, rather than considering the individual self, focuses on social groupings and institutions.

In *Theses on Feuerbach, No. 10*, Marx clearly took a stand:

> The standpoint of the old materialism is civil society; the standpoint of the new is human society or social humanity.
>
> *(Theses on Feuerbach, No. 10)*[13]

The idea of humanism has evolved time and again over the era and advances a philosophical and ethical understanding arguing for freedom of mankind in true sense, not in terms of material gains but to realize one's full potential.[14] The idea could be encapsulated by portraying human species as social creatures. However, from the womb of the scientific and ideological standpoint that conceives humanism, we can simply interpret humanism as a space which creates an opportunity for all. It is operated not at the mercy of a few powerful groups, and it upholds the human spirit to achieve its full potential. Therefore, humanism is to be reckoned as an important pillar of cohesive development.

c. Institution

The entry of institution as a factor of socioeconomic outcome or development is a relatively new phenomenon. North (1991, p.97) defines institutions as 'the humanly devised constraint that structures political, economic and social interactions'. The constraints, as North mentions, are both informal (sanctions, taboos, customs) and formal (constitutions, law, property rights). Missing in all analyses of institutions, however, is the power relation inherent to any institution (Ray and Bijarnia 2007).

Cohesive development is a long-term dynamic phenomenon which needs to be sustained. Therefore, an institution should be built to serve the common interest. Transaction cost (TC) in economic exchange plays an influential role in determining the volume of economic activities. This cost includes information cost, bargaining cost etc. In a perfectly competitive market situation, it is assumed that a transaction cost of zero is desirable. But in reality, it exists nowhere in society. There is always some degree of transaction cost involved in the market. An institution is an organization that may reduce the transaction cost to boost economic activities.

Therefore, an institution is required that will work for the interest of common people in a way that diminishes the transaction cost. One of the components that can reduce the transaction cost is the smooth flow of information. But as noted earlier, an in-built power relation within institutions impedes this reduction. Lui Althusser analyzes power through a top-downwards model, in which ideological state apparatuses function rather than repressive state apparatuses (Ferretter 2007). Michel Foucault, focusing on a bottom-up model of power, criticizes this idea (Mills 2003). He was particularly critical of the conceptualization of power as the 'capacity of powerful agents to realize their will over the will of powerless people' (Mills 2003, p.34). To Foucault, power is not processed but performed by devising a chain of net (ibid). This net is nothing but the institution. Therefore, to build an appropriate institution, this power relation must be broken. The question is how to break it. Foucault answers this in his book *The History of Sexuality*, 'where there is power there is resistance' (*ibid*, p.40). Therefore, resistance comes up as the main weapon to break the power relation. CPRs have the property of non-excludability. But they face the problem of free riding. Consequently, the indiscriminate use of CPRs causes depletion and ecological imbalances which ultimately affect the source of livelihood generation. Therefore, a regulatory mechanism needs to be devised. The building of a local-level institution can make certain rules and regulations to control and sustain the use of CPRs.

In the case of India, the 73rd and 74th constitutional amendments ensure local self-government at the grassroots level. However, two decades after the creation of these amendments, local government is dominated by those groups who are powerful in terms of having land or assets in the countryside of India, with few exceptions to this bleak picture. Bagchi (2005) appreciated the democratic and participatory functioning of panchayati raj institutions in West Bengal and Kerala. In these two states, these institutions foster the cohesive character of development, though having many limitations. But the breaking of the power structure through land reform is the real basis of success, whatever the degree may be.[15] Therefore, an institution that can function independently without having any stake in the vulnerable section of the society is a prerequisite for cohesive development.

d. Problematic

Problematic is a concept developed by Luis Althusser (Althusser 1969). The idea is that any concept cannot be isolated from the 'theoretical or ideological framework' within which it functions. If it is isolated, the concept's essence will be misplaced. As Althusser (1969, p.62, cited in Ferretter 2007, p.34) said, 'Every ideology must be regarded as a real whole, internally unified by its own problematic, so that it is impossible to extract one element without altering its meaning'.

Therefore, implicit internal unity is found in the system of thought. This unity, Althusser termed, is its problematic (Ferretter 2007). Therefore, while conceiving cohesive development, all the constituents mentioned are interlinked. They are not mutually exclusive. The change in the meaning of any idea will collapse the very idea of cohesive development.

These four pillars conceive the idea of cohesive development. The question remains regarding the ethics or morality to operationalize cohesive development. In the case of cohesive development, the end result is important. This implies that all actions will be judged by the final outcome. However, this does not mean at all that the *process* is not important and the understanding of deontological morality is fully eliminated (Sen 1999; Bagchi 2000). In fact, Amartya Sen took a middle view. He declared himself to be sensitive to the consequence without denying the process. This model strongly asserts the framework of consequentialism.[16]

IV. Conclusion

This chapter is an attempt to conceptualize the idea of cohesive development. It shows that conservation of common property resources by people together at the local level creates positive externalities leading to dismantling existing power relations. Drawing lessons from different studies, the chapter shows the extraordinary strength of the collective action that can resist the onslaught of the present hegemonic international economic order.

This collective action manifests in the form of social capital that needs to be nurtured. However, the biggest challenge of the resistance movement has revolved around question of sustainability. The aggressiveness of the capital accumulation process with the help of the state apparatus largely has been able to bewilder the resistance movement at the local and national levels. The fundamental reason the movement has abated is the weak or no solidarity among different kinds of movements. Bagchi (2003) distinguishes this movement into two parts: (i) Political resistance: This group believes in waging battle against global finance capital that has established control over major government policy making. Therefore, a long-term strategy is required that can reverse the present process. (ii) The other group wants to initiate a movement immediately against the policy that has crippled the lives of people.

This division has done nothing but weaken the resistance movement. There has been a lack of trust among these movements. Consequently, none of these resistance movements could recognize their real friends. As a result, it leads to diminishing the intensity of the movement, indirectly helps the capital intensification process, and gives enough space to capital for systematizing their strategy to rupture the movement. Moreover, the lack of trust halts the expansion of the organization. Resentment of the people is expressed in many election results. Due to the absence of a credible alternative, people have been choosing political parties which shamelessly propagate racist, fascist, semi-fascist, and communal agendas, be it in India, the United States, or the United Kingdom. This development is essentially an outrage against the neo-liberal policy which has pushed millions of people to live in sub-human conditions and increases inequality.[17] Capital uses this anti-establishment resentment of people to continue its expansion and oppression (Bhaduri 2005). This appears to be a real danger to the human civilization and therefore calls for solidarity among different movements (Bagchi 2003; Ray 2012).

The resentment of the common people, eagerly waiting for a real alternative, needs to be organized.[18] Therefore, a solidarity network has to be built among different kinds of movements. Otherwise, it will be difficult to reverse the present political movement, and cohesive development will emerge as a utopian idea which can be hoped for but not touched. As Bagchi (2007, p.11) commented, 'There is no golden age in the history of mankind, but a majority dreams of it' (author's translation), the examples given here clearly show that it is possible to build a brighter and *golden* tomorrow, taking all the people together. It is possible for cohesive development to emerge as an alternative paradigm.

Notes

1 www.oxfamindia.org/sites/default/files/EVEN%20IT%20UP%202017%20 REPORT.pdf accessed 19/12/19
2 The interested reader may see Dreze and Sen (2013) for detailed data.
3 The concentration and centralization of capital, on the other hand, reducing options of the people to a very limited choice, results in instability and economic crisis (Piketty 2014)
4 In fact, Piketty (2014) shows that the rate of return on capital is greater than the rate of economic growth over the long term. According to him, this is the reason for the concentration of wealth.
5 However, when Thomas More paints an egalitarian fictional society on an island in his fifteenth-century book *Utopia*, it advances new ideas or dreams for an equal and just society.

6 The Human Development Reports (HDRs) published from 1990 onwards gained popularity in advancing the idea that economic growth cannot be the end of any development process but should be a means for fostering human development.

7 After the collapse of the Soviet Union and Eastern European countries, Francis Fukuyama's arrogant thesis of 'end of history' and Thomas L. Friedman declaration that the world has been flattened through the process of globalization are dismissed and reversed as reflected in recent political developments in different countries.

8 The *Communist Manifesto* rightly foresees, 'The bourgeoisie has torn away from the family its sentimental veil, and has reduced the family relation to a mere money relation' (Marks and Engels 1848).

9 This reminds us of the famous job interview scene of Satyajit Ray's film *Pratidwandi* (*The Adversary*) in which the main protagonist of the film, Siddartha Choudhury, in replying to the question of the interviewer to name the most significant world event in the last ten years, answered 'the plain human courage shown by the people of Vietnam' against USA imperialist force, instead of man landing on the moon, as expected.

10 Marx developed the 'Theory of Alienation' in *Economic and Philosophical Manuscripts* of 1844 (Marx 1932). It was never published in his lifetime, but it gained immense popularity across the different schools of thought after its publication in 1932.

11 Althusser argued that Marx's thought got a radical turn in *Theses on Feuerbach and The German Ideology*, in which Marx completely abandons the problematic of humanism. Althusser termed it as 'epistemological break'. However, Althusser himself later and others rejected this idea of any 'break' (Ollman 1971; Sayers 2017).

12 In the economic sense, it also represents a kind of Pareto optimal condition since essentially humanism intends to do better for everybody without harming anybody. Therefore, in this sense, humanism cannot eliminate inequality.

13 www.marxists.org/archive/marx/works/1845/theses/theses.pdf (accessed on 18.03.2020)

14 In this context, Sen (1999) cited the classic study conducted by Fogel and Engerman (1974), in which they discuss the living conditions of the slaves in the nineteenth-century US South. The material condition of the slaves was better than that of free agricultural labourers. The dichotomy shows the contradiction between material gain and real fulfilment of a dignified human life.

15 During the first three-tier panchayat elections in 1978, the Left Front had called for the uprooting of the existing hegemonic power relations in villages to remove the impediments to real development.

16 In *Mahabharat*, the activities of Krishna, be it the murder of Jarasandha or Duryodhan, the attempt to attack Bhishma, the plan for Shalya, or many other countless activities, established him as a consequentialist. But ironically enough, in *Gitaa* he said, "*Karmanye vadhikaraste Ma Phaleshu Kadachana*" (You have the right to work only but never to its fruits. Let not the fruits of action be your motive, nor let your attachment be to inaction), which go against the spirit of consequentialism. In Greek mythology, Prometheus stole the fire from the god. Morally it is not ethical, but he performed a noble job for human civilization. These mythological examples delineate the spirit of consequentialism being judged by the end result.

17 The different nations, such as the US and the UK, are choosing governments which clearly favour a protectionist economic policy. This clearly reflects the growing rejection of neo-liberal policy, executing the mega project of unipolar conversion of the globe.

18 Mrinal Sen, internationally acclaimed filmmaker, in his movie *Calcutta 71*, depicted the turmoil of 1970s Kolkata through an anthology of four stories. In the first story, he deals with a lower-middle-class family, struggling to be protected from heavy rain in their cottage that hardly has a roof. The head of the family, even in this chaotic situation, tries to enjoy smoking and expresses his anger to other family members. His anger ultimately is expressed to a street dog named Bhulu. Finally, the head decides to move with the family to a safer place where he has to share the same room with Bhulu. Sen, in fact, tried to articulate how the wrath of the middle class is misdirected, not targeting the real enemy.

References

Althusser, Lui (1969): *For Marx*. London: Allen Lane.

Amin, Samir (2012): "Contemporary Imperialism and the Agrarian Question", *Agrarian South: Journal of Political Economy*, Vol. 1, No. 1, pp. 11–26.

Bagchi, Amiya Kumar (2000): "Freedom and Developments as End of Alienation?" *Economic & Political Weekly*, pp. 4408–4420.

Bagchi, Amiya Kumar (2003): "The Parameters of Resistance", *Monthly Review*, Vol. 55, No. 3.

Bagchi, Amiya Kumar (2005): *Perilous Passage: Mankind and the Global Ascendancy of Capital*. Lanham, MD: Rowman & Littlefield.

Bagchi, Amiya Kumar (2007): *Sanskriti Samaj Arthoniti (Culture Society Economy)*. Kolkata: Anustup Prakashani.

Beck, Tony and Madan G. Ghosh (2000): "Common Property Resources and the Poor", *Economic and Political Weekly*, pp. 147–153, January 15.

Bhaduri, A. (2005): *Development with Dignity: A Case for Full Employment*. New Delhi: National Book Trust.

Bon, E. (2000): "Common Property Resources: Two Case Studies", *Economic & Political Weekly*, pp. 2569–2573, July 15.

Clark, B. and S. B. Longo (2017): "Marxism and Ecology", in David M. Brennan, David Kristjanson-Gural, Catherine P. Mulder and Erik K. Olsen (eds.), *Routledge Handbook of Marxian Economics*, pp. 399–408. London: Routledge.

Dasgupta, Partha (2005): "Common Property Resources: Economic Analytics", *Economic & Political Weekly*, pp. 1610–1622.

Dreze, J. and A. Sen (2013): *An Uncertain Glory: India and Its Contradictions*. New Delhi: Allen Lane, Penguin Group.

Ferretter, Luke (2007): *Luis Althusser*. London: Routledge.

Fogel, Robert William and Stanley L. Engerman (1974): *Time on the Cross: The Economics of American Negro Slavery*. Boston, MA: Little, Brown.

Giddens, Anthony (1984): *The Constitution of Society: Outline of the Theory of Structuration*. Cambridge: Polity Press.

Gordon, H. S. (1954): "The Economic Theory of Common Property Resource: The Fishery", *Journal of Political Economy*, Vol. 62, pp. 124–142.

Hardin, Garrett (1968): "Tragedy of the Commons", *Science*, Vol. 162, No. 3859, pp. 1243–1248.

Harvey, David (2012): *Rebel Cities*. London: Verso.

Heinrich, M. (2013): *An Introduction to the Three Volumes of Karl Marx's Capital (Translated by Alexander Locascio)*. New Delhi: Aakar Books.

Iyengar, Sudarshan (1989): "Common Property Land Resources in Gujarat Some Findings about Their Size, Status and Use", *Economic and Political Weekly*, Vol. 24, No. 25, 24 June, pp. A67–A77.

Jodha, N. S. (1985): "Population Growth and the Decline of Common Property Resources in Rajasthan, India", *Population and Development Review*, Vol. 11, No. 2.

Jodha, N. S. (1986): "Common Property Resources and Rural Poor in Dry Regions of India", *Economic and Political Weekly*, Vol. 21, No. 27.

Jodha, N. S. (1990): "Rural Common Property Resources Contributions and Crisis", *Economic & Political weekly*, Vol. 25, No. 26, pp. 65–78, June 30.

Jodha, N. S. (2000): "Waste Lands Management in India", *Economic & Political Weekly*, Vol. 35, No. 6, February 5.

Kurien, J. and A. J. Vijayan (1995): "Income Spreading Mechanism in Common Property Resources: Karanila System in Kerala's Fishery", *Economic & Political Weekly*, pp. 1780–1785, July 15.

Marx, Karl (1932): *Economic and Philosophic Manuscripts of 1844*, Progress Publishers, Moscow, 1959.

Marx, Karl and Frederick Engels (1848): *Manifesto of the Communist Party*, Foreign Language Publishing House, Moscow, 1953.

Mills, Sara (2003): *Michel Foucault*. London: Routledge.

Mishra, Pradeep Kumar and Mukul Kumar (2007): "Institutionalising Common Pool Resources Management: Case Studies of Pastureland Management", *Economic & Political Weekly*, Vol. 42, No. 36, pp. 3644–3652, September 8.

Nagel, T. (1986): *The View from Nowhere*. Oxford: Clarendon Press.

North, Douglass C. (1991): "Institutions", *The Journal of Economic Perspectives*, Vol. 5, No. 1, pp. 97–112.

Ollman, B. (1971): *Alienation*. Cambridge University Press, Cambridge, London

Ostrom, E. (1990): *Governing the Commons: The Evolution of Institutions for Collective Action*. New York: Cambridge University Press.

Öztürk, M., J. Jongerden and A. Hilton (2014): "Commodification and the Social Commons Smallholder Autonomy and Rural – Urban Kinship Communalism in Turkey", *Agrarian South: Journal of Political Economy*, Vol. 3, No. 3, pp. 337–367.

Piketty, T. (2014): *Capital in the Twenty-First Century*, Translated by Arthur Goldhammer, Harvard University Press, Cambridge, Massachusetts, London, England

Polanyi, K. (1957): *The Great Transformation*. Boston: Beacon Press.

Ray, S. (2012): "Economics of Solidarity: Economics of the 21st Century", *Economic & Political Weekly*, Vol. XLVII, No. 24, pp. 39–48.

Ray, S. and M. Bijarnia (2007): "Power Relations and Institutional Outcome: A Case of Pastureland Development in Semi-arid Rajasthan", *Ecological Economics*, Vol. 62, No. 2, pp. 360–372.

Rousseau Jean Jacques (1762). On the Social Contract; or, Principles of Political Rights, Translated by G. D. H. Cole (accessed from https://www.ucc.ie/archive/hdsp/Rousseau_contrat-social.pdf on 18.03.2020)

Sayers, S. (2017): "Alienation", in David M. Brennan, David Kristjanson-Gural, Catherine P. Mulder and Erik K. Olsen (ed.), *Routledge Handbook of Marxian Economics*, pp. 135–142. London: Routledge.

Sen, Amartya (1993): "Positional Objectivity", *Philosophy and Public Affairs*, Vol. 22, No.2 pp. 126–145.

Sen, Amartya (1999): *Development as Freedom*. New York: Oxford University Press.

Kurien, John and A.J. Vijyan (1995): "Income Spreading Mechanisms in Common Property Resource: Karanila System in Kerala's Fishery", *Economic and Political Weekly*, Vol.30, No. 2, pp. 1780–1785.

10 Formal, informal, social and unsocial economy

Waste and the work and politics of women[1]

Barbara Harriss-White

1. Introduction: three subfields in development

This chapter has two purposes and is divided into two distinct parts. The first part introduces and critiques the concept of the solidary economy, whose capacity to provide an alternative model of development to capitalism is at present being widely discussed and questioned in India, as elsewhere. I will introduce three separate subfields in the study of development that must be conjoined if the potential of social solidary organisations is to be assessed in India's economy. In the second part, I integrate these subfields and use ethnographic evidence from women's work in the waste economy of a South Indian town to answer questions about solidary organisation.

The three subfields are the solidary economy, the informal economy and the politics of subaltern women. The question at issue is whether, in the overlap between the solidary and the informal economy, distinctive forms of empowerment for women may be generated which challenge both the logic and modes of expansion of capitalism and the movement towards Polanyi's destructive market society.[2]

1.1. Solidary/solidarity economy

Rather than covering an entire economy, the solidary or solidarity economy (SSE) is a fuzzy term denoting a subset of economic activity and of civil society consisting of distinctive organisations. As well as economic objectives, social (and now environmental) ones are pursued through forms of self-organisation in co-operative, associative and solidarity relations (Utting, 2013). Not only is the term subject to multiple meanings, multiple terms are mobilised for similar practices. The conceptual literature includes the solidar(it)y economy, the social economy and social enterprise, the moral and ethical economy, the human economy (Hart, 2008), the popular and share economies and cohesive development. Laville's authoritative review of its institutional genealogy (2010) frames the SSE through a range of forms of *organisation* and poses their *economic and political contexts* in history as both enablers and obstacles to them.

Through this method we see that *trades unions* have mobilised workplace – and class – solidarities. In some rare circumstances their objectives have developed from the class-based improvement of work conditions to the cross-class and democratic governance of capitalist entities through works councils and worker representation on boards. *Worker self-management* has developed direct economic democracy through co-operatives and collective action (most advanced in the service sector). Self-managed organisations, however, are prone to be disunited over the question whether private property should be abolished (and the position of self-managed activity in struggles between classes). They are contextually threatened from monopolies on information, from the prevalent felt need for functional specialisations and increasing formalism in the delegation of work practices. *Worker acquisitions of companies* have tended to be driven by the motive of need rather than political choice: forced on workers by threats to livelihoods by the relocation of multinational corporations and the development of global supply chains. Trades unions then navigate alternative logics either of support or of opposition to these collective forms of management.

Faced with 'austerity' (cuts and privatisation of public services), deindustrialisation and unemployment, *proximity services* have been organised along collective – and often voluntary – lines, maintaining childcare crèches, libraries, community transport, prisoner support groups and mutual domestic help. Then the fusion of environmental politics with those of worker justice has motivated the *collective provisioning* of 'fair trade' and organic products. *Microfinance* has diffused widely through the formation and management of groups, not only in response to group collateral but also for other solidary purposes such as the transformation of daily life, political consciousness and ecological and social change. For the latter objectives it is next to impossible to assign money values, but *from* the latter perspective the restriction of objectives to the minimising of risk through collective collateral/collective responsibility for repayment is reductionist and does not do justice to the social scope of microfinance groups. *Local currencies* involve the calculation of exchanges according to values specific to each 'convivial' group, often with the additional aim of confronting and avoiding the national money supply (and its tax system).

Laville's analytical genealogy is derived from evidence for sustainability. With very few exceptions, the size of the SSE relative to the national workforce or GDP is not relevant to his argument about the conditions of existence of solidarity organisations. It is enough that these institutions all involve collective management and are embedded in 'reflective' activity 'for the common good' – though the common good may be qualified by class interests and by scale. Whether run for profit (not necessarily for profit maximisation), for a return exceeding or equalling costs, or according to a system of values where such concepts are irrelevant, the SSE has to resist pressures to develop from being in opposition to or an alternative to what is variously called 'market organisation'/'modern capitalist markets'/'globalisation' towards what Laville calls 'pragmatic realism' and public recognition as components of the neoliberal economy and its market-driven politics. While Polanyi saw market transactions as one of three modalities of exchange (markets, reciprocity and redistribution), and while later redactions of Polanyi cast these three as mutually exclusive, SSE organisations negotiate non-market behaviour – reciprocity and/or redistribution – in hybrid institutional forms. They operate in the circuits of capitalism as combined and contradictory institutional forms (Laville, 2010). Indeed John Davis (1990, 1996) comparing Melanesian exchange with that of contemporary Britain through nearly a century found that the Trobrianders had names for 80 kinds of exchange (according to goods, people and their relationships, and time periods) of which just one was for profit maximisation according to market rationality. And in contemporary Britain, he describes repertoires of exchange varying with motive and purpose, status differences in transacting parties and contexts, etiquettes, deceits, moral norms and legal regulations. All three of Polanyi's modes of exchange are seen to interact. It is the arrogance of mainstream economics to reduce economic motivations to self-interest – amenable to formal mathematised modelling. Davis concludes from a wealth of evidence that all economic activity is conditioned by culture and ethics. They have real consequences.

Some of the consequences of SSE activity are stylised by Laville as embodying four kinds of unavoidable tensions: (i) between Polanyi's three modes of exchange; (ii) between social and political power and challenges to it (which is as close as he gets either to class struggle or to emancipation from gender subordination); (iii) between direct participation and indirect representation in democratic management; and (iv) between contradictory public policy behaviour. While this is a powerful template for the analysis of SSE institutions and practice, at the same time it is a cast iron case for the need for empirical specifics.

1.2. The informal economy

One of these specifics is the status of the forms of the regulatory authority without which none of Polanyi's three types of exchange can function. Plural modes of regulation can co-exist, be combined, be captured as resources or be strategically neglected. Turning to economic activity that is not regulated by state law, and using evidence from Latin America, Laville sees the informal economy as a *refuge from threats* to livelihoods from authoritarian domination, debt crises and social de-regulation. With Chile as his outstanding example,[3] informal, community-based, associational forms of solidarity have acquired/appropriated and managed agricultural land, industrial workshops and consumer provisioning, infrastructure, utilities, housing and the disposal of waste. In productive activity these informal solidarity organisations face continual damage from the forces to which they pose alternatives. They must negotiate the competitive dynamic of capitalist outsourcing and the difficulties of raising productivity and standards of living. They need resources for training and seed funds for productive activity (which can be mobilised from formal-informal relations of hybridity with NGOs). Laville also finds that SSE organisations in the unregulated economy tend to face incomplete citizen rights: access to rights becomes a political goal. And women's sections have additional struggles against the dichotomies between 'public and private, productive and reproductive' spheres; for within the informal SSE they tend to be disproportionately allocated to unpaid work. SS organisations involving women may grapple with internal equality.

But in India, the term 'informal economy' is subject to many other contextual meanings. For some it is all small-scale activity below the annual tax threshold of Rs 3 lakhs. For others the unorganised economy is activity with fewer than 10 workers. This does not mean it is disorganised or unregulated, it means it is socially regulated (Basile, 2013; Harriss-White, 2003). It involves unregistered or even registered but unincorporated firms (the latter being 72% of all firms and gaining access to a mere 4% of formal sector finance). It is small firms not bound by the labour laws. It is the 93% of all the Indian workforce that works without a written contract or access to work rights. And not only does this informal labour toil in small firms but since 2000 it has also become the largest single component of the labour force in the corporate sector and in the workforce subcontracted to the state itself. The informal economy is also unrecorded activity (rent, interest, profit and wages – which includes the black economy (estimated at between 25% and 62% of GDP)).[4]

Like the SSE the informal economy is indeed a fuzzy term. Like the SSE it is also variously labelled: as the economy, a sector, an activity or a kind of work; as the local, mobile, real and actually existing economy;[5] and as medium, small and micro enterprises (MSME), village industries, precarious labour, and lately the 'need-economy'. Given that the latter is defined as non-capital, non-market activity, imbued with a logic of provisioning and not profit maximisation (Sanyal 2007), it may be seen as part of the SSE. Indeed, Sanyal argues that non-polar classes are part of a non-capitalist circuit, hence his term need-economy, which he argues typifies developing economies in general. Ancillary classes (in law, education, health, bureaucracies etc.), domestic reproductive work and petty producers are forms necessary to society which populate Sanyal's need-economy. However, insofar as they are unable to reproduce outside the circuits of capital, they must be considered integral to these circuits and part of the diversity of actually existing capitalism (Jan, 2011; Gidwani and Wainwright, 2014).

1.2.1 India's informal economy

In *India Working* and in *Capitalism and the Common Man*, the socially regulated, informal economy is also argued to be an integral part of India's contemporary capitalism (Harriss-White, 2003, 2012). Substantively, India's informal economy long predates its being identified as such, which has shaped the very poor evidence we have about it: pieced together from economic ethnography and ad hoc surveys. *The Economist* estimates its current contribution to GDP at anywhere between 25% and 70%. It thrives despite poor infrastructure and access to utilities – challenging the textbook view that public and private investment feed on each other (UNCTAD, 2010). It embraces all of Indian agriculture except for plantations, which are however rapidly informalising their workforces (Mishra et al, 2012). Whereas India's formal economy suffers jobless growth, it is the informal economy that has generated almost all the jobs and a significant part of consumer demand (Raj and Sen, 2016). It has a longstanding informal banking sector. It is innovative and expands through the multiplication of tiny businesses. The informal economy is also the cash economy: 80%–90% of the workforce is paid in cash. (For many reasons (itemised in Ghosh et al, 2017), the demonetisation of late 2016 will change this only very slowly.)

Scores of millions of firms operate informally, some wealthy: 5% with wage labour forces exceeding five workers, the vast remainder simply making ends meet. Between 1990 and 2011 the average number of employees per firm dropped from three to two, often family members, and the rapidly expanding majority of India's livelihoods consists of self-employed people. But, unable to withdraw from market exchange for both productive and reproductive purposes, they are not part of a separate need-economy, nor what Paul Clough (2014) has called 'indigenous, non-capitalist' accumulation. They form an essential element in what Prabhat Patnaik has termed India's 'perverse transformation' (2012). The Indian economy expands on two tracks: accumulation (with the concentration and centralisation of capital) and multiplication (with the proliferation of tiny firms seeded by savings, inheritances and marriage transfers). Despite an active debate over whether petty production/trade/services are wage labour in disguise, these two trajectories are, with few exceptions, segmented (Adnan, 1985; Harriss-White, 2014; Srinivasan, 2016).

REGULATION BY SOCIAL IDENTITY AND STATE

A growing literature has explored the ways in which institutional expressions of culture are – or have developed to become – hard regulators of informal economic activity. Caste, ethnicity and religion embody specific kinds of social authority which regulate exchange. In a new literature, language is being added to India's social structure of accumulation. The largest literature however is focussed on the gender division of labour and gender subordination. The engagement with state regulation by firms regulated through social institutions has developed in ways which have become complicated. These days, firms with employees (even if they comprise a family labour force) are usually registered with the local government, and most will have one or more bank accounts (in fieldwork I have found up to 10). But without social sanction, they under-contribute to revenue from tax (evading local taxes on property and profession, income tax and commercial tax (being 'systematised' as GST)). They tend to ignore building regulation and to flout environmental laws. They abuse the labour force and they follow customary norms about contracts and standards. When provoked, their business associations activate rules about market behaviour that are still governed in large measure by caste and ethnicity.

In minimising costs, especially those of labour, in under-cutting and out-competing the formal sector, India's informal economy generates competitive advantages. Of India's manufactured exports, some 40% are from urban gullies and alleys. Domestically, the informal economy is dominated by trade and services, some of which are sophisticated but still mediated through verbal contracts. It runs on cash plus 'rolling', trust-based credit (Guérin et al, 2013). This flexibility also substitutes for the lack of state social protection. At the same time, a larger scale of subnational business is poised to turn small-town India's bazaars into franchises, branches and agents using banks.

The SSE and the informal economy (IE) are technically fuzzy terms which overlap conceptually, just as Polanyi's forms of exchange overlap in practice. However attributes such as small size (below thresholds for tax or licensing), non-market exchange, unwritten contractual arrangements and lack of state protection or regulation do not imply collective self-organisation, the defining attribute of the SSE. And if culture shapes the economy, as it does, it does not follow that the motivations and behaviour embodied in social institutions trumps the logic of accumulation in the way it is formally defined as doing in SSEs. The threshold between moral and immoral economy is a matter of empirical evidence and its contested interpretation. Informal business associations for example may be self-managed civil society organisations, but their objective is to secure the collective conditions for competition and accumulation.

Scholarly evidence is now emerging that India's informal economy does not only indicate the limits of the state's capacity to enforce its own dense skeins of regulative law, it has long been the result of a deliberate concession to both corporate and local/intermediate capital. Because this is both far-reaching in its implications and also not widely understood, let us summarise the arguments. Research on two of the most important enabling acts for India's capitalist economy, prefiguring by decades what most scholars identify as liberalisation (the Industrial Disputes Act of 1947 and the Companies Act of 1956) shows they were vocally opposed in draft form by the All India Organisation of Industrial Employers, concerned about lack of provisions to ease lay-offs in the former and threats to the managing agency form of 'collective management' of capital in the latter. State regulation has never stopped the expansion of informal 'zones of non-intervention' and the progressive informalisation of the corporate industrial labour force. (Das Gupta, 2016). Meanwhile Karuna's meticulous scrutiny of the

Madras archives for the period from Independence into the early 50s, and of bodies of historical research rarely consulted by economists and scholars of contemporary labour, traces a battle for the size and shape of the non-corporate informal economy (forthcoming). While trades unions were at pains to improve poor physical and economic working conditions, while Gandhian support for small-scale industry made political efforts to protect it, and while certain elements in the bureaucracy supported both forms of regulation, the combined weight of many organisations of small capital and the state resulted in provisions in the Madras Non-power Factories Act of 1947 and the Madras Shops and Establishments Act of 1947 to privatise the regulation and discipline of the workforce and to deny it protection on the grounds of practicality and a fear of rising costs. Legislation was then riddled with loopholes (powers conferred on the state to exempt sectors from the reach of these Acts and to halt prosecutions under it) and strategic vagueness (as in the definitions of factory, of worker and of work). Judicial discretion then led to further exclusions of workers from these Acts' protection and after decades of political dissipation, by the 1970s, the unorganised economy was safely ring-fenced for exploitation by capital fettered only by norms and practices of caste, ethnicity, religion, gender and local business associations. Not only is the informal economy a deliberate artefact but also, because it is deliberate, there is much continuity in the modes of operation of the informal economy before and after the so-called kink point of 1991 and the so-called liberalisation of the Indian economy. This continuity in informal economic behaviour will only be affected by the current drive to cashlessness via the modalities of commodity transactions; other dimensions of regulative law are proof against formalising the informal economy.

A final point of comment concerns women's work – for women are rarely active owners and managers of property. Both the IE and SSE are thought to overlap in care work and other non-market work that is dominated by female labour. The concept of care work covers activity ranging from domestic reproductive work to the 'housekeeping' (clearing) of hospital waste. But a crucial distinction between these activities is that while the former is unpaid, the latter is paid work. Reproductive labour is not separate from the circuits of capital; rather the reproductive sphere is conjoined with circuits of production-distribution-consumption-investment and is also being commodified.

Not for nothing does Karuna (forthcoming) observe that at Independence, '[w]omen who were [thought] vulnerable due to extreme poverty and patriarchal structures were perceived to need protection from labour laws rather than through them' so they could work safely at home! So, along with productive work, large numbers of women work in private sites in the paid and unpaid labour of reproduction/care. And this is taken to reflect their subordinated status. Such work is also stigmatised so that irrespective of supply and demand, wherever tasks can be compared (which is unusual given gender divisions of labour), women get worse terms than do men.

Why this might be so and how women react to it are questions for the final subfield of development addressed in this paper.

1.3. The 'subaltern politics' of Dalit women

Given the sites and positioning of women's work, there are particular forces constraining their organisation, for the SSE 'women are in direct competition with each other and are located at different intersections of inequality in terms of class, race, caste and legal status' (Thara, 2017).

In the case of caste and gender, Karin Kapadia (2017a) has revisited a large literature on Dalit women's politics, meshing it with a new collection of diverse, positioned ethnographies in a Gramscian feminist analysis. While her project does not make for easy generalisations either about subaltern politics of work or about women's subaltern politics, certain processes appear with regularity and we summarise them here.

First, in India, the very upper caste and class patronage relations, which enable formal democracy, work to impede substantive democracy. Dalits – and Adivasis – are incomplete citizens in Marshall's political, economic and social dimensions (Prakash, 2015). While the social meaning of caste is specific to caste status and may have morphed into 'difference' among the upper castes, it is the upper castes which practise choice-denying, persistent and oppressive behaviour towards Dalits, behaviour that is extremely resistant to change. As for destitute people so for Dalits and Adivasis, state, society and economy act either actively or ambivalently against them. The poor are increasingly disproportionately Dalit, Adivasi and Muslim. Studies of new access to banks and relations with the police confirm that for Dalits the state remains an upper caste fortress.

So, in the absence of changes in behaviour by upper castes, Dalits have to mobilise defensively against acts of exclusion, denial of rights, oppressive agricultural, sanitary, sewer, carcass and forced/unpaid work for property owners; against sexual abuse, accusations of promiscuity and the trafficking of girls and women; and for emancipating plasticity in the gender division of labour at times of family breakdown. The social instruments they are recorded as using range from political parties and empowerment through religious conversion to migration and flight. These are institutions unmentioned both in Laville's analysis of SSE or in our earlier account of the informal economy here, just as the work of Dalits is hard to unearth in official economic statistics.

For Kapadia, the politics of Dalit women is produced through *constant struggles in their daily lives*, a politics of resistance to naturalised social deference, a politics involving all social relations. The collection edited by Anandhi and Kapadia provides evidence not so much for class-based collective action against capitalist bosses as for daily struggles against the bearers of patriarchy: husbands and bureaucrats. These have brought mixed results. On the one hand, Anandhi (2013, 2017) has revealed a paradox that while peri-urban Mathamma men and women struggle jointly against caste stigma and practice, success on that front brings with it a new male patriarchal control over women. Here economic mobility for male Dalits results in a reduction of women's autonomy. On the other, Ciotti (2017) and Kapadia (2017b) both find in their urban research that upward mobility for Dalit families is bringing improved rights, roles and autonomy.

So far, Dalit women's politics has made progress in transforming Dalit women's social consciousness and in challenging their identity in the eyes of non-Dalits not only through Ambedkar's injunction for change in dress, adornment and comportment but also through developing a sense of women's honour. Pentecostal conversion in urban settings has led to Dalit women becoming leaders of prayer groups and wider religious activity (Roberts, 2016). Other collective means to empowerment include self-help groups and women's groups, often conscientised/organised and resourced by NGOs. They are examples both of Lavillle's SSE and of formal-informal hybridity. Sometimes riven by internal divisions, it is in urban sites rather than rural areas that such forms of action are likely to transform the paradox of power and patriarchy into a synergy of women's power and challenges to patriarchal domination.

Kapadia (2017a) concludes that Dalit women's politics develops everyday praxis in the slippages, openings and contradictions of historically specific forms of bourgeois hegemony. But that justice continues to be denied.

This review of three subfields of development suggests three sets of questions about the intersection of the gendered informal and solidary economies.

I   (From 1.2) how is the economy institutionally regulated? (From 1.1) to what extent is the informal economy a refuge which operates with a logic different from that of capitalist accumulation?
II (From 1.3) how are property ownership and the labour process gendered? What are the economic and social consequences?
III (From 1.1) what is the gendered significance of collective, self-managed activity in the 'everyday praxis' of caste and ethnicity?

Positioning SSE research

All empirical research is grounded and positioned. Empirical research on the solidary economy is normally positioned by finding, analysing and making visible instances of solidary organisation. This type of research design is inappropriate for questions about the relative importance of SSE in GDP, in a local economy or in employment; it omits the context in which these organisations may fail, which is as important as the conditions which nurture such activity. Without a wider context it is also hard to measure impact, and positioned research focussed on SSEs may lead to exaggerated inferences about cause and effect – as when an SSE is credited with raising literacy levels way outside its sphere of action. Other ways of knowing are also needed. Here, our position is derived from a spatial territory – a small town – and a sector – the waste economy, on which field research was carried out in 2015 and 2016.

2. Work and gender in a small-town waste economy

2.0.1 *The significance of waste*

All human activity generates waste,[6] and in contemporary capitalist society the way in which raw materials are obtained and waste is later generated and disposed of makes a rift with the material and energy balances of nature – a 'metabolic rift'. Waste is without value, but the moment it spends without value might last a few minutes before it is recycled as raw material or last for all eternity. India's waste is among the fastest growing in the world and ranked third after the US and China is terms of volume. Hoornweg et al. (2013) in *Nature* expect 'peak waste', the moment when efficiencies in waste production and disposal in India outweigh the absolute physical mass of waste driven by growth as yet 100 years into the future. Not only is waste experienced as chaotic as it piles up on all kinds of land, whatever its tenurial status, it is epistemologically incoherent. The ways in which it is classified and understood vary with positioning and are incoherent and probably wasteful too.[7]

Yet the waste economy is, like the informal and solidary economies, a specialised subfield in development whose literature is focussed on manual scavenging, solid waste management and technology, and the relations between the formal and informal sectors. This literature is rich in calls for solidary action, given the manifest failures of state and market to control urban waste. Two years before manual scavenging was made illegal in 1993, Anil Agarwal (1991), ever sensitive to appropriate technology, argued for peoples' participation in waste management 'at the mohalla level', after which there have been regular demands for participatory institutions, citizens' decision-making, and the formation of co-operatives of waste workers to gather, segregate and compost (e.g. Annapu, 2012; Eswaran and Hameeda, 2013). The allure of solidary organisations of informal workers takes several forms: the protection of livelihoods, cost saving for corporations and municipalities, reductions in landfill with the enhancement of supplies for recycling, improvement in public health and reductions in GHG emissions due to reuse rather than incineration, vital public services.

The growing literature on achievements in the informal and SSE of waste points to the importance of collective responses to triggering events: such as collective strikes and strategic public sleep-ins by waste workers to secure insurance payments for the families of workers asphyxiated in sewers – and to claim permanent employment status; or cross-class protests at pollution and loss of livelihoods from waste incinerators, or from landfill (Demaria and Schindler, 2015; de Bercegol and Gowda, 2016; Jagtap, n.d.). Informal waste economy workers are also organised in NGOs, often supported by environmental justice movements and trade unions, to lobby for the protection of their livelihoods and for the provision of safety equipment at work. In India some 30 are federated in a lobbying alliance.[8] Workers' co-operatives have been awarded collective contracts for the first stage of urban waste collection (ibid; Annapu, 2012; WIEGO, 2017). Trade unions of self-employed informal waste workers have skilled themselves politically to hold rallies, demonstrate and lobby to protect livelihoods, resist the entry of large-scale private capital and secure citizenship rights (Demaria and Schindler, 2015); they have also proved capable of securing portable waste-sorting sheds, allocating work and monitoring it via short message service (SMS) technology, and investing in composting and biogas (Jagtap, n.d.). The SSE organisation whose leader won the prestigious Magsaysay award in 2016, Safai Karmachari Andolan (SKA), has – in an ongoing and constant struggle – transformed the disposal of human waste. Over three decades SKA has mobilised over 6,000 volunteers, campaigned for safe working conditions, liberated 600,000 manual scavengers, rehabilitated and reskilled them for alternative livelihoods, secured cash assistance, made use of courts to outlaw manual scavenging and secure redress for state crime and negligence, lobbied the then National Advisory Council (NAC), local and national legislators, organised direct action to demolish dry latrines and exposed and attacked caste prejudice (Singh, 2013; Wilson, n.d.). NGOs focussing on retraining and alternative livelihoods have added literacy and language competences too (RoyChaudhury, 2013). Case studies emphasise that women are capable of collective action for social purposes in the waste economy: for protests against pollution and the organisation of waste work (Annapu, 2012; WIEGO, 2017).

The waste economy is clearly a useful, exemplary sector in which to examine the intersection of informality, SE and women's politics. The literature, however, whether for advocacy, celebration or analysis, is replete with case studies that are scattered. It tends, with exceptions, to record spasmodic responses to upheavals in the urban waste economy, and is notably confined to metros. It generally avoids the friction and conflicts over the 'public bad' of waste among informal workers, between them and the local municipal workers, and between both and the state and the new large scale of family or corporate capital in waste, conflicts confronted in Cavé's situated ethnography (2015). To provide a contrast, the rest of this paper contributes field material from a small-town waste economy.

2.0.2. The significance of small town India

Almost all research into all aspects of waste is metropolitan, only research into open defecation is at all rural. Urban India is thought to produce 62m tonnes per year, 70% of which collected – of which but 30% is thought to be 'treated'. Of urban human waste, a mere 12% is treated. So it is as a neglected development problem as well as a manifestation of the 19th-century metaphor for the metabolic rift, 'town and country', in which social progress is focussed in towns but at the expense of rupturing essential cycles of stocks and flows of nutrients and chemicals, that a small town was selected as a unit for research.

This is a South Indian town whose official population in 2011 was about 70,000. The town generates about 35 tonnes of waste per day (Municipal Data 2014–15) though one sanitation engineer's estimate was double that. It is sited close to new transport arteries, under rapid outwards and upwards expansion from an early 20th-century core of wholesale and retail markets, administration, public and private education, health and newer services for entertainment (10 cinemas and 23 halls for large marriage events). Socially cosmopolitan, packed with local and long-distance in-migrants from professional and labouring classes, it is residentially differentiated. A congested central area yields outwards to a periphery of houses and apartment blocks in compounds, interspersed with lines of small single-storey terraces for poorer workers where new build is engulfing local villages and residential 'colonies' for Dalits – ex-untouchables and other 'backward' and very low castes. All spare land everywhere is littered with waste.

The fieldwork reported here (and see Harriss-White and Rodrigo, 2016) indicated that about half this waste cannot be recycled and is left to nature's sinks: river beds (and the sea), sub-soil and, increasingly, socially produced land surfaces including verges and a 7-acre, pestilential, overflowing dump-yard.

2.0.3. *Circuits of waste production and disposal*

Since the classifications and meanings of waste follow such a wide range of principles so incoherently that they defy the concept of a 'system', for analytical and practical purposes a conceptual order has to be imposed on matter and activity which may in practice be disordered or have many kinds of order. One coherent analytical order can be imposed by following the generation of waste in the sub-circuits of capital (in industrial production, distribution, consumption, the production of labour and the reproduction of society).

In our discussion here, the sub-circuit of production generates waste in activity exemplified by clothing accessories, rice mill and industrial alcohol industries; that of distribution involves waste in Indian Railways and the wholesale vegetable market; consumption waste occupies the municipal sanitation workforce, that of a private subcontracted cleaning company, a hierarchy of private waste recyclers and informal workers; waste in the production of labour is focussed on those disposing of human waste; and the sub-circuit of social reproduction (the long-term perpetuation of classes) examines the generation of waste in the provision of public and private health services essential to social reproduction and the delivery of alcohol (without which the waste workforce would not work and society would also not be able to reproduce). Coherence was also derived from the systematic inquiry into the livelihoods, enterprises and collective action evoked by waste: physical trajectories and social processes have been researched through the life-worlds of those working directly with it in the sub-circuits of capital – those who supply waste, receive gifts of waste, and gather, share, barter, buy, sell, bulk, dump and dispose of it.

2.0.4. Exploratory fieldwork

Exploratory fieldwork involving interviews with more than 80 waste workers (mostly individually, while a few spoke in small informal groups) was carried out in January–February 2015. While the sectors of the Indian economy are often spatially concentrated (Stanley, 2015), the waste economy (WE) is not a site: the waste-generating sub-circuits of capital form a set of dispersed spaces, places, concentrated nodes, physical flows and social networks pervading the town and transgressing its built, political-administrative and social boundaries. Since much of the WE is unregistered and its totality is unknown to any single individual, qualitative exploratory fieldwork ventured 'outwards' from the formal municipal labour force into the informal economy of waste using a snowball sampling method plus early-morning traverses of the town together with observation. For each of the very many livelihood niches discovered, despite several interviews at strategic points like the municipal sanitation labour force, resources had to halt the snowball after a minimum of two separate respondents, usually a man and woman, providing corroboration of their evidence and experience. In this exploratory fieldwork, the need for representation has had to precede the principle of representativeness.

Waste workers are among the poorest and most stigmatised in India. So 10 agents of change – lawyers, activists in movements and NGOs, caste and business association presidents and politicians – were also interviewed in 2015; and 15 town-level officials met us individually in 2015 and January 2016 – over a hundred respondents in all. We had further conversations about waste with householders and businessmen.

In the account that follows, the evidence derived from the circuits of capital (analysed elsewhere: Harriss-White, 2017, 2019) is reassembled, and where possible gendered, to address the thematic questions listed at the end of section 1.

2.1. (From 1.2 and 1.1) institutions and the modes of regulation of waste

The WE may be socially marginalised but it is not a non-capitalist refuge nor is it an exclusively Dalit domain. It is institutionally complex. Here we examine the institutions of class, regulation, social identity and agency.

2.1.1. CLASS

The list that follows shows that the WE has developed a hierarchy of accumulation. It maps both the diversity of waste enterprises and the formation of classes. Apart from the polar classes of capital (a small number of accumulating firms) and labour (small to large informal wage-labour forces) (as in models 1.2 and 1.3), most firms are located in between: as own-account enterprise (OAE) and self-employment (SE) (as in models 1.4 to 1.7). OAE and SE are forms of petty production which has in turn been theorised either as in transition to the polar class of labour (Bernstein and Byres, 2001) or micro-capital (NCEUS, 2007) or as already part of the wage-work force in 'disguised' relations of dependence, which rob this labour of freedom (Banaji, 1977).

There is no doubt that some SE waste gatherers are locked into debt relations of disguised wage labour (DWL). But while others are paupers, trapped in low incomes and excluded by both risk and lack of collateral from tied DWL, autonomy in self-employment is an aspiration of many (Harriss-White, 2013). However, whether dependent or not, the returns to SE and the balance between consumption and investment rarely allow accumulation; yet SE persists and expands by multiplication rather than accumulation. Where market exchange exists, SE workers in the WE also faces adverse exchange relations on markets other than labour: markets for the sale of gathered waste; markets for credit; and markets for plots of land. So there are several fault-lines preventing mobility and blocking the formation of polar classes in the WE: first, between capitalist asset-owners who accumulate and SE firms which do not; second, between autonomous SE, SE tied as DWL and those too poor for this; third, between capital and wage labour; fourth, between on the one hand municipal labour that is formally entitled and unionised but actually threatened with insecurity and deteriorating entitlement, and on the other the bulk of wage work which is casual, unentitled, un-unionised and paid at poverty wages. While the WE shows that class formation is a process marked by economic segmentation, within classes it is further striated by informality.

LIST OF BUSINESS MODELS IN THE WASTE ECONOMY, 2015 (with indicative examples)

1.1 Public sector labour force

  i   Large labour force (130+), full rights at work, unionised (e.g. municipal sanitation workers or MSW);
  ii Small labour force (<5) – variable work rights – some permanently casualised (e.g. government liquor shops and glass bottle recycling)

1.2 Private business

  i   Registered joint family with 10–500 wage workers – local and migrant (e.g. scrap yards, medical waste, gunny bag depot)

    ii   Private companies subcontracted to state (30–300 wage workers) – local and migrant labour, no union, no work rights, side jobs (e.g. urban consumption waste and 'municipal' rubbish, hospital cleaning and security, railway sanitation)

1.3 Waste 'departments' inside big companies

Specialised labour (3–40) to clean-up, segregate, pack – disproportionately Dalit/Adivasi (e.g. clothing accessories, industrial alcohol, paddy milling, wedding halls, private hospitals, big meals hotels)

1.4 Own account enterprise

Family labour with 1–2 wage labourers and more or less tied suppliers (some with bikes/vans) (e.g. general waste wholesalers, second-hand goods, septic tankers)

1.5 Self-employed agent

As in reprocessing; vehicle/two-wheeler (e.g. scrap, glass bottle recycling)

1.6 Self-employed – barter

With cart or scooter – (e.g. cloth for plastic kitchenware, iron waste for salt, dates, turmeric, onion and tomatoes)

1.7 Self-employed individual

Gathering on foot, with bike or cycle cart [e.g. hundreds in general waste (scavenging before and after the MSW), scores on dump-yard, scores in vegetable market, clearing up slaughter sites and meat/fish sales]

Source: author's field survey, 2015

2.1.2. MODES OF REGULATION – FORMALITY AND INFORMALITY

Over the last quarter-century while the volume of waste has increased by a factor of 8–10 and shifted decisively to being non-biodegradable, the formal municipal sanitation labour force has declined by 60%. Tax evasion starves the local government of resources. Technologies and labour productivity have hardly changed, so an informal economy has ballooned which is now indispensable to the waste system – and so to the rest of local society and economy. The compulsions of new public management, corporate privatisation and 'contractualisation' are replacing public sector employment in waste – in the municipality, in Indian Railways and in the government hospital (with full ILO-style work rights at Rs 15–25,000 per month) – by private sector jobs on verbal contracts, sometimes involving bondage, fetching half to a third the income with no rights and few, discretionary welfare favours.

Not only does this rapidly growing, formally registered private sector operate with an informalised labour force, but also further informal side jobs are essential to supplement the abrupt formal-informal shift in earnings and rights due to privatisation. After the long stints, the workday lengthens further with the sorting and bagging up of waste for it to regain value in transactions with private wholesale recyclers.

For every decent job in waste disposal there must be in the region of 15–20 in the informal economy. Rounds of gatherers mostly on foot, sometimes by cycle or (bonded) cycle carts scour the town before dawn and after the municipal labour force has finished their shift to supply dealers who sort, bulk up and supply a massive depot where recyclable waste is redefined by scores of workers into hundreds of categories for onwards reprocessing. Small fortunes are made by the few Nadar wholesalers dominating the local informal waste economy.

2.1.3. CASTE AND ETHNICITY

The WE is further segmented by social identity. The work is always disgusting, physically dirty, smelly and often dangerous (conditions to which workers never become immune).[9] The WE is naturalised as work for Dalits either because Dalits, freed from ritually polluting work, are nonetheless devoid of choices to leave tasks that are closely related to their original caste-related tasks,[10] or because public space involves the impure mingling of castes whose waste is left 'to fester until someone of the right caste comes by to clean up' (Doron and Raja, 2015, p. 195, discussing Rodrigues, 2009). In the formal WE we studied, about a third of the workforce is not scheduled caste (SC) or scheduled tribe (ST). In the informal WE, most workers are from the lowest castes and tribes. But it is not a domain exclusive to them: other backward castes are allowed entry because the raw material is increasing so quickly that exiguous livelihoods are not yet threatened by the supply of workers. People who have forfeited the social right to be dependent upon others due to addictions, disease, elopement and crime – those who define themselves as 'transients' but who may be transient in one place for years – are allowed to subsist from their livelihoods in the informal waste economy. An estimated 200 such waste workers wash in water holes and tanks and sleep rough, in shacks and under awnings. Remarkably many urban residents choose not to see these workers, just as they avoid seeing physically and socially dirty public space. Capital assets (from firms resizing cement and gunny bags to the ownership and management of the big scrap yard and its fleet of trucks) are in the hands of upwardly mobile other backward castes (OBC) Nadar migrants from the South.

2.1.4. HUMAN AND NON-HUMAN AGENCY

'We are machines'. Here an FMSW[11] refers to the inhuman physical drudgery of her work. 'I live two lives. I am human outside work' (said a Kattunaicker FMSW). But the Irular waste collectors,[12] who may number 150–200, are distinguished by all the other elements of the Dalit and Adivasi WE workforce. 'We never talk to them' (FMSW – Paraiyar). 'We have no contact with them' (ST association president).

Their work is segregated in time (before and after the MSW have cleared the streets of the town) and in space (on the dump-yard after non-recycled waste reaches its resting place). They are looking for usable plastic, polythene, paper, iron and other metals, boxes and wrecked furniture not collected by others. 'They are not really humans' (female Paraiyar informal scavenger). 'We are treated like animals' (self-employed dump-yard Irula). Paraiyars and people from other scheduled tribes called them 'beggars' and 'drunkards'. Of Irulars, we were told 'a dog is still a dog even if you bathe it'.

There is a difference between feeling like a machine and being treated like – and feeling like – an animal.

Why are Irulars thought by others not to be fully human? This is not an easily answered question. Irulars have a unique permutation of attributes, many of which are individually associated with other groups of Dalits or Adivasis or low-paid workers (Charsley, 1997). First, their closeness to nature: their past association with rat and snake catching, their knowledge of the world they 'share with animals' as stewards, hunters and fishermen; their make-shift settlements in hilly forest habitats (after multiple evictions), or pushed to the tops of urbanised hills ('their' territory encroached upon by others) or squatting on municipal land – never with title. Irulars wash in water holes or tanks (for most have not been provided with water). Their combination of fluent oral expression but extensive lack of formal education (with few of their children in school even now) is unusual even among local Dalits and Adivasis. The relative independence of their women, the routine consumption of alcohol by almost every adult, marks them out. But by themselves, none of these attributes is unique to them.

Whether as cause or as effect of their 'marginalised humanity' in the eyes of others, those who need their entitlements – ration cards and ST certificates – most for access to basic utilities, education and employment, are by far the most poorly enfranchised as citizens. Addicted to alcohol, unable to afford rice at market rates, their few ration cards have to be circulated between households.[13] 'Socially excluded', they are discriminated against by being ignored and shunned by others in the waste economy. They are actively socially expelled by encroachers and are brutally treated with regularity by the state.

In this town, upwards of 500 livelihoods are generated from the edible waste which supplies raw material for its animal economy. 'Animal agency' is also deployed to sort waste. Hundreds of pigs, goats, cows and chicken are produced using the biodegradable waste of the vegetable market, meals hotels, hostels, wedding halls and clinics. Animals tend to be revered by their owners: many are housed, fed and treated far better than are the Irulars. Animals are essential to the waste economy and the *status* of the animal affects that of those who rear them.

We see that the answer to the first question indicates two paradoxes which in turn contain a further paradox. First, although the WE is ignored by society and marginalised by the state, it has developed great institutional complexity through which it is economically and socially segmented. Second, although it is studied separately as an exception in the research literature, it is as seamlessly integrated in the local capitalist economy as any other economic sector. Third, its segmented structure and stigmatisation are not inconsistent with its seamless articulation.

2.2. (From 1.3) the gendering of waste: property and work

2.2.1. MASCULINITY AND PROPERTY IN WASTE

Property ownership in the WE is male. All public property is managed by men as are the control and direction of the corporate private company formally subcontracted to the municipality and the ownership of all the formally registered but informally operated wholesale and warehouse recycling businesses. The exception is a private company on contract to Indian Railways which is managed by a woman. In the municipal labour force, both men and women are forced to buy from their pay equipment (such as clothing, gloves and masks) that is inadequately provided by the municipality, or not at all. These tiny 'informal' private assets in the public waste economy are widely dispersed. Liquor[14] is widely regarded by women and men as essential to consume before work to brace labour for their experiences and after work as therapy for aching bodies and emotional disgust. Of course rather than an asset, this practice is a costly private liability, one never conceptualised by authority as an essential public investment for work in waste.

2.2.2. THE GENDERING OF THE WORKFORCE

The International Monetary Fund reports that 30% of Indian women work, contrasted with 50% globally (Das et al, 2015, p. 5). Tamil Nadu approximates the All-India average (ibid). Female participation in India is declining, a trend which Heyer (2014) has explained in terms of a standard of living paradox observed among agrarian Arundathiars near Tirupur, Tamil Nadu: as working-class incomes rise, so women tend to be removed from wage work in public spaces and secluded for domestic work and childcare. This reduces their energy expenditure but raises both household status as well as child welfare. Anandhi (2017) has confirmed this behaviour in Dalit households but attributes it to patriarchal force. Kapadia finds radically different forces operating to increase female workforce participation in Chennai where Dalit women aspire for English medium education for children and their own education matches the kinds of jobs available.

In the WE, rough estimates for the formal registered workforce and for the informally contracted workforces of formally registered private firms suggest that, whatever the local participation rate, workforce participation in waste is relatively feminised.

In the formal municipal sanitation labour force a third of the 125 workers are women. The female workforce has been declining ever since manual scavenging was abolished in the early 1990s. The rule that expenditure of municipal revenue on waste should not exceed 49% means that 60 female positions are vacant, but the rule that there should be four female workers per 1000 population indicates a shortage of 80 women. These inconsistent administrative barriers to entry mean that the workforce is chronically short of women. The driving of machinery is male, as is supervisory work. The 285 workforce cleaning the government hospital is 75% female while its supervisors are 50% women. The 40 station and track cleaners in the private company contracted to Indian Railways are 95% women – day-time shift workers – while their supervisors and the night shift are all male. The 50 informal, migrant, bonded workers employed by the private company contracted to the municipality are 50% female, while their supervisors are all male. The labour force of the monopolist scrapping company is 40% local women while the men it employs are all migrants and the supervisors are male. Between them, the four firms washing/'sterilising' used liquor bottles employ 160 workers, all women.

The size of the informal WE labour force is unknown but larger, while the proportion of female workers may be smaller: For instance, 10% of the Kattunaicker scheduled tribal pig herders and just 7% of the collectors of vegetable waste are women. Meanwhile entire families work the surface of the dump-yard, couples are employed to clean the waste of wedding halls and many 'self-employed' women gather household waste with their menfolk at dawn in the town's residential and commercial areas.[15]

Women work throughout the WE but tend to be concentrated in arduous manual labour.

2.2.3. TERMS AND CONDITIONS OF WOMEN'S WORK

The exacting work conditions of the WE are gendered. The municipal workforce performs two shifts a day totalling 8 hours, women clearing dry waste while men gather wet waste. When men fail to turn up (which is said to be not unusual) women have to substitute for men; but the reverse never happens. So work groups are often 'under-manned'. Female sanitation workers also gather, sort and sell waste informally between morning and afternoon shifts, 'saving to educate our daughters'. They bathe and eat only after the work shifts have finished. No drinking water is provided for municipal waste workers in the local government HQ; there are no washrooms for women sanitation workers, nowhere for menstrual cloths or pads. Women have to 'beg access' to private latrines or – 'what an irony' – defecate on the verges. The lack of sanitation often forces women to work short shifts while menstruating, for which they report abuse from roadside households.

The private company deploys bonded migrant married couples in pairs on 8-hour shifts. Some women report having to take their children with them for lack of supervision. A woman paid to manage public latrines near the migrants' shacks said she minds workers' children for free 'but they are always running away' – clearly without access to nurseries or school.

Women cleaning the railways on incomplete, often verbal, contracts with a private employer carry out daytime shifts of 8 hours in which they jet-clean human waste into an (open) drain, clear the 'dustbin' of the station platforms and tracks, and then informally lengthen their day by segregating and selling waste when their shift has ended.

While in the public hospital, the waste shift is 12 hours, in the private clinics and hospitals the shift varies between 8 to 12 hours. The tasks are also fluid, mixing waste work with nursing and even tasks in theatre, and the contract is verbal, shaped by relations of loyalty, age, discretion and patronage. One cleaner in her fifties with adult children emphasised that her work is 'not compatible with family life: the journey and the shifts are so long and tiring'.

Whether in the formal or informal WE, women's work is arduous and hard to combine with childcare and household reproductive work. Little to no provision is made in the workplace for the biological and social needs of women.

2.2.4. EARNINGS AND POVERTY

While the permanent municipal sanitation workers, the only labour paid directly by the state, earn between Rs 15,000 and 25,000 per month plus benefits irrespective of gender, they are being replaced by 'ad hoc' or 'permanently temporary' contracts which discriminate by about 20% against women. In general, holding tasks constant, women working for registered private companies are also paid 20% less than men (Rs 210 against Rs 240),[16] while in the unregistered informal economy they are paid about 40% less (Rs 100–150 against Rs 240–260 (sometimes with food and lodging) for men). Self-employed earnings aren't gendered because where women work they are coupled with their menfolk. Informal self-employment yields between Rs 4–6000 per month, less in the rainy season when self-employed workers report routinely cut back on food. Where we can hold the task constant, women are paid less than men are.

The urban minimum wage in Tamil Nadu (Rs 180 per day in 2015–16) would generate Rs 4500 for 25 days (Rs 5400 for a no-rest month) so waste livelihoods hover above and below the minimum. The minimum wage is not set to provision a family, so these incomes require a minimal ratio of dependents to workers – which explains the appearance in the waste economy of labouring children and the aged.

By contrast the urban poverty line (PL) has been revised upwards (by the Rangarajan Committee using data from the Centre for Monitoring the

Indian Economy) from the Tendulkar-Planning Commission's Rs 33 per day (Rs 990 per month) to Rs 47 per day (Rs 1400 per month) (Jitendra, 2014). By this yardstick, earnings in this essential part of the economy are mostly in excess of the revised poverty line. But clearly for people to reproduce at the PL level of income their basic needs have to be available and subsidised, which is not the case here.

In the past waste workers have had to beg for food. Some women waste workers still report accepting gifts of food from householders (though they no longer take it in their hands or pick it from the ground when householders place it there). However, in addition to food and shelter and time-consuming searches for poor-quality fuel and water, private health, education and dowry costs are now well established to eat into the conventions of 'essential expenditure' of even the lowest status and poorest labouring people (Cavalcante, 2015). The neediest people work in the informal waste economy and the neediest waste workers are the most imperfectly entitled to the social safety net.[17]

2.2.5. STIGMA AND DISCRIMINATION

The social structure in which the WE is embedded is experienced as a structure of violence that forces people who have the lowest social status and the least choice to work without options of exit. While few of those we interviewed experienced discrimination among themselves across caste and tribe at work, more instances were reported in their work-related contact with the rest of society (e.g. passengers expressing annoyance at Indian Railways' subcontracted cleaners if they even touch the inside of compartments and specially abusive commands by medical patients to hospital housekeepers). But there is a long way to go before discrimination is eliminated from what the Reserve Bank of India's governor described in early 2015 as people's 'preparation' for the economy: in housing, school, access to health, transport, temples etc.

In social relations of production, discrimination against waste workers is rife. Though, as seen earlier, one tribe was routinely abused as a group, many other waste workers are now reporting experiences of discrimination not as a result of 'ascribed', group-based identity (their caste or tribe) but rather as the product of 'acquired' characteristics such as poverty, illiteracy, the dirt of this work and the need to drink alcohol that it inevitably leads to.

Female gender, however, is with rare exceptions an ascribed identity that remains the butt of discriminatory patriarchal practices. Apart from the subordination expressed through lower pay, over-long shifts and reproductive work afterwards, and whatever their caste/ethnicity and the exact type of waste work, women report derogatory name-calling – even by other women; but they are unclear over whether this is due to their inferior gender or to the filthy work. Being gifted by female householders (waste producers) with used sarees at festival times is felt as an insult. Mockery and harassment lead women to avoid working alone in public space. Women report obstruction and 'subtle' forms of harassment in new sites, access to which is also claimed as a social achievement: in queues and in engagement with tellers in banks and in interactions with the police.

Yet the most historically stigmatised work, the disposal of human waste, is no longer reserved for women. It is now Paraiyar and Kattunaicker men who void septic tanks or heave the undifferentiated 'wet waste' from open drains into dump-yard trucks. When male workers are seconded to other government departments, or off sick, women take over the modern form of manual scavenging, though none work underground.

Although the shit-work itself is disgusting and dangerous, if they are municipal employees they report being more 'properly treated' outside the workplace than in the past – as government workers the precise nature of whose job may not be known. 'It is a symbol of our dignity and it's *disciplined* work'. If they are migrant workers for private companies, they are isolated and out of contact with local society due to the barriers of language.

So individual discrimination exists alongside group-based discrimination and may be replacing it – or may be a modern mask for persistent ritual pollution. In India, waste policy is discussed as a problem of technology and finance, rarely one of caste discrimination (Rodrigues, 2009, being an early exception).

While the entire sector is stigmatised, the legal status of women's municipal work in the WE tends to carry authority derived from incomes that are equal to men's. It is clear that in this respect the state is progressive. However, when women with formal contracts supplement their incomes with informal work they struggle against the same social obstacles as those working full time in the informal economy. Sometimes the abusers of women are women. And, with privatisation, the Indian state is dismantling its achievements for women.

From this glimpse of women's work in the waste economy it appears that the starting hypothesis cannot be other than that most livelihoods in waste, the worst tasks and the poorest paid waste work, are done by women.

2.3. (From 1.1 in) the SSE: collective action for social purposes

The question of SSE in waste can be addressed in three ways. First, the means by which motivations and objectives other than profit – or wage – maximisation relate to – or oppose – the dynamics of capitalism in the WE. Second, the conditions under which collective organisations exist for social purposes other than profit maximisation. Third, the specificities of women's SSE in the waste economy.

2.3.1. PROGRESSIVE SOCIAL FORCES

First among forces competing against profit-making is the struggle against the structural violence of caste and tribal identity. Scholars of Dalits have identified the expansion of caste-neutral work, migration and education as the progressive solvents of Dalit subjugation (Gorringe, 2010). Caste-neutral work generates new economic opportunities; migration to urban sites allows anonymity and new forms of self-presentation and reinvention of identity; education potentiates escape from the WE and changed social attitudes to caste. To this list, our fieldwork suggests self-employment.

Property and self-employment Waste workers regard self-employment as important for self-esteem. Dalit waste workers aspire to a quantum leap not as labour ('at best as nurses or construction workers' . . . 'shinning up electricity poles will always be a Dalit job') but in self-employment. 'In this town we have set up in auto-rickshaws, lorries, sand, vehicles maintenance and sales, chauffeuring, tourism, construction, beef and mutton', said a Dalit social worker forgetting to mention the two septic tankering businesses. Although the sectors he named are evidently distant from the launch pad of the WE, they act as examples of the liberation offered by the town. Self-employment provides work, accumulation possibilities and esteem.

The social collectivities most sustained by these progressive social and economic forces are ascribed rather than acquired and confined selectively to Paraiyar Dalits, rather than Adivasis. They promote empowerment and enable individual mobility more than collective mobility. Women are not in the vanguard of these processes. Waste work is also definitely at the rear. While the state offers skeletal social protection for the victims of the market economy, none of these social processes are in opposition to the logic of actually existing capitalism. They are all consistent with it.

2.3.2 COLLECTIVE ORGANISATION

Laville's listing of prominent forms of SSE (in part 1 here) frames the discussion of SSEs in which WE workers participate.[18]

Trades unions In a new phase of labour mobilisation, trades unions are moving out of factories and cities into India's smaller towns. Three quarters of the municipal labour force are members of the Centre of Indian Trade Unions (CITU). Public sector workers who join unions often hedge their bets (a matter of risk aversion, of maximising possibilities for gains) and belong to more than one. 'Multiple membership weakens the unionised (public) sectors' (said liquor men).

'Unions don't deal with discrimination' (MSW). But according to the leaders of the waste work section, unions like CITU[19] have indeed 'protected municipal waste workers against the charge that discrimination is an individual matter', arguing instead that it is due to *class* (and not to caste). The TU has achieved modest gains in work conditions. 'Officials no longer persecute us. Supervisors no longer skim our pay. And the unions stopped us accepting demeaning treatment'. CITU has also played a key role in negotiating bank access for MSW. But the outcome is contradictory. On the one hand union members have registered with banks; on the other hand their treatment by bank staff and clients is experienced as discriminatory.

Self-management through caste associations   Caste and ethnicity are ascribed at birth and hard to exit. But this identity is often collectively organised in associational form. The pig-men's association, for instance, is preoccupied with three objectives: dispute resolution within the caste – currently about the theft of piglets and the sharing of water; the organisation of long-term collective aspirations (the temple, a wedding hall); and the representation of the ST to the state: ST certificates, patta, housing subsidies and bank loans. Even though solidarity in caste and tribal associations prevails among people in different class positions, there is no federation between caste associations, quite the reverse, and actually a strained contact between this (officially) tribal association and other local low-caste associations.

Self-management through kinship   Meanwhile the oppressed Irulars' collective organisation is not through a formal association but through kinship – 'we are united' – as an ethical unit as well as a practical unit of work. Internal negotiations take place over mutually exclusive routes for waste gathering and times of day, sharing the take, respecting the stacked-up verge-side waste property of others etc. Yet they have little mediated access to their ST certificates and know nothing of the nearby political mobilisation of Irulars against police scapegoating, published in the English press, let alone the work opportunities provided by Madras Snake Park further north.

Alternative currency/exchange   A restricted kind of waste recycling is famously governed by barter at fixed and customary, not market, rates of exchange. While there is no formal organisation to manage barter rates, men on bikes, cycle-carts or scooters patrol residential areas in institutionalised, mutually exclusive circuits, making bilateral exchanges: waste cloth for plastic kitchenware; or waste metal for fruit, vegetables or spices.

Small in scale, multipurpose in objectives, SSE in the waste economy is not recognised by its members as economic or non-economic. Non-economic collective objectives extend to work (e.g. respect in transactions). There is also no division between collective activity in the productive and reproductive spheres. Collective economic objectives may play out in the sphere of social reproduction (e.g. access to citizenship rights, agreement over the costs of marriages). Women participate in this activity but are marginalised. These niches for the collective preconditions for economic activity are not to be interpreted as opposition to the market economy, rather as attempts to make it work better in the socially fractured collective interests. Despite such collective activism, or because of it, the manifold problems of waste workers as *waste workers* are only represented through their ascribed identities as Dalits and Adivasis. And then, fragmented through the lenses of caste and ethnicity, their interests and grievances at work and out of work fall to the foot of local associational agendas.

2.3. Women's solidarity economy

While Laville (2010) defines the SSE in formal terms, Kapadia (2017a) sees female solidarity expressed through individual struggles in 'everyday praxis' bridging work sites, productive work in public space and domestic labour.

2.3.1. EVERYDAY PRAXIS

Wherever sited in the WE women dislike working alone and prefer to work with other women or family groups. Non-kin male-female work groups imposed by employers are accepted by women workers. During the working day women then regularly manage work, switches of task, frequent substitution for absent male labour and ad hoc child care. Every morning, women MSW routinely wait until informal Irular waste gatherers have completed a first round of the town's waste, a concession regulated by custom. Groups of women also protect themselves against physical dangers and patriarchal social threats. These groupings are not to be conflated with 'self-help groups' or even chit-funds (which were not mentioned); they are mere zones of freedom from caste and gender harassment at work in which women help one another.

2.3.2. CITU WOMEN'S SECTION

While the CITU is unable to organise labour on informal contracts to private firms subcontracted by the municipality, and while it also cannot organise the informal workforce of self-employed, all the female municipal workers are members of the CITU waste section – in which, according to their women leaders, they seem to operate over many issues independently of male comrades.

The TU is actually a bureaucratic organisation that has had ad hoc achievements and systematic failures. Illiterate women members have been trained as leaders: one Paraiyar, one Arundathiar. They have mobilised CITU women successfully to stop persecution by male TU officials. They have also forced the TU to negotiate the prosecution of the attacker of a female sanitation worker who refused to clean human waste from a verge. After an un-unionised informal worker fell from a bouncing truck and died, TU women threatened strike action and won ad hoc compensation from the municipality for the victim's family. While gender is ascribed, these achievements involve organising across the ascribed status of caste. And while unions are said to be focussing on citizen's rights outside work because of the difficulties of organising at work (Lerche, 2012), these achievements of women are work-related.

However, despite mobilisation by women, the TU is unable to rectify the contraction of the permanent municipal labour force, nor its casualisation and masculinisation. Likewise, it has failed to get non-discriminatory treatment for ill health in the government hospital, though women have campaigned inside the TU about the need for therapy for alcohol addiction and the problems of wet season work and peak disease. Women are never collectively consulted about technology or work conditions by the municipal engineers. Nor has the TU figured out tactics to enforce formal regulations and supervisory discipline among the many state agencies complicit in their neglect.

Waste is a low-status sector for the union, but the solidarity of women waste workers spans caste and ethnicity. Solidarity acquired through work has prevailed over the several forms of ascribed status which pervade the waste economy. The TU's armoury of political action also spans labour in the public and the private sectors. The public sector employer, the municipality, operates with a Polanyian distributive logic (in mobilising resources through tax, organising their allocation and operating redistributive transfers), but, although the unionised workforce acts under terms and conditions incomparably nearer those of the ILO's Decent Work than do workers in private registered companies and informal self-employment, the capitalist logic of commodification, privatisation, contractualisation and casualisation is diffusing through the state and prevailing over the logic of public service.

3. Conclusions

Research designs are always positioned and exclusive. Research focussing on SSEs may not reveal the conditions under which SSE is, or is not, able to thrive: for this, a research design with a wider lens is needed. Our differently positioned research, taking a sector of an urban economy, finds but little SSE. It also finds conditions antithetical to SSE.

3.1. The SSE

There is scant evidence for the existence of acquired solidarities niched within the market economy.

The informal and SSE overlap through ascribed collectivities such as caste associations (when the latter are unregistered, which is rare), and through kin and work groups (which, although they are commonly imposed by supervisors with registered contracts onto workers with informal ones, are not resisted by workers themselves). Like other economic sectors, that of waste is collectively regulated in a multiplicity of ways in which social objectives operate within the capitalist system rather than in opposition or resistance to it. Other social objectives are more important than opposition to capitalism: above all, vanquishing the disrespect meted out to tribal, low-caste and female-gendered workers in and outside work. Social objectives such as respect and autonomy, or environmental responsibility, might form a platform for opposition to capitalism in the future; but of this, in this town, there is currently no sign.

Our field research has generated instances of Laville's tensions: first, in hybrid forms of exchange. Market exchange meshes with principles of distribution – par excellence in the municipality faced with the invasion of new public management practices. Reciprocity and market exchange characterise the rolling of loans and the Irulars' practice of sharing their product. Reciprocity and distribution are combined when the trades union pools resources and engages with reciprocal support to workers.

But non-economic motive(s) cannot be read off collective organisational forms. Business associations for example are collective SSEs, but they seek to control and disempower labour, to regulate markets and to develop countervailing power over the regulations of the local state.

This is not to deny Polanyi's classification of the three modes of exchange or his pendulum swing towards market exchange and commodification. But it is to argue – with John Davis – that these modes are not mutually exclusive – just as the formal and informal economies are not mutually exclusive. Laville's contradictions over power are mostly starkly reflected in low takings, wages and bargaining power in the labour force contrasted with accumulation and concentration in registered private firms that exploit informal wage labour.

Tensions between direct participation and indirect representation affect all the SSEs in the waste economy. Caste associations and TUs represent the interests of working members through a union bureaucracy (which often fails), while their female membership thrashes issues out through direct participation at work. By definition the SSE is autonomous from the state but in practice the state acts in tension with it – illustrating Laville's tensions of social and political power and public policy practice. On the one hand, the verge-side work camps of itinerant WW in the centre of town are not the object of raids or harassment because the police and municipality need their collective work. On the other hand, by abolishing reserved jobs in waste, entry is no longer a collective right and must depend on the individual mercy of a bureaucratic patron.

We conclude from these instances of SSEs that Laville's theorisation of power struggles and of institutional politics relates convincingly to a small-town WE that is currently under-developed in SSE organisations. But schisms between ascribed identities and occupational identities together with ambivalent behaviour from local government prevent interests in SSE from thriving. Without comparative research and further positioned research, both on waste and on small towns, we cannot conclude whether either are unusually lacking in SSEs.

3.2. *The informal economy of waste*

While there is strong evidence that this segmented waste economy is an informal labour sponge and capable of being an economic refuge of last resort for socially expelled people, it is not (*pace* Sanyal or Laville) an SSE refuge from threats from capital – a refuge operating with a different logic from other parts of the economy. On the contrary, the informal economy has long been deliberately entangled in the local capitalist economy, to which it is vitally important. The rare cases of exit from the informal economy to the formal economy are not acts of opposition to capital, they express aspirations to increase wage income or to accumulate within the system. And just as production and waste are inseparable, so are the formal and informal economies of productive activity and of waste, and so is male and female work.

3.3. Gender

Though the official data is flimsy, the WE appears to be disproportionately feminised. Many women find livelihoods in the WE in the fractured niches evoked by Kapadia for Dalit women's work in general. Nevertheless, despite the entire WE being stigmatised, the terms and conditions of their work are clearly more oppressive than are those for men. Women work harder for longer hours, lower pay and fewer social entitlements. The social processes described here as 'solvents' work on caste rather than on patriarchy. Where women are found to group together, their objectives are to improve the terms and conditions under which they are incorporated into the capitalist economy and reduce patriarchal oppression – and not (yet) to oppose, transform or abolish either. Outside their waste work, women face continued patriarchal discrimination, and in new forms and sites. Only women on contract to the state are able to organise, and while the union is blind to caste and ethnicity it is still a patriarchal institution where gains for women have been matched by failures.

The social objectives defining the SSE are melded with economic ones since, like the rest of the economy, India's waste economy is a cultural artefact. Only when the practices and economy of waste are disengaged from caste and patriarchy is the WE likely to be technologically transformed and might SSEs have a greater role to play. Meanwhile waste will become one of India's most obtrusive and intractable development problems.

Notes

1 This chapter has been developed from a keynote paper for the conference 'Solidarity/Moral Economic Practices of Women in India', Jindal Global University, India, March 4–5, 2017. It is offered in memory of the late John Davis. I wish to thank Isabelle Guerin, Karin Kapadia, Swagato Sarkar and Ratna Sudarshan for their useful comments on earlier versions. Field research was carried out in 2015 and 2016 with Gilbert Rodrigo under the London School of Economics' research programme on Poverty and Inequality, directed by Alpa Shah to whom I am also grateful. The usual disclaimers apply.
2 Polanyi argues that market society is a state impossible to attain in a pure form.
3 Where half the workforce was said in 2010 to be working in the informal solidary economy.
4 See Harriss-White, 2012, 2018 for discussions of sources for these data.

5 Of this, Harriss-White wrote: "It has been called 'real', 'actually existing', and even 'authentic', to distinguish it from the imagined economy that is so often inferred from official data in a selective way to support orthodox economic theories. However, 'real' is also a term used to distinguish productive activity from financial capital; and the implication of 'authentic' – that the top of the economy is *in*authentic – is unacceptable." (2003, p. 3).

6 So does biological activity, but that is outside the scope of this essay.

7 See Harriss-White 2018 for an illustrated review of the massive literature on waste.

8 See the Global Alliance of Waste Pickers on its Indian allies: http://globalrec. org/who-we-are/ and see http://wasteportal.net/en/events/workshop-comment-optimiser-la-contribution-des-petits-entrepreneurs-priv%C3%A9s-pour-am%C3%A9liorer-l%E2%80%99a, accessed 19/12/19

9 The dump-yard is toxic slaughterhouse waste – pigs, chicken, mutton and fish scrapings go putrid rapidly and seethe with maggots, drains collapse, verge-side and workshop dust pollutes the atmosphere, and moving vehicles have hit waste workers.

10 See Harriss-White 2003 and Harriss-White and Rodrigo 2016 for the socially specific nature of relations of caste authority

11 MSW = municipal sanitation workers; M and F = male or female.

12 Also known as Kattukar (forest people who migrated south from Andhra several centuries ago).

13 A situation far from confined to Irulas (Ehrenrich, 2014).

14 There is much social hypocrisy about alcohol consumption and status. Rich young women are well known to drink liquor but in private hotel bars, not in public streets.

15 The ridicule of women generates high turnover in the male wage labour force of septic tank cleaning lorry fleets.

16 Supervisors were reported by CITU leaders to skim as much as Rs 80/day from the migrants' wages.

17 The public distribution system was frequently praised as a nutritional safety net for SC and ST waste workers and its rations are often shared among kin without ration cards.

18 Solidary/collective organisations such as business associations, chambers of commerce, political parties, Dalit panthers, and civil society, Ambedkar Paserai and Dalit legal activism are currently not relevant to the waste economy so are omitted here (see Harriss-White and Rodrigo, 2016).

19 Few MSW members of CITU are members of the political party – the CPI(M) with which CITU is associated.

References

Adnan, S. 1985, 'Classical and contemporary approaches to agrarian capitalism', *Economic and Political Weekly*, vol. XX, no. 30 pp. PE53–PE64

Agarwal, A. 1991, 'Karachi's Gandhi: The sanitary revolution', *Sanitary Insights*, New Delhi, Centre for Science and Environment

Anandhi, S. 2013, 'The Mathammas', *Economic and Political Weekly*, vol. 48, no. 18, 4 May

Anandhi, S. 2017, 'Gendered negotiations of caste identity: Dalit women's activism in rural Tamil Nadu', in (eds) S. Anandhi and K. Kapadia, *Dalit women: Vanguard of an alternative politics in India*, New Delhi, Routledge

Annapu, R. 2012, *Sustainable solid waste management in India*, New York, Columbia University and Waste to Energy Research and Technology Council

Banaji, J. 1977, 'Capitalist domination and the small peasantry: Deccan districts in the late Nineteenth Century', *Economic and Political Weekly*, vol. XII, no. 33–34 (special number)

Basile, E. 2013, *Capitalist development in India's informal economy*, London, Routledge

Bernstein, H. and T. Byres. 2001, 'From peasant studies to agrarian change', *Journal of Agrarian Change*, vol. 1, no. 1, pp. 1–56

Cavalcante, M. 2015, 'Feeling rich on an empty stomach: Agrarian crisis and rural consumption choices', chapter 10 in (ed) B. Harriss-White, *Middle India and urban-rural development: Four decades of change*, New Delhi, Springer

Cavé, J. 2015, *La ruée vers l'ordure. Conflits dans les mines urbaines de déchets*, Rennes, Presses Universitaires de Rennes

Charsley, K. 1997, ' "Children of the Forest" or 'Backwards Communities? The ideology of tribal development', *Edinburgh Papers In South Asian Studies Number 7*, Centre for South Asian Studies, Edinburgh University

Ciotti, M. 2017, 'For another difference: Agency, representation and Dalit women in contemporary India', in (eds) S. Anandhi and K. Kapadia, *Dalit women; Vanguard of an alternative politics in India*, New Delhi, Routledge

Clough, P. 2014, *Morality and economic growth in rural West Africa: Indigenous accumulation in Hausaland*, Oxford, Berghahn Books

Das, S., S. Jain-Chandra, K. Kochhar, and N. Kumar. 2015, *Women workers in India: Why so few among so many?* IMF Working Paper 15/5, Washington, IMF

Das Gupta, C. 2016, *State and capital in independent India: Institutions and accumulation*, Cambridge, Cambridge University Press

Davis, J. 1990, *Exchange*, Oxford, Oxford University Press

Davis, J. 1996, 'An anthropologist's view of exchange', *Oxford Development Studies*, vol. 24, no. 1, pp. 47–60

de Bercegol, R. and S. Gowda. 2016, 'Le recyclage informel des déchets à Delhi', photoessai et commentaire, available at http://mouvements.info/recyclage-informel-delhi/

Demaria, F. and S. Schindler. 2015, 'Contesting urban metabolism: Struggles over waste-to-energy in Delhi, India', *Antipode*, vol. 48, no. 2, pp. 293–313

Doron, A. and I. Raja. 2015, 'The cultural politics of shit: Class, gender and public space in India', *Postcolonial Studies*, vol. 18, no. 2, pp. 189–207

Ehrenreich, B. 2014, 'It is expensive to be poor', *The Atlantic*, January 13, available at www.theatlantic.com/business/archive/2014/01/it-is-expensive-to-be-poor/282979/

Eswaran, A. and C. Hameeda. 2013, 'The waste picking community: Some issues and concerns', *Economic and Political Weekly*, vol. XLVIII, no. 22, available at www.epw.in/node/127929/pdf

Ghosh, J., P. Patnaik, and C. Chandrasekhar. 2017, *Demonetisation decoded: A critique of India's currency experiment*, New Delhi, Routledge

Gidwani, V. and J. Wainwright. 2014, 'On capital, not-capital, and development after Kalyan Sanyal', *Economic and Political Weekly*, vol. XlIX, no. 34, pp. 40–47

Gorringe, H. 2010, 'Shifting the "grindstone of caste?" Decreasing dependency among Dalit labourers in Tamil Nadu', chapter 12, pp. 248–266 in (eds) B. Harriss-White and J. Heyer, *The comparative political economy of development: Africa and South Asia*, London, Routledge

Guérin, I., S. Morvant-Roux, and M. Villarreal (eds). 2013, *Microfinance, debt and over- indebtedness: Juggling with money*, London, Routledge

Harriss-White, B. 2003, *India working: Essays on economy and society*, Cambridge, Cambridge University Press

Harriss-White, B. 2012, 'Capitalism and the common man', *Agrarian South: Journal of Political Economy*, vol. 1, no. 2, pp. 109–160

Harriss-White, B. 2013, 'Credit, finance and contractual synchrony in a South Indian market town', in (eds) I. Guerin, S. Morvant and M. Villareal, *Microfinance, debt and over-indebtedness. Juggling with money*. London, Routledge

Harriss-White, B. 2014, 'Labour and petty production', *Development and Change Special Issue: FORUM 2014 September*, vol. 45, no. 5, pp. 981–1000

Harriss-White, B. 2017, 'Formality and informality in an Indian urban waste-economy', *International Journal of Sociology and Social Policy*, vol. 37, no. 7/8, pp. 417–434

Harriss-White, B. 2018, *India's informal waste economy and urban informality: An illustrated tour of the epistemological horizon*, Work in Progress Research Paper 23, School of Interdisciplinary Areas Studies, Oxford University, available at www.southasia.ox.ac.uk/sites/default/files/southasia/documents/media/bhw_waste_rev_lit_2018.pdf, accessed 19/12/19

Harriss-White, B. 2019, 'Waste, social order and physical disorder in small-town India', *Journal of Development Studies* Vol. 55, pp. 1–20, available at https://doi.org/10.1080/00220388.2019.1577386

Harriss-White, B. and G. Rodrigo. 2016, 'Discrimination in the waste economy: Narratives from the waste-workers of a small town', *Journal of Social Inclusion Studies*, vol. 2, no. 2, pp. 3–29.

Hart, K. 2008, *The human economy*, ASA On-line no. 010.1

Heyer, J. 2014, 'Dalit women becoming "housewives": Lessons from the Tiruppur region, 1981/2 to 2008/9', in (ed) C Still, *Dalits in neoliberal India: Mobility or marginalisation?* New Delhi, Routledge

Hoornweg, D., P. Bhada-Tata, and C. Kennnedy. 2013, 'Waste production must peak this century', *Nature*, vol. 502, pp. 615–617

Jagtap, S. n.d., *Best practice Initiatives in waste management–Pune City*, Pune, Pune Municipal Corporation

Jan, M. A. 2011, 'Ideal-types' and the diversity of capital: A review of Sanyal', Work in Progress Research Paper 12, School of Interdisciplinary Areas Studies, Oxford University, available at https://pdfs.semanticscholar.org/3c9d/1b9cd213f94f1d663dbdb0c70b738c96fb20.pdf, accessed 19/12/19

Jitendra, C. 2014, 'The new poverty line', *Down to Earth*, available at www.downtoearth.org.in/news/new-poverty-line-rs-32-for-rural-india-rs-47-for-urban-india-45134

Kapadia, K. 2017a, 'We ask you to rethink: Different Dalit women and their subaltern politics', in (eds) S. Anandhi and K Kapadia, *Dalit women: Vanguard of an alternative politics in India*, New Delhi and London, Routledge

Kapadia, K. 2017b, 'Improper politics: The praxis of subalterns in Chennai', chapter 10 in (eds) S. Anandhi and K. Kapadia, *Dalit women: Vanguard of an alternative politics in India*, Delhi and London, Routledge

Karuna, D-W. forthcoming, 'The emergence of the informal sector: Labour law and politics in South India, 1940–1970', *Modern Asian Studies*

Laville, J-L. 2010, 'Solidarity economy: An international movement', *Rivista Critica de Ciensas Sosias*, vol. 2, no. 2, pp. 1–30

Lerche, J. 2012, 'Labour regulations and labour standards in India: Decent work?' *Global Labour Journal*, vol. 3, no. 1, pp. 16–39.

Mishra, D., V. Upadhyay, and A. Sharma. 2012, *Unfolding crisis in Assam's tea plantations: Employment and occupational mobility*, New Delhi, Routledge

NCEUS. 2007, *Reports on the financing of enterprises in the unorganised sector and creation of a National Fund for the unorganised sector*, New Delhi, National Commission on Enterprises in the Unorganised Sector (NCEUS), Government of India.

Patnaik, P. 2012, 'The perverse transformation', 22nd Rajan Lecture, IRMA, Gujarat (January), available at www.youtube.com/watch?v = Vy39RVvV_c4, accessed 19/4/2012

Prakash, A. 2015, *Dalit capital: State, markets and civil society in urban India*, New Delhi, Routledge

Raj, R. and K. Sen. 2016, *Out of the shadows? The informal sector in post-reform India*, New Delhi, Oxford University Press

Roberts, N. 2016, *To be cared for: The power of conversion and foreignness of belonging in an Indian Slum*, Oakland, University of California Press

Rodrigues, V. 2009, 'Untouchability, filth, and the public domain', pp. 108–123 in (ed) G. Guru, *Humiliation: Claims and context*, New Delhi, Oxford University Press

RoyChaudhury, S. 2013, 'Scavengers unveil a new life', *Times of India*, November 17, available at http://timesofindia.indiatimes.com/city/delhi/Scavengers-unveil-a-new-life/articleshow/25905018.cms, accessed 19/12/19

Sanyal, K. 2007, *Rethinking capitalist development: Primitive accumulation, governmentality and post-colonial capitalism*, London and New Delhi, Routledge

Singh, B. 2013, *Unseen–The truth about India's manual scavengers*, New Delhi, Penguin

Srinivasan, M. V. 2016, 'Arni's workforce: Segmentation processes, labour market mobility, self-employment and caste', chapter 3, pp. 65–96 in (ed) B. Harriss-White, *Middle India and urban-rural development: Four decades of change*, New Delhi, Springer

Stanley, J. 2015, 'A future not so golden: Liberalisation, mechanisation and conflict in Arni's gold ornaments cluster', chapter 5 in (ed) B. Harriss-White, *Middle India and urban-rural development: Four decades of change*, New Delhi, Springer

Thara, K. 2017, 'Feminist analysis of social and solidarity economy practices: Views from Latin America & India', Conference Concept Essay, Jindal Global University

UNCTAD. 2010, 'Employment, globalisation and development', in *Trade and development report*, Geneva, UNCTAD

Utting, P. 2013, 'What is social and solidarity economy and why does it matter?' *Oxfam*, available at https://oxfamblogs.org/fp2p/beyond-the-fringe-realizing-the-potential-of-social-and-solidarity-economy/, accessed 19/12/19

WIEGO. 2017, 'Four strategies to integrate waste pickers into future cities', *WIEGO, Harvard*, available at www.wiego.org/informal-economy/occupational-groups/waste-pickers#org, accessed 19/12/19

Wilson, B. n.d., *Manual scavenging*, New Delhi, Safai Karamachari Andolan

11 Integrating the informal with the formal

A case of cohesive development in urban waste chains

V. Kalyan Shankar and Rohini Sahni

A female waste picker typically evokes two kinds of impressions in the urban public mind. In the first, she is mobile, moving through public spaces, carrying a sack across her shoulder, rummaging through garbage, picking up bits of waste with her bare hands. In the second, she is static, sitting in an alley amidst a pile of waste surrounding her, sorting the value hidden in this lump. Beyond this isolated imagery acquired from fleeting encounters, we know precious little of her work. Yet, for understanding the afterlives of waste in the many forms we produce it, she remains a key entry point. It is through her subaltern lens that we seek to frame our arguments on cohesive development. As a constituent of a bottom-of-the-ladder labor form, what kind of cohesion is she seeking and with whom? What would result from it? At the outset, these are important questions to address.

As a working definition, cohesion could be understood as a greater formal or informal recognition of the role of different stakeholders, an integration of their interests and concerns in arriving at a desired outcome. Accordingly, depending on the stakeholders involved and the extent of cohesion achieved, the outcomes of cohesive development would vary. From the perspective of waste pickers, the following examples could help explain this further. The waste disposed by households becomes the primary source for materials recovery for waste pickers. This waste is often in a lumped form – combining not just organic and inorganic forms but also contaminated with sanitary waste (such as diapers and sanitary napkins). Greater integration with households could not only improve access to waste but also add to the dignity of their labor. Further, waste pickers are dependent on scrap dealers for the purchase of the retrieved recyclables. In some cases, waste which is potentially recyclable ends up being discarded either because waste pickers do not find it economically viable or because of a lack of market at the scrap dealers' end. A greater cohesion with scrap dealers could not only provide for better economic returns but also ensure higher recycling. At a macro-level, waste pickers derive value from the discarded resources of the city and transform them for the better. Urban local bodies can recognize and formalize their labor, integrate them into the municipal waste chains and governmental schemes of welfare. Cohesion is thus a desirable outcome not only for waste pickers but also for the city at large. The difficult part, however, is to achieve it. While we do not emphasize on any singularity of approach, some of the characteristics of cohesion are worth outlining.

The blueprint of cohesion is a cryptic one, involving multiple, parallel processes of negotiation between different stakeholders. The strategies involved would vary from one stakeholder to another. As a note of caution, all stakeholders may be less than amenable to cohesion and resistant to change. For instance, households have never had to pay for waste collection services. At the same time, they have traditionally had little incentive to segregate waste unless it is profitable to do so, as in the case of newsprint or other forms which could be sold further. How to convince them otherwise? In addition, even though household segregation into dry and wet waste is mandatory under the Municipal Solid Waste Management Rules, its implementation is abysmal. The urban local bodies remain inept at identifying and penalizing cases of non-compliance. How to ameliorate this problem? Such discrepancies are not uncommon across the waste chains, where the role of participants may be either ill-defined or not complied with. Given the positionality of a stakeholder, some linkages may work out better than others. We also have the issue of who should take the lead in pursuing cohesion. Should it happen from the state in a top-down manner? Or would a movement from the grassroots work better? There could be primary and secondary stakeholders, strong and weak ties across them, active versus redundant coalitions between them. Also, cohesion is a matter of evolution. So long as the different parties are functioning in relative isolation, their engagement would be marginal or confined to issues of common ground. They could benefit from the actions of others without having to acknowledge them. With integration emerges a newfound scrutiny and newer points of friction. Even while some broader consensus may be achieved, the underlying terms of engagement continue to evolve towards an agreeable functional homeostasis. Achieving cohesion would thus constitute both the means and ends of development.

For elaborating on our arguments, the chapter is structured as follows. In Section 1, we discuss the usage of the term 'cohesive development' in existing literature and contextualize it to waste flows in a city. In Section 2, we outline the journey of waste pickers in Pune (India), their unionization and integration with door-to-door waste collection from households. As can be concluded from their trajectory, just as development needs to be inclusive and sustainable, it also needs to be cohesive.

Section 1: cohesive development: existing definitions and relevance for waste chains

In literature, a host of adjectives has been used to qualify development. Inclusive development, equitable development, sustainable development, pro-poor development, dynamic development, balanced development, incremental development – the terms in usage are diverse. How would 'cohesive development' be any different from the versions of development already framed? For answering this question, the present usage of the term and its varying contexts require careful examination. In the context of this paper, it would also be imperative to relate these meanings to waste and waste pickers in a city. Two specific aspects of cohesion viz. spatial and social are discussed further.

Cohesiveness in spatial terms. Geographers have historically framed "cohesive development" in relation to regional development. The underlying spatial cohesion could be between a city and its periphery, between an industrial zone and its vicinity, or between two regions that are grossly imbalanced in their prospects of development. Industrial growth is known to be dominated by networks or clusters, which inherently leads to an unevenness of spatial development and harbors inequalities. This unevenness could be traced to the "cumulative causation" argument of Myrdal (1957: 27), where markets left to themselves will drift towards regional inequalities through "backwash effects". The better-off region would end up attracting further resources at the expense of the less-developed one.

"Urban cohesion" is also a valuable allied term to explore – combining elements of spatial and social cohesion and referring to the internal dynamics of the city. Urban spaces can be sites for both "social separation" and "social cohesion" (Toye, 2007). As argued in Vranken (2005: 258), a "cohesive social unit would be an organization, group or city in which a variety of forces are active that are strong and lasting enough to hold that unit together". In the context of the urban, such forces can be spotted in the form of strong local networks of communities or neighborhoods. Correspondingly, the dismantling of the neighborhoods (through processes of gentrification or otherwise) becomes "a hindrance for urban cohesion" (Vranken, 2005: 257).

In the context of waste, spatial cohesion (or the lack of it) becomes relevant at several levels. Waste in its concentrated form is predominantly an urban output. As urban agglomerations grow in size, waste volumes multiply. Given that a city may not be realistically in a position to handle its own waste, some forms of spatial tensions are inevitable. The first visible lack of cohesion involves a city and its periphery. Across India, the dumping of waste in peri-urban landfills has been the trigger for increasing conflicts between local residents and municipal authorities (see The Hindu, 2016, 2017a, 2017b for instances of landfills turning into proverbial battlegrounds). The second layer of mismanagement emerges within the city, from the spatial unevenness of municipal services. Slums in cities are often neglected pockets for waste collection. Further, as cities expand, they bring in adjacent localities/villages into municipal limits. The services of waste collection and disposal remain poorly addressed in these newly integrated peripheries. Third, service providers for waste collection within city wards could differ. In some parts, the services could be handled directly by the municipal body. In others, it could be delegated to private parties or left to the citizens to make arrangements of their own. The nature of services may also differ, ranging from manual door-to-door collection to placement of common public bins to use of motorized vehicles for collection. These operational differences may lead to variations in costs incurred by citizens for managing their waste or alternatively, create different standards or benchmarks. The absence of a 'one city, one model' approach to waste management leads to spatial differences in service delivery.

On a positive note, citizenry and civil society groups in some wards of a city could be more progressive/receptive for experimentation and introduction of newer approaches in waste management. Such pockets exemplify urban cohesion. Decentralization of waste handling, for instance, is a spatial exercise involving creation of localized facilities of segregation and disposal at a ward level. This would not be possible without active support from citizens and their elected representatives.

Cohesiveness in social terms. References to the term "social cohesion" are found passim in literature and carry a wide set of nuanced meanings (see Easterley, Ritzen and Woolcock, 2006; Buck, 2005 for an overview of definitions). Elaborating on its outcome-based orientation, Ritzen and Woolcock (2000: 9) define social cohesion as "a state of affairs in which a group of people . . . demonstrate an aptitude for collaboration that produces a climate for change". How can this integrative process be achieved in the case of waste pickers? Who are the stakeholders whose collaboration can bring this change? Alternatively, should we rely on "cohesive capitalism", which seeks to place the advancement of social inclusion in capitalist hands and relies on the ethics of firms (see Wheatcroft, 2010)? Would privatization of waste be the answer? While the need for social cohesion in waste management is recognized, a host of such questions prevail regarding the processes of achieving it.

In urban waste, the lack of social cohesion is only too apparent. Households are primary producers of waste and yet their participation in efficient waste disposal remains voluntary. The urban local body has the onus of collecting and disposing waste but is often constrained in terms of both finances and labor. Urban waste pickers play a crucial role in diverting recyclable waste forms into the recycling channels and away from landfills. Yet, they receive little recognition for their role in resource recovery and environmental sustainability. Moreover, they are tied in exploitative relationships within the waste chains, especially with the scrap dealers. From the perspective of waste pickers, given their marginalization socially and in the waste chain, their challenges for social cohesion are diverse.

First, waste pickers are self-employed, itinerant labor. As part of the urban poor, they are competing among themselves for access to waste. Waste picking is often engaged by poor migrants in their quest for livelihoods. The activity poses little capital requirements and few entry barriers. As newer waves of migrants take to the occupation, too many people could chase the limited quantity of waste available. Therefore, any internal cohesion among waste pickers is not without its constraints. Second, as a segment of informal labor, how can waste pickers articulate their rights? If they are the right holders, who are the corresponding duty bearers? Should they align with other labor forms in the informal sector or with workers in the formal sector? As argued in Holman and van der Pijl (1996: 55), classes are "social forces whose cohesion derives from the role played in a mode of production". However, achieving such cohesion among informal labor is an arduous task. Among segments of informal labor, there may be little recognition of their own labor or its broader consequences – waste pickers are a case in point. Creation of a common work consciousness remains the key to rallying them. Further, should waste pickers wage an independent struggle or can they possibly align with municipal labor in waste, given their functional similarities? While both segments handle waste, the possibility of this larger coalition is scuttled because of other differences of identity. The latter are formal workers, deriving the benefits of unionization, drawing their incomes from the urban local bodies and engaged in working class struggles – a relatively more privileged lot. Informal waste pickers, on the other hand, typically remain unorganized and form a more disadvantaged segment of labor compared to the municipal cadres. They are also substantially larger in numbers. Third, waste pickers across India have traditionally come from socially disadvantaged and marginalized communities – the Matangs in Maharashtra, Valmikis in Delhi, Paraiyars in Tamil Nadu. Should caste become the basis for social cohesion, where they become part of caste-based alliances for forwarding their struggle? Questions remain on how waste pickers, given the stigma of their occupation, will be perceived and integrated with others. Fourth, the voluntary labor of waste pickers benefits the city at large. Keeping this in mind, in what way can they seek cohesion with the state and households from a position of strength? The urban local body is a passive beneficiary of waste pickers' labor. And yet, recognizing the labor of waste pickers may amount to greater budgetary provisions for their welfare. Would the urban local bodies be able to prioritize social justice over its fiscal considerations? Unfortunately, most city governments in India are unlikely to do so.

Given the previously outlined challenges, what is the recourse for waste pickers? Further in this paper, we discuss their journey for solidarity among themselves and cohesion with other stakeholders in waste as witnessed in the city of Pune (India). Methodologically, we base our arguments on fieldwork and interactions (2014–17) with two interrelated organizations of waste pickers operational in the city.

Section 2: waste pickers and a case in cohesive development

Waste management remains a sore point in urban governance in India. Across Indian cities, the rapid pace of urbanization and economic growth has led to a commensurate increase in both quantity and diversity of waste forms. As per estimates in 2010–11, Delhi generated 6800 tons of municipal solid waste per day; Mumbai generated 6500 tons; a host of cities fell in the range of 1000–3000 tons (Central Pollution Control Board, 2013). The volumes are expected to grow rapidly, making it imperative to devise sustainable waste management solutions. Municipalities in India spend anywhere between 10 to 50 percent of their annual budgetary expenditure on solid waste management (Asnani and Zurbrugg, 2008: 51). The results are far from satisfactory. In 2011–12, urban India generated 127,486 tons of solid waste every day; 89,334 tons of this waste was collected but only 15,881 tons treated (Central Pollution Control Board, 2013). The numbers summarize the problems of waste at three levels – collection, segregation, and disposal.

Across urban India, waste chains can be segregated into two types. The first are the official or formal chains operated by the municipal bodies, employing a combination of its own staff and private contractors. For collecting household waste, municipalities have conventionally provided public bins/receptacles. Gradually, they progressed to operating pushcarts and trucks covering certain defined routes within the city and gathering waste. This aggregated mass, through a fleet of trucks, is disposed of at the landfills or worse still, incinerated in the open. The absence of a robust last-mile-collection system remains responsible not only for the leakages in collection but also for the lack of waste segregation in the official channels. Municipalities remain inadequately equipped to recover recyclables from the mass of mixed waste. Across Indian cities, this task has been taken over by a second, parallel form of waste chains. These are informal ones, fragmented in their operations and involving a network of waste pickers, scrap dealers, and recyclers who are bound loosely and profit from the arbitrages of selling further in the chains. An anonymous body of waste pickers initiates these chains by performing the functions which should ideally be the responsibility of the urban local body. They derive their incomes through collection and segregation of myriad forms of waste – paper, plastic, metal, glass, electronics – and selling them off to informal scrap dealers. Given the functional disconnect across the chains, how can any cohesion be achieved between them?

Several governmental policy documents in India have acknowledged the need for integrating waste pickers in urban solid waste management. As stated in the Report of the High Power Committee on Solid Waste Management in India (Government of India, 1995), "private agencies/NGOs, ragpickers or their cooperatives may be involved in primary collection of solid waste from house-holds/community bins". How can these policy recommendations be realized on the ground? A functional prototype of this formal-informal integration emerged in the city of Pune. First, the waste pickers were collectivized to form a trade union of their own. Second, through the union, the waste pickers could reach out to other stakeholders of waste – the urban local body in particular – for safeguarding their economic and social interests. From this engagement emerged an alternative model of governance that carved a space for the informal waste pickers in the formal/municipal waste chains. The reorganization of the waste chains not only led to an improvement in working conditions for the waste pickers but also provided them with a more legitimate channel for accessing waste.

Internal cohesion. In 1993, Kagad Kach Patra Kashtakari Panchayat (KKPKP), a trade union of those collecting paper, glass, and metals, was formed in Pune. It constituted an important watershed event in the collectivizing of labor associated with waste. In the early 1990s, waste gatherers in the city constituted a heterogeneous lot. Certain transactional forms of waste existed in the market, marked by a gender divide. The *bhangarwala* or *raddiwala* were male dealers who purchased scrap and newsprint respectively from households. The female *dabbabatliwali* purchased glass and other utensils. Some barter forms existed, as in the case of exchange of old clothes for steel utensils or waste for onions and garlic (the traders were referred colloquially as the *kandalasoonwaale*). In some of the industrial pockets of the city, some men would carry large magnets and scout for iron filings which would be sold as iron scrap. These niche forms aside, a large pool of labor comprising of women rummaged from the bins and other public dumps of waste to gather what they perceived as valuable chunks of recyclables. The bulk of those who joined the union belonged to this segment; they were the ones whose work previously lacked any identity.

Chikarmane and Narayan (2010) provide an account of the genesis of the trade union. As they argue, the organizing of waste pickers was centered on an important inversion of outlooks on waste. The endeavor was to "establish an alternate identity for waste-pickers as 'workers' premised on the belief that scrap collection was socially relevant, economically productive and environmentally beneficial 'work'" (p. 3). This internal cohesion paved the way for reforming the organizational and functional aspects of waste collection in the city. The union was able to curb the presence of child labor in the trade. The strategy adopted was to engage with scrap dealers, threatening to boycott such dealers who purchased from children. The creation of a credit society of its own was an equally important intervention. Conventionally, waste pickers were not considered creditworthy given their inability to furnish collaterals. The only lines of credit were through scrap dealers and informal money lenders, which mired them in exploitative financial transactions. The indebtedness with scrap dealers also tied them occupationally, compelling them to sell their waste to the particular dealer and reduced their bargaining power. With the formation of the Kagad Kach Patra Kashtakari Nagri Sahakari Pat Sanstha in 1997, an alternative credit channel formed for waste pickers for their loan requirements. In 2017–18, the credit society handled the savings of over four thousand waste pickers and operated with a turnover of close to 75 lakh rupees.

Engagement with the state. For the waste pickers, the union served as the vehicle for articulating their demands with the state and citizens. In public perception, waste picking overlapped with thieving; waste pickers would be commonly harassed by the police on the grounds of suspicion of theft. The underlying problem was of identity and lack of recognition of their labor. To counter this problem, the union issued identity cards to its members, which were subsequently endorsed by the Pune Municipal Corporation (PMC) and Pimpri Chinchwad Municipal Corporation (PCMC) in 1995–96. This was an important step in the recognition of waste picking as an occupation by the state.

The union was also able to quantify the free, unrecognized labor that waste pickers were providing to the state. As stated in Chikarmane (2012), "each waste picker in Pune contributed US$5 worth of free labour to the municipality every month, and their combined labour saved the municipality US$ 316,455 in municipal waste transport". Similar figures are in place for Delhi, where waste pickers "handle almost twenty percent of the waste generated, reducing the burden of the municipal authorities, saving the Municipality over Rs.6 lakh (US $ 14 thousand) daily" (Chintan, 2006). In Pune, the savings estimate formed the basis for seeking welfare benefits from the state, especially medical insurance. In 2003, PMC acceded to the demand and became the first urban local body in the country to provide insurance coverage for informal waste pickers.

Tripartite engagement with the state and households. In 2007, a strategic, functional realignment of waste pickers was effected by the union through the formation of SWaCH – India's first wholly owned co-operative of self-employed waste pickers and other urban poor. In October 2008, SWaCH entered into a memorandum of understanding (MoU) with PMC. As per the agreement, PMC was to provide the collection equipment and gear, facilitate and pay for the management of operations, and create a special budget for training waste pickers and citizen outreach. The role of SWaCH workers was to engage in the collection of segregated dry and wet waste directly from households. A similar contract was inked with PCMC in 2010.

SWaCH represents a progressive, experimental model of cohesive development, upholding the interests of the state, citizens, waste pickers, and the city at large. In the first phase, 80 elected corporators (*nagar sewak*) signed up for SWaCH, expressing their support and paving the way for door-to-door collection of waste through waste pickers. Within the first few years of its operations, SWaCH expanded rapidly to most of the city wards. In the initial years, some citizens' groups protested against the inclusion of waste pickers in what they saw as a state responsibility. However, the model couldn't have worked without citizen support and the experience has been largely positive. Through the contracts with PMC and PCMC, waste pickers became the official interface between the state and households. They acquired a right to the recyclable waste collected by them while deriving additional income through user fees from households. SWaCH has around 3000 members today, largely women drawn from the KKPKP fold. The organization has been responsible for transforming itinerant waste pickers into waste workers. On the ground, two to three workers collect waste from around 250–300 households. As per latest figures (2018), the organization covered some 610,000 households in the city on a daily basis and was responsible for diverting some 170 tons of waste per day towards recycling.[1]

Negotiating the fine print of social and spatial cohesion. While a broad consensus prevails over the positives of SWaCH, certain points of friction continue to be negotiated between the stakeholders. At an operational level, the lack of segregation and delayed payment (or non-payment) of user fees by households are key issues of contention. While SWaCH workers are mandated to collect segregated dry and wet waste, they also have to contend with substantial volumes of mixed waste. The SWaCH waste collectors are placed at the fist node in the municipal chain, interacting directly with households. In this new equation, households are in a position of power to pass over the onus of segregation to waste workers. For fear of retaliation, the latter are less likely to report cases of non-compliance. The role of the municipal body becomes important in mediating and streamlining these interactions.

With the municipal officials, the struggles of SWaCH are more strategic. As per the PMC-SWaCH contract, the municipal body has the responsibility of building sheds for the sorting of waste. This would require decentralized earmarking of urban spaces for waste-related services. For ensuring efficient recycling, waste needs to sorted, graded, and even cleaned at times. Each recyclable form of waste poses its distinct challenges of accumulation. Glass for example is both fragile and bulky; plastics are voluminous; metals are high in value but sparsely retrieved from household waste. Once segregated, the economic viability of these waste forms lies in selling only after sufficient quantities have been accumulated. In the intermediate period, waste is required to be stored. For this purpose, SWaCH has managed to negotiate and access 66 sites from PMC and PCMC altogether – 32 of them are sorting sheds, the remaining are storage facilities. However, waste pickers have faced resistance from other stakeholders in using these spaces.

For households, waste disposal was a practical necessity; waste had to be pushed out of sight and out of mind. Having waste sorting sheds near residential spaces ran contrary to this perception, leading to protests for their removal or relocation elsewhere. The presence of waste sheds was also argued as a threat to public sanitation and hygiene. The utility of the sorting sheds as spaces for finer gradation of waste was lost upon them. Elected representatives (corporators) echoed similar sentiments, fearing a backlash from households in their respective wards. Municipal officials too were not favorably disposed towards providing sorting sheds for waste pickers, citing opposition from households and corporators. This gradual scaling up of resistance to sorting sheds and efficient waste management practices had to be systematically negotiated and reasoned by SWaCH.

For the waste pickers, having official access to spaces is vital for other strategic interests. Scrap dealers have been the missing parties in the discussion on cohesion so far. Any collective negotiation with them is limited by the fragmented nature of their operations and lack of internal cohesion. Meanwhile, waste pickers continue to remain dependent on them for the sale of waste, exposing themselves to unfair trade practices and economic exploitation. The trade union presently operates two scrap shops in the city, on sites provided by PMC and PCMC respectively. For waste pickers, these shops provide the benchmarks for waste prices in the city. Through accessing more space, the union is seeking to create an expanded decentralized network for the purchase of waste. These fair trade shops would reduce the dependency on scrap dealers (or in the very least, provide for alternative avenues for sale of waste), while providing for higher returns and better terms of purchase. With the assistance of the state and other stakeholders, the union is seeking to counter some of the market-related vulnerabilities of waste pickers and increase their bargaining power.

Conclusion

In the literature on development, the quest for inclusion and sustainability remain paramount. Inclusion is necessary for addressing inequalities; inclusive development is meant to tackle the redistributive challenges of growth. Similarly, sustainable development is vital for addressing the excesses of the Anthropocene and the rapid depletion or contamination of natural resources. In the words of the Brundtland Commission, any development has "to meet the needs and aspirations of the present without compromising the ability to meet those of the future" (WCED, 1987). However, in the sequence of development, inclusion would be the starting point, where all stakeholders are brought to the table. Achieving long-term sustainability through their coordinated action would be the desired outcome. Straddled in between would be the processes of cohesive development – ones that address the concerns of multiple stakeholders and imparts them a voice in the decision making. Arguably, if development has to be cohesive, it cannot be disruptive of present livelihoods in the hope of an uncertain future prosperity. This would be particularly true of the marginalized stakeholders, waste pickers in our case.

As the journey of waste pickers in Pune would illustrate, cohesive development has a transformative potential, adding to the processes of inclusion and sustainability. Cohesion would have to imply something more than inclusion; it would involve mobilization of the marginalized on the ground, imparting them with a sense of self-empowerment and recognition from the state and other stakeholders. The linkages between cohesion and sustainability are equally important. Efficient management of the urban environment and waste cannot be achieved without active participation of the urban poor, especially those laboring in the informal waste chains.

Despite the mutual benefits, presuming that cohesion of waste pickers in urban waste management would happen without a struggle would be wishful thinking. Cohesive development is not a definitive state of being; forces of disruption have to be factored in. Urban local bodies remain predisposed towards private entities taking over parts of the municipal waste chains. The expected outcomes are centralized, capital-intensive, waste-handling solutions – like waste to energy plants. These developments threaten the cohesion achieved by the union with other stakeholders over the years. How do waste pickers, with their decentralized mode of operations through the informal chains, convincingly argue about the value they offer? This is a question for perpetual negotiation with one stakeholder or the other. For waste pickers in Pune, their journey of cohesion has corresponded to a series of claim making from the state and other stakeholders. Some of their demands have been met in the form of greater recognition of work identities. If development has to be meaningful and imbued with social justice, negotiating this cohesion remains the way forward – both in principle and in the fine print.

Note

1 www.swachcoop.com/ accessed on 10 August 2017

References

Asnani, P.U. and Chris Zurbrugg (2008), *Improving Municipal Solid Waste Management in India: A Sourcebook for Policy Makers and Practitioners*, Washington, DC: The World Bank

Buck Nick (2005), 'Social Cohesion in Cities', in Nick Buck, Ian Gordon, Alan Harding and Ivan Turok, ed. *Changing Cities: Rethinking Urban Competitiveness, Cohesion and Governance*, Hampshire and New York: Palgrave Macmillan, pp. 44–61

Central Pollution Control Board (CPCB) (2013), 'Status Report on Municipal Solid Waste Management', Website: www.cpcb.nic.in/divisionsofheadoffice/pcp/MSW_Report.pdf, accessed on 29 June 2017

Chikarmane Poornima (2012), 'Integrating Waste Pickers into Municipal Solid Waste Management in Pune, India', WIEGO Policy Brief No. 8, July Cambridge, MA

Chikarmane Poornima and Lakshmi Narayan (2010), 'Organizing the Unorganized: A Case Study of the Kagad Kach Patra Kashtakari Panchayat', Website: www.inclusivecities.org/wp-content/uploads/2012/07/Chikarmane_Narayan_KKPKP_Organising_the_Unorganized.pdf, accessed on 15 January 2015

Chintan (2006), 'Privatising Waste Services: Clearing Waste or People', *Jahan-e-Kabadi: The World of the Waste Recyclers*, 1

Easterly, William, Josef Ritzen and Michael Woolcock (2006), 'Social Cohesion, Institutions and Growth', Working Paper No. 94, Centre for Global Development, Website: http://cgdev.org.488elwb02.blackmesh.com/sites/default/files/9136_file_WP94.pdf, accessed on 2 April 2018

Government of India (1995), *Report of the High-Power Committee: Urban Solid Waste Management in India*, New Delhi: Planning Commission

Gunnar, Myrdal (1957), *Economic Theory and Under-developed Regions*, London: G. Duckworth

The Hindu (2016), 'Mandur Observes Bandh, Continues Protest Against Garbage Landfill', 2nd June 2016, 15.24 IST, Website: www.thehindu.com/news/cities/bangalore/mandur-observes-bandh-continues-protest-against-garbage-dumping/article6075579.ece, accessed on 30 April 2018

The Hindu (2017a), 'No Break in Pune's Garbage Impasse', 2nd May 2017. 23.06 IST, Website: http://www.thehindu.com/news/national/other-states/no-break-in-punes-garbage-impasse/article18359729.ece, accessed on 10 May 2018

The Hindu (2017b), 'The Tipping Point: Where Must Our Solid Waste Go?' 16 September 2017, 22.59 IST, Website: www.thehindu.com/sci-tech/energy-and-environment/the-tipping-point/article19691563.ece, accessed on 30 April 2018

Holman, Otto and Kees van der Pijl (1996), 'The Capitalist Class in the European Union', in George Kurvetaris and Andreas Moschonas, ed. *The Impact of European Union: Political, Sociological and Economic Consequences*, London and Westport, CT: Praeger, pp. 55–74

Ritzen, Jo and Michael Woolcock (2000), 'Social Cohesion, Public Policy and Economic Growth: Implications for Countries in Transition', Address for the Annual Bank Conference on Development Economics (Europe), Paris, June 26–28, Website: http://documents.worldbank.org/curated/en/914451468781802758/820140748_200404140033848/additional/28741.pdf, accessed on 5 August 2017

Toye, Michael (2007), 'Social Cohesion: International Initiative for Cities', Parliamentary Information and Research Service, Library of Parliament, PRB 07–46E, Website: https://lop.parl.ca/content/lop/ResearchPublications/prb0746-e.pdf, accessed on 15 May 2018

Vranken, Jan (2005), 'Changing Forms of Solidarity: Urban Development Programs in Europe', in Yuri Kazepov ed. *Cities of Europe: Changing Contexts, Local Arrangements, and the Challenge to Urban Cohesion*, Malden, Oxford and Victoria: Blackwell, pp. 255–276

WCED (1987), Report of the World Commission on Environment and Development, United Nations General Assembly, Website: http://home.agh.edu.pl/~awyrwa/Regulacje/UNFCCC/1987_brundtland.pdf, accessed on 10 August 2017

Wheatcroft Patience (2010), 'Cohesive Capitalism has a Following', *The Wall Street Journal*, 5: 44, 27 January p.m. ET, Website: www.wsj.com/articles/SB10001424052748704094304575029120305252544, accessed on 10 August 2017

12 Organizing among informal workers

Can pragmatism invoke cohesive development?

Neetu Choudhary

I. Introduction

Labour unionizing is a weakened phenomenon today, yet there are new forms of organizing that have engulfed the world under neoliberalism. These organizing incidences represent the stories of the numerous poor who have begun to assert themselves in heterogeneous forms. Of course, labour is an integral part of 'the poor' and 'the poor' are informal workers in one way or the other. It is observed rightly therefore that neoliberal capitalism has now reached the point where its spontaneous tendency for keeping down class resistance, through the promotion of fragmentation, is no longer sufficient to do so (Patnaik 2017).

Contextualized case studies exemplify how informal workers organize as a class but not against capital, rather with the tendency is to bargain with the state (Agarwala 2013, Kabeer 2013). Further, this organizing does not negotiate only with nation states; it is crossing boundaries, forging partnerships and taking recourse also in multilateral institutions and relevant international agreements such as the ILO conventions. In other words, traditional unionizing based on radical class struggle does not define the new trend of organizing. The question then is, what could be the new theory of informal workers' organizing?

There is a huge body of research on organizing among informal workers that explain exquisitely how the nature, forms as well as strategy of this organizing have transformed (see for example Sarmiento et al. 2016, Chen et al. 2015, Feingold 2013, Sen 2012, Sundar Shyam 2011, Agarwala 2013, Kabeer et al. 2013, Lindell 2009, Scully 2008, Sandoval 2007, Sanyal 1991). However, it primarily represents a microscopic examination that falls short of offering a theoretical foundation to the process. This chapter attempts to theorize this context-specific and organic response to changing labour relations.

Based on a contextualized and coherent analysis for the Global South, this chapter argues that the new trend of organizing under neoliberal conditions has theoretical underpinnings of pragmatism. The argument is that this organizing, although a struggle of the informal worker, is mediated by interests and the approach of classes 'other' than the informal labour, in particular the state, civil society, trade unions and so on. The question is whether such a process represents a real potential to articulate an alternative development agenda. Given that capital thrives through its nexus with the state, can the state be expected to work on an alternative agenda? If not, can such an agenda be implemented without involving the agency of the state? This chapter explores these questions vis-à-vis organizing of the informal workers across the Global South with particular reference to India. The central concern is to theorize the process of informal organizing while linking it with possible implications for an alternative development paradigm.

Methodologically, this is a qualitative reflection based on a survey and triangulation of existing literature along with the author's individual interaction with some of the trade union and civil society representatives from several countries, including India, Ghana, Brazil, Thailand and Uruguay. The chapter is organized into three broad sections. Section I, the introduction, provides an overview on the issue while also reflecting upon the philosophy of pragmatism. Section II discusses labour organizing under neoliberalism. Finally, the chapter winds up with section III while interlinking pragmatism to cohesiveness.

Pragmatism: does it negate ideology?

Pragmatism owes its origin to the United States of the early 19th century and in the works of Sartre, Dewey and Pierce, among others. The fundamental contention of pragmatism is that the role of a theory is not just to define, illustrate or predict, rather it is also to deal with real-world problem solving. Theories are to be judged by their practical consequences, as per the pragmatists. Pragmatism refutes Cartesians' quest for certainty and would rather concentrate on what people experience. Thus, what matters for pragmatism is what people see and experience in their life world. According to pragmatism, there is no universal truth and all theories are working hypotheses subject to modifications as per the needs of humans.

Often, pragmatism and ideology have been conceptualized as polar types. Sartori (1969:411) described ideologies as 'the hetero-constraining belief systems par excellence . . . the crucial lever at the disposal of elites for obtaining political mobilization and for maximizing the possibilities of mass manipulation.' In contrast, beliefs and belief systems, pragmatists would hold, are guides to actions and should be judged against outcomes rather than abstract principles (Karlson 2010). However, pragmatism does not refute any theory, but it questions the permanence that a theory may claim to have. Pragmatism is a philosophical movement claiming that an ideology or proposition is true if it works satisfactorily and that the meaning of a proposition is to be found in the practical consequences of accepting it. It may therefore be contended that pragmatism does not have an inherent problem with ideology as far as the latter can have consequences for the world as people experience it. Moreover, pragmatism does not necessarily negate ideology, neither is it value neutral. What pragmatism emphasizes instead is the significance of doing away with the dichotomy between fact and value or theory and action. As such, it may be able to offer a potential theory for the present global scenario, where ideology-driven labour movements have lost a firm basis and capitalism with all its crises and challenges appears to be the dominant reality.

II. Labour organizing under neoliberalism: pragmatism in practice

Labour organizing has traditionally been defined as having a negative basis[1] wherein resistance (e.g. in response to wage cuts, poor working conditions etc. by the employer) has been its immediate objective. But the current form of organizing is different from traditional unionizing in at least two ways – firstly, the boundary between the poor and (informal) labour is blurred, so informal workers' organizing is often co-terminus with various forms of organizing among the poor. Secondly, as evident from existing evidence, this organizing is directed towards bargaining from the state rather than towards confrontation with capital (Agarwala 2013). Informal workers today are aware of their weakened bargaining position under liberal economic policies, and on their part pragmatism is reflected in subdued militancy in their resistance. Their involvement in industrial disputes in India, for example, has declined during the post-reform period. According to a recent survey on informal labour conducted and shared by the Thozhilalar Koodam[2] (Workers' Forum) blog on labour issues in Tamil Nadu, the majority of workers sought government support in terms of social security, health care, food security and so on. Although union representatives gather to offer strong critique of government moves to reform labour laws,[3] this does not seem to have invoked a sense of radicalism in organizing on the ground. While workers themselves have been pragmatic in their action, other stakeholders – the state, civil society and formal trade unions – also reflect pragmatism in their approach, and informal workers' organizing has manifested on the convergence on these approaches.

International development order, civil society and informal labour

Informal workers' organizing has often been facilitated by or is co-terminus with social movements and civil society activism – as the wheels of democracy and democratization process. The new international development order during neoliberalism has supported civil society growth – first – to stimulate democratization in non-democracies as a prerequisite to expansion of free market policies and second to appease subsequent neoliberal discontents reflected in anti-globalization movements across countries. The convergence of democratic struggles and anti-neoliberalism movements in Latin American countries like Argentina and Brazil has been an opportunity for the international development order to retain its hold in the countries – now through partnership with the civil society. These convergences culminated into what has been expressed as 'neoliberal democracy'[4] in a Latin American context. For example in Chile, popular organizations of the urban poor were formed to protest against conditions of political authoritarianism or dictatorial rule and to push for a democratic opening (see Foweraker 2001). In Brazil, social discontent out of authoritarianism fuelled massive grassroots mobilization, and labour was an important actor in the process, which is said to give rise to a new form of organization called 'neo-unionism' (Sirohi 2017). Since the authoritarian government in Brazil had taken an anti-labour stance and the country was under economic shock, the governance upheaval had to take care of the interests of the labour and the poor at large. For this, labour and social movement representatives chose to acquire access to state apparatuses. Consequently, we see a pro-labour government in Brazil which itself promotes labour solidarity in the form of cooperatives.

In fact, in Latin America, the urban poor as a whole organized themselves against neoliberalism and lack of statesmanship and formed many cooperatives as an alternative to advance their own well-being (Veltmeyer 2009). These urban poor are the informal workers, who in the previously discussed contexts have been organizing to develop alternative economic experiments. Thus, what is seen in Latin America is not so much the growth of unionism as that of cooperatives and associations of informal workers. A similar observation can be made for South Africa as well in its anti-apartheid struggle. Workers' organizing in general and among informal workers in particular got impetus after the fall of Suharto regime in Indonesia in 1998 (Folkerth and Warnecke 2011).

In democracies like India, the same development discourse emphasized the role of civil society, initially as a vehicle of alternative development to the state and lately as development partner of the state (sees Connolly 2007). The civil society has been conceptualized as the true guardians of democracy and good governance everywhere (UNDP 1997). The emergence of a donor–recipient relationship has also been a major catalyst for growth and strengthening of civil society organizations, which have been field contact in the South for operationalizing the (development) agenda of the North. This process has been empowering for civil society in India, wherein now even the government departments do not hesitate to outsource their activities to various NGOs.[5] Moreover, democratic freedom and an independent judiciary have positively mediated the process of strengthening civil society in India, of which the organizing of informal workers has been a central agenda. When social protection does not come from work status, it has to be derived from citizenship status, which concerns rights championed by civil society (see White 2013). The organizing of informal street vendors for example – under the aegis of NASVI[6] and subsequent formulation of the National Policy – is a case in point. Civil society freedom has been eventually upheld by an independent judiciary (see Sundar 2011), as indicated in the Supreme Court's verdict favouring informal workers' right to livelihood in public spaces. While international development organizations have attempted to co-opt the anti-globalization movements to retain their influence, civil society has been pragmatic in collaborating with their attempt. In doing so, civil society has been able to mobilize resources which can be channelized, at least fractionally, to the causes of the political society. This process that has given impetus to informal workers' organizing has in turn been mediated positively by democracy or democratic struggles.

Thus, the relationship between civil society and poor informal workers is not uniform across countries. In Thailand, for example, the growth in NGOs post liberalization was facilitated by the process of devolution, wherein municipalities overwhelmed with tasks that were once the central government's responsibility began to turn to NGOs (Balassiano and Pandi 2013). Yet civil society remained subordinate to the Thai government (Kuhonta and Sinpeng 2014). Thailand demonstrates a background of conflicting policies and practices: a constitution that specifies freedoms, devolution of authority and public participation that contrasts sharply with regular military crack-downs on political demonstrations by civil society organizations (Balassiano and Pandi 2013). In fact, despite its adoption of free market policies, countries like Thailand and China have not allowed international development relationships to influence their internal dynamics. Also, civil societies have been dissuaded from international partnerships and, therefore, could not witness growth as they have in India. Ostensibly, the pragmatism that encouraged organizing of the poor and the informal workers with support from democratic forces could not be fostered under an authoritarian political structure. Moreover, as Partha Chatterjee (2008) explains, the organization of the informal sector – which he conceptualizes as the *political society* – directly depends on successful operations of certain political functions, and this process is facilitated by democracy. This is because to a certain extent democratic beliefs represent enduring ideologies for organizing human collective action (Novak and Harter 2008).

Trade unionism and informal workers' organizing

To the extent the effectiveness of informal workers' movements could be a function of the presence of a formal workers' movement (Agarwala 2013), countries with a history of strong trade unions offer a favourable context for informal workers to organize. This is expected due to the cultural legacy of activism that formal trade union movements offer to informal workers. But this is also happening because of the pragmatic shift in approach of formal trade unions, which now have begun to extend support to informal workers – primarily to deal with the declining trend in their membership base, as more labours work informally under the liberal economic framework. For example, in 1996, the Ghana Trade Union Congress (GTUC) adopted six policies – one of which was organizing informal workers – to help the organization confront challenges of declining membership (Chen 2013). Franklin O. Ansah of Trade Union Congress of Ghana explains,

> Earlier informal workers were not in the consideration of our unions. But now we are carrying out campaigns to mobilize these workers – as their share in labour force has increased significantly.[7]

In India, organizations such as the Trade Union Centre of India (TUCI, Mumbai), Trade Union Coordination Centre(TUCC, Bengaluru), the All India Central Council of Trade Unions (AICCTU), and the Self-Employed Women's Association (SEWA) organize contract and other forms of non-regular workers (Sundar 2011). The secretary-general of the Indian National Trade Union Congress (INTUC), S. Q. Zama, in a recent interview with *Business Standard*, explains that the union is trying to expand its membership among contractual workers.[8] Similar trends are observed in Brazil. According to Ana Paula Melli of CUT, Brazil,

> trade unions are strong in Brazil and even though they did not directly engage with informal workers' earlier, they have used their influence to get social security coverage for informal workers as well.[9]

Thus, the informal workers' movement has benefitted wherever trade unions have been relatively strong. This resonates quite a bit in the Indian case also, where the formal trade unions have enlarged their protest agenda to cover not only issues relating to organized sector workers, but also those concerning the unorganized workers and livelihood issues (see Folkerth and Warnecke 2011, Sundar, 2011), though in India this has not resulted in as much success as in Brazil or Uruguay. According to Ariel Ferrari of the National Trade Union of Uruguay,

> there is strong partnership between the [left] government and Trade Union, which has resulted into a decline in informal employment from 53% in 2005, to 17% at present. Bargaining is not looked at enterprise level now and the focus is on social security. There is universal social security for all workers including informal labour. The national union is also engaged in organizing street sellers for advancing economic gains.[10]

Lack of a history of labour unions has been one of the weaknesses that discouraged the growth of organizing among informal workers in Thailand. Democratic upheavals at the level of government have failed to accommodate the labour movement in an independent political space and as an independent social force (Hutchison and Brown 2001). Similarly, in China workers' right to organize is severely curtailed due to legal restrictions and subsequent administrative action on workers (Estlund 2013). Through their activism within civil society, workers do manage to get wage revisions, but overall labour unions' ability in Thailand or in China to organize and embed in political space remain weak. This is obviously strategic on the part of the authorities to dissuade the growth of labour movements that often partner with and reinforce democratic struggles.

Promoting solidarity? Decent work and transnational pragmatism

Among the international responses that harsh labour implications of neo-liberalism invited, those emerging from the ILO's international convention on decent work have been at the forefront. The decent work framework of the ILO has been able to get involvement from formal trade unions as well as informal workers' representations. These representations come from workers who do not necessarily seek a structural change in labour relation; instead, they attempt to carve out their own space within the given frame-work. As Veltmeyer (2007) aptly explains, radical transformation never became the agenda of those who wanted a change. Given that the right to form associations and to bargain is one of the constituents of the decent work criteria, ILO and other such agencies have begun to engage with labour-centric organizations and trade unions and encourage them in turn to associate with informal workers. As a part of its decent work agenda, increasingly the ILO[11] is organizing platforms that bring together repre-sentations from policy, unions as well as academia. Creation of a Global Labour University as a collaborative project among Brazil, India, Germany, South Africa and the United States of America is a unique initiative to pro-vide a platform for labour unions, which offers a platform for knowledge and experience sharing as well as training of informal and formal unions representatives. Concern has been expressed that this is a part of interna-tional development agencies' move to co-opt the labour's agenda against global capital (Kumar 2008).

However, the concomitant opportunity is being pragmatically utilized by workers' associations as a platform to negotiate, bargain and create pres-sure on nation governments. This process of pressure building of course has greater momentum in democratic countries, while workers in non-democratic countries like Thailand have failed to associate with the main-stream trend. Wherever possible, workers' organizations are increasingly integrated into the international framework, and across countries they have begun to enter into various forms of partnerships (as with formal trade unions as discussed earlier) to advance their agenda. Associations of infor-mal workers in the South are increasingly establishing international links and creating international movements (Chen et al. 2015, Lindell 2010). Thus, sector-specific international networks have been formed that have local organizations as affiliates. StreetNet International, Home Net International, Latin American Waste Pickers Network, International Domestic Workers' Network etc. are among these networks and regional alliances that spread awareness and recognition and engage in advocacy for informal workers. At a local level, access and exposure to such networks have been instrumental in strengthening informal workers' organizations. For example, the Self-Employed Women's Union (SEWU) in South Africa was created based on experience sharing from SEWA in India. That is, the more the informal workers partner with such networks, the better they organize and gain policy acceptance (Chen et al. 2015, Feingold 2013). Informal workers' associations are not aiming to transform the labour relation necessarily, but they certainly are trying to bring the element of security and protection in it. Starting from SEWA, which has taken networking to another level (Folkerth and Warnecke 2011), many informal workers' organizations in India are an active part of international networks. As pragmatic ideologues, government in countries like India encourage such partnership as an obligation to ILO's decent work agenda.

The state and the informal: appeasement or pragmatism

The scale of their existence under neoliberalism has also opened up the opportunities for informal workers to organize. At the level of informal workers, organizing activity has been a response to unfavourable labour relations – deprived of certainty, security and protection. It is argued that within the national and international framework discussed in the previous section – to what extent informal workers engage in organizing depends upon the extent of neoliberal ramifications as well as state interventions in the form of social protection etc. In Latin America it has emerged[12] as a necessary response to social deprivation (Allard and Matthaei 2008), while in Africa, solidarity and cooperation are reflected in civil society involvement in initiatives of poverty alleviation, social exclusion etc. (Tremblay 2009). In Asia, cooperatives and solidarity-based innovations are attempting to fight economic discrimination and exclusion – for example, in Japan, solidarity initiatives (Alcorta 2009).

Clearly, when workers' organizing is a response to the deprivation and insecurity they face, then the intensity of response depends upon the extent of deprivation. It is here that the state's approach becomes important. Wherever authoritarianism partnered with deprivation or where governments have completely failed to respond to people's needs, the state machinery has been attacked by the poor and informal workers. Moreover, the state, if it wants to sustain, has to see that resistance does not culminate in revolution and that the poor remain attached to its system. For example, one of the goals of informal workers' organizing activities in Latin America has been to secure greater social protection coverage and organizing support from the government, which has ended up lending support to cooperative organizing through favourable legislation, partnerships and social protection leading to decline in informalization (Maurizio 2014). These governments have undergone administrative experiments to deal with social protection and people's cooperation.[13] Solidarity and consultative councils in Brazil are such administrative innovations that have promoted informal workers' organizing in terms of cooperation and solidarity units. It has been argued that in a class-divided society, the role of the state is to maintain social order that is already skewed in favour of the elite (Fisk 1989). To this end the state tilts towards the interests of the popular masses, depending upon the latter's political activity (Sirohi 2017).

In India, which is largely a case of crony capitalism but also an electoral democracy, the state has avoided overt and outright projection of an anti-labour stand. In fact, India is also a signatory to several international conventions on labour rights and is, in principle, in agreement with the social protection agenda propounded by the international development system. Thus, as *pragmatist ideologue*, it espouses the social protection agenda towards formalization of informal workers as advocated by the international development agenda today. The state's submission to forces of capitalism seems to manifest in several social protection programmes initiated in India to support the informal workers. Among these, the Mahatma Gandhi National Rural Employment Guarantee Act (MNREGA) and the National Food Security Act are the largest ones. MNREGA in particular has received widespread appreciation and in fact other countries such as South Africa are attempting to come up with a similar programme.[14] However, the commitment of governments to such programmes depends upon the compulsions of electoral politics that they face. The then government enacted MNREGA in 2005, due to pressure of coalition politics and civil society, but the current government with parliamentary majority has been reducing the budgetary allocation to the programme (Dreze 2016). As Hedges (2011) illustrated, popular pressure enables liberals within the elite to press for reforms. In its absence the state reverts to policies that support the supremacy of capital (DuRand 2014). However, even with the voting majority the government cannot completely do away with such programmes, since to sustain it must give people the hope to have an opportunity to grow. To protect the capital, the state has to sustain itself. In other words, for capital to sustain, the state has to mediate and maintain governability (DuRand 2014).

The state therefore acts pragmatically to divert some resources to the poor and the informal workers and actually does satisfy a large segment of population, including civil society, activists and academia, which is of the opinion that the free market and informalization is going to stay, therefore it is at least better to have public support mechanisms given the extent of poverty and deprivation in India. This segment represents the lot of *ideological pragmatists* that speaks for social protection of the poor and support their organizing as a tool to fetch the same. Another section, a minority, perceives this as the state's populist policies to appease its people – the voting majority. For example Kumar (2008: 82) argues,

> Despite such impoverishment and exploitation there is an absence of any powerful movement today in the cities (in India). . . . It is the power of capital to atomize the collective that impedes the growth of any ideologically structured resistance.

Even in non-democracy countries like Thailand, the government has worked on economic security that has been helpful in averting major resistance from workers. Thailand was one of the centres of economic crisis in 1997, resulting in large-scale labour layoffs and informalization. Yet the country is noted to have been relatively quick in reviving from the crisis (Lafferty 2010). According to Poonsap Toolaphan of HomeNet Thailand,

> economic opportunities in the country have been sound enough to keep people especially labour silent rather than confront the government for their rights as labourers. . . . Because of lucrative economic alternatives, it is difficult in Thailand to find people willing to work for the cause of labour or for civil society in general.[15]

This is not surprising given that the poverty line at around 578 US dollars per person per annum in Thailand and 360 US dollars in China is much higher than the set international cut-offs. The poverty line in India is 130–180 US dollars per person per annum. At the same time, workers in the informal economy of Thailand are entitled to social protection schemes which provide basic, social and economic security (Nirathron 2013). A study by Nirathron (2006) revealed that 85% of survey respondents expressed satisfaction with their job and autonomy, which is very different from the picture, though very limited, available on India (Bhowmik 2005). The economic condition of informal workers in Thailand is relatively better than their counterparts are in other countries from the South, and the need for organizing has not been felt intensely. Historically unaccustomed to assertion of their identity as labour, workers in Thailand reflect pragmatism in their preference for economic security. The state in such contexts reflects *political pragmatism* inasmuch it avoids a subscription to the ideals of individual liberty, freedom or justice but is considerate in its actual impact of policies (primarily in economic terms).

III. . . . but can pragmatism invoke cohesiveness?

Organized action has been the mechanism for labour to express itself. In the current context, when the world is preoccupied with its search for an order away from neoliberalism and a growing proportion of informal workers is being associated with organizing activities and solidarity-based initiatives, it is pertinent to identify whether and how the new trend of organizing can implicate the pathways to cohesive development. It is in this context that this chapter has attempted to explore the nature and dynamics of informal workers' organizing in the Global South.

As discussed in the foregoing sections, organizing of informal labour is starkly different from traditional unionizing processes. What is unique in this process is that it is not an isolated act, rather it can be conceptualized as an act of cooperation and reinforcement not only on the part of the workers but also on the part of the state, trade unions and the larger gamut of civil society – in varying degrees. While informal labour has been pragmatically negotiating with the state, trade unions have opened up to informal labourers and the state, often crony with capital –pragmatically engaging with the poor and the informal – to keep them tied to its system and mechanism without antagonizing capital. International agencies like the ILO have been seen as co-opting the anti-globalization wave to advance their agenda in the name of social protection and development, and civil society has leveraged this pragmatically. For pro-capital countries like India that are compelled to live under the shadow of socialism, the state has displayed pragmatism of varying degree to pacify discontents emerging from unbridled accumulation of capital. In countries like Thailand, where the military has been the predominant form of governance, the state leverages economic opportunities arising out of neoliberalism to suppress discontents that may emerge from deprivation. This is in a way similar to the hegemonic pragmatism pursued in Singapore (see Tan 2012). In Brazil also, pragmatism – rather than politics or ideology – has been the main driving force behind market reforms (Pinheiro et al. 2015) under the phenomenon of 'neoliberal democracy'.

Evidently, albeit in varying degree, pragmatism perhaps has begun to gain empirical support as most reforms consist of marginal adjustments to existing policies (Lindblom 1959, Wildavsky 1988, Jones et al. 1997). As Ellarman (2010: 4) states, pragmatism views the social world as being actively constructed by people so, at each point in time, it is radically incomplete and in a state of becoming. Hence, the notion of there being some predefined 'one best way' does not occur. Informal workers organizing with its continuity, gradualism and contextual mediation can be defined through the philosophy of pragmatism.

Thousands of poor and workers engulfing the street in protest against neoliberal extremities are not valueless people. They seek justice and security for themselves in the global world, and this is the ideology underlying their pragmatism. Co-option or appeasement could be alternative explanations for the approach, international development order or the state have adopted towards labour under neoliberalism. Yet on the part of these stakeholders, their approach certainly reflects pragmatism and reinforces the new form of organizing among labour. It is through such a lens of pragmatism that this chapter has attempted to offer a theoretical mould to the organizing of informal labour in the contemporary world. While the global economic order appears to have succumbed to capitalism despite its recurrent crises, and where the quest for alternative development is increasingly gaining voice at the grassroots, pragmatism of the labour and the poor in congruence with other stakeholders can perhaps evolve as an articulation of the cohesive development agenda.

Notes

1 Several studies show that the basis of labour union organization is essentially negative – i.e. labour form a group to protect themselves from the outside world instead of associating for greater causes (Bowden 2009).
2 Thozhilalar Koodam is an independent blog representing the working-class in India with their website https://tnlabour.in/
3 All trade union conference, on February 23rd for "Equal Wages for Equal Work" and implementation of labour laws, Tamil Nadu (India), http://tnlabour.in/factory-workers/4796 accessed 19/12/19.
4 Palacios (1999) in Veltmeyer (2004).
5 Of course, there have been strong criticisms also (see White 2013). It is questioned whether this is just a way for the state to absolve its obligations to the citizens – commodification of the state's functions.
6 For example, more than 300,000 street vendors across India are affiliated to the National Alliance of Street Vendors in India (NASVI). The legislation of the National Policy on Urban Street Vendors 2009, Government of India and legislations in several states of India broadly oriented towards regulation as well as the protection of the livelihoods of street vendors are the corollary of an organized action on the part of street traders and civil society.
7 In the interview conducted on July 13, 2016, during the first Academy on South-South and Triangular Cooperation, held in Turin.
8 See Rakshit (2016)
9 In the interview conducted on July 13, 2016, during the first Academy on South-South and Triangular Cooperation, held in Turin.
10 In the interview conducted on July 14, 2016, during the first Academy on South-South and Triangular Cooperation, held in Turin.
11 For example, several academies on the social and solidarity economy have been held by the International Training Centre of the ILO in different parts of the world – which include a discussion on union strategy and informal workers' organizing.
12 Veltmeyer and Petras (2011), Kumar (2008).
13 The South American Council on Social Development, established in 2009, can be seen as a platform for coordinated state-supported initiatives.
14 Interview with Stanley W. Henderson, Deputy Director-General, Public Works Department, Republic of South Africa, on July 13, 2016, Turin.
15 Interview conducted on November 25, 2015, at HomeNet Thailand Office in Bangkok.

References

Agarwala, Rina (2013). *Informal Labour, Formal Politics and Dignified Discontent in India*, New Delhi: Cambridge University Press
Alcorta, Juan A. (2009). *Neo liberal Cycles and Solidarity Economies: A Comparative Study of Argentina and Japan* (Unpublished Doctoral Dissertation), National

Institute of Informatics, Tokyo, accessed from http://dspace.lib.niigata-u.ac.jp/
dspace/bitstream/10191/8409/1/09_0004_JAA.pdf on 29/11/2015, 19/12/19

Allard, J. and Matthaei, J. (2008). Introduction. In J. Allard, C. Davidson and
J. Matthaei (Eds.) *Solidarity Economy: Building Alternatives for People and
Planet* (pp. 1–18). Papers and Reports from the U.S. Social Forum 2007, Chicago:
ChangeMaker Publications

Balassiano, Katia and Pandi, Asha R. (2013). Civic space and political mobilization:
Cases in Malaysia and Thailand, *The Journal of Development Studies*, 49(11):
1579–1591

Bhowmik, Sharit (2005). Street vendors in Asia: A review, *Economic and Political
Weekly*, 40(22): 2256–2264.

Bowden, B. 2009. The organising model in Australia: A reassessment, *Labour and
Industry*, 20(2): 138–158.

Chatterjee, Partha (2008). Democracy and economic transformation in India, *Economic and Political Weekly*, 43(16): 53–62

Chen, Martha A. (2013). Informal workers in the developing world: Organizing in
the global economy, *New Labour Forum*, 22(1): 67–73

Chen, Martha A., Bonner, Chris and Carre, Francoise (2015). Organizing Informal
Workers: Benefits, Challenges and Successes, Background Paper, Human Development Report Office, UNDP

Connolly, Eileen (2007). The Role of Civil Society in Poverty Alleviation: perspectives
from Tanzania, Ethiopia and Central America, Research Findings: Governance,
Trade and Aid Effectiveness, vol 1., Advisory Board for Irish Aid, 2007, accessed
from http://doras.dcu.ie/2108/1/Irish_Aid_journal.pdf on August 16, 2016

Dreze, J. 2016. *Stagnant wages, payment delays and eroding support: Jean Dreze
on MGNREGA @10* [Interview] (3 Feb. 2016), accessed from http://www.catch
news.com/india-news/stagnant-wages-payment-delays-and-eroding-political-sup
port-jean-dreze-on-10-years-of-mgnrega-1454471238.html on February 14, 2017

DuRand, Cliff (2014). Contradictions of global neoliberalism, *Perspectives on
Global Development and Technology*, 13: 36–42

Ellarman, David (2010). Pragmatism versus economics ideology in the post-socialist
transition: China versus Russia, *Real World Economic Review*, (52)

Estlund, Cynthia (2013). *Will Workers Have a Choice in China's Socialist Market Economy? The Curious Revival of the Workers Congress System*, Working
paper no. 13–180, Public Law and Legal Theory Research Paper Series, New York
University

Feingold, Cathy (2013). Building global worker power in a time of crisis, *New
Labour Forum*, 22(2): 45–50

Fisk, M. (1989). *The State and Justice: An Essay in Political Theory*, Cambridge:
Cambridge University Press

Folkerth, John and Warnecke, Tonia (2011). Informal labour in India and Indonesia:
Surmounting organizing barriers, *Labour, Capital and Society*, 44(2): 131–153

Foweraker, Joe (2001). *Grassroots Movements, Political Activism and Social Devel-
opment in Latin America: A comparison of Chile and Brazil*, Civil Society and
Social Movements–Programme Paper no. 3, United Nations Research Institute on
Social Development, Geneva

Hedges, C. (2011). *Death of the Liberal Class*, New York: Nation Books.

Hutchison, Jane and Brown, Andrew (2001). Organizing labour in globalizing Asia:
An introduction. In Hutchison and Brown (Eds.) *Organizing Labour in Globalizing Asia*, Routledge: London

Jones, Bryan D., True, James L. and Baumgartner, Frank R. (1997). Does Incrementalism stem from political consensus or from institutional gridlock. *American Journal of Political Science*, 41(4): 1319–1339

Kabeer, Naila, Milward, Kirsty and Sudarshan, Ratna (2013). Introduction. In Naila Kabeer, Ratna Sudarshan and Kirsty Milward (Eds.) *Organizing Women Workers in the Informal Economy: Beyond the Weapons of the Weak*, London: Zed Books

Karlson, Nils (2010). *The Limits of Pragmatism in Institutional Change*, paper presented during the seminar on "Philosophy, Politics and Economics of Public Choice: Reflections on Geoffrey Brennan's Contributions", in Turku (Åbo)

Kuhonta, M. Erik and Sinpeng, Aim (2014). Democratic regression in Thailand: The ambivalent role of civil society and political institutions, Contemporary Southeast Asia, 36(3): 333–355

Kumar, Ravi (2008). Globalization and changing patterns of social mobilization in urban India, Social Movement Studies, 7(1): 77–96

Lafferty, George (2010). In the wake of neo-liberalism: Deregulation, unionism and labour rights, Review of International Political Economy, 17(3): 589–608

Lindblom, Charles E. (1959). The science of 'muddling through. Public Administration Review, 19(2): 79–88.

Lindell, Ilda (2009). Glocal' movements: Place struggles and transnational organizing by informal workers, *Human Geography*, 91(2): 123–136

Lindell, Ilda (2010). Informality and collective organising: Identities, alliances and transnational activism in Africa, *Third World Quarterly*, 31(2): 207–222

Maurizio, Roxana (2014). Labour formalization and declining inequality in Argentina and Brazil in 2000s, ILO Research Paper No. 9, International Labour Office, Geneva

Nirathron, Narumol (2006). Fighting Poverty from the Street: A Survey of Street Food Vendors in Bangkok, Geneva: International Labour Organization

Nirathron, Narumol (2013, May). Social Protection for the Workers in the Informal Economy: A Move towards Social Inclusion, paper presented during Conference on "Social Quality in Asia: Moving from Concepts to Practices", Kind Prajadhipok Institute, Thailand

Novak, David R. and Harter, Lynn M. ((2008). Flipping the "scripts" of poverty and panhandling: Organizing democracy by creating connections, Journal of Applied Communication Research, 36(4): 391–414

Palacios, Paulino. (1999). Limites y posibilidades de la acción política: El proyecto neoliberal. Boletín ICCI "RIMAY", 1(1):1–8

Patnaik, Prabhat (2017). A Climacteric for Capitalism, Annual A N Sinha Memorial Lecture delivered at the A N Sinha Institute of Social Studies, Patna, July 27

Pinheiro, Armando, C., Bonelli, R and Schneider, B. N. (2015). *Pragmatic policy in brazil: The political economy of incomplete market reform*, Discussion Paper No. 1035, Institute for Applied Economic Research (IPEA), Brazil

Rakshit, Avishek (2016). Contract workers will help Coal India tide over September 2 strike, Business Standard, Kolkata, August 24, 2016.

Sandoval, S. A. L. (2007). Alternative forms of working class organization and mobilization of informal sector workers in Brazil in the era of neoliberalism, *International Labour and Working Class–History*, (72): 63–89

Sanyal, Bishwapriya (1991). Organizing the self-employed: The politics of the urban informal sector, *International Labour Review*, 130(1): 39–56

Sarmiento, Hugo et al. (2016). The unexpected power of the informal workers in the public square: A comparison of Mexican and US organizing models, *International Labour and Working Class–History*, (89): 131–152

Sartori, Giovanni (1969). Politics, ideology and belief systems, *The American Political Science Review*, 63(2): 398–411.

Scully, Benjamin (2008). *Strong Union, Weak Labour Force: Responses of the South African Labour Movement to Marginalization in the Labour Market*, Paper presented at the annual meeting of the American Sociological Association Annual Meeting, Boston, accessed from http://citation.allacademic.com/meta/p241086_index.html on 23/08/2016

Sen, Ratna (2012). Unionization and collective bargaining in the unorganized sector, *The Indian Journal of Industrial Relations*, 47(4): 598–616

Sirohi, Rahul (2017). Alternate paths to economic development: A comparative analysis of Brazil and India in the era of neoliberalism, *Brazilian Journal of Political Economy*, 37, n° 2 (147): 304–323

Sundar Shyam, K. R. (2011). *Non- regular Workers in India: Social Dialogue and Organizational and Bargaining Strategies and Practices*, Working Paper no. 30, International Labour Review, Geneva

Tan, K. Paul (2012). The ideology of pragmatism: Neo liberal globalization and political authoritarianism in Singapore, *Journal of Contemporary Asia*, 42(1): 67–92

Thozhilalar Koodam (2016). What workers think of the upcoming general strike: a general survey, August 24, 2016, http://tnlabour.in/?p=4014 accessed 19/12/19

Tremblay, Crystal (2009). Advancing the Social Economy for Socio-economic Development: International perspectives, Public Policy Paper Series No. 01, Canadian Social Economy Hub, University of Victoria

UNDP (1997). *Governance for sustainable human development: A UNDP policy document*, New York, PNUD

Veltmeyer, Henry (2004). Civil Society and Social Movements: The Dynamics of Intersectoral Alliance and Urban, rural Linkages in Latin America, Civil Society and Social Movements, Programme Paper No. 10, United Nations Research Institute on Social Development, Geneva

Veltmeyer, H. (2007). *Illusion or opportunity? Civil society and the quest for social change*, Halifax: Fernwood Books

Veltmeyer, H. and Petras, J. (2011). Beyond pragmatic Neoliberalism: From Social Inclusion and Poverty Reduction to Equality and Social Change, UNESCO Conference on "Rethinking Development: Ethics and Social Inclusion", 17–18 August 2011 Mexican Ministry of Foreign Affairs Mexico City

White, Barbara-White (2013). Comments and perspectives. In Gerry Rodgers (Ed.) *Aligning Economic and Social Goals in Emerging Economies: Employment and Social Protection in Brazil, China, India and South Africa*, New Delhi: Academic Foundation

Wildavsky, Aaron. (1988). The New Politics of the *Budgetary Process*, Glenview: Scott, Foresman & Co.

13 Does community-driven development empower the powerless?

The case of urban Bangladesh

Parvaz Azharul Huq

1. Introduction

This chapter explores some of the promises and perils of community participation within the framework of community-driven development (CDD) in an urban setting in Bangladesh. Stemming from critiques against state-led top-down models of development, a renewed interest in participatory development in the 1990s led a number of development agencies to implement projects using participatory mechanisms. This second wave of participatory development tended to be informed by broad-based social inclusion and empowerment discourses. More recently, participation has been related to the concept and practices of participatory local governance, aiming at bringing transformation in institutional relations within the local governance sphere. Against this backdrop, this chapter presents and analyses the findings of a qualitative study on the Urban Partnerships for Poverty Reduction (UPPR) project, a CDD intervention in Bangladesh with an urge to make practical links between the theories and practices of participatory development. It examines how members' participation in community groups (as invited spaces) influenced their level of agency (asset endowment) and the structural factors (socio-economic and political relationships) leading to transformation in institutional relationships. It is argued here that the absence of trans-local linkage may make CDD projects incapable of inducing a broad-based social transformation process leading to cohesive communities which are marked by a high level of social inclusion, social mobility and social capital.

After presenting a brief discussion on the theoretical aspects of participation, empowerment, CDD and the UPPR project, the chapter first presents an overview of the socio-political and institutional context within which the development intervention was initiated. Then it reports and analyses the perceived impacts of the group savings and credit programme and the community contracting process on collective and personal asset endowments. Afterwards, the discussion moves on to focus on issues related to the participants' choices and actions that influenced the existing socio-economic and political relationships. The chapter ends with a critical review of the findings and a conclusion.

2. Participation: a transformative concept

Participation, for some, is a transformative concept in which the purpose is collective action for social change (Ledwith and Springett 2010:14–15; Osei-Hwedie and Osei-Hwedie 2010). Despite the great potential of participation as a means of combating many of the social and political problems like social exclusion, political apathy and uneven distribution of resources, the second wave of participatory development practices has also been criticised severely during the last two decades. Many have portrayed participatory development – the way it has been managed – as tyranny. Some of such tyrannies have been highlighted by Cooke and Kothari (2001) and Miller and Rein (2011). According to Hickey and Mohan (2004:11), the backlash against participatory development generally has four lines of arguments: first, failing to relate local issues with the broader structure; second, inadequate understanding of power relations; third, limited understanding of the role of structure and agency in social change; finally, treating participation as a technical method rather than as a political methodology of empowerment. However, Hickey and Mohan (2004) and Ledwith and Springett (2010) indicate that certain approaches of participation, located within the immanent process of development, possess the potential of transformation.

'Transformation' in this context means transformation of traditional development practices (top-down or the old generation community development) and, more radically, changes in social relations, institutional practices and minimisation of capacity gaps which cause social exclusion (Hickey and Mohan 2004:13). From this perspective, it might seem that transformation is meant to be a radical power reversal in social relations. But, the writings of Williams (2004), Masaki (2004), Cornwall (2004) and Ledwith and Springett (2010) signify that such a narrow understanding of transformation might detain us from understanding the subtle process of transformation, because transformation does not necessarily involve a radical reversal of power relations but a strengthening of the bargaining power of the disadvantaged within the relations.

To be transformative, as Hickey and Mohan (2004:12) argue, firstly, participation must be based on clear ideological exposure and sound theoretical background and secondly, it must be involved in changing both institutions and structures. It is becoming evident that deepening democratic governance needs to work both sides of the equation: strengthening the process of citizen participation through mobilisation and building the political capabilities of the participants, and on the other hand, changing institutional designs to make public institutions more responsive to citizens' demands (Gaventa 2003:2). Thus, the transformative potential of local participatory practices are conditional to changes at the broader political, economic, social and institutional spheres that go beyond the locale. This must be a 'radical development project' (Hickey and Mohan 2004:14–15). Here we find that although the practices of participation in development have been criticised severely, a few of the authors claim that participatory spaces can be transformative when participation coincides with changes in the capabilities of the participants and also in institutions conducive to democratic governance.

3. Community-driven development: leading to transformation?

Community-driven development is a new type of community-based development (CBD)[1] approach through which beneficiaries are given more direct control over project decision-making, implementation and evaluation processes. In recent times, this has been one of the most popular mechanisms among donor communities for channelling development resources to developing countries (Mansuri and Rao 2012). The proponents of this approach claim that it is a response to the failure of previous CBD approaches, for example, community development, integrated rural development (The World Bank 2000:5) and area development programmes (Binswanger-Mkhize *et al.* 2009:1). According to Dongier *et al.* (2002), CDD is an approach that confers upon community groups better control over planning, decisions and investment resources for local development projects. The most operative and distinguishing words here are 'approach' and 'control over planning, decision and resources', which make CDD different from the other versions of community-based participatory projects. The first difference is that CDD is an approach and a process – 'not a project' (Binswanger-Mkhize *et al.* 2009:3) – which can be applied to various socio-economic contexts to revitalise democratic local governance and participation (Economic and Social Commission for Western Asia 2004:2). Secondly, it gives community groups more authority and control over resources to enrich social capital and strengthen the accountability of all actors in local development. Often the community groups work in partnership with other actors in local development, e.g. local government, national or regional government agencies, NGOs and the private sector, where local communities and local governments remain in the driving seat in the overall development process and are bestowed a new set of powers, rights and obligations (Dahl-Ostergaard *et al.* 2003, Binswanger and Nguyen 2005).

Since local development is a co-production of communities, local governments and supportive sector institutions, with collaboration from the private sector and non-government organisations (Binswanger-Mkhize *et al.* 2009:1), CDD emphasises community empowerment, enabling the local governments and synergy among government and non-government efforts (including NGOs and the private sector) in local development to make the local development process self-sustaining (Kumar 2003:5). The theoretical underpinnings of CDD come from three theoretical propositions in the development literature: decentralisation, democratisation and collective action (Beard and Dasgupta 2006). Since the mid-1990s the CDD approach has emerged as one of the fastest growing investments by NGOs, aid organisations and multilateral development banks (Mansuri and Rao 2004; Platteau 2004; Dasgupta and Beard 2007). The World Bank's lending for such projects increased from US$325 million in 1996 to $2 billion in 2003 (Mansuri and Rao 2004:2). During the years 2000–2005, approximately 190 projects worth up to US$9.3 billion have been supported by the Bank (Tanaka *et al.* 2006). The scale of some CDD projects, for example, the Kecamatan Development Program (KDP) in Indonesia, the KALAHI project in the Philippines and the Northern Mountains Poverty Reduction Program (NMPRP) in Vietnam are especially notable. The success of many of these projects has been described on the World Bank's official website.[2]

The earlier discussion on CDD shows that this particular approach to participatory development seems to be informed by changes in relationships between the participants and the state institutions. Therefore, it holds the promise of transformative participation where the participants become 'makers and shapers' instead of being the mere object of development. However, a number of studies (for example, Cooke and Kothari 2001; Platteau and Gaspart 2003; Mansuri and Rao 2004; Platteau 2004; Dasgupta and Beard 2007; Dill 2009) suggest that many of the large-scale CDD projects are indulged with lack of organisational capacity at the community level as well as lack of ownership of the projects by the beneficiaries. Projects are susceptible to elite capture because participants come from unequal positions of power. The contemporary development literature suggests that local elites may distort the outcomes of participatory processes by biasing local decisions and resources toward their own self-interested preferences (Labonne and Chase 2009). Despite the inherent potential for elite domination, a number of studies (for example, Owen and Domelen 1998; Domelen 2002; Dasgupta and Beard 2007) show that a large majority of social fund/CDD projects succeeded in addressing at least one of the pressing local needs and were distinguished by high levels of beneficiary satisfaction.

4. Participation and empowerment: a conceptual framework

Generally, community participation is a process wherein people in the community have access to decision-making, implementation and benefit sharing. But the concept of community participation is contested, and there is a great debate if it is a 'means' or an 'end'. Participation can be used as a means to enhance efficiency, effectiveness and sustainability of a project by incorporating local knowledge and resources, or an end where participation itself is counted as a goal so that a community could have greater control over resources and regulative institutions in a given social situation (Moser 1983). Recently, there is a great impetus all over the world to seek participation as an end in itself (Miller and Rein 2011:90). It ultimately requires redistribution of power. Therefore, participation, for some, is a transformative concept where the purpose is collective action for social change (Ledwith and Springett 2010:14–15; Osei-Hwedie and Osei-Hwedie 2010). Participation in its transformative aspect has to be able to produce outcomes in a manner that overcomes existing unequal economic, social and political power relations (Cornwall 2002:50). As such, effective and genuine participation has to empower.

In general, empowerment can be understood as a process of increasing people's control over their lives which means more freedom of choice and action (Lyons *et al.* 2001; Narayan 2002). It entails the process of enhancing individual or group capacity to make choices and transform those choices into desired actions and outcomes. Edwards and Hulme (1992:24) define empowerment as: "the process of assisting disadvantaged individuals and groups to gain greater control . . . over local and national decision-making and resources, and of their ability and right to define collective goals, make decisions and learn from experience". It is implied here that someone can act in favour of others to make them empowered. It also concedes that empowerment is relevant both at individual (for example, personal assets and capabilities) and collective levels (for example, voice, organisation, representation and social capital), and closely related to power relations that call for actions to change unequal institutional relationships both formal and informal. According to Lyons et al. (2001:1245), community empowerment is a process through which communities achieve greater control over their own affairs. This meant, firstly, an increase of the collective ability to negotiate with external agents, and secondly, an increase in the ability to manage internal affairs. Therefore, community empowerment entails both individual and collective human development (Partridge 2008:161).

In the political context, empowerment is a combination of power and authority. Political empowerment of communities drives from two kinds of changes for the citizen: one is the development of citizens' capacities (power resources) for exercising power and the second is acquiring the rights (delegation of authority) to exercise power (Smith 2008:4). Enhancing citizens' capacity, both at the individual and group levels, entails acquiring some basic knowledge and skills, such as developing negotiating skills and the ability to co-operate, listening, assertiveness, exploiting expertise, dealing with difficult people, enabling newcomers to get involved, broadening the basis of involvement, creating well-accepted representative organisations, building social capital, accumulating knowledge, raising consensus, demystifying political power and so on. To utilise these capacities in public affairs, people need to have the authority (rights) to take part in the formal decision-making process (Smith 2008:4–5). Therefore, we can summarise the process of empowerment into four models: 'power within', 'power to', 'power with' and 'power over' (Nelson and Wright 1997; Stewart 2001; Sabhlok 2007). Empowerment is a process of building self-confidence and self-worth at the individual level – 'power within'. It is also a process of increasing the capability to make decisions and solve problems at the collective level, which can be termed as 'power to' and 'power with'. Finally, empowerment again entails a process of gaining access to political decision-making and control over resources, often in the public forum, which can be termed as 'power over'.

5. The Urban Partnerships for Poverty Reduction project in Bangladesh

The UPPR project (2007–2015) was the largest urban poverty reduction initiative in Bangladesh and one of the largest in the world. It covered 30 towns and cities (out of 64 district towns) of the country (Urban Partnerships for Poverty Reduction 2012). This was a typical community-driven development project co-sponsored by the United Nations Development Programme (UNDP) and the UK Department for International Development (DFID). Creating new community-based organisations and introducing participatory planning and implementation process were integral to the UPPR, so that community people could make collective claims on the resources of the programme which would be characterised by popular democracy, accountability and transparency. The intervention intended to support partnership among urban poor community groups, the government, local government bodies, civil society and the private sector (Urban Partnerships for Poverty Reduction 2006). The UPPR project had three main components: (i) providing grants for the construction of basic services and physical improvements; (ii) providing support for livelihood development programmes in the communities through a community contract system;[3] and (iii) capacity building of local government to address the needs of the urban poor. A four-tier implementation structure – community, ward,[4] *Pourashaval* city and national level – had been developed to support the fundamental principle of the project that decision-making will take place at the community level (Urban Partnerships for Poverty Reduction 2008:4).

At the community[5] level, there were two types of groups: primary group (PG) and community development committee (CDC). A primary group was composed of a group of 15–20 persons in the community who wanted to address a development issue of common interest (Government of the People's Republic of Bangladesh 2001:15). On the other hand, a CDC was comprised of the group leaders and secretaries of the PGs in a community and represented 200–300 families. CDC chairperson, vice-chairperson, secretary and treasurer were elected as office bearers[6] for two years by the members of the CDC. CDCs were the focal point for carrying out all the development activities and addressing the common development issues faced by the entire community. At the ward level there was the project implementation committee and CDC-Cluster at the cluster level.

A savings and credit programme was one of the most important activities undertaken by the community groups. The community contracting process espoused by the project was an effective mechanism for community capacity-building by providing a focus for community action and empowering community people, especially women, in the processes of decision-making, planning and contract management (Urban Partnerships for Poverty Reduction 2006). There were two types of community contract: settlement improvement fund (SIF) and socio-economic fund (SEF). SIF finances all physical investments in the project communities. It supports five types of services: (i) improved water supply and hygiene; (ii) sanitation; (iii) access and environmental improvements; (iv) sheltered space; and (v) urban food production infrastructure (Urban Partnerships for Poverty Reduction 2009). SEF espoused four main programmes: apprenticeships grants, business start-up grants, education grants and social-development activities grants (Urban Partnerships for Poverty Reduction 2009).

6. Research methodology

This chapter is based on a case study research method within the framework of a qualitative research approach. It draws on both primary and secondary data. Primary data were collected through face-to-face in-depth interviews. The respondents included 29 community people from four project communities in the Rajshahi City Corporation (RCC) area, i.e. Alampur, Salampur, Jogotpur and Sripur.[7] Interviews were also conducted with five project officials. The interview sessions were conducted during a five-month-long field study from October 2009 to February 2010. A purposive sampling technique was used to select the respondents. Employing purposive sampling allowed the researcher to do two things: firstly, to select unique information-rich respondents for in-depth investigation, and secondly, it enabled the researcher to select easily accessible respondents who are generally identified as 'difficult-to-reach-specialised population'. While analysing, interview data has been 'triangulated' with data collected from various secondary sources, e.g. academic books, academic journal papers and newspaper contents.

7. The context: local power structure

Historically Bangladeshi society is a hierarchical as well as a low trust society. The hierarchical structure of the society is an imprint of the Hindu caste system as well as the colonial heritage which was based on master-slave rapport (Rahman 2000). On the other hand, as a low trust society, there is a low level of popular trust in various public institutions because of their dysfunctional role in providing services to the people in general. These institutions are historically vested with corruption, nepotism and rigidity and thereby have become inaccessible to the most disadvantaged groups of the society. One of the manifestations of such hierarchism and low trust in public institutions is the presence of the patron-client relationship between the advantaged (patrons) who have control over resources and the disadvantaged (clients) who always seek their favour to get access to the resources (Rahman 2000). The logic of clientelistic and patronage politics have greatly influenced the local governance process by shaping the design of the local government institutions in Bangladesh. As such, the existing urban local governance process is more about consolidating a local political power base through the local government system than sharing power down to the local levels following democratic decentralisation. There is a clear patron-client relationship between the national government and the local government. This patron-client relationship is again reflected within the city corporation's power structure. Within the corporation a culture of patronage has developed where the councillors are connected to national-level politics through the mayor (Huq 2014).

Accordingly, the elected ward councillors held an important position in the community power structure in the four study communities. But their dominance in the community-level power structure was influenced by some factors: for example, the level of political connection of the councillors above the ward level and the presence of other influential local elites in a community and their political profiles. Thus, political affiliation with the ruling political party and the level of political influence were two of the important power resources for the local elite (including the councillor) at the community level. In many respects, community people were connected with the local power elites according to the logic of the patron-clientelistic relationship than being in a dyadic relationship. The ward-level governance process in general was marked by the power distance between the councillors and community people. In the absence of formal channels of participation, community people were only able to influence councillor's decisions through various informal means.

8. Participation, empowerment and the UPPR project

One of the prime objectives of participation in a CDD intervention like UPPR was to expand the assets and capabilities of the poor to participate in, negotiate with, influence, control and hold accountable the institutions that affect their lives. Therefore, power, achieved through acquiring various power resources (asset endowment), in its different manifestations, then, had to be converted into forms of economic, social and political power that could lead to social transformation conducive to a pro-poor development. The following discussion has been organised under two broad headings: power and agency, and social transformation.

8.1. Power and agency

8.1.1. Savings and credit programme

Getting access to savings and credit facilities was one of the important motivating factors for community people in joining the community groups formed under the project. This indicates that the CDCs, as community-based organisations, were providing an incentive that the members valued. But the experience of the savings and credit programme in each of the four study CDCs was different. The programme was more stable in Salampur and Jogotpur than it was in the other two communities. In Alampur the savings and credit operation went through a great setback when a few of the office bearers mismanaged group savings. However, when the second phase of the UPPR project came into operation, that CDC managed to settle down the issue and made a fresh start. Although Sripur encountered a similar situation, it could not resolve the problem and all kinds of group activities stopped in 2006. In the other three CDCs, most of the group members, except a few, drew loans for various purposes. The purposes can be divided into two broad categories: for investment and for withstanding crisis. Some female borrowers handed over the money to their husbands for investing in their business. According to them, those were worthy investments to increase their family income. Some used the loans for building concrete houses, and they considered it as an investment for additional income by renting out extra rooms. A few borrowers started tailoring business and petty trading. Some other borrowers spent the money for withstanding crisis like meeting the educational costs of their children, paying medical bills for their family members, spending on a daughter's wedding ceremony or other similar purposes. Whatever the purposes of the loans, data show that the availability of group loans provided group members with the opportunity to either increase their financial and material assets base or to withstand crisis. Thus, they were in the process of gaining power in determining the life pathway that they valued.

For many, the availability of group loans enhanced their bargaining power in the micro-credit market. It was evident that a good number of group members turned down credit offers made by various NGOs working in the study area for a number of reasons, for example, high interest rate, rigid repayment options and tough conditionality. Under the circumstances, a few research participants opined that taking a loan from CDC was their first preference. Many of them especially mentioned flexibility of repayment as one of the important factors. At the same time, some members valued the issue of their ownership over the fund. Some of the respondents, mainly a few of the office bearers, talked about their future plans and dreams with group savings. One of the office bearers from Salampur said that at the cluster level they had decided to start a group business. She also talked about her own dream of buying public buses for a group business. Another office bearer from Jogotpur talked about their group's plan to start a business of some kind. Therefore, the group savings and credit programme was not only contributing to increasing economical and material assets, but was also developing some participants' capability to envisage change – a psychological asset.

However, in Sripur where the CDC programme remained stopped for years, group members experienced a different reality. According to one of the office bearers of the CDC, many members lost their savings, because there were many who did not draw loans but made savings. On the contrary, there were many who drew loans of 2000 BDT against, for example, a saving of 500 BDT, and they were not interested in repaying the loans. Therefore, there was a group of members who gained at the expense of a few other members, which was against the spirit of collective action. While in the other three CDCs under the study, some UPPR group members were leaving the memberships of other credit-giving NGOs, in Sripur, according to some of the respondents, people were relying more on the credit facilities provided by those NGOs, despite the fact that people in this neighbourhood had had a number of bad experiences in dealing with those external service providers. Thus, instead of expanding agents' choices, the mismanagement of the savings and credit programme in Sripur squeezed members' choices and reinforced their dependence on external service providers.

8.1.2. Community contracts

Community contract was one of the key project strategies towards physical improvement and increased income and assets of the poor. Beside this, at the local level, the issue of building partnerships among local government bodies, the private sector and communities was realised through community contracts. As mentioned earlier there were two types of community contract: settlement improvement fund and socio-economic fund.

8.1.2.1. SETTLEMENT IMPROVEMENT FUND

The SIF benefited the group members in two major ways: (a) through infrastructural development and (b) through skill and knowledge development. A total of 309 latrines, 44 tube-wells, 168.55 meters of drain and 468.55 meters of footpath were constructed using the SIF in the study communities. According to the project estimation, a total of 927 households were the beneficiaries of shared latrines and 880 households of tube-wells. Community assets, such as footpaths and drains, were considered to benefit the whole community and thus benefited 1565 households in total. Interview data indicate that the services provided through the community contracts outweighed the services that had been provided by the Rajshahi City Corporation in those communities in terms of quantity and number of beneficiaries. Community people as a whole highly valued the project's contribution in infrastructure development. The sanitation facilities in the study area were very poor in general before the project came into operation. People made latrines by digging holes with temporary fences around them or building bamboo platforms over the ponds or river. Beside these, a huge number of people used open spaces (drains, riverbanks and bushes). Accordingly, building sanitary latrines brought a fair improvement in public health conditions by reducing water-borne and seasonal diseases like dysentery, cholera and diarrhoea. Installing deep tube-wells ensured the availability of safe water for domestic use throughout the year. Building footpaths and drains provided easy accessibility and reduced waterlogging problems in the respective communities.

Therefore, it is obvious that the project enabled local people to play a crucial role in developing a healthy environment through infrastructural development. The community groups' activities had been contributing to the increased material and financial assets of the members and the community people as a whole. This goes beyond acquiring assets (power resources) because people were participating actively in the local development process including planning, implementation and evaluation, which was previously an absolute official domain of the city corporation personnel.

8.1.2.2. SOCIO-ECONOMIC FUNDS

According to the official documents, the project envisaged that the partnership between communities and private sector service providers would grow in more concrete forms through community contracts under the SEF. For example, under the apprenticeship programme, selected group members or their family members received on-the-job type vocational training in tapestry, batik printing and making silver pots in various small factories. A few of the trainees continued their work after the training period was over, but a majority of them discontinued due to low salaries offered by the employers and an unfavourable work environment. This suggests that group members' ability to increase their assets (skills) was dependent more on the labour market situation which was outside the control of the community groups, as well as the project management. Besides this, there were some incidents of corrupt practices of some the office bearers in administering the apprenticeship programme. On some occasions, group members valued the monthly cash allowance provided by the project more than receiving training and acquiring new skills. And some of the office bearers selected some of those members as beneficiaries based on personal relationships. For favouring some members over others, some office bearers even manipulated official records. Therefore, community contracts also helped in developing favouritism and corrupt practices. During the project lifetime a number of income-, skill- and awareness-building workshops and training programmes were organised by the community groups. Research data show that group members acquired valuable knowledge about various social, political, legal and income-generating skills. But those training and workshop sessions were mainly participated in by the office bearers and primary group leaders.

8.1.3. Community groups and social capital

Trust and social networks are important factors in collective action. These are also by-products of successful collective action. Therefore, these are two of the important asset endowments (organisational assets) for empowerment. The discussion first focuses on the issue of trust followed by networks.

Research data, in general, speak in favour of the positive impact in heightening the level of social trust among the group members in Alampur, Salampur and Jogotpur where the project groups were functional throughout the project lifetime. Trust building in these three communities was a long process which had been developed and reinforced gradually through the establishment of good practices in managing group activities like savings and credit programme, community contracts and so on. But this kind of trust was fragile in nature. People became encouraged to trust each other by seeing successful collective action. Benefit sharing was one of the important factors in the trust-building process. When members received benefits through collective action, inter-personal trust developed among the group members. On the contrary, trustworthiness declined when members missed services provided by the groups. But the demand for group resources usually remained higher than supply. Therefore, the decision-making of resource distribution had to be more participatory and transparent so that all the group members were able to have the scope to take part in the process as informed participants. This would enable the members to know who were getting what and on what basis. In contrast, the experience of Sripur shows how the failure of collective action caused mistrust among the group members that impacted their interpersonal relationships negatively.

Social networks, an important property of social capital, influence an actor's social capital through the actor's direct and indirect ties afforded them by virtue of the overall structure of the broader network within which they are embedded. UPPR project group members were directly tied to each other in groups within a CDC. At the same time they were also tied to the wider network (cluster level and city level) mainly through the office bearers. Therefore, the level of social network gain was different for general group members, primary group leaders and office bearers. While the office bearers talked about various types of people ranging from various levels of project officials, ward councillors (WCs) of different wards, city corporation officials and members from different CDCs, those with whom they were closely tied and interacted frequently, the general primary group members talked about mainly the concerned community development workers and the few other people who occasionally visited the CDCs. Therefore, the size of the social network of group members increased as a whole where the general primary group members were tied to the broader network through the office bearers. Because of group activities, CDC office bearers were actively linked with a range of influential persons beyond the communities, for instance, the mayor of the Rajshahi City Corporation, UPPR project officials, officials of various government departments and members of other CDCs. When we consider network building as a source of power and influence, the CDC office bearers and thus the project community group members acquired power resources. On the downside, by considering the fact that power was concentrated in the hands of a few office bearers and was not generally shared by the group members, the network gained through group activities become more of a personal attribute than a group property.

8.2. Social transformation

People may acquire various kinds of asset endowments (e.g. psychological, informational, organisational, material, financial and human assets) through participating in community groups. These asset endowments (power resources) may not improve the state of empowerment on their own until they are used to bring about desired outcomes favourable to bringing changes in asymmetrical social relationships. The following discussion focuses on the effects of participation in changing gender relations, reconfiguring the mode of community-level governance and influencing various community level social affairs.

8.2.1. Gender relation

Women's presence in various political and social organisations in Bangladeshi society is generally limited by gender-biased social norms and practices. In this context, UPPR group membership provided the women members with legitimate roles and positions in managing local development issues. Within a patriarchal context, women's ability to acquire political and social power (collectively or individually) is dependent on their ability to exercise some form of legitimate power, or gain 'power within' or 'power with' through improved status, assertion of identity and changes in traditionally defined gender roles in a society. The structural framework of UPPR and the group activities provided women members with the opportunity to acquire collective power, which could lead to women acting against domination and improving their subordinate status. Again, at the individual level, women need to gain two forms of power: positional and personal (Stamm and Ryff 1984, cited in Sabhlok 2007:212–213). Positional power stems from specific positions and roles in a society. It is formal authority delegated to the holders of the positions. On the other hand, personal power is related to the potential of individuals to exert influence and control which is sanctioned implicitly through the acceptance of an individual's right to make decisions about a particular aspect of social life. UPPR aimed to change the positional power of women through group membership and assigned roles (through forms of 'power with', 'power over' or 'power to') and personal power through self-confidence and self-awareness ('power within').

The changing role of women in society was well acknowledged by the research participants. In the context of Bangladeshi society, husbands' consent and co-operation was crucial for the female members' participation in group activities. All the female project group members (interviewees), except one, mentioned that their family members (including husbands) were co-operative and appreciative of their involvement and activities in the groups. A number of group members considered the co-operation of their husbands meant getting recognition of their work by their families. Group membership was a source of self-esteem, building self-confidence and self-awareness. A number of respondents talked about their good feelings in terms of positive changes in their identity. Women's involvement in group activities was also found to be conducive to changing the traditional gender-biased norms and practices. Thus, some women members appeared as change agents in the process of changing gender-biased social views. Many respondents mentioned that as women they did not face any resistance from community people. This was a sign of societal acceptance of women's roles in the local development process. Such societal acceptance carries significant value from a women's empowerment viewpoint.

8.2.2. Participation in the ward-level governance process

Elected ward councillors were one of the most powerful actors within the ward-level governance process. Except in Sripur, the initial community group formation process was greatly intervened by the concerned councillors for some practical reasons. For example, the project community development workers – responsible for initiating the community mobilisation process – were outsiders and unknown to the community people. Therefore, the concerned ward councillors and their nominated persons, who eventually occupied the group leadership positions on many occasions, were a source of confidence and trust for the local people in building faith in the proposed project intervention. Therefore, as local people's representatives, councillors had an important role in overseeing the functions of the CDCs. Their formal involvement in group activities was seen as an integration process of the community groups in the wider decision-making sphere, as the CDD approach promises to do so.

Interview data show that the concerned councillors influenced the functioning of the community groups in many ways. Any kind of group decision had to be endorsed by the councillors. Where group members disagreed with the councillors' wishes, severe clashes occurred. Some of the community group members and UPPR project officials identified the roles of many of the local councillors as impediments to the proper functioning of many of the community groups. Some of the primary group leaders and office bearers were not giving back group savings that they had siphoned in a number of CDCs in Rajshahi city. They could do this since they were in a good relationship with the concerned councillors, and the project officials were unable to take any action against them. On a few occasions the concerned local councillors were a source of power for a few of the group members in influencing the group activities in undue manners where the majority of the group members as well as the local project office had little to do. This resembled the continuation of the existing asymmetrical relationships among the actors involved in the local governance process. However, this was one side of the coin. Research findings also illustrate that in many instances, the group members could exercise their influence on the councillors as well. There were some incidents where the community group members exercised their agency (power over) through successful protest against the undue behaviour of the councillors.

Due to the absence of the formal mechanism of direct citizens' participation in the ward-level governance process in the urban areas of Bangladesh, informal means of participation were the only ways for the local people to interact with the councillors. In this context, the project intervention opened a formal avenue for the group members to interact with them. This enabled some of the group members to be in close touch with the local elected representatives. Those members opined that they were more aware of various local development issues than before because of their participation in group activities. Some of the project activities, for example, community contracts, indeed provided the groups with the opportunity for taking part in the ward-level decision-making on a consensus basis. One of the respondents from Salampur shared one of her experiences. She reported that the main walkway in her community was already included in the city corporation's annual development programme, but it was uncertain when the corporation tendering process would take place. Under the circumstances, considering the urgency, the street was constructed by her CDC upon the recommendation of the concerned councillor. In fact, the community groups became an influential actor in the ward-level governance process.

Nevertheless, we can see that it was predominantly the office bearers who were exercising 'power over' or sharing 'power with' the local councillors. General group members were connected with the WCs through the primary group leaders and CDC office bearers. This phenomenon became apparent by the comments made by a number of general primary group members, who reported that when they needed help from the councillors, they first contacted the chairpersons of the concerned CDCs because they were intimate with them. The issue denotes two different perspectives. Firstly, this can be seen as the enhancement of collective agency of the group members through which group members enjoyed better access to elected representatives. Secondly, on the contrary, when we consider the fact that power was hardly shared within the group, this could be seen as the reproduction of the pre-existing patron-clientelistic relationship, where some of the group members, mainly the CDC office bearers, appeared as agents of the local councillors and acted as intermediaries between the general primary group members and the councillors.

8.2.3. Involvement in the management of social affairs

When we consider empowerment as a process through which communities achieve greater control over their own affairs, it entails that power resources should also be converted into social and political actions. There were some good examples where a community group actively took part in resolving various social problems, for example, family conflict, dealing with local police and so on. In one study community, the group members took an extraordinary initiative in cooperation with the concerned councillors to diminish alcoholism and other crimes in their community. In another community the group members resisted a number of incidents of violence against women. After sharing a similar type of experience, one of the respondents from Salampur reported that in many instances people came to them to settle petty disputes, which was previously a sole prerogative of the local elites in those communities. Therefore, data show that the collective ability to negotiate with external agents and to manage internal affairs was acquired by some of the community groups and its members. Consequently the group members, except in Sripur, gained some kind of collective power which they converted into social and political actions to deal with various social issues.

9. The promises and perils of CDD: a critical review

The research findings demonstrate, subject to the successful functioning of the group savings and credit programme, some of the members benefited through the acquisition of psychological, material and financial assets. It was not only important to enrich their material and financial asset base, but it also helped to develop psychological assets for some of the members (mainly group leaders) to increase their capacity to envisage change. From Sen's (1999) 'Development as Freedom'[8] perspective, the group savings and credit programme expanded the group members' capabilities in terms of increasing their access and opportunity to do things that they valued. In those communities where the project groups were functional, members were getting access to a healthy environment as well as the opportunity to develop income-generating skills and build awareness on various socio-economic issues through community contracts. Participation in community groups benefited the members by providing them with easy access to elected local people's representatives, societal acceptance of their roles in local development, self-confidence, self-esteem, personal experience, trusted relationships and social networks. These asset endowments helped some of the group members in sharing power with the concerned councillors and with other local power elites. The collective ability to negotiate with external agents and to manage internal affairs was also gained by some of the community groups. By engaging in and influencing various community affairs, some of the female group members emerged as change agents in altering the traditional gender-biased views of the society. Consequently, the community group members acquired some kind of personal and collective power which they could convert into social and political actions by solving various community-level social problems. This gives an indication of positive change towards an inclusive local governance process following a subtle process of transformation in institutional relationships by strengthening the collective bargaining power of the community people.

However, findings also show how the failure of collective action could bring adverse consequences in terms of disempowering the group members. While the savings and credit programme was pivotal in the successful functioning of project groups in two study communities, it was a bone of contention in two others. The same programme design and strategies worked differently in a changed community context. Again, the experiences of using the SEF for employment creation through internship programmes highlighted the issue that the ultimate outcomes depended largely on the labour market situation and the judicious use of the members' agency in selecting beneficiaries. While it was found that participating in various workshops and seminars was conducive to increasing participants' informational, psychological, organisational, financial and human asset endowments, the benefits were largely enjoyed by only some of the group members – more specifically the CDC office bearers. If we measure the level of power and control in terms of asset endowments acquired through the membership of the groups, we will find that there was a great discrepancy between the general group members and the CDC office bearers. Thus, the level of asset endowment (power resources) was unequal among the group members, and, therefore, the empowerment effect was more visible in the actions of some of the office bearers in the study CDCs.

The downside of this situation was two-fold: firstly, concentration of power in the hands of a few perhaps contributed towards the practices of alleged corruption in distributing group resources following the logic of nepotism and favouritism. It means that some of the office bearers exerted disproportionate influence over the collective action process; secondly, there was an indication that on many occasions some of those office bearers had been co-opted by the existing local power structure and were reproducing the pre-existing asymmetric relationship instead of becoming an agent of change. Existing literature suggests that such co-optation exerts a serious threat of 'elite capture' – a condition where the project decisions, planning and resources are totally monopolised by the elites (Cooke and Kothari 2001; Platteau and Gaspart 2003; Mansuri and Rao 2004; Platteau 2004; Dasgupta and Beard 2007; Dill 2009).

While the 'elite capture' poses a serious threat, the theoretical propositions as well as socio-political realities of the Bangladeshi society imply that local elites' involvement is sometimes necessary for the functioning of a community-based participatory process. The involvement of the local elites (i.e. elected councillors/their selected persons) was important in building trust among the community people in an externally initiated development intervention. One cannot deny the fact that local communities are sites that are neither sealed off from relational and trans-local linkages (broader networks) nor homogeneous. Communities are often sites of power struggle, featuring a culture of patron-clientelistic relationships that are embedded in social networks and governance institutions whose nature and outcomes affect the community-level power structure. Therefore, a sudden endeavour to mobilise community people, while bypassing the local power holders, with a desperate aim of revising the prevailing asymmetric power relations, might not work in a context where the local governance system generally reflects the logic of a patron-clientelistic relationship which flows in a cascade manner from the national level down to the community level (Huq 2014).

10. Conclusion

The chapter aimed at examining whether the community group members – individually and collectively – exercised or acquired any form of power and control over their lives. More precisely, the prime quest was to explore how people's participation in a CDD project may influence their level of agency and the structure within which they operate. In general, the UPPR project provided the community people with an opportunity of building personal as well as collective capacity. It also granted a legitimate role in managing local affairs through creating a new type of participatory space where the participants were bestowed with a new set of responsibilities, resources and authority. The findings of this study and the subsequent analyses indicate that inducing participation through CDD projects may have the potential of empowering community people. Failure of collective action, however, may disempower the people to an extent that can outweigh the potential benefits. Moreover, it could be a process of producing a new type of power elites who later might or might not be co-opted by the traditional power structure. Therefore, inducing participation and empowering communities through CDD projects is a tricky job to accomplish.

To conclude, CDD-type development interventions might propel the subtle process of social transformation along with a high level of beneficiary satisfaction upon the adoption of context-specific sensible programme strategies and practices, but such endeavours alone may fall well short of building a cohesive community, marked by a high level of social inclusion, social mobility and social capital. This demonstrates the limitation of a community development programme which is not linked with a state-sponsored 'radical development project' aiming to change the broader political, economic, social and institutional spheres that go beyond the locale.

Notes

1 CBD is an umbrella term encompassing a wide range of projects that actively include beneficiaries in their design, management and implementation.
2 https://www.worldbank.org/en/topic/communitydrivendevelopment.
3 Community contract is a process whereby common amenities are built by the community as a contractor.
4 A town/city is divided into wards according to its population, and representatives are elected from each ward.

5 The idea of community in the project was similar to the idea of neighbourhood. The project identified communities mainly based on geographical boundaries. The minimum number of households in a community was 30.
6 Either the chairperson or vice-chairperson must be a female member. This is strategic policy to ensure more females in the leadership position.
7 The names of the study communities (CDCs) representing them are pseudonyms.
8 "the expansion of the 'capabilities' of people to lead the kind of lives they value – and have reason to value" (Sen 1999:18).

References

Beard, V. A. and A. Dasgupta (2006). "Collective Action and Community-driven Development in Rural and Urban Indonesia." *Urban Studies* **43**(9): 1451–1468.

Binswanger-Mkhize, H. P., J. P. de Regt, and S. Spector (2009). "Introduction and Conclusions." *Scaling Up Local and Community-driven Development (LCDD): A Real World Guide to Its Theory and Practice.* H. P. Binswanger-Mkhize, J. P. de Regt, and S. Spector. Washington, DC, The World Bank.

Binswanger-Mkhize, H. P. and T.-V. Nguyen (2005). "A Step by Step Guide to Scale Up Community Driven Development." *International Workshop on 'African Water Laws: Plural Legislative Frameworks for Rural Water Management in Africa'.* Johannesburg, IWMI Books, International Water Management Institute.

Cooke, B. and U. Kothari (2001). *Participation: The New Tyranny?* London, Zed Books.

Cornwall, A. (2002). *Making Spaces, Changing Places: Situating Participation in Development*, IDS Working Paper. Sussex, Institute of Development Studies.

Cornwall, A. (2004). "Spaces for Transformation? Reflections on Issues of Power and Difference in Participation in Development." *Participation: From Tyranny to Transformation? Exploring New Approaches to Participation in Development.* S. Hickey and G. Mohan. London, New York, Zed Books: 75–91.

Dahl-Ostergaard, T., D. Moore, V. Ramirez, M. Wenner, and A. Bonde (2003). *Community-Driven Development: What Have We Learned?* Washington, DC, Inter-American Development Bank.

Dasgupta, A. and V. A. Beard (2007). "Community Driven Development, Collective Action and Elite Capture in Indonesia." *Development and Change* **38**(2): 229–249.

Dill, B. (2009). "The Paradoxes of Community-based Participation in Dar es Salaam." *Development and Change* **40**(4): 717–743.

Domelen, V. J. (2002). "Social Funds: Evidence on Targeting, Impacts and Sustainability." *Journal of International Development* **14**(5): 627–642.

Dongier, P., J. V. Domelen, E. Ostrom, A. Rizvi, W. Wakeman, A. Bebbington, S. Alkire, T. Esmail, and M. Polski (2002). "Community-driven Development." *A Sourcebook for Poverty Reduction Strategies.* J. Klugman. Washington, DC, The World Bank: 301–331.

Economic and Social Commission for Western Asia, U. N. (2004). *Community-Driven Development as an Integrated Social Policy at the Local Level.* Retrieved 6 April 2009, from www.escwa.un.org/information/publications/edit/upload/DRIVENE.pdf.

Edwards, M. and D. Hulme (1992). "Scaling-up the Developmental Impact of NGOs: Concepts and Experiences." *Making a Difference: NGOs and Development in a Changing World.* M. Edwards and D. Hulme. London, Save the Children and Earthscan.

Gaventa, J. (2003). "Towards Participatory Local Governance: Assessing the Transformative Possibilities." *Participation: From Tyranny to Transformation*. Manchester, Zed Books.

Government of the People's Republic of Bangladesh (2001). *Implementation Guideline, Local Partnerships for Urban Poverty Alleviation*. Ministry of Local Government Rural Development and Cooperatives, Local Government Division and Local Government Engineering Department, Dhaka.

Hickey, S. and G. Mohan (2004). "Towards Participation as Transformation: Critical Themes and Challenges." *Participation: From Tyranny to Transformation? Exploring New Approaches to Participation in Development*. S. Hickey and G. Mohan. London, New York, Zed Books.

Huq, P. A. (2014). "The Politics of Local Policy-Making in Urban Bangladesh: The Case of Rajshahi City Corporation." *Asian Journal of Political Science*: 1–20.

Kumar, N. (2003). *Community-Driven Development: Lessons from the Sahel, An Analytical Review*. Washington, DC, The World Bank Operations Evaluation Department, The World Bank.

Labonne, J. and R. S. Chase (2009). "Who Is at the Wheel When Communities Drive Development? Evidence from the Philippines." *World Development* 37(1): 219–231.

Ledwith, M. and J. Springett (2010). *Participatory Practice: Community-based Action for Transformative Change*. Bristol, The Policy Press.

Lyons, M., C. Smuts, and A. Stephens (2001). "Participation, Empowerment and Sustainability: (How) Do the Links Works?" *Urban Studies* 38(8): 1233–1251.

Mansuri, G. and V. Rao (2004). "Community-based and -driven Development: A Critical Review." *World Bank Research Observer* 19(1): 1–39.

Mansuri, M. and V. Rao (2012). *Can Participation be Induced? Some Evidence from Developing Countries*, Policy Research Working Paper. Washington, DC, The World Bank.

Masaki, K. (2004). "The 'Transformative' Unfolding of 'Tyrannical' Participation: The Corvée Tradition and Ongoing Politics in Western Nepal." *Participation: From Tyranny to Transformation? Exploring New Approaches to Participation in Development*. S. Hickey and G. Mohan. London, New York, Zed Books: 125–139.

Miller, S. M. and M. Rein (2011). "Community Participation: Past and Future." *The Community Development Reader: History, Themes and Issues*. G. Craig, M. Mayo, and K. Popple. Bristol, The Policy Press: 83–90.

Moser, C. O. (1983). "The Problem of Evaluating Community Participation in Urban Development Projects." *Development Planning Unit Working Paper: Evaluating Community Participation in Urban Development Projects*. C. O. Moser. London, University College London.

Narayan, D., Ed. (2002). *Empowerment and Poverty Reduction: A Sourcebook*, Washington, DC, The World Bank.

Nelson, N. and S. Wright (1997). "Participation and Power." *Power and Participatory Development: Theory and Practice*. N. Nelson and S. Wright. London, Intermediate Technology Publication: 1–18.

Osei-Hwedie, K. and B. Z. Osei-Hwedie (2010). "Participatory Development." *Social Development: Critical Themes and Perspective*. M. S. Pawar and D. R. Cox. New York, Oxon, Routledge: 57–75.

Owen, D. and V. Domelen (1998). *Getting an Earful: A Review of Beneficiary Assessments of Social Fund*, World Bank–Social Protection Discussion Paper. Washington, DC, The World Bank.

Partridge, W. L. (2008). "Praxis and Power." *Journal of Community Psychology* **36**(2): 161–172.

Platteau, J. P. (2004). "Monitoring Elite Capture in Community-driven Development." *Development and Change* **35**(2): 223–246.

Platteau, J. P. and F. Gaspart (2003). "The Risk of Resource Misappropriation in Community-Driven Development." *World Development* **31**(10): 1687–1703.

Rahman, M. T. (2000). *The Role of Parliamentary Committees in Ensuring Bureaucratic Accountability in Bangladesh*. M. Phil Dissertation, University of Bergen.

Sabhlok, S. G. (2007). *Women and NGOs' Participation in Development: Partnership and Control in India*. PhD, The University of Melbourne.

Sen, A. K. (1999). *Development as Freedom*. New York, Alfred A. Knopf.

Smith, B. C. (2008). "The Concept of Empowerment." *Centre for Study and Research Journal* **1**(3).

Stewart, A. (2001). *Theories of Power and Domination: The Politics of Empowerment in Late Modernity*. London, Thousand Oaks, New Delhi, Sage Publications.

Tanaka, S., J. Singh, and D. Songco (2006). *A Review of Community-driven Development and Its Application to the Asian Development Bank*. Manila, Asian Development Bank.

Urban Partnerships for Poverty Reduction (2006). *Urban Partnerships for Poverty Reduction, Bangladesh: Technical Annex 1 (Description of Project Components)*. Dhaka, Government of the Peoples' Republic of Bangladesh, and United Nation Development Programme.

Urban Partnerships for Poverty Reduction (2008). *Project Document*. Dhaka, Government of the Peoples' Republic of Bangladesh, and United Nations Development Programme.

Urban Partnerships for Poverty Reduction (2009). *Annual Progress Report 2009*. Dhaka, Urban Partnerships for Poverty Reduction.

Urban Partnerships for Poverty Reduction (2012). "Official Website of the Urban Partnerships for Poverty Reduction Project." Retrieved 1 April 2012, from www.upprbd.org/.

Williams, G. (2004). "Towards a Depoliticization of Participatory Development: Political Capabilities and Spaces of Empowerment." *Participation: From Tyranny to Transformation? Exploring New Approaches to Participation in Development*. S. M. Hickey. London, New York, Zed Books: 92–107.

The World Bank (2000). "The Community Driven Development Approach in the Africa Region: A Vision of Poverty Reduction Through Empowerment." Retrieved 17 April 2009, from http://siteresources.worldbank.org/INTISPMA/Resources/383704-1153333441931/cdd_approach_africa.pdf.

14 Neo-community formation, contestation and policy making in India

Narratives from Chilika

Lalatendu Keshari Das

Introduction

During the 2014 and 2017 general elections in India and the United Kingdom (UK) respectively, two slogans emerged as central discussion points: the *sabka saath, sabka vikash* slogan of the right wing Hindutva nationalist Bharatiya Janta Party (BJP) in India and *For the Many, Not the Few* slogan of the centre-left Labour Party in the UK. The former emerged from the anti-corruption movement that polarised the imagination of voters during the last phase of United Progressive Alliance (UPA) rule at the centre, while the latter was articulated at the aftermath of the Brexit referendum, in which a majority of voters wished the UK to leave European Union. The puzzling part of the aforementioned narrative is how to make sense of this conjuncture, a situation in which both the political left and right are appealing to their audience with a similarly constructed rhetoric. Does this mean that significant ruptures have emerged in the earlier vision of an imagined community (Anderson, 2006) based on shared language and culture (Gellner, 1983)? Can we now argue that this indicates the emergence of a new paradigm, one in which, notwithstanding one's political ideology, economic and social development needs to cater to the greatest number of people and not just a few castes, classes or ethnic groups? In other words, have we reached a stage in which 'cohesive development' is the only way forward? This chapter, through empirical investigation of a counter-movement in Odisha, attempts to understand this conjuncture by problematising the idea of 'community' vis-à-vis the discursive practices of development.

In what follows, I first discuss the recent theorisations on community formations for bringing cohesiveness to policy making in India. Then by discussing a counter-movement that took place in the Chilika region of Odisha against shrimp cultivation in the lake, I show the problematic in the articulation of 'community', which I call 'neo-community', by both the subaltern groups and the legal and political elites. Drawing from my case study, I finally discuss whether 'cohesive development' is the idea which has become inevitable to the survival of communities, locally, nationally and globally.

Community and contestation

Community, as a standalone category, has been a mainstay for sociologists and anthropologists since the colonial period. 'Community development' in the post-colonial regimes has also been discussed elegantly. However, the shifting pattern of work from primarily agriculture-related activities to a multiplicity of work (Haan, 1999; Breman, 2007) has complicated this hitherto accepted idea of community. The fragmentation of locations, because of the new work regimes as well as developmental activities of the state and corporate capital, for both households and kinship relationships, has given rise to new forms of relationships. This has brought ruptures in the imagination of community bonding contra state and capital, as was articulated by an earlier generation of scholars. Commenting on the emerging processes, Chatterjee (2008a) argues,

> [i]f such incidents had taken place 25 years ago, we would have seen in them the classic signs of peasant . . . Here were the long familiar features of a peasantry, tied to the land and small-scale agriculture, united by the cultural and moral bonds of a local rural community, resisting the agents of an external state and of city-based commercial institutions by using both peaceful and violent means. Our analysis then would have drawn on a long tradition of anthropological studies of peasant societies, focusing on the characteristic forms of dependence of peasant economies on external institutions such as the state and dominant classes such as landlords, moneylenders and traders, but also of the forms of autonomy of peasant cultures based on the solidarity of a local moral community.
>
> (54)

Rather, for Chatterjee, state is no more an alien agent for the peasants/fishers/forest dwellers in the Indian hinterland. The previous description of their struggles would merely be a caricature of a bygone era. Through what the rights discourse calls 'subsistence rights' and Chatterjee (2008a) and Sanyal (2007) termed governmentality, namely, 'education, health services, food, roadways, water, electricity, agricultural technology, emergency relief', among others, the state has reached out to most of the dispersed communities in India. So, the notion of community for these groups is no more in terms of 'negation' of the 'external agency' like the state, rather it has become relational to strategically locating the state's nodes of power to use them for one's own benefit. For this, it is no longer necessary for the individuals or groups to belong to the same caste, class or even religion or physical location. Rather, the formation of a community is more contextual and meant for specific purposes.

On a similar note, Agarwala (2006, 2013) and Chandra (2015) propose that instead of interpreting resistance and community formations as forms of 'negation', something Ranajit Guha eloquently describes in his classic work *Elementary Aspects of Peasant Insurgency in Colonial India* (1994), we need to look at it as 'negotiation'. This will free the researcher from totalising tendencies of the subaltern studies works (Dhanagare, 2016), which tried to create rigid boundaries between discourse and strategies of subaltern groups. Struggles by the subaltern groups are meant to negotiate the terms of engagement with the state, particularly in the neoliberal era when corporate capital is taking hegemonic form in India.

The contextual and ephemeral nature of these communities is further highlighted as, unlike in the past in which community-based institutions of arbitration were preferred over an alien legal system (Cohn, 1965; Srinivas, 1994), the present communities formed over certain issues do not hesitate to use courts of law to further their demands as citizens (Vallinder, 1994; Nielsen, 2015a). This process, it is argued, not only gives the subaltern groups a handle to manoeuvre the policy-making mechanism of the state and its ruling elites, but also it provides these communities an audience, wherein the policies would 'resonate with their aspirations' (Nielsen, 2015b).

Does this mean that the neo-communities have finally broken the chains of servitude prevailing in the anthropological village republics and the antiquated nature of communities, glorified and vilified at the same time over the past two centuries, something our aforementioned theorists have harped on? Unlike Chatterjee (2008b, 2011), who argued that people belonging to different classes, castes and gender come together to form a 'community' and assert their rights against the capital and the state, Harriss-White and Gooptu (2009) have pointed out the peculiar nature of capitalist development in post-colonial India. They argue that with state regulations not keeping up with the penetration of capital into the Indian hinterland as well as urban areas, much of capitalist growth has taken place in the unorganised sector. This has resulted in a large segment of the workforce still deprived of basic training in terms of education and skills development for various apprentice jobs. Without such standardisation of the workforce, Indian labour is not only poverty stricken and unskilled, but also remains substantially deprived of its basic rights under the ill-defined labour laws. Under these circumstances, caste and regional affinity to the capitalist (Breman, 2013) become crucial for the workers to get work, on the one hand, and capitalists to ascertain their control over the working population on the other. So, glorifying the formation of these neo-communities does not augur well for the future of development in India. As class issues or 'politics of the labour' have been replaced by the so-called politics of the poor or governmentality and identity politics, the central problematic of such political formations is their tendency to showcase an individual and homogenous 'community' (Chaudhury, 2014). But the fact of the matter is that such constructed communities do not necessarily change the internal contradictions within them. As our case of Chilika will show, cohesiveness constructed in the form of neo-communities around governmentality could become handmaiden of the state and elites to make the hitherto old communities compete with and against each other for a share in the resources.

The counter-movement in Chilika

Administratively, Chilika Lake falls under the jurisdiction of eight community development blocks, namely Krushnaprasad, Brahmagiri, Kanas, Tangi, Chilika, Banapur, Khallikote and Ganjam located in the three districts of Puri, Khurda and Ganjam, respectively, in Odisha (Ghosh and Pattnaik, 2006; Nayak, 2014). There are approximately 137–140 villages in the eight blocks, which are predominantly inhabited by people belonging to fishing castes (consisting of Kaibartya 67.1%, Kandara 14.3%, Kartia 2.7%, Khatia 3.0%, Tiara 7.0%, Gokha 0.2% and Nolia 6.8%) (Mitra and Mahapatra, 1957; Iwasaki and Shaw, 2008). These villages are surrounded by upper- and middle-caste villages. Of them, the three upper castes of Brahmins, Karans and Khandayats are the largest landholders.

Chilika, particularly since the late 1980s, has seen systematic dissent against the imposition of new economic policies of the Odisha state government. The period between 1985 (when the results of the first phase of shrimp aquaculture were realised) to 1993 was crucial for Chilika as the region witnessed a phase of rapid intensification of shrimp cultivation activities. During this period not only the village Sunamuhin (where the Odisha state government with financial assistance from the World Bank created shrimp cultivation ponds for distribution to the poor fisher households), but also every shallow area in the lake, called *dian* and *uthapani*, were converted to aquaculture fields. Pen enclosures were installed within the lake for intensive and extensive shrimp cultivation encompassing hundreds of hectares of water area. Meanwhile, first in 1986 during the Congress government under the chief ministership of J. B. Pattanaik and then in 1991 under the Janata Dal Chief Minister Biju Pattanaik, the Tata group came to occupy a central role in aquaculture activities in the lake, when Chilika Aquatic Farms Limited (CAFL) was conceived as a joint venture between the Odisha state and the Tatas. Six hundred hectares of shoreline in the Chilika area were earmarked for this project in the Krushnaprasad block of Puri district. To further exploit the economic prospects of the lake, in 1991, the Odisha state government changed the access regime in Chilika. It divided the lake area (of approximately 19148.88 hectares) into a 60:40 ratio of capture and culture fisheries, respectively, and allotted a majority of the culture sources (5665.59 hectares) to the non-fishing castes.

The subsequent enclosure of the lake from villages Panaspada to Mudiratha by the CAFL for culture ponds ignited the first phase of movement in the surrounding areas of the project. The movement drew upon the language of moral economy and constitutional provisions of social and environmental justice to contest the statist claims for marketization of natural resources. The involvement of civil society organisations from Bhubaneswar in the form of 'Meet the Students' group (under Chittaranjan Sarangi) and the

Odisha Krushaka Mahasangha (under Banka Behari Das, an ex-minister with the Congress government in Odisha) made the movement gain national and international attention under the banner of *Chilika Bachao Andolan* (Mohanty, 2000; Pattanaik, 2003). At the same time, the *Chilika Matsyajibi Mahasangha*, the trade union of fisher groups representing all the fishing villages in the lake, was active in mobilising different castes and classes of fishers (Adduci, 2009), under the banner of *Matsyajibi Bachao Andolan* (MBA) against aquaculture activities in the lake and the imminent threat of dispossession to the fishers. The fishing communities, with their primary fishermen cooperative societies (PFCS) and city-based civil society organisations, formed the core group of this movement.

One thing that needs to be taken into account is that the class character of *Chilika Matsyajibi Mahasangha*'s mobilisations saw more importance given to the livelihood discourse of the fishers. It also questioned the right of the state to interfere in the hitherto followed moral economy of the Chilika fishers. As one of its pamphlets asks, '[i]n a situation where commercial use of resources comes into conflict with the livelihood pursuit of poor people, what should be the priority of the state?' (cited in Mohanty (2000: 14)). The central purpose of this movement, according to its activists, was to prevent the decoupling of markets from the social and cultural roots of the fishing communities, as Chilika was also their main source of livelihood and which through generations of care and affection they have nurtured and received nurture in return. This way a strong bond of sustainability between the lake and its fisher people has been created. The *Odisha Krushaka Mahasangha*–led *Chilika Bachao Andolan*, on the other hand, emphasised on the environmental fallout of the Chilika Aquatic Farms Limited.

Supreme Court and the environmental discourse

The environmental discourse of *Chilika Bachao Andolan*, particularly the one headed by Banka Behary Das, received support from similarly positioned social action groups in India when in 1995 they filed a writ petition in the Supreme Court, *S Jagannathan vs. Union of India* (AIR 1997 SC811),[1] on the impact of intensive shrimp cultivation by industrial houses in the coastal areas and other ecologically fragile water bodies. The petition did not specifically argue the Chilika case. However, it requested extensive regulation of the coastal areas for sustainable and meaningful use. The court evoked the protection of Coastal Regulatory Zones (CRZ) under the Coastal Regulation Notification of 1991 and Environmental (Protection) Act of 1986 to ban shrimp cultivation within 500 meters of the CRZ[2] and 1,000 meters from Chilika and Puliket lakes, respectively. Citing the CRZ notification of 1991, it banned (S. Jagannathan vs. Union of India 1996),

i   Setting up of new industries and expansion of existing industries, except those directly related to water front or directly needing fore-shore facilities.

ii Manufacture or handing or storage or disposal of hazardous substances as specified in the Notification of the government of India in the Ministry of Environment & Forests Nos. 0.59.1(E) dated 28 July 1989, S.O. 966(E) dated 27 November 1989 and GSR 108(E) dated 5 December 1989.
iii Setting up and expanding fish processing units including warehousing (excluding hatchery and natural fish drying in permitted areas).
iv Discharge of untreated wastes and effluent from industries, cities and settlements. Schemes shall be implemented by the concerned authorities phasing out the existing practices, in and within a reasonable time period not exceeding three years from the date of this notification. (Para 17)

Moreover, the court also suggested that there should be a free passage for fishers and tourists through the shrimp ponds, as this would minimise social conflicts. This was so, the court argued, because shrimp farming would not require waterfront lands. Rather it could involve pumping of brackish/salt water into ponds, created at suitable distances from these waterbodies. So, the court asked the state implementing agencies to demolish all shrimp ponds and pen enclosures in these areas and ensure that the polluting industries compensate the affected communities following the 'polluter pays' principle. The judges, however, allowed various forms of 'traditional extensive'[3] methods of shrimp cultivation to continue with the clause that these farms have to be carefully regulated. An environmental impact assessment (EIA) and a social impact assessment (SIA) were made mandatory for construction and functioning of these farms. Showing concern towards growing opposition to environmental issues involved in shrimp aquaculture, particularly in Odisha, Andhra Pradesh and Tamil Nadu, the court reasoned that the revenue generated out of such activities within the CRZ was not remunerative enough to compensate for substantial environmental degradation.

This verdict of the Supreme Court was hailed by activists as a landmark judgement for protecting the fragile ecosystem of CRZs and helping the poor fishers in these areas to gain meaningful subsistence following their traditional craft. Notwithstanding the judgement, the shrimp-processing industry continues to thrive within the CRZ zones, including Chilika, where in the commercial town of Balugaon new shrimp-processing units have come up right in front of the state enforcement agency buildings with the backing of local ruling party lawmakers (an engraved marble plaque on the outer wall of a processing plant, officially inaugurated in late 2015, announced the grand opening of the plant by the local Member of Legislative Assembly (MLA)).[4]

The contradiction is apparent because the environmental discourse of both the petitioners and the Supreme Court left gaping discrepancies as they ignored the political economy of the individual regions in India. By putting aside the class and caste contradictions of the communities living within these CRZs, the court merely followed a mechanical interpretation of the issue, obfuscating the relations of power underlying these economic activities.

The verdict of the Supreme Court of India created uncomfortable situations for the dominant classes involved in Chilika, as the changed policies had legitimised their hitherto illegal shrimp cultivation activities in the lake. Many more investors had also made substantial investments in the lake for shrimp farming after the policy changes. Meanwhile, a few PFCS (primarily on the east side of the lake), owing to lack of funds to engage in shrimp farming, had sublet their share of culture fisheries sources to private parties (Das, 1993), from which the PFCS (mainly the leadership) were getting a steady supply of revenue (Das, 2014). In other words, they had become petty landlords themselves. So, both the dominant classes and certain PFCS faced a difficult situation owing to the Supreme Court verdict. Nevertheless, as mentioned before, shrimp cultivation continues unabated in the lake and its surrounding areas.

Fishers in the north-west and west sides of the lake (mainly engaged in capture fisheries), however, were rejuvenated by the Supreme Court's directive. Taking the court's verdict at its face value, the fisher leaders challenged the non-enthusiasm of the state enforcement agencies to implement the judgement. In 1999, under the *Chilika Matsyajibi Mahasangha* banner, more than 3,000 fishers ferried into the lake and demolished hundreds of pen enclosures belonging to the non-fisher castes. The ensuing mayhem resulted in the death of four fishers in police firing. The judicial commission report (Tripathi, 2005) headed by a sitting judge of the Odisha High Court, Justice P. K. Tripathi on the violence, however, blamed the fishers for this tragedy. It rejected all evidence and names provided by the leadership of *Chilika Matsyajibi Mahasangha* of shrimp mafia and their coterie in Chilika without attempting even to investigate the matter. Justice Tripathi pointed out,

> I feel that mere denial by them to participate in the inquiry cannot give rise to such a presupposition so as to pinpoint the accusing finger against them when there is no other evidence on record to establish that they were/are in the helm of making such encroachments and prevailing the 'Mafiaraj' in Chilika . . . I do not feel proper to record any further findings in that respect in the absence of positive evidence and merely on the basis of bald allegations.
>
> (2005: 74)[5]

While brushing aside all allegations of the fishers, the commission, however, reiterated the state government, the Odisha High Court and dominant classes' stand that the only way to solve the Chilika dispute was to divide the lake into culture and capture fisheries and auction the latter portion to the highest bidder. With this partition, all the parties concerned could make meaningful use of the lake's resources. The state government had already attempted in 2001 and 2004 to legalise the partition. Now, bolstered by the Tripathi Commission report it again tried to do so in 2007 and 2011.

However, the activist nature of a few fishing communities ensured that the bill was not even tabled in the Odisha Legislative Assembly in the first place.

Meanwhile, the number of petitions in the Odisha High Court, as well as district-level courts, have increased considerably, regarding continued encroachment or non-possession of legally allotted fishery sources to the PFCS. See, for example, *Ambika PFCS vs. State of Odisha and Ors* (WP (c) 9014 of 2014, WP (c) No. 18006 of 2010, W.P. (c) No. 16156 of 2008, and W.P. (c) No. 6536 of 1998) in the Odisha High Court.[6] In all these petitions, the High Court cited the previously discussed Supreme Court verdict to direct the state agencies to implement the former's order. However, as is witnessed in the four writ petitions spread over a period of 15 years, on the ground the issue remains unresolved. Similar cases are recorded for many other PFCS in the lake as well.

The differences between the fishing and non-fishing communities

Another reason for the decline of the movement and continued dependence on the litigation strategies is generally seen in the inter-caste relationship between the fisher and non-fishers in Chilika. Adduci (2009) has argued that the inter-caste relationship in this region is qualified by caste-based allegiance to the 'neo-rentier class' (belonging to the two upper castes of Karan and Brahmin) in Odisha. This class controls the lake's political economy, and by violence and credit facilities it has managed to make Chilika the 'largest illegal aquaculture complex in the world' (SeafoodNews, 2011). Adduci's conclusion, broadly on the lines of the Das Committee report (the report terms the 'neo-rentier class' as 'mafia') and the general rhetoric of the leadership of *Chilika Matsyajibi Mahasangha* (CMM), tilts heavily on a top-down narrative of the state-level power elites controlling the subaltern groups for the former's gain.

Adduci's description of the chain of product-market linkage from PFCS at the village level to fish exporters at the top, as an ex-secretary of CMM told me, holds true for not more than 20% of the land under shrimp cultivation in the lake (personal interview 22/02/2015). The PFCS get these portions of the lake as 'capture sources', however they sublet them, illegally, to shrimp mafia and a few others for shrimp cultivation. But the 5,665 hectares (almost 40%) of Chilika, which were converted to culture fisheries in 1991, were not renotified as capture sources. Rather, this portion of the lake was earmarked by the district revenue departments as 'disputed lands' and was made out of bounds to fishing cooperatives for sublease. This decision of the administration has effectively kept Chilika in the hands of dominant classes/castes of the region who are engaged in shrimp cultivation. The upper castes had been operating in the lake since the pre-independence period; however, their contribution was mainly limited to the market yards. As both the fishers and the non-fishers engaged in different occupations, traditionally there were no visible conflicts between the two groups. The conflicts emerged with the processes of globalisation making Chilika resources highly remunerative. The upper castes then did not shy away from entering the lake to take advantage of the same.

The differences within the fishing community

Though one does not deny the significance of the *inter-caste* relationship for the decline of the anti-dispossession movement, I argue that the *intra-caste* relationship within the 'fishing community' is as important as the former. The penetration of capital in Chilika did not happen just by taking advantage of the gap between judicial pronouncements and implementing agencies. Rather, it was done by exploiting the internal contradictions within the judicial verdicts regarding development and subsistence and by widening the historical differences within the fishing community itself. Meanwhile, within the *Chilika Bachao Andolan* itself, there were two factions, one dominated by the *Chilika Matsyajibi Mahasangha* and the other by *Odisha Krushaka Mahasangha*. During the period of struggle, the friction between the two was obvious, as the *Chilika Matsyajibi Mahasangha* leaders felt that Banka Behari Das was trying to appropriate the movement to suit his fancies (Mohanty, 2000). They even accused Das of working for the corporates. By the end of 1993, the two factions had parted ways (Adduci, 2009).

The 'fishing community' created by the *Chilika Bachao Andolan* also followed this pattern. As we discussed before, the fishers in Chilika was constituted of more than seven sub-castes. Each one of them has residence in particular geographical locations in and around Chilika and used specific gear to fish in the lake. Until the advent of the shrimp culture, the Kaibartya and Khatia sub-castes among the fishers, inhabiting mostly the northern, western, and southern parts of the lake, dominated the lake's economy of production and distribution in capture fisheries. Their practice of fisheries led them to move around the lake to fish. Most of the major market towns, whether it was Balugaon and Kalupadaghat in the west or Rambha in the south of the lake, were located in the areas of their domination. Even the villages of Satapada and Mainsa-Berhampur are located near the artificial sea mouth, which has become the main channel for the transit of fish juveniles in and out of the lake. These towns were also located on major railway and highway routes. Even within the *Chilika Matsyajibi Mahasangha*, almost all the leadership positions were/are held by this sub-caste. Their numerical and political domination led them to go unchallenged by other fisher sub-castes.

This unrestricted domination was shattered first with the advent of shrimp culture in the lake and then by ecotourism and other infrastructural facilities in the eastern side of the lake. Although the number of fisher caste villages is much smaller in the east in comparison to other parts of the lake, most of the fishing grounds, whether for capture or culture, are located in the eastern side. The sea mouth is also located in the east, from where almost 85%

of the fish travel inside the lake. A restriction or capture of juveniles in the sea mouth area severely limits the number of species entering and spreading across the lake. Although a few of the Kaibartya caste fisher households prospered under the new regime by diversifying their economic activities and making use of state's policies towards reservations in government jobs and engaging in fisheries business itself, the new economic regime was a mixed bag for most other Kaibartyas.

It was not so with the Kandara and Tiara sub-castes of fishers. The encroachment of their *sairats* by the non-fisher groups in the earlier phase and thereafter legal conversion of these *sairats* to culture fisheries by the Odisha state government created conditions wherein they were posed to lose everything they had. The declaration of several patches of the lake, such as the Nalaban bird sanctuary, the dolphin sanctuary, among others, as protective areas further restricted the movement of the Kandara and Tiara fishers. While for the Kaibartya fishers loss was predicted in the long term, contrarily for the Kandara and Tiara fishers, loss of livelihood was imminent. Over the years their produce of shrimp and crabs and some low-value fish had little value in the market. This kept them under perpetual poverty and on the verge of starvation. Anticipating the changed circumstances (in the 1980s) in which their produce would be highly remunerative for the first time in history, some of the Kandara and Tiara PFCS had gone into partnership with the upper-caste shrimp cultivators and the local corporate houses to engage in shrimp cultivation in the lake. However, the incoming of CAFL and legal conversion of the capture into culture sources was to destroy this deal. Therefore, they were at the forefront of the *Chilika Bachao Andolan*.

The Kandara and Tiara formed one group covering almost 21% of the fishing population. However, despite their population, these two sub-castes were relegated to be mere followers of the other two dominant castes. The poverty between these two castes was also comparatively higher than the Kaibartya and Khatia sub-castes. Within the caste hierarchy too, Kandara and Tiara are considered to be among the lowest in the ritual status. So, both in terms of class position and caste status positions, castes other than Kaibartya and Khatia were at a marginalised position.

Such precarity of fishers' situation was not hidden to their social superiors. So, by both coercion and patronisation the lower castes among the fishing community were made to cooperate with the corporate houses for shrimp cultivation. The internal rivalry between the sub-castes within the fisher community paved the way for accumulation of capital and decline of the anti-dispossession movement in Chilika. Capital, with the help of the dominant social groups in the lake, preyed on the contradictions of both the judicial activism and the differences within the fishing community to co-opt the anti-dispossession movement for an unhindered accumulation of capital. As Harriss-White and Gooptu (2009) reasoned, in the struggle between fragmented capital and fragmented workers, it is the fragmented capital which witnesses cohesiveness, while labour's internal divisions lead to further fragmentations. This does not mean that the workers, for Harriss-White and Gooptu, and fishers in our case are not conscious of the overwhelming nature of their exploitation. Rather, it is the diversity within themselves which perpetually keep them fragmented. Therefore, 'legality/judicial activism' and 'community', which were supposed to create covalent bonds between divergent subaltern groups to protect them from the vagaries of capital, nevertheless failed to do so. Thus, the anti-dispossession movement in Chilika fell apart.

The possibility of a cohesive development?

At the beginning of this chapter, we raised a question whether 'cohesive development' is the new paradigm by citing anecdotes from the recently concluded general elections in India and United Kingdom, respectively. The purpose was to verify the neo-claim-making mechanisms of the political elites in these two countries, miles apart in terms of developmental forbearance and international standing but linked to each other by a shared history of colonialism. As both our review of literature and the case study of Chilika shows, 'development' in a post-colonial country is underlined by contradiction based on class, caste, identity, gender and region. For example, the fishing co-operatives in Chilika, created first during the late colonial period and subsequently revived and rejuvenated during the 1950s and 1960s, were meant to bridge the gaps between the haves and the have-nots. However, since the beginning of the neoliberal period, a majority of these co-operatives have seen complete breakdown in governance.

The fishing co-operatives, with all their problems, primarily were caste/class-based associations. They provided the fishers a sense of belonging and a language of politics. By undermining these associations and depoliticising them to cater to the needs of governmental largesse, as and when they appear, the class-based politics of the fishers was trumped. Which boded well for the social and political hegemons of the region, as they did not see any direct threat to their hegemony in any substantial way from the renewed activities of the fisher co-operatives.

As the labour in the informal sector are perpetually deprived of their class-based politics (notwithstanding the so-called dignified discontent of Agarwala (2013)), similarly, the class-based demands of the co-operative societies in Chilika to give exclusive rights on Chilika to the traditional fishers is brushed aside by the state. 'Citizenship rights', therefore, in the neoliberal era is contingent upon the state's policies of privatisation and liberalisation. The reason for marginalised groups to come to the negotiating table is more often than not their inability to fight against the state's power.

But does that mean 'cohesive development' is an antithesis to Indian society? My answer is 'No'. Rejecting the very discourse of 'cohesive development' is tantamount to throwing out the baby with the bathwater. Rather, as we discussed in this chapter, cohesive development is equivalent to human dignity and democracy, which essentially means that the subaltern groups have to remain vigilant. The fragmentation of the neo-communities on the one hand and cohesiveness of the capital, on the other, has, nevertheless, not resulted in the complete takeover of the former by the latter. Rather, despite of the multiple attempts by both an overbearing state and expanding capital in conjunction with each other, neither of them have been able to completely overthrow the fishers from the lake. This is true with the classes of labour in India too; capital, howsoever cohesive it might have become, it is not able to dominate labour and mould it as per its needs. Cohesive development, even if it has come in the form of governmentality, has benefited the subaltern masses. Only a democracy like India can force both capital and the state to opt for taking even the deprived sections of the country with them along the path of development.

Notes

1 S. Jagannathan, a recipient of Jamnalal Bajaj Award for Constructive Work in 1998, was the chair of the Gram Swaraj movement in Tamil Nadu. His organisation took on issues such as Bhoodan and Gramdan of Vinoba Bhave as well as Total Revolution of Jayaprakash Narayan for rural reconstruction in India.
2 The distance between low- and high-tide zones.
3 Improved traditional is a form of shrimp cultivation in which the shrimp ponds, created by making enclosures in brackish water lakes or creeks, have stock entry control mechanisms. Desired species of shrimp are artificially implanted in these ponds or pen enclosures and left to grow under 'natural' conditions. For more on the different types of shrimp cultivation methods see Alagarswamy (1995).
4 For similar (mis)treatment of the CRZ and the emerging precariousness of the artisanal fishers in the Mumbai metropolitan region see (Chauhan, Parthasarathy, and Pattanaik, 2016).
5 The report also lists the names of witnesses and people responsible for the spread of shrimp mafia in the lake. The latter names include some of the top leaders of the Odisha state government.
6 In the WP (c) No. 6536 of the 1998 case, the Ambika PFCS of village Chandraput in western Chilika fought against the corporate house of Maa Prawn Culture Industry to retain its *sairat* in the lake. The Odisha High Court citing the Supreme Court judgement evicted the corporate house. However, as it emerged during my discussion with the petitioner PFCS, the corporate house is now functioning by taking the help of a local strongman. The later petitions in the High Court and district sessions' court were filed by the PFCS to regain the lost *sairats*. However, even after a decade they have not been able to gain it back.

References

Adduci, M. (2009). Neoliberal Wave Rocks Chilika Lake, India: Conflict over Intensive Aquaculture from a Class Perspective. *Journal of Agrarian Change*, 9(4), 484–511.
Agarwala, R. (2006). From Work to Welfare. *Critical Asian Studies*, 38(4), 419–444.
Agarwala, R. (2013). *Informal Labour, Formal Politics, and Dignified Discontent in India*. New Delhi: Cambridge University Press.
Alagarswamy, K. (1995). The Current Status of Aquaculture in India: The Present Phase of development and Future Growth Potential. *Regional Study and*

Workshop on the Environmental Assessment and Management of Aquaculture Development. Bangkok: Food and Agriculture Organisation.

Anderson, B. (2006). *Imagined Communities: Reflections on the Origin and Spread of Nationalism* (Revised and extended ed.). London: Verso.

Breman, J. (2007). *The Poverty Regime in Village India: Half a Century of Work and Life at the Bottom of the Rural Economy in South Gujarat*. New Delhi: Oxford University Press.

Breman, J. (2013). *At Work in the Informal Economy in India: A Perspective from the Bottom Up*. New Delhi: Oxford University Press.

Chandra, U. (2015). Rethinking Subaltern Resistance. *Journal of Contemporary Asia*, *45*(4), 563–573.

Chatterjee, P. (2008a). Democracy and Economic Transformation in India. *Economic and Political Weekly*, *43*(16), 53–62.

Chatterjee, P. (2008b). Classes, Capital and Indian Democracy. *Economic and Political Weekly*, 89–93.

Chatterjee, P. (2011). *Lineages of Political Society: Studies in Postcolonial Democracy*. Ranikhet: Permanent Black.

Chaudhury, M. (2014). What is 'New' in the New Social Movements? Rethinking Some Old Categories. In Savyasachi and R. Kumar (Eds.), *Social Movements: Transformative Shifts and Turning Points* (pp. 159–185). New Delhi: Routledge.

Chauhan, H. A., Parthasarathy, D., and Pattanaik, S. (2016). Coastal Ecology and Fishing Communities in Mumbai: CRZ Policy, Sustainability and Livelihoods. *Economic and Political Weekly*, *51*(39), 48–57.

Cohn, B. (1965). Anthropological Notes on Disputes and Law in India. *American Anthropologist*, *67*(6), 82–122.

Das, G. (1993). *Report of the Fact-Finding Committee on Chilika Fisheries*. Cuttack: Government of Odisha.

Das, L. K. (2014). Privatisation of the CPRs and the Informal Sector: A Case of Chilika Lake. *Economic and Political Weekly*, *49*(40).

Dhanagare, D. (2016). *Populism and Power: Farmers' Movement in Western India, 1980–2014*. New Delhi: Routledge.

Gellner, E. (1983). *Nations and Nationalism*. Oxford: Basil Blackwell.

Ghosh, A. K., and Pattnaik, A. K. (2006). *Chilika Lagoon: Experience and Lessons Learned Brief*. Retrieved September 12, 2016, from http://projects.inweh.unu.edu/inweh/getdocument.php?F=583009942_4bac326f33a146.79942142

Guha, R. (1994). *Elementary Aspects of Peasant Insurgency in Colonial India*. New Delhi: Oxford University Press.

Haan, A. D. (1999). Livelihoods and Poverty: The role of Migration- a Critical Review of the Migration Literature. *The Journal of Development Studies*, *36*(2), 1–47.

Harriss-White, B., and Gooptu, N. (2009). Mapping India's World of Unorganised Labour. *Socialist Register*, *37*, 89–118.

Iwasaki, S., and Shaw, R. (2008). Fishery Resource Management in Chilika Lagoon: Study on Coastal Conservation in the Eastern Coast of India. *Journal of Coastal Conservation*, *12*, 43–52.

Mitra, G. N., and Mahapatra, P. (1957). *Bulletin on the Development of Chilika Lake: Survey Report on the Fishing Industry*. Cuttack: Orissa Government Press.

Mohanty, R. (2000). *Chilika Bachao Andolan (Save the Chilika Movement): A Case Study of People's Resistance to the Integrated Shrimp Farm Project in Chilika, Orissa*. Civil Society and Governance Programme. London: Institute of Development Studies.

Nayak, P. K. (2014). The Chilika Lagoon Social-Ecological System: An Historical Analysis. *Ecology and Society*, 19.

Nielsen, K. B. (2015a). 'Community' and the Politics of Caste, Class, and Representation in the Singur Movement, West Bengal. In A. G. Nilsen and S. Roy (Eds.), *New Subaltern Politics: Reconceptualising Hegemony and Resistance in Contemporary India* (pp. 202–224). New Delhi: Oxford University Press.

Nielsen, K. B. (2015b). Law and Larai: The (De)judicialisation of Subaltern Resistance in West Bengal. *Journal of Contemporary Asia*, 45(4), 618–639.

Pattanaik, S. (2003). Tradition, Development and Environmental Movement of the Marginalised: A Study of Fishing Community's Resistance in Orissa. *Indian Anthropologist*, 33(1), 55–70.

S. Jagannathan vs Union of India & Ors. (1996). https://indiankanoon.org/doc/507684/ (Accessed 24 January, 2017)

Sanyal, K. (2007). *Rethinking Capitalist Development: Primitive Accumulation, Governmentality & Post-Colonial Capitalism*. New Delhi: Routledge.

SeafoodNews. (2011, February 11). *Small-scale Fishermen Destroy Shrimp Farms around India's Chilika Lake: The Largest Illegal Aquaculture Complex in the World*. Retrieved November 20, 2015, from Seafood News International www.shrimpnews.com/FreeNewsFolder/FreeNewsBackIssues/2011Backissues/FreeNewsFebruary201111.html

Srinivas, M. (1994). *The Remembered Village*. New Delhi: Oxford University Press.

Tripathi, P. (2005). *Report of the Commission of Inquiry: Related to Incident of Police Firing at Village Soran on 29/30.05.1999*. Bhubaneswar: Government of Odisha.

Vallinder, T. (1994). The Judicialisation of Politics: A World-Wide Phenomenon: Introduction. *International Political Science Review*, 15(2), 91–99.

15 Community network for cohesive development in rural India

An exploratory study

Meghadeepa Chakraborty

1. Introduction

Non-cohesive society is a threat to the peace and survival of the people. Communities of all kinds experience threats and polarized ideas from their immediate environment. Despite being located in different socio-ecological contexts, communities are embedded within collective identity and sense of community belonging. The acknowledgement of commonness comes with the community acceptance of similarity and mutuality between the individual members who get space for development while maintaining diversity. Divisiveness of the society adversely impacts development. Hence, social integration and cohesion facilitates cohesive development.

Putting forth the argument that the community network is significant in developing community solidarity, cohesiveness and integration, this chapter discusses the critical role and interdependent functions of these networks for building a cohesive society. The basic questions that the present chapter raises are the following: Can we think of a cohesive society without community network? How do these networks form and function? What are the challenges these networks face? Does public policy adequately recognize the vital role the community network plays? While addressing these questions the chapter mainly focuses on social relations in the community – for example, how they develop, how exchanges occur, what mechanisms build trust among people and how the social network functions as social insurance. Thus, in short, the central question is how community networking is instrumental in achieving cohesive development. The chapter is discussed within the larger theoretical framework of social capital and moral economy. Four villages were selected in four states of India viz., Gujarat, Rajasthan, Assam and Tripura, in order to examine the questions raised earlier. Two of them are in a semi-arid zone where people's livelihood challenges are primarily associated with the problems of dry climate and inadequate rainfall. Culturally, the two states have many commonalities between them. The other two states have a wet climate and largely common cultural traits as well. Following the constructivist approach, the study uses a qualitative methodology.

The applied methodology helps in understanding the social phenomenon in which participants interpret their situation and construct meaning of their lived experiences through interaction, development of shared meaning and communication (Neuman, 1997).

The chapter is divided into four parts. The first part of the chapter sets up the context in that it explains the background, research concerns and methodology. The second part attempts to conceptualize the network and its characteristics and explains its relevance to individual lives in the contemporary era. This part further examines the close relationship between social network and economic performance and explains how social capital and morality play an important role in creating a better society to live in. The third part of the chapter highlights the major findings and explains how valuing diversity, shared vision, creation of space for generating knowledge and so on form pathways for building a cohesive society. The fourth and last part concludes the chapter, arguing for the need to have proper institutional mechanisms and conducive policies to enhance the community network so that cohesive development, which is equally beneficial for all in the community, can be achieved.

2. Understanding network: an overview

Human society does not exist in isolation. It is embedded in a network of relationships. As Fritjof Capra writes, the network is a pattern that is common to all life. Wherever we see life, we see networks (cited in Castells, 1996). Networks, both social as well as technical, have been created by human beings since long time. The social networks are created by individuals, groups, organizations and even societies at large whereas telecommunications and computer networks links are created by communicative (inter) action (van Dijk, 2006: 25). The term network was first used in the context of the dynamics and significance of social living (Warner and Lunt, 1942). Further, network can be understood as a set of interconnected nodes that involves relational and embedded ties (Castells, 1996). Starkey (1997: 14) defined network as a group of individuals or organizations who engage voluntarily in the process of exchanging information or undertake joint activities, and who organize themselves without affecting each other's individual autonomy.

Castells (1996) discussed network society as a social structure constructed by a network empowered by technology-based information and communication. By social structure, Castells referred to the organizational arrangements of human relations in the process of production, consumption, reproduction, experience and power expressed in meaningful communication coded by culture (3).

The defining characteristics of network as described by Kilduff and Tsai (2003) are embeddedness, social capital, structural holes and centrality, which play a significant role in the process of community cohesiveness. Thus, understanding the network has the benefit of reflecting on daily life and thinking about community in the context of the everyday. The literature on networks, specifically social networks, portrays personal, social, economic and political reasons for the formation of a networking relationship (Adler and Kwon, 2002). Bell (1992) further explained that the network becomes a crucial component for the community to have sustained development, as this creates a new stratum in the power structure which offers the possibility for long-term and important change. The actors in the network derive their power from the relations with others along with the actor's own attributes and strategies in acquiring that power (Brass, 1984).

In the contemporary era, the term network has created its own relevance in every individual's life and has many powerful and pervasive factors in all aspects of people's social lives (Greve et al., 2014). It can be considered as a medium that supports the process of individual earnings, learning and trading, ensures a secured and protected life and serves as insurance in crisis and conflicts.

2.1. Social capital and economy

Social capital in the form of networks of interrelations has the capability to enhance the performance of an individual or a group by improving both income-generating capacity and the ability to compete (Barr, 1998). Fountain (1998: 89, cited in Malecki, 2000) asserted that the constituent elements of social capital are trust, norms, and networks, absence of which negatively affects the lives and livelihoods of people. Economy is one of the most important drivers for development where the market economy plays a significant role. In this regard, Granovetter's (2005) work establishes significant relevance where he looked at the connection between the social network and labour market and argued that, in labour markets, social networks play a significant role in pursuing the economic activity smoothly. He further discussed that social networks affect the economic outcome in three major ways – first, networks have their own implication in the flow and quality of information where individual actors have more faith in people they know than in impersonal sources. Second, networks are important sources of reward and punishment, and third, people trust those known to them and whom they expect will conduct action in the right direction despite any odd situations.

While discussing the use of network in the economy, in the current situation, significant understanding is emerging on solidarity networks. Solidarity networks play an important role for people attempting social and political change and encourage values for human and ecological survival (Lewis, 2007: 3). These networks embody an ethic of social responsibility, plurality and empowerment, working towards the realization of a more just, democratic and sustainable world.

2.2. Interlinkages between social capital and the morality approach: uncovering possibilities

The contemporary era experiencing a wide dichotomy due to the aftereffects of globalization. Undoubtedly, globalization has made the world smaller in terms of communication and global interaction, enhanced mobility of people, and ease in exchanging goods, ideas, information and knowledge to all corners of the globe. However, on the other hand, it has also increased the level of uncertainty in people's lives and enhanced vulnerability because of fluctuating global financial markets imposing threats to human security. There is a constant drift from a simple to complex society where society is further polarized in wealth, income and power, threatening people's lives and destroying natural resources. In such a situation, networks play an important role which can be considered as a tool to bind people together and support each other to attain cohesive development as an alternative paradigm for development. Two major components that could influence the community network in helping to strengthen cohesive development are social capital and moral economy. The inter-linkages between social capital and moral economy that comes within the morality approach appear to be particular for the study.

Social capital is resources (networks, memberships of groups, relationship of trust, access to wider institutions of society) accessed through an individual's social connection for which the individual has to be in relation with other individuals, that are the sources of their advantages (Hofferth and Iceland, 1998). Bebbington (1999) and others argued that social capital facilitates gaining access to resources to ensure livelihood security. Social capital is an important resource for household members that greatly affect their ability to act and their perceived quality of life (Coleman, 1988). According to Portes (1998), social capital functions in three contexts – as a source of social control, as a source of family support and as a source of benefits through extra-familial network. Social capital is the social institutions and relationships that facilitate this process (ibid) relation with the community where they exhibit their inclusiveness in society at large. According to Woolcock (1998), social capital is a major asset upon which individual and families rely during crisis. It is argued that households with a rich stock of social networks and associations are in a stronger position to deal with poverty and vulnerability (ibid) compared to one who lacks such resources. Thus, for the underprivileged groups of people, maintaining better relationships and creating social capital are important and valuable. The presence of good relations at times steers the behaviour of individuals and groups, who are then morally guided to further support and strengthen the relationships.

In conditions where poverty and dependency are rampant, moral concerns and morally motivated behaviour become important as these behaviours support an environment in which human communities meet their needs and create livelihoods together (Pennartz and Niehof, 1999). This, in a way, is the approach for achieving a solidarity economy. The broader canvas of the morality approach covers the idea of care, the moral economy and the morality of give and take. These ideas are very much relevant in the context of a community network, where care for each other in the community, transactions in different forms both material and non-material and exchange of gifts are very much relevant for enhancing the relations among one other and for the cohesive development of the community. As Mckee (1987, as cited in Pennartz and Niehof, 1999) pointed out, in times of distress, individuals and households make their own choices where moral dimensions and normative principles underlie reciprocity and sharing. Thus, while talking about community network as a means to have cohesive development, the idea of care and moral economy within the larger canvas of the morality approach needs to be understood. Other than morality, the solidarity economy too plays a significant role.

An emphasis is placed on understanding the economic version of the society in a linear fashion, citing that we live within one single economic system. The economy means "capitalism" or the "market system", which are regulated by the law of supply and demand and whose philosophy is based on rational, self-interested groups of people pursuing maximum profit even in the situation of a resource scarcity (Miller, 2010). There is a limited view on the other kind of economy lying beyond the market and state that follows different kinds of economic activities, motivations and behaviours (ibid). This economy, called the solidarity economy, is based on building relationships and ethics of care, cooperation and solidarity that supports the community in meeting and creating their livelihood needs together (ibid). The solidarity economy can be conceptualized as an alternative path between market and state, which is filled by the active connotations of "community participation" expected to support local development with people's active participation.

3. Discussion on the case studies

3.1. *The geographical context*

The study was conducted in four villages from four states of India. While two villages from the states of Gujarat and Rajasthan are located in the dry climatic region, two other villages from the states of Assam and Tripura are located in the wet region. The objective is to examine how community networks play a role in ensuring the survival of the communities living in such harsh climatic conditions. The villages from the states of Rajasthan and Gujarat are located within a semi-arid, drought-prone zone, whereas the villages from the states of Assam and Tripura have prodigious rainfall and as a result are flood-prone zones. The nature of vulnerabilities, cultural practices, lifestyle and so on shows differences which may have implications for the various forms and functions of community network. Secondly, in the previous two villages (Kutch district of Gujarat and in Rajasthan), the researcher took the help of an interpreter during the interview process.[1] Therefore, the researcher decided to collect data from a known location where they researcher knows the language and is accustomed to the culture. A village from Assam and one from Tripura were selected. Both come under the rainfall area where people's livelihood challenges are different from the other selected villages.

The aforementioned field setting gives an impression of the diversity that prevails among the studied villages. Arguing for the need of an alternative paradigm of development, i.e. cohesive development, it is of utmost importance to understand in what ways the existence of a community network contributes in shaping the foundation for the cohesive development in any society.

3.2. *Valuing diversity*

All the communities studied had marked differences in terms of social structure, fashion, terrain and other cultural significances. Even then, the communities maintained a close network among themselves. This is especially true of the village of Bhoominagar, in Kutch. The village is a cohabitation of communities from diverse religions, Hindus and Muslims; and even among Muslims, there are four sub-categories. It was interesting to note the amicable interaction among different groups, and the community took pride in the fact that even during the Gujarat riot, the village remained unaffected. The question is, what intriguing factor helped them to retain peace and maintain a strong social network among themselves under such circumstances? Interdependence for secured livelihood is one of the major reasons. The traditional pastoralists from the Muslim community of the village were found to be no longer confined to the practice of animal husbandry as their source of livelihood; rather they began to learn to practice agriculture on their own land or on someone else's land. This change was observed among the Ahir, who were always engaged in agriculture but recently had begun to engage in animal husbandry. This change in the village appears to have developed interdependence between the Hindu and Muslim communities, in terms of sharing occupational knowledge, skills and information with each other. However, in the other village, which is not as diverse as Bhoominagar in terms of religion and caste, diversity was observed in terms of economic class.

Despite such differences, it is evident that there was a support structure where the notion of care for each other did exist. This care was carried out by every individual who was a part of the larger community network. Care is about regular practice of attentiveness, responsibilities, competence, responsiveness which are born out of social concern rather than seeing care just as a disposition or an emotion which is often sentimentalized and

Table 15.1 Characteristics of the Villages

Village[1]	Anandwari	Bhoominagar	Chetanagar	Durlabhwadi
State	Rajasthan	Gujarat	South Assam	North Tripura
District	Tonk	Kutch	Cachar	Dharmanagar
Block	Dewli	Nakhatrana	Katigorah	Kadamtala
Climatic Condition	Drought prone	Drought prone	Flood prone	Flood prone
Total Households	147	118	90	35
Total Population	724	578	433	137
Religion and Caste	ST (Meena), few houses of OBC (Bherwa)	Muslim (Theba, Saiyad, Verar and Samaja), Hindu (Ahir)	Dominated by Scheduled Caste	Inhabited by SC and a few houses of OBC
Main occupation	Agriculture and livestock rearing, casual labour, Mahatma Gandhi National Rural Employment Guarantee Act (MGNREGA)	Agriculture and livestock rearing, casual labour, MGNREGA	Fishing and agriculture, casual labour, petty business, selling of by-products, MGNREGA	Fishing and casual labour, MGNREGA

Source: Panchayat office and ICDS centres

1 Anonymous names have been designated to the villages to maintain the principle of confidentiality.

privatised, which has been discussed by Tronto in the new ethics of care (cited in Pennartz and Niehof, 1999).

However, the issue that needs attention is the existence of conflicts in the presence of the diversities. It was observed that at the community level inequalities and incompatibilities among the members of the communities led to conflicts for longer or shorter periods. Who are the people who create such a non-cohesive environment and breed conflicting situations? The field survey revealed that the people from the privileged class in the community remained less associated with the community network and showed less care towards others. They were less bothered to understand the hardships others faced and considered the poor and underprivileged people pitiful. They were never respected. The social relation between them as a result was never reconciliatory and had a tendency to give rise to conflicts at different levels. However, in order to resolve such conflicts, the community took support of their network, developed it further and made sure that such conflicting situations never occurred. Hence, social networking in the villages under study was found to have developed not necessarily for meeting economic needs. There were several social common needs and interests around which the community organized themselves to meet the interest of all.

It is true that village communities under study had bifurcated layers in respect of socio-cultural and economic lives competing and conflicting with each other. However, there was a tendency to negotiate with diversity, since interdependence between the diversified groups of the population existed for social and economic reasons. Hence, in the event of any common problem that the community faced, it was desirable on their part to develop a collective understanding despite the differences they had with each other and to work towards a common goal to solve such problems. Similarly, in case of sharing a similar kind of occupation and areas of interest, the community network supports identifying and understanding the common thread of interest among the group as well as individual members and acting accordingly. This is important, as the skill sets, competence, knowledge base and information access may not be equal among all; different levels will exist irrespective of social, economic and cultural differences. In such a situation, the community network supports making a judicious assessment and attempts to bring people together considering their level of curiosity, engagement and commitment. People in the network show their care through responsiveness towards each other, as they believe that all the members in the network have a more or less similar background or common experiences which need empathy based on moral values and cultural practices.

Therefore, what we have learned from the field survey when I questioned how a community network could contribute to cohesive development was that valuing diversity was an important prerequisite. However, unleashing more attention to the practice of care for each other, which was embedded with the moral concern of the community, was equally significant. This will not only strengthen the bond among members but will enhance the capability of the community to resist the growth of hierarchies within the communal lives and restore equality.

3.3. Shared vision through community network

In the context of community development, wellbeing is achieved through mutual responsibilities, where members in the communities make compromises with their individual interests and develop through the process of collective action and exchanges. The community network, which is also an ongoing process of engaging people in purposeful physical connectivity, facilitates people sharing the vision. In all the studied villages, it was observed that people share a common vision to achieve overall development of the community by sharing their dreams of what is possible, learning to build their self-esteem and confidence, making commitments by engaging themselves in networks such as women's groups, farmer groups, religious groups or in day-to-day interactions, and supporting each other.

In the context of the villages under study, women's association with groups set up an exemplary engagement, which depicts the shared vision that has enhanced social relations among members and their families and collective responsibilities to achieve welfare for the community. Getting financial support is not the only support groups provide, rather affiliation with groups has improved women's abilities and also improved the socio-economic conditions of the village. In villages where groups are not active, however, such changes have not taken place. Women have generated their economy through solidarity networks especially in the villages of Anandwari and Durlabwadi through milk cooperatives, which largely support the overall development of the households and village community as a whole.

Despite prevailing limitations, the community addresses their issues at their own level and solves their own issues by themselves. The formal institutions are approached only when a large amount of money is required for bigger projects, which have been found in only a handful of households. Poor households find an informal source to be more user friendly and the money easily accessible in less time during crisis. They borrow from one another to help one another during crisis. Trustworthiness among individuals or households over time is central to any kind of transaction. The trust for households with better asset holdings has been observed to be higher than for those with poor assets.

From the observations it is understood that the well-connected communities, like in the villages of Anandwari and Bhoominagar where women's groups took institutionalized form, transformed the lives of community people, unlike the other two villages which were comparatively less connected. The villages with better organized structure have an advantage in organizing themselves in different situations whenever they want, which in a way contributes in the construction of community welfare where personal responsibilities and actions are transformed into a responsibility of impersonal collectivist.

Thus, community networks facilitate people in mobilizing resources, improvising communication, supporting resource pooling and bringing overall benefits to the community.

3.4. Creating space for knowledge generation

The informal network in any community is a continuous source of information and knowledge building through debate and discussion, sharing of ideas and sharing of experiences over any issue. In a way, the network creates a free environment for members that enables individuals, as well as groups, to learn, broaden their perspectives and extend their horizons. Through this, they eventually break the barriers of hesitation, fear and prejudice and act as bridge even if there are differences of opinion or conflict of ideas or disagreement over any issues due to any form of difference. This phenomenon was very much evident in all the villages under study. In every way, people are in continuous interaction with each other over the issues of their life, whether about the knowledge of how to follow good agricultural practices, recent changes in the market, which livestock breed to buy, how to rear them, community-level problems, and many other aspects. There is continuous transfer of traditional knowledge related to each other's occupation, sharing of information, rendering support, engaging in village level planning etc. It was also observed that the prevailing groups which are working with NGOs also collaborate with the groups from other villages, and because members visit each other, they build up a common perspective and understanding by expanding their horizons, not only in terms of geographical location but also in terms of their knowledge domain, expansion of their network and strengthening their network.

3.5. Intricate relationship between moral economy
and social capital

Investment on social capital is always based on expectations from informal sources, and therefore trustworthiness plays a vital role in sustaining the moral economy in the community. The study shows that households take special care in maintaining trust among one another by completing transactions as per the scheduled time frame, maintaining commitments, being available to support as and when it is sought and so on. These mechanisms develop the level of trust that smoothen the interaction between inter-household and community as a whole.

It is also observed that people make their decisions about rendering support and assistance to others in the light of attempting to show their responsible behaviour towards each other. Getting work opportunities, information and financial support, as well as emotional and social support, provide the avenues through which household members who belong to local groups or organizations maintain effective networks and support take advantage of their social capital. Women's association with groups not only enhances their network and strengthens their social relations, but also expands their opportunity to ensure their relation for the future and draw benefit from the network. Households without association, however, fail to form a network from which they can draw benefits. This means that there is a different experience between households with and without organizational membership.

The transaction for investment follows interesting ways like giving gifts, helping each other in domestic activities, rendering support in livelihood activities, providing support in cash or kind, participating in one another's social functions, etc. The return comes in similar fashion whenever there is idiosyncratic risk. It is interesting to look at the process of exchanges depicting how family obligations are embedded in the values and norms which are directly endorsed from moral principles influenced by cultural context, which Cheal (1988) discussed with reference to the moral economy (Pennartz and Niehof, 1999).

Usually, it has been observed that when there is covariate risk, the situations of all the members become more or less similar, because of which the support system slackens and households have to be dependent upon external sources. Moreover, in many occasions, investment in the form of gifts become stressful for others as they may not be fulfilled or forcefully fulfilled, which can lead to indebtedness. Similarly, association with the organization sometime makes too much credit available that households without any specific target use fail to repay, which make them indebted for a longer period. While investment in social capital is found to be positive, it also has negative aspects, in that instead of making a household's position stronger, it makes the situation stressful and weak.

The intention behind investing on social capital is explained in the works of scholars like Lin (1999), Coleman (1988), Adler and Kwon (2002) and Narayan and Pritchett (1999), where it is emphasized that the investment in social relation supports individuals to gain resources and, in return, expect some action in future. The studies highlighted the significance of social capital during crisis, when rural people deal with the situation by using resources from the network, whether from kinship relationships or from friends. It reiterates the fact that rural poor households in the community find their affiliation with the informal community network that supports them in crisis, guards their livelihood and supports their day-to-day living. Relatives, neighbours and friends are the most immediate circle whom households approach in need. The findings pointed out that social capital created by humankind develops with time and effort, with the expectation that the future will be more secured and will see an increase in capital. Moreover, investment in maintaining the social network helps to access effective sources of information regarding job opportunities, recent developments in the respective activities, credit benefit whenever required and so on. There is a tendency to develop negotiations over time, which is beyond direct payment and agreed explicitly or implicitly to help one another as per specific needs and events.

Even though the network is crucial to the lives of the people and of the community as a whole, there are also compulsive situations in which a community could incur higher cost on social spending to be inclusive and to exhibit status in the network.

3.6. Status conferring spending

Spending on social occasions (such as weddings, funerals, festivals, etc.) is a common phenomenon (Chen and Zhang, 2012) in the Indian villages. These occasions are such that every household either hosts or participates in their community. Such occasions are unavoidable as they keep households connected with their community, maintaining societal norms and traditions. Work of scholars such as Rao (2001) and Arcodia and Whitford (2007) find that households or their community look at social spending as their investment towards building a strong and sustainable social network and to generate private economic return.

It appears from the field survey that spending on social occasions is a common phenomenon among households irrespective of their economic condition. They do not explicitly identify this spending as a problem. However, heavy spending undoubtedly leads to a crisis situation; it comes as an internal shock and takes away their earning or drives them to debt. For example, the practice of organizing a big feast after the death of a family member contributes to a dual burden for households. The phenomenon has been observed among the tribal community (Meena) in Anandwari. Here households are bound to follow the tradition of organizing a big feast. It is interesting to question why households, even after experiencing a financial crunch, make a heavy expenditure on social events. The traditional practice remains the norm that directs participation in social events like funerals (Brown et al., 2011). For households already facing an emotional crisis, arranging money for the funeral services creates even more stress due to the death of a financially active member.

Interestingly, it can also be argued that as households are in constant interaction with the society, it strengthens their social network and relations, so it is important to make such an investment. The spending is considered as an investment, which they indirectly make in order to strengthen social capital, which they believe will serve as insurance for them during a crisis.

Other than strengthening social capital, this spending is made with an assumption that it will enhance the social status of the household and make their position better in the community. The engagement in organizing social events like marriages or religious ceremonies includes households in the network and benefits them. Works in the literature (Hayden, 2009; Brown et al., 2011; Van der Geest, 2000) look at the practice of hosting lavish funerals in other countries like China, Ghana and Africa and attempt to find the reasons behind it. It has been seen that this spending is made to maintain and affirm people's social status, show love and respect for the deceased and display their social, economic and political strength. This helps the families to have an advantage in building relations and to remain included in society.

Similarly, marriages and religious activities are other areas where households undertake heavy expenditure. Several studies show that people observe a festival as a mechanism that increases cooperation and cohesiveness and strengthens bonds across families to build social capital (Arcodia and Whitford, 2007). In the same way, giving gifts rather than hosting a feast is another important activity. The burden of social spending is not only borne by the households, even the invitees to the event are put under stress as they have to bring gifts. Excessive spending on gifts creates a financial burden and stress on the households. Gift exchange remains as a practice enacted by all the households in the community.

Some studies (Offer, 2012; Chen et al., 2012) raise the issue of the risk of social exclusion, indebtedness, imbalance in social relations and inability to participate in mutual social exchanges of material or other resources. However, for poor people, their mutual relation is the strongest asset, so they do not want to put that at risk. So, households make all efforts to spend on occasions and maintain reciprocity, even under extreme pressure. Thus, it is untrue that social capital cannot be sour. Maintaining social relation and reciprocation becomes a burden that lessens the span of good relation, which goes beyond the exchange of material. The practice of giving gifts on different occasions becomes a burden for households and leads them to heavy financial crisis. To have one asset (social relations), they have to put the other assets at risk (financial stock), and this creates imbalance. It is also observed that the livelihood of households whose main bread earner has died or is headed by a female (widow, deserted or divorced) or has members with disability or chronic illness gets adversely affected due to this social practice. These families are already suffering from their socio-economic vulnerabilities. The additional burden deepens their struggle for livelihood.

3.7. *Improving economic situation*

Rural communities encounter economic crisis due to regular deficit of cash in hand, low means of earning, challenges and hardship with the traditional means of production, and above all an imperfect market. In such a situation, often large groups of people resort to migration and move out of their place in search of jobs, or get into the trap of indebtedness with a strong loop of creditors. The imperfect credit market is another reason why the community network works well, where people become dependent on each other based on mutual trust. Thus, the network becomes a safety net for them, which is maintained for securing their livelihood.

The community network appears to be an excellent instrument that attempts to rescue and protect individuals, families and groups from misery, which many formal institutions often fail to deliver. For example, it has been observed that when people from a community decide to migrate for better sources of earning and become job seekers, their own network, which is probably kinship based, activates well in terms of information dissemination, guidance and support in these new destinations. Information about availability is mostly disseminated among the members in the group, who are closely known to the informants and about whose skill set and commitment the informant is well-versed. This arrangement works in two manners – first, the job seeker shows a relatively good level of commitment towards their job, as the stake of their relative is involved and second, a good skilful worker is obtained from a known source. This phenomenon has been observed majorly in the village of Rajasthan, where cases of migration are high. Here the nature of network is based on level of commitment which strives to bring economic efficiency, which is well discussed in the work of Munsi (2014).

Thus, we can say that by having an effective community network, one can address community issues and problems in a more systematic and logical manner that increases collective efficacy (Bandura, 2001; Sampson et al., 2002). Collective efficacy, as Gilchrist (2009) mentioned, is a way of explaining the shared belief that by working together, people can change situations and challenge any form of injustice. It is further elaborated that the combined experience shared and reinforced through community networks creates a virtuous spiral of learning, confidence and mutuality.

4. Conclusion

The study shows how social cohesion through networking within the community enables people to express their ideas, exchange goods and services, cooperate and operate based on shared values. All these together play a significant role in bringing about development. People's own ways to bond ties, establish relation and nurture the relation through different mechanisms of sharing values, belief system, resources, trust and mutual understanding are considered to be prerequisite for the community and society to develop. Thus, there is the need for better pro-poor policies to enhance and strengthen these ties at the community level. Moreover, emphasis should be given to strengthen different resource bases, which should not be limited to financial assets. Government organizations must work towards better governance so that the poor can have better access to the services that come under the institutional networks.

Note

1 PhD fieldwork, 2011–2013.

References

Adler, P.S., and Kwon, S. (2002). Social capital: Prospects for a new concept. *Academy of Management Review*, 27(1), 17–40.

Arcodia, C., and Whitford, M. (2007). Festival attendance and the development of social capital. *Journal of Convention & Event Tourism*, 8(2), 1–18.

Bandura, A. (2001). Social cognitive theory: An agentic perspective. *Annual Review of Psychology*, 52, 1–26.

Barr, M.A. (1998). *Enterprise performance and the functional diversity of social capital.* (No. WPS/98–1). Centre for the Study of African Economies, Institute of Economics and Statistics, University of Oxford.

Bebbington, A. (1999). Capitals and capabilities: A framework for analyzing peasant viability, rural livelihoods and poverty. *World Development*, 27(12), 2021–2044.

Bell, J. (1992). *Community development team work: Measuring the impact.* London: Community Development Foundation.

Brass, D. (1984). Being in the right place: A structural analysis of individual influence in an organisation. *Administrative Science Quarterly*, 29, 518–539.

Brown, P.H., Bulte, E., and Zhang, X. (2011). Positional spending and status seeking in rural China. *Journal of Development Economics*, 96(1), 139–149.

Castells, M. (1996). *The rise of the network society: The information age: Economy, society and culture.* Oxford: Blackwell Publishers.

Chen, X., Kanbur, R., Zhang, X. (2012). Peer Effects, Risk Pooling, and Status Seeking: What Explains Gift Spending Escalation in Rural China? *CEPR Discussion Paper No.* DP8777.

Chen, X., and Zhang, X. (2012). *Costly posturing: Relative status, ceremonies and early child development in China* (No. 2012/70). WIDER Working Paper.

Cheal, D. (1988). *The gift economy.* London/New York: Routledge.

Coleman, J.S. (1988). Social capital in the creation of human capital. *American Journal of Sociology*, 94, S95–S120.

Fountain, J.E. (1998). Social capital: Its relationship to innovation in science and technology. *Science and Public Policy*, 25(2), 103–115.

Gilchrist, A. (2009). *The well connected community: A networking approach to community development.* Bristol, UK: The Policy Press.

Granovetter, M. (2005). The Impact of Social Structure on Economic Outcomes. *Journal of Economic Perspectives*, 19(1), 33–50.

Greve, H., Rowley, T., and Shipilov, A. (2014). *Network advantage: How to unlock value from your alliances and partnership.* San Francisco CA: John Wiley & Sons Ltd.

Hayden, B. (2009). Funerals as feasts: Why are they so important. *Cambridge Archaeological Journal*, 19(1), 29–52.

Hofferth, L.S., and Iceland, J. (1998). Social capital in rural and urban communities. *Rural Sociology*, 63(4), 574–598.

Kilduff, M., and Tsai, W. (2003). *Social networks and organizations.* London: Sage Publication.

Lewis, M. (2007). *Constructing a sustainable future: Exploring the strategic relevance of social and solidarity economy frameworks.* Alberta: Balta, Alberta Social Economy Research Alliance.

Lin, N. (1999). Building a network theory of social capital. *Connections*, 22(1), 28–51.

Malecki, J.E. (2000). Symposium: New directions in regional science: Soft variables in regional science. *The Review of Regional Studies*, 30(1), 61–69.

Miller, E. (2010). Solidarity economy: Key concepts and issues. In E. Kawano, T. Masterson, and J. Teller-Ellsberg (Eds.), *Solidarity economy I: Building alternatives for people and planet*. Amherst, MA: Center for Popular Economics.

Munsi, K. (2014). Community networks & the process of development. *Journal of Economic Perspectives, 28*(4), 49–76.

Narayan, D., and Pritchett, L. (1999). Cents and sociability: Household income and social capital in rural Tanzania. *Economic Development and Cultural Change, 47*(4), 871–897.

Neuman, W.L. (1997). *Social research methods: Qualitative and quantitative approaches*. Boston: Allyn & Bacon.

Offer, S. (2012). The burden of reciprocity: Processes of exclusion and withdrawal from personal networks among low-income families. *Current Sociology, 60*(6), 788–805.

Pennartz, J.J.P., and Niehof, A. (1999). *The domestic domain: Chances, choices and strategies of family households*. Aldershot, Hampshire, England: Ashgate Publishing Limited.

Portes, A. (1998). Social capital: Its origin and applications in modern sociology. *Annual Review of Sociology* 24: 1–24.

Rao, V. (2001). Celebrations as social investments: Festival expenditures, unit price variation and social status in rural India. *Journal of Development Studies, 38*(1), 71–97.

Sampson, R., Morenoff, J., and Gannon-Rowley, T. (2002). Assessing Neighbourhood effects: Social processes and new directions in research. *Annual Review of Sociology, 28*, 443–478.

Starkey, P. (1997). *Networking for development*. London, UK: Intermediate Publication Ltd.

Van der Geest, S. (2000). Funerals for the living: Conversations with elderly people in Kwahu, Ghana. *African Studies Review, 43*(3), 103–129.

van Dijk, J.A.G.M. (2006). *The network society: Social aspects of new media* (Second Edition). London, UK: Sage Publication.

Warner, W.L., and Lunt, P.G. (1942). *The status system of a modern community*. New Haven, CT: Yale University Press.

Woolcock, M. 1998. Social capital and economic development: Toward a theoretical synthesis and policy framework. *Theory and Society* 27(2): 151–152.

16 Implementation of the Forest Rights Act 2006 and its implications for cohesive development

The case of Telangana and Andhra Pradesh

M. Gopinath Reddy

I. Introduction

Historically, there exists a symbiotic relationship between nature (forest) and the tribals who live with it. Both of them exist by way of mutually reinforcing each other's sustenance. In the precolonial era this relationship was not disturbed to a great extent by the feudal chiefs as they never looked towards forests for generating revenue. From the colonial period on, especially after the British established their supremacy all over India, the country started exploiting forest resources, particularly forest wood for infrastructure projects like shipbuilding, laying the railway network and so on. Slowly, tensions and conflicts arose between colonial rulers and indigenous people, who depend solely on this resource for their sustenance. Massive resistance movements were built by various leaders (drawn from both tribal and non-tribal communities) to resist this exploitation by British colonialists. Central India, Eastern India and South India witnessed such resistance movements against the British. Notable among them were the Gonds Rebellion, the struggles in the Chota Nagpur region in Jharkhand and the Rampa Rebellion in the Eastern Ghats of Andhra Pradesh.

Unfortunately, the rulers of post-colonial independent India continued this exploitation of the tribals and forest resources. A number of forest policies, such as the Indian Forest Policy, the Wildlife Act and the Forest Conservative Act, were all brought by the Indian ruling establishment to 'protect' so-called forests from being exploited by the tribals. Most of these policies were invoked in the name of forest resource conservation and protection. But the exploitation of forest resources has been continued by the forest contractors and industrialists with the tacit help rendered by the forest bureaucracy. The forest dwellers, particularly tribals, were being marginalized and were alienated gradually from their resource and habitat.

The 'Panchsheel' Doctrine put forth by the first prime minister of India, Jawahar Lal Nehru, for tribal development and their integration into mainstream society, remained elusive despite large sums of money spent in the name of tribal development. In particular, cohesive development that exists between forests and the tribals was being weakened by the various policies pursued by the ruling parties in independent India.

Context

It is against the backdrop of large-scale alienation of the forest from the actual inhabitants that one must realize how it inflicts damages to the process of tribal development, particularly during the post-liberalization era. Two decades of globalization have resulted in more displacement. One estimate shows that the number of tribal inhabitants would have exceeded 65 million by 2010 (Walter Fernandes et al, 2019). Sadly, the original inhabitants of the forest are made to live by the state as 'encroachers'. A long-drawn-out battle by civil society groups in alliance with progressive political parties succeeded in building pressure on the then United Progressive Alliance (UPA) government to bring the legislation, popularly known as the Forest Rights Act 2006 (henceforth FRA or FRA-2006), to undo the 'historical injustice' perpetrated against this section of population by the state. This chapter tries to unfold this story of FRA in percept and practice to see to what extent the historical injustice is being undone by the government. While doing so, it is intended to examine whether the issue of cohesive development is adequately addressed through the implementation of this act. The cohesive development in the present context refers to the development of tribals in every respect without destroying the inalienable bond they have had for generations with the forest. It is the solidarity between them and nature that they nurture for their sustenance and growth. Hence, any intervention sought for the development of tribals may boomerang if the element of cohesiveness is not embedded. What it means is whether the co-evolution of human and nature (here tribals and forest) is implicitly or explicitly recognized as an integral part of the development process sought through enactment of the act.

FRA-2006 and its salient features

The Forest Rights Act was passed by India's Parliament in 2006, finally recognizing the fact after 60 years of independence that across India almost one-quarter of its land has been encroached by the state causing injustice to the people living there for generations. The act provides the legislative basis for redressing this injustice, and so has major implications across states, promising a more secure basis for forest people's livelihoods.

The act (Ministry of Tribal Affairs, 2007), as quoted next, clearly shows how it has bestowed rights to the forests dwellers, who receive individual or community tenure or both.

(a) right to hold and live in the forest land under the individual or common occupation for habitation or for self-cultivation for livelihood by a member or members of a forest dwelling Scheduled Tribe or other traditional forest dwellers; (b) community rights such as nistar, by whatever name called, including those used in erstwhile Princely States, Zamindari or such intermediary regimes; (c) right of ownership, access to collect, use, and dispose of minor forest produce which has been traditionally collected within or outside village boundaries; (d) other community rights of uses or entitlements such as fish and other products of water bodies, grazing (both settled or transhumant) and traditional seasonal resource access of nomadic or pastoralist communities; (e) rights including community tenures of habitat and habitation for primitive tribal groups and preagricultural communities.

The single most important aspect of the act is that by bestowing the right to tribal groups to own land either individually or communally or both, it intends to resurrect the bond between the tribals and the forest. Further, it may be mentioned that FRA-2006 reforms have ushered in significant steps to restore the land base of the Adivasis as a right by conferring them their land rights legally, especially when their land and livelihood base are increasingly being eroded in the post-liberalization era. By ushering in this reform, which was taken place mainly at the initiative of civil society organizations in close collaboration with tribal groups, one has reasons to hope that such an inalienable bond between forest and its people will never be destroyed.

However, serious obstacles are being encountered when it comes to the implementation process. The wildlife fundamentalists and environmentalists, forest bureaucracy and corporate class interested in mining natural wealth have become a serious hindrance and obstacle for achieving cohesive development of tribals with the forest (Karat, 2016). Within the implementation spectrum of the act itself, serious flaws came to the forefront. The emphasis on individual rights over community rights has diluted the elements of cohesive development. This chapter tries to address these questions based on a field survey being undertaken in Andhra Pradesh (AP) and Telangana.

Key questions

Against the backdrop of the previous discussion on FRA-2006, the chapter addresses the following questions: (1) Do FRA-2006 provisions adequately cover the range of forest right deprivations in the state of AP? (2) Does implementation of FRA-2006 actually result in meaningful and pro-poor institutional reforms at the local level? and (3) Does FRA justify cohesive development between the tribals, the actual inhabitants of the forest and the forest? Before shedding critical reflections on these questions in the discussions being carried out in the following sections, it may be worthwhile to discuss briefly how civil societies and political parties reinforced the process of the act to come into being while they were waging movements for the forest rights at different points of time. Section II is devoted to this topic. Section III discusses FRA implementation across India and the few fault lines in its implementation and examines their implications for achieving cohesive development between tribals and the forest. Section IV examines state-specific (Andhra Pradesh) implementation of FRA; Section V discusses the recent Supreme Court judgement that will have far-reaching consequences to the tribal rights and finally Section VI suggests steps to be taken for proper implementation of the act that restores cohesion of the tribal groups and the forest as a strategy to bring about overall development of the latter.

II. Political contestation over rights deprivation and emergence of the FRA

The processes through which forest peoples have been expropriated have led to a range of responses, from resignation to non-violent protest movements to outright insurrection in tribal uprisings such as the Gudem-Rampa rebellions (1839–1924), the Gond revolt of 1940, the Naxalite (Maoist) insurrectionary movement of 1970s, and indeed ongoing insurgency in forest areas to this day. These movements have not, in recent years, been led by tribals, but have undoubtedly received their sympathies due to their challenging the authority of the state, which has routinely persecuted them.

However, there has been very limited political self-organization of tribal groups within the democratic process to seek redress. Forest people are remote and fragmented, having limited education and literacy or acculturation into the socio-political processes. Nevertheless, the absence of political organization remains very surprising. There are currently only two strong tribal organizations, namely *Adivasi Samkshema Parishad* and '*Tudumdebba*' (the regional outfits fighting for tribal rights), who are not associated with NGOs, are primarily taking up land conflict issues between tribals and non-tribals (rather than forest based land issues) and are also evincing keen interest on tribal employment issues.

Most political representation of forest people's interests have come from NGOs and activist groups working on behalf of tribals. These agencies express concerns over a range of grievances including violation of their rights (particularly lands, forests and other natural resources), lack of development service delivery, negligence and lapses in government functioning, and exploitation by non-tribal moneylenders, traders and public and private industries. These NGO groups also work towards strengthening tribal communities, in their assertion for self-rule and governance, and protecting their cultures and customary rights. However, few NGOs are actually involved in direct field-level advocacy on land and forest issues in tribal areas. The majority of these NGOs lack field capacity, but instead engage in articulating issues through print media and court litigation rather than mobilizing the community themselves to raise the issues.

Due to very limited self-organization, external political groups have also stepped in to organize forest peoples, although this may have led to a tendency for outside agendas to be imposed upon them. The Communist Party of India (Marxist-Leninist) affiliated with *Ryutu Coolie Sanghams* encouraged tribal communities to clear the forests for their survival across the tribal areas of AP, and the political organizations later mobilized the tribal communities to resist the forest departments' objections (a phenomenon widely seen across areas). Political organizations supported the tribals to fight against the forest cases booked by the department.

The extreme left 'Peoples War Group' has also supported and helped defend tribal settlers in forest areas. It is hard to say whether the so-called Naxalism has led to the furthering of forest peoples grievances. Certainly, organized insurgency has forced the government to be more sensitive to the development issues of the tribals, the most significant of which is land rights. On the other hand, excessive policing of the forest has led to perpetrating massive oppression to the tribal community. Even peaceful non-violent opposition to such repression as a mark of protest being organized by the same tribal community has labelled them as 'Maoists' or Naxalites.

Across India the main impetus for the civil society forest rights campaign (coordinated by the Campaign for Survival and Dignity) was the 2002 countrywide wave of evictions by forest departments, prompted by the MoEF (Ministry of Environment and Forests) Directive to evict 'illegal encroachers' (which covers the rights deprived forest peoples) in response to a Supreme Court enforcement request. At the national level, 1,3433,000 ha of forests lands are categorized as under 'encroachment' by the forest departments. In AP alone 295,383 ha are categorized in such a way (Trinadha Rao, 2007). However, the APFD (Andhra Pradesh Forest Department) did not use the 2002 MoEF demand to evict these occupiers due to legal hurdles, particularly due to the 'Samata' judgement delivered by the Supreme Court of India. Nevertheless, forest peoples' extreme insecurity of losing their rights on land has been a major factor in the mobilization for rights reforms (Springate et al, 2009).

Although direct political organization and mobilization of forest peoples has been limited, the discontent and disaffection have resulted in unrest that finally snowballed into supporting political extremism. The state of Andhra Pradesh gradually realized it not as a simple law and order problem. It understood how perpetual injustice was meted out to the tribal community of the state and felt it was necessary to take remedial measures.

Furthermore, the extreme rights deprivations situation has led the tribal groups to actively participate and support the civil society organizations that led their Campaign for Survival and Dignity. The left extremism working in the forest areas for championing the cause of the tribal community and the campaigns by the aforementioned civil society organizations together could sensitize the political class to the extent that the latter finally gave cognizance to the grievances of the tribal community. This culminated into sanctioning the bill.

III. Implementation of FRA-2006

The efficacy of implementation needs to be understood in terms of (1) how much land is claimed, how much is distributed (%) and how much is finally rejected (rejection/claimed and rejection/distributed); (2) the distributive pattern between community and private; and (3) the extent to which the incidence of deprivation of the forest rights of tribal groups is minimized and ensures sustainability of the inalienable bond between them and the forest.

A brief account of mplementation process at the All India level shows that a few states, including AP, Odisha and Maharashtra, have distributed land among tribal groups more than the All India average. However, what is intriguing is that the incidence of rejection of the claim is equally discouraging. It makes mockery of the act.

A higher incidence of the rejection rate has become a contentious issue in the forest rights implementation process. Through various bureaucratic institutions such as SDLC (sub-divisional level committee) and DLC (divisional level committee) (revenue centric), the Forest Department is usurping tribal rights over land by denying them their genuine claims over land by citing technical grounds on which innocent tribals have no knowledge and are unable to challenge the bureaucracy. In addition, the grievance redressal mechanism is also very weak or non-existent, which further deprives the tribals to have their rights on land.

The All India data on FRA (Ministry of Tribal Affairs, Government of India 2014) indicates that in terms of the extent of forest land distributed in absolute terms (in acres), Andhra Pradesh accounts for the highest distribution of the land (1,456,542 acres) (as compared to other states) followed by Madhya Pradesh for 1,081,426.65 acres of forest land, Maharashtra for 798,630.70 acres (236,633.28 individual and 561,997.42 community), Odisha for 666,050.11 (514,886.02 individual and 151,164.11 community) acres, Tripura for 416,555.58 (416,498.79 for individual and 56.79 community) for 116,100 titles, and Uttar Pradesh for 139,778.04 acres. The rest of the states have distributed less than one lakh acres in total. The overall macro picture of the claims received and titles distributed and rejected shows 3,654,420 (3,578,040 individual and 76,380 community), and the total number of titles distributed is 1,418,078 (1,395,647 individual and 22,431 community) and 15,864 ready for distribution, while the total number of claims rejected is 1,688,612 (1,678,318 individual and 10,294 community).

However, equally disturbing is the incidence of rejection of claims of ownership across the states. It was found that rejection takes place at various stages of implementation of the act across all states. The rejection rate is as high as 87.5% in Karnataka followed by Uttar Pradesh (79.0%), Maharashtra (67.5%), West Bengal (58.2%), Madhya Pradesh and Chhattisgarh and Bihar (56.0%) and Andhra Pradesh (40.3%). The large-scale rejection rate raises serious apprehension about the commitment of the states to grant inalienable rights to the tribals to land and restore their bond with the forest. (Reddy and Nagaraju, 2015).

A close look at the All India scenario shows how the implementation process and its outcomes are in conflict with the basic interest of the tribal community. What appears glaringly is that alienation of the tribals from the forest is forced upon them, against which they all were fighting. Its far-reaching consequences in their co-evolution with the forest that ensures cohesive development are apprehended to be adverse due to the following reasons. Firstly, large-scale rejection of claims across the states (nearly 45% and more in some tribal-dominated states such as Madhya Pradesh, Jharkhand and Chhattisgarh, Odisha, AP) by various institutions such as Gram Sabhas, SDLC and DLC is irreconcilable. Often, local foresters, as reported by tribals during the field survey, influence or rather intimidate the Gram Sabhas for not granting rights to the genuine forest dwellers on trivial technical grounds (such as GPS – geo-positioning systems – maps not supporting tribal claims, etc.).

Secondly, the large-scale rejection across the majority of the states including AP and Telangana by revenue institutions such as SDLC/DLC arbitrarily left the innocent tribals (with no literacy and legal knowledge) helpless as to how to defend their rights in the absence of a proper grievance redressal mechanism.

Thirdly, overemphasis placed on granting individual rights ('pattas') rather than community rights have gravely undermined the collective ethos of development. Community rights mean a lot to the tribal masses who manage forests resources on a collective basis rather than an individual basis as occurs in non-tribal regions. The tribal ethos places great importance on collective management of natural resources. This is at stake in the present implementation process.

IV. Andhra Pradesh and Telangana

The status report of Andhra Pradesh (as on 31 July 2014) shows that the government of AP has appointed a nodal officer besides forming various committees – SDLC, DLC and SLMC (state level monitoring committee) apart from creating awareness among people regarding the provisions of the act and rules on the ground. The AP government also has accomplished the task of translating the act and rules in the regional language in addition to passing on the FRA guidelines to Gram Sabhas and forest rights committees. There are 3,744 FRCs (forest rights committees) formed by conducting Gram Sabhas. FRC trainings and awareness campaigns are also being organized in the state. The progress of implementation of the act in the states concerned is briefly shown in Table 16.1.

In Andhra Pradesh including Telangana, there are 3,841 Gram Panchayats that are closely linked to the forest. In order to implement the act, Gram Sabha meetings are being conducted at all forest-linked interface Gram

Table 16.1 Progress of FRA (by Activity and Action Taken) in Andhra Pradesh and Telangana (as on 30-09-2014)

Sl. No.	Activity	No.	Extent (in acres)
1	No. of Gram Panchayats having a close forest interface	3,841	–
2	No. of Gram Sabhas convened	3,841	–
3	No. of FRCs constituted	3,841	–
4	No. of DLCs constituted	46	–
5	No. of SDLCs constituted	44	–
6	No. of individual claims received	402,132	1,207,272
7	No. of community claims received	11,089	1,265,581
8	No. of claims recommended by the Gram Sabhas to SDLC	244,910	
9	No. of claims recommended by SDLC to DLC	195,926	
10	No. of claims approved by DLC for title distribution	177,769	
	Total Claims Received	1,043,439	2,472,853
	Action taken		
1	Titles Distributed–Individual Claims	169,238	481,626
2	Titles Distributed–Community Claims	2,282	979,252
1	Cases Rejected–Individual Claims	163,339	486,186
2	Cases Rejected–Community Claims	3,825	41,514
1	Cases Pending–Individual Claims	69,214	234,699
2	Cases Pending–Community Claims	4,982	24,4785

Source: TCRTI (Tribal Centre for Research and Training Institute), Hyderabad

Panchayats. In addition to it, FRCs are formed under the jurisdiction of each Gram Panchayat. There are 44 SDLCs constituted to monitor the FRCs and to verify claims and recommend the verified claims to the DLCs. Forty-six DLCs have been constituted at the district level for again verifying the claims and distribution of entitlements.

The implementation process carried out in AP and Telangana is almost similar to what is observed at the All India level. The high rejection rate (more than 40%) of both individual and community rights by various implementing agencies is equally disturbing as it appears from the detailed account presented next.

In AP, claims received (as on 30-09-2014) stood at a total of 413221 (both individual and community) over an area of 2,472,853 acres (individual claims add up to 402,132 over an area of 1,207,272 acres, while community claims add up to 11,089 over an area of 1,265,581 acres).

It appears that 169,238 titles have been distributed in respect of individual claims, over an area of 481,626 acres (around 40%, or 481,626/1,207,272) whereas 2,282 titles have been distributed in respect of community claims over an area of 979,252 acres. As for the rejection of claims, 163,339 individual claims over an area of 486,186 acres (40.3%) have been rejected due to various reasons, while 3,825 community claims over an area of 41,514 (3.3%) have been rejected. In the case of pending claims, 69,214 individual claims over an area of 624,699 acres have been put on hold due to reverification and other reasons, and 4,982 community claims over an area of 244,785 acres have also been put on hold (see Table 16.1).

It is evident from these figures that in many cases officials have not accepted all the claims and they rejected many claims, sometimes on spurious grounds. The biggest limitation on improved livelihood security so far is the rejection of legitimate claims or providing titles for reduced areas than those claimed.

In all villages, many individual and communal rights claims have been submitted. However, officials have not accepted all the claims; rather they rejected many claims on different grounds such as lack of sufficient evidence. If the claims are to be accepted properly under this act, the poor definitely stand to benefit in a number of ways. (Gopinath Reddy et al, 2011).

It is paradoxical that the state is seeking to control the use of lands for which it has transferred rights to local people. In some districts where rights are conferred on land (through 'Pattas'), tribal groups are forced by the government to go for plantation crops by giving a subsidy. Many community groups are expressing concern that such an initiative may not increase household livelihood options; rather it will force them to adopt plantations through again compromising their new rights and livelihood/food security. The contest between the state and forest people for control of forest lands seems destined to continue, albeit in changing forms.

The Forest Rights Act, passed by the Indian Parliament at the end of 2006, was the result of an intensely contested drafting process (Bose, 2010). The subsequent implementation rules bringing the act into force were issued on 1 January 2008. Overall, the FRA's key institutional reform is that legal rights will be accorded to private occupation and to village common property resources currently in state forest land, subject to checks and proofs (Sarin, 2010).

Private land is not the only rights issue that local people are eager to have reformed. Access to common lands has also been legally denied by the state through a range of policies, and under the FRA local people have the right to their common resources and are hoping to secure them through implementation. In one of the study villages (Reddy et al, 2011), there are ad hoc JFM/CFM groups through which the APFD allows NTFP (non-timber forest products) collection; there are no legal rights, and so local people seek to put forest product collection and grazing on a legal basis, taking over their village forests from Forest Department control. The act, however, is not a panacea, as it constrained in terms of the extent to which it can fully redress rights deprivations. Furthermore, its provisions are limited in some significant ways.

Firstly, overall the rights ensured under the act remain subject to the right of the state to continue 'eminent domain' principles for its acquisition of lands in the name of development projects (as with any land rights, although acquisition has been a particular problem in upland areas).

Secondly, the forest land titles assured under the act are inalienable, and as such the titles granted to the claimants have no absolute and alienable right over the property. Private titles awarded under the Forest Settlement Rules under the A.P. Forest Act gave absolute title over the forest lands under occupation by claimants during the forest reservation process. Therefore, the titles granted under the act do not give ownership over the lands in the same way.

Thirdly, although the private rights to be granted are heritable under Sec4(4), there is no provision to promote gender equity in inheritance. The act ensures the joint title in the name of the spouses in case of married or single title in the name of a single person, and in the absence of a direct heir, the heritable right shall pass on to the next of kin. However, who that successor would be is not specified. Neither the Hindu Succession nor the Indian Succession Act are applicable to Scheduled Tribes in view of specific bars under the said laws. Only customary law is applicable for the tribal communities in succession of properties, and most tribal communities practice customary law, which ensures patrilineal succession of properties. These customary laws exclude the tribal women to claim their share in the inherited property. This is a clear case of gender discrimination.

Fourthly, the FRA is not explicit whether the claimant should be in actual possession of land or control over land. The act's Sec.4(3) gives eligibility to claim forest rights to STs and other traditional forest dwellers if they had occupied forest land before 13 December 2005. However, Sec4(6) restrains the claimant to claim forest lands which are not under cultivation. The provision ensures title to the "actual occupant" of forest land to the extent of four hectares. Tribals typically shift their cultivation plots from place to place over time to allow fallows.

Fifthly, the FRA has put a cut-off period, i.e. 13 December 2005, which means that rights deprived after that time will not be considered for redress.

Finally, the rules made under the act (Rule 11) fix a three-month period for filing claims. This provision restricts the claimants to make their right to claim. Although Rule 14 enables an aggrieved party to file appeals within the limited period (60 days) against the resolutions passed by various levels of committees, the law is silent about the communication of the decision of such bodies to the parties.

Thus, there is a range of concerns over the extent to which the act may fully redress rights deprivations. Evidently a major part of its potential remains contingent on how it is interpreted and followed during implementation. Yet the implementation provisions in the rules (2008) themselves also leaves a large number of ambiguities to the discretionary power of the implementing agencies (Sarin, 2010). The problem of implementation of the act seems to have become severe with the recent pronouncement of the Supreme Court.

V. Recent Supreme Court judgement: further setback to tribals' rights

The Supreme Court, on 13 February 2019, asked the state governments to report on steps being taken by them in cases of claims being rejected under the Scheduled Tribes and Other Traditional Forest Dwellers (Recognition of Forest Rights) Act, 2006 (FRA) and to complete the review works of such rejections within four months. Meanwhile, the Union government failed to defend the act in the court. The order came in response to a petition that the apex court was hearing. The petitioners claimed before the court that everyone whose FRA claim had been rejected was an "encroacher" and should be evicted. There are nine court cases filed by retired forest officials from Andhra Pradesh, Odisha, Maharashtra and Karnataka, along with conservation organizations like the Wildlife Trust of India, the Nature Conservation Society, the Tiger Research and Conservation Trust and the Bombay Natural History Society. Their demand is to get the FRA or orders under it struck down as unconstitutional.

In January 2015, the Supreme Court transferred all the High Court cases to itself and clubbed the cases together. In this context Mr. Tushar Dash of Community Forest Rights–Learning and Advocacy, an advocacy group of experts and activists working for creating awareness about FRA says that "More than 50 per cent of claims have been rejected by states without following due procedure. The rejected claims need to be reviewed by the states to correct illegal rejection of claims. The proceedings in the Supreme Court raise genuine fears of eviction of lakhs of tribals and forest dwellers, particularly those whose claims have been illegally rejected. This will also impact the ground level implementation of FRA" (Down To Earth, 2019). Meanwhile, the Union government failed to defend FRA during the hearing. The Centre ('Union of India'), the Union Ministry of Tribal Affairs and the Union Ministry of Environment, Forest and Climate Change, which are respondents in the case, are reported to have been keeping silent in the hearings in all consecutive hearings of the apex court. The aforementioned ruling will have serious implications on the lives of the millions of tribals whose bonding with the forests and nature will be disturbed forever. The judgement will further aggravate the alienation process between the tribals and their land rights without correcting the historical injustice meted out to them.

VI. Way forward

The foregoing analysis of implementation of FRA-2006 shows how inherently constrained it is to facilitate the tribals to continue to nurture their unbreakable bond with the forest. Although the act has clear pro-tribal and pro-poor biases, the serious flaws in certain provisions of the act seem to be hindering the prospect of preserving the cohesion between tribal groups and the forest. The chapter shows how the principle of 'eminent domain' in the name of development projects seriously hinders the endowment of land rights to the tribals. In the same way, another important clause in the act states that forest land titles assured under the act are inalienable and as such titles granted to the claimants have no absolute and alienable right over the property. This condition once again puts a question mark on the intentions of the governments, whether they really desire the tribals to be empowered. Yet another lacuna of the act is that although private rights to be granted are heritable under Section 3 clause (4), no provision exists in the act to promote gender equity in inheritance. The emphasis on individual entitlements at the cost of community rights brings in divisiveness in the unified compact culture of the tribal community that has learnt from their tradition how to survive and grow together with the forest. It is needless to mention that the market economy is more associated with individual rights. It helps market forces to determine property relations and their management. Once the trend intensifies, it may have an adverse impact on the customary practices of property management that have been helping the tribals to maintain their social equilibrium.

In order to implement the act to the purpose for which it was enacted, it may be worthwhile to take the following steps to design the intervention mechanism appropriately.

(1) The large-scale rejection of individual claims needs to be addressed through a continuous redressal mechanism. The process should be sustained until all the claims have been properly resolved. (2) There is an urgent need for resolving the contradictions between the area controlled by JFM committees (converted under CFR amounting to nine lakh acres and declared as community resources) and the community rights claimed under the FRA over local resources such as grazing and NTFP etc. (3) Although FRA-2006 promises the granting of individual and community rights over forest land, a host of other development-related interventions need to be launched by both the state governments as part of supporting the forest dwellers in terms of provision of irrigation, extension services, access to institutional credit from banks and cooperatives (farmers can pledge land 'pattas' as collateral) and infrastructure facilities which were not available in the reserved forest areas before the FRA-2006 was launched. Sadly, as our field observations reveal, not much progress is discernible on this front. Unless such complementary interventions (as mentioned earlier) are initiated, one cannot expect substantial income-benefits from the existing land endowments. Land development activities should be undertaken by the departments concerned under the NREGS program or through any other new intervention that the beneficiaries who have got ownership rights over their 'podu lands' are able to cultivate their lands and possibly improve crop yields in future.

Since the tribals are tied to the land not only for their livelihood needs but also for various cultural and spiritual needs (ecosystem services), any attempt to dilute this bonding will have serious consequences to their well-being.

The current unrest emanating from the tribal ecology, especially in recent years (because of opening up this resource to mining corporates and industrialists), clearly indicates how their livelihood is threatened. Much more important, they constantly fear how their inalienable bond, their solidarity with the forest, will be destroyed once and for all.

References

Bose, Indranil (2010), *How Did the Indian Forest Rights Act, 2006, Emerge?* http://re.indiaenvironmentportal.org.in/files/forest%20rights%20act%202006-emerge.pdf Accessed 19 December 2019.

Down To Earth (2019), *SC Seeks Reports on Rejected Forest Rights Claims from States*, www.downtoearth.org.in/news/forests/sc-seeks-reports-on-rejected-forest-rights-claims-from-states-63233 Accessed 20 February 2019.

Government of India (2007), *The Scheduled Tribes and Other Traditional Forest Dwellers* (Recognition of Forest Rights) Act, 2006, Ministry of Tribal Affairs (MoTA), New Delhi.

Karat, Brinda (2016), Rights for the Rightful Owners, *The Hindu*, December 15.

Rao, Trinadha P. (2007), Persisting Alienation of Tribal Lands, in Fr. Thomas Pallithanam Sdb (Editor), *Rekindling Hope? Access, Retention and Development of LAND: A Dalit Perspective*, Dalit Bahujan Shramik Union, Andhra Pradesh Social Watch, Hyderabad.

Reddy, Gopinath M. and C. Nagaraju (2015), *Forest Rights Act-2016: A Resurvey of Implementation and Impact Analysis in Andhra Pradesh and Telangana*, CESS Research Monograph 40, October, Hyderabad.

Reddy, Gopinath M., et al (2010), *Access to Forest Justice the Implementation of Institutional Reform (FRA-2006) in Andhra Pradesh's Forested Landscapes*, CESS Research Monograph 13, July.

Reddy, Gopinath M., et al (2011), Issues Related to Implementation of the Forest Rights Act in Andhra Pradesh, *Economic & Political Weekly (EPW)*, vol xlvi, no 18, April 30.

Sarin, Madhu (2010), *India's Forest Rights Act -The Anatomy of a Necessary but not Sufficient Institutional Reform*, IPPG Discussion Paper Series 45, July.

Springate, et al (2009). *Redressing 'Historical Injustice' Through the Indian Forest Rights Act 2006: A Historical Institutional Analysis of Contemporary Forest Rights Reform*, Discussion Paper Series 27, August, www.ippg.org.uk

Walter Fernandes, et al (2019), *Displacement and Marginalisation in Andhra Pradesh and Telangana1951–2010*, NESRC Displacement Series-6, by North Eastern Social Research Centre, Guwahati, Laya Resource Centre, Vishakapatnam.

Index

Note: Page numbers in **bold** refer to tables.

Printed in the United States
by Baker & Taylor Publisher Services